Strategic Learning in a Knowledge Economy

D0061127

Resources for the Knowledge Based Economy Series

KNOWLEDGE AND STRATEGY
Michael H. Zack

KNOWLEDGE AND SPECIAL LIBRARIES
James M. Matarazzo and Suzanne D. Connolly

RISE OF THE KNOWLEDGE WORKER
James W. Cortada

KNOWLEDGE IN ORGANIZATIONS
Laurence Prusak

KNOWLEDGE MANAGEMENT AND ORGANIZATIONAL DESIGN
Paul S. Myers

KNOWLEDGE MANAGEMENT TOOLS
Rudy L. Ruggles, III

THE STRATEGIC MANAGEMENT OF INTELLECTUAL CAPITAL
David A. Klein

Strategic Learning in a Knowledge Economy: Individual, Collective and Organizational Learning Process

Edited by
Robert L. Cross, Jr and Sam B. Israelit

BUTTERWORTH
HEINEMANN

Boston   Oxford   Auckland   Johannesburg   Melbourne   New Delhi

Library of Congress Cataloging-in-Publication Data
Strategic learning in a knowledge economy : individual, collective, and organizational learning process / Robert Cross, Sam B. Israelit, editors
    p. cm.
  Includes bibliographical references and index.
  ISBN 0-7506-7223-4 (pbk. : alk. paper)
   1. Knowledge management. 2. Organizational learning. 3. Strategic planning. I. Cross, Robert, 1967-II. Israelit, Sam B.

HD30.2 .S789 1999
658.4'038—dc21
                                    99-049844

British Library Cataloguing-in-Publication Data
A catalogue record for this book is available from the British Library.

The publisher offers special discounts on bulk orders of this book.
For information, please contact:
Manager of Special Sales
Butterworth–Heinemann
225 Wildwood Avenue
Woburn, MA 01801–2041
Tel: 781-904-2500
Fax: 781-904-2620
For information on all Butterworth–Heinemann publications available, contact our World Wide Web home page at: http://www.bh.com

10 9 8 7 6 5 4 3 2 1

Table of Contents

Introduction: Strategic Learning in a Knowledge Economy: Individual, Collective and Organizational Learning Process

Robert Cross[1]
Boston University & The Institute for Knowledge Management

Sam Israelit[2]
Arthur Andersen Knowledge Business Solutions Practice

Many organizations have recently turned to knowledge management in an effort to improve business performance (Nonaka and Takeuchi 1995; Stewart 1997; Davenport and Prusak 1998). Despite the richness and promise of this way of thinking, to date most initiatives have focused on identifying important knowledge in various pockets of an organization and building a technical

---

[1] Rob Cross is a Research Manager and Consultant in the Institute for Knowledge Management where he consults with organizations on issues of organizational learning, knowledge-based strategy and organizational design. He is also an advanced doctoral candidate and part time faculty member in Boston University's Organizational Behavior Department. His current research interests include organizational learning, knowledge-intensive teams and social cognition. Please address correspondence to: Robert Cross, Boston University School of Management, 595 Commonwealth Avenue, Boston MA 02215. rcross@bu.edu.

[2] Sam Israelit is Partner in charge of the Knowledge Services Business Solutions Practice where he consults with organizations on issues of strategic planning, organizational learning and system dynamics modeling. Prior to joining Arthur Andersen, he attended the Sloan School of Management and worked for Hughes Aircraft Company for six years designing dynamic computer simulations to assess missile system effectiveness.

infrastructure to support knowledge capture, dissemination and collaboration. Such efforts generally entail implementation of groupware or intranets and occasionally more sophisticated technologies such as neural nets, data mining or case-based reasoning.

Less frequently, organizations develop a human infrastructure to support knowledge management initiatives (Ruggles 1998). While some have developed new roles (e.g. the CKO) or mechanisms for screening knowledge (e.g. a panel of recognized experts), few have paid attention to the crucial role of learning as a key enabler to knowledge management. This is troubling as learning processes define the quality of knowledge entering these distributed technologies as well as the effectiveness with which knowledge from these repositories is put to use. As outlined by Tom Davenport (1997, 9), "people turn data into information . . . knowledge . . . is valuable precisely because someone has given the information context, meaning and a particular interpretation." Today's knowledge worker is valued precisely for his or her ability to contribute unique knowledge, skills and perspectives—a highly subjective process that at best can only be enabled by technologies forming the heart of what most organizations are calling knowledge management. To truly leverage knowledge, we must work with the subjective nature of learning and the idiosyncrasies of all those people we find in organizations—a task requiring greater attention to individual and social processes of learning in organizational settings.

This introductory chapter will serve to identify often overlooked individual and social processes shaping how knowledge is developed and applied to business initiatives in organizational settings. The remainder of the volume will address the challenges of learning at different organizational levels. Throughout, we are primarily interested in identifying how best to promote learning from experience at an individual level and then ensure that such knowledge is both applied to business initiatives and moved to higher levels within an organization such that other members benefit.

ORGANIZATIONAL LEARNING TODAY

In today's business environment, most people agree that an organization's ability to learn faster than its competition is a significant source of competitive advantage (Stata 1989; McGill and Slocum 1993; Slocum, McGill, and Lei 1994; Nevis, Dibella, and Gould 1995). In this vein of thought, the successful organization is one that can "assimilate new ideas and transfer those ideas into action faster than a competitor" (Ulrich, Jick, and Von Glinlow 1993, 55). Key to this process is the transformation of important experiences, such as new product development or delivery of innovative client solutions, into knowledge that benefits the rest of the organization. History has shown this to be an effort requiring more than just technology. Effective learning from experience requires attention to the ways in which organizations learn at the individual, group and organizational levels.

Unfortunately, experience is not a kind mentor. Important learning events are often sporadic or unique, hampering an organization's ability to establish validity and generality of knowledge acquired (March, Sproull, and Tamuz 1991). Further, experiences worth learning from are often critical business initiatives that pressure participants to survive the present rather than increase organizational learning for future initiatives. Translating such experiences into knowledge actionable for organizational members requires planning and resources to define and pursue learning worth expenditure of effort (Moingeon and Edmondson 1996; Sanchez and Heene 1997). Yet while companies readily purchase knowledge management technologies, they are frequently reticent to make investments of time in these "softer" processes of learning.

Even if effective learning from experience occurs at an individual or team level, important barriers often keep other organizational members from putting such newly acquired knowledge to use. Though frequently unrecognized, a significant impediment to knowledge transfer is that users often do not understand the implications of another person's lesson or best practice for their own problem (Szulanski 1996). Whether this is an issue of poor teaching practices on the part of the sharers or insufficient knowledge on the part of the users, such cognitive barriers profoundly impact an organization's ability to move lessons from its members' experiences across boundaries of time and space. Even when knowledge is successfully moved from one individual to another, action does not necessarily ensue. For example, individual learning can be "role-constrained" such that knowledge has no effect on individual or organizational action (March and Olsen 1975). Similarly, use of knowledge can be restricted by cultural norms or political dynamics in an organization (Pentland 1992).

Clearly, the process of learning from experience and making such learning actionable for other organizational members is fraught with potential biases and inconsistencies. While, recent work on individual and organizational learning has addressed the topic from a semi-utopian perspective (Senge 1990; Wheatley 1994; Wick and Leo'n 1993), it fails to address what people need to learn about and how learning will influence organizational performance. If nothing else, history continues to remind us that management interventions must be at least aimed in the direction of business problems to be sustainable over time. As a result, learning initiatives must be both (1) guided by strategic objectives and (2) integrated with important business initiatives.

This anthology was developed to remind us of the importance of and ways that learning occurs at various levels within organizations. Many of these ideas are not new, but are increasingly important as we wrestle with how to make knowledge management effective for organizations. Two premises underlie this volume. First, organizational learning, in the sense of strategic capability or competence development, is becoming increasingly important as we evolve into a knowledge economy. Many early adopters of knowledge management were not selective in the forms of knowledge they acquired and so overloaded their servers and the minds of their employees. As we move forward, identifying and developing mechanisms for pursuing specific, strategically important forms of

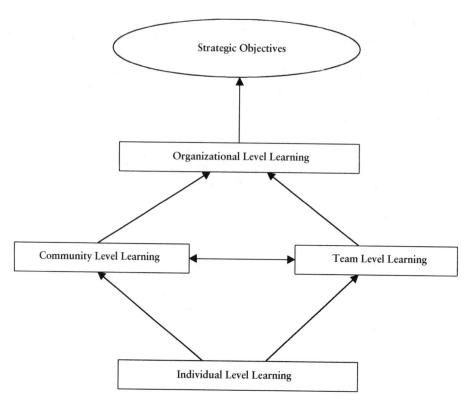

FIGURE 0.1 Levels of Learning

knowledge is taking on increasing importance. The world is moving too fast and the stakes are too high not to be increasingly precise about how strategy affects organizational learning and what an organization will be competitive at in the future. Second, learning in organizational settings is a more complex and fragile process than we sometimes acknowledge. Learning occurs within and is influenced by a host of social contexts, such as communities of practice or cross-functional teams. The ways in which these structures influence learning are different from each other and certainly from our notions of individual learning. To be truly effective, knowledge management initiatives must help individuals learn more effectively and also attend to the social processes that shape how knowledge becomes actionable in such contexts as cross-functional teams or communities of practice. The true pay off for knowledge management lies with putting newly created knowledge into action—often via a team or community—and then ensuring that lessons from the experience benefit others within the organization. Since learning looks different at various organizational levels, we need to employ appropriate mechanisms to ensure that valuable knowledge flows from an individual to a truly organizational level. Figure 0.1 delineates these levels and provides the orienting framework for this volume.

STRATEGY AND LEVELS OF LEARNING

Strategy

Learning and knowledge management initiatives should be, first and foremost, strategically driven. As organizations struggle to keep up with the pace of change today, it is increasingly important that capabilities be developed for future competitive advantage. Without focus, organizations learn in a path dependent fashion, thus potentially evolving into suboptimal markets or capabilities (Cohen and Levinthal 1990). Environmental scanning and active strategy formulation processes that acknowledge the importance of learning and knowledge help counter this tendency.

The advent of the resource-based view of the firm has helped us begin to think in terms of core competencies and capabilities, as opposed to strictly market position (Wernerfelt 1984; Barney 1991; Prahalad and Hamel 1990). From this perspective, a crucial element of strategy lies with identifying core competencies and important tacit and explicit knowledge necessary to support such competencies. Once knowledge critical to future competitive success has been identified, it is a relatively straightforward task to determine appropriate learning strategies. Such strategies may entail internal development or acquisition via processes such as Research and Development (R&D), hiring, mergers, or external development via such mechanisms as partnerships or alliances.

A competence-based approach to strategy helps an organization identify and target important forms of knowledge necessary for future success. This is an important planning process as knowledge critical to future success is often not developed in the course of day-to-day operations. With plans in place for acquiring strategically important knowledge, organizations should then focus on optimizing organizational learning from important business initiatives.

Organizational Learning

What does it mean to say an organization can learn? How would we know if one did? These and other questions have concerned researchers and practitioners for some time (Cyert and March 1963; Argyris and Schon 1978; Daft and Weick 1984; Fiol and Lyles 1985; De Guess 1988; Dibella and Nevis 1998). Rather than digress into a quagmire on whether an organization can learn outside of its members, one constructive way to think about this topic is to consider learning as a process of development to organizational memory (Walsh and Ungson 1991). By organizational memory, we are referring to various structures within an organization that hold knowledge in one form or another, such as databases and other information stores, work processes, procedures, and product or service architecture. As a result, when we say an organization can learn, we

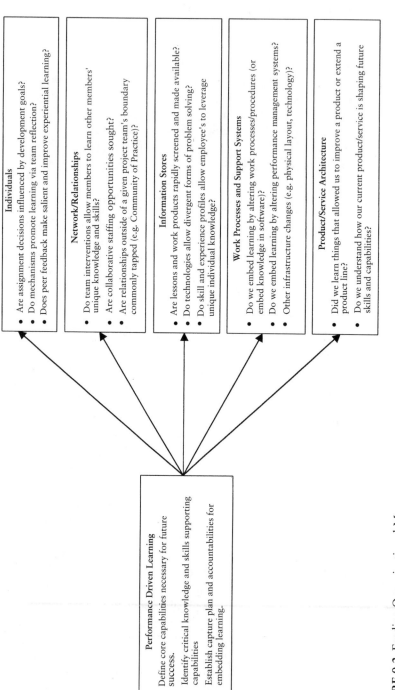

Individuals

- Are assignment decisions influenced by development goals?
- Do mechanisms promote learning via team reflection?
- Does peer feedback make salient and improve experiential learning?

Network/Relationships

- Do team interventions allow members to learn other members' unique knowledge and skills?
- Are collaborative staffing opportunities sought?
- Are relationships outside of a given project team's boundary commonly tapped (e.g. Community of Practice)?

Information Stores

- Are lessons and work products rapidly screened and made available?
- Do technologies allow divergent forms of problem solving?
- Do skill and experience profiles allow employee's to leverage unique individual knowledge?

Work Processes and Support Systems

- Do we embed learning by altering work processes/procedures (or embed knowledge in software)?
- Do we embed learning by altering performance management systems?
- Other infrastructure changes (e.g. physical layout, technology)?

Product/Service Architecture

- Did we learn things that allowed us to improve a product or extend a product line?
- Do we understand how our current product/service is shaping future skills and capabilities?

Performance Driven Learning

- Define core capabilities necessary for future success.
- Identify critical knowledge and skills supporting capabilities
- Establish capture plan and accountabilities for embedding learning.

FIGURE 0.2 Feeding Organizational Memory

are concerned with more than just individual cognition and expanded social networks. We are interested in the way in which knowledge becomes embedded (and sometimes stuck) in business processes, formal reporting structures, performance management systems, and resource allocation processes that guide the overall direction of the firm.

With an understanding of important components of memory, an organization can better appreciate how it is currently learning from its key experiences such as core work processes or new product development (see Figure 0.2). Targeting important learning allows management to ensure that relevant knowledge becomes embedded within the future operations and practices of the organization. For example, a new product development effort provides an opportunity not only for individuals engaged in the experience to learn and document lessons, but also to change processes and procedures or even a product's architecture. Such changes ultimately are reflected in future efforts and serve to shape learning and knowledge accumulated by an organization over time.

While a powerful guide to increase organizational learning from experience, this view of memory focuses primarily on capturing the outcomes rather than supporting the processes of experiential learning. To truly support learning within organizational settings, we must attend to important social contexts where learning occurs.

Communities of Practice

Most people agree that organizations themselves cannot learn, but rather that individual learning migrates to the organizational level in social interaction of some form (Kim 1993). One social structure within organizations attracting the attention of both academics and practitioners today is the community of practice (Orr 1990; Lave and Wenger 1991; Brown and Duguid 1991; Wenger 1998). While often an elusive concept, communities are being either found or established to facilitate collaboration in such diverse settings as professional services, R&D, and manufacturing. In many cases, these communities are effective forums for individuals with specialized knowledge to collaborate and learn from each other. In others, they provide means of developing strategic capabilities or technologies and facilitating change processes.

Communities of practice provide a powerful mechanism for problem solving and integration of specialist knowledge—particularly for organizations that have transitioned from functional to cross-functional team structures. However, these groups also pose significant organizational challenges that we are only beginning to work through in practice. For example, while technology can help support communities of practice, both research and consulting experiences have shown that the social bond of these groups is the more important determinant of success. Development of this bond takes significant effort and time as most organizations' performance management systems value either team or individual performance and do not easily accommodate or value what can emerge from communities. To obtain the benefits anticipated from communities of practice, organizations must invest both time and some hard resources to identify, nurture, and maintain these groups.

However, we must also remember that despite the promise of communities, they are still not the primary means by which work is accomplished today. We spend considerably less time in formal communities obtaining important advice or knowledge than we do in cross-functional teams trying to apply our knowledge to measurable goals and expected work outcomes. As our ultimate interest lies with ensuring that learning becomes actionable for an organization, we must look not only to communities of practice where learning may occur, but also to work teams where this knowledge is applied to important business initiatives.

Teams

Many organizations have turned to team-based structures in an effort to improve collaboration, integrate specialized functional and technical knowledge, and increase responsiveness to demanding stakeholders (Hirschorn 1991; Mohrman, Cohen, and Mohrman 1995; Mankin, Cohen, and Bikson 1996; Fisher and Fisher 1998). However, while teams can be effective in minimizing cross-functional inefficiencies and improving decision-making, they also represent diverse social contexts that make both learning and putting knowledge into action a challenge. It is one problem to "learn" a piece of knowledge in an open discussion forum with others who think like you (such as in a community of practice). It is another to then introduce this new knowledge into a cross-functional team where people often do not share a common vision, language, metrics of performance, or even understanding of the problem itself. Such cognitive barriers often restrict cross-functional team members from leveraging members' knowledge and expertise (Lakoff 1987; Dougherty 1992).

Problems in effectively leveraging the collective knowledge and experience of a team's members are more than cognitive. Team structure, in the sense of established roles and responsibilities, often determines how knowledge enters a team (i.e. through which individuals) and also how such knowledge may come to be shared by the group as a whole. Similarly, social factors in a team such as a sense of safety, or skills such as problem solving or dialogue, can influence both learning and performance (Edmondson 1996). For example, political or cultural factors can dramatically influence which voices are heard in a team setting and thus how accessible the entire team's knowledge is in being brought to bear on a problem.

Mechanisms such as the Army's After Action Review and a culture of openness, can help counter both cognitive and emotional biases by making other facts and perspectives available to a group (Baird, Holland, and Deacon, 1999). It is in this sense that an ability to hold one's own knowledge loosely and engage in constructive dialogue are crucial to team level learning and effectiveness. While this skill is often manifested in group interactions, it fundamentally requires an individual to be aware of his/her own biases and tendencies in these interactions. Thus, while we are interested in building dialogue and problem solving skills in work groups to effectively leverage the collective intellect of these teams, we must do so on a foundation of the individual learning tendencies that shape these behaviors.

Individuals

Most would agree that individual learning precedes or at least co-occurs with any form of collective knowledge in an organization. At an individual level, experiential learning follows a cycle of experience, reflection, concept formation, and testing of implications (Kolb 1984). Yet what is learned from an experience is subjective and can often be fundamentally different for individuals even when engaged in the same event. Aspects of an experience capture peoples' attention and warrant their engagement with a topic differently (Louis and Sutton 1991; Dutton 1993). This is in part a product of the extent to which existing knowledge shapes what we see in a situation, as well as the way in which current concerns or goals impact what we attend to. Without a concerted effort to counteract the subjectivity inherent in the interpretation of events, what may be learned from an experience and passed on to the organization by way of stories or technical channels may be dramatically removed from the actual event.

In addition to purely cognitive constraints, emotion itself plays a profound role in learning as it shapes how we attend to a situation (Goleman 1995 and 1998). The simple decision to mentally bring ourselves into or remove ourselves from the activities of a group or task is often done tacitly yet can dramatically impact what we learn from a situation (Kahn 1988). Further, emotions and well-worn cognitive processes can erect defensive routines that keep us from learning in situations (Argyris 1982 and 1993). Without an awareness of our own personal tendencies, as well as the time to reflect on and learn from events, little effective and actionable knowledge can emerge from experience (Weick 1995; Daudelin 1996; Schon 1990). And, of course, lack of learning at the individual level precludes any ability to effectively move such knowledge to higher and thus more profitable organizational levels regardless of the technology or other organizational programs thrown at knowledge management.

CONCLUSION

If nothing else, learning from experience and moving important lessons to higher organizational levels is an enormously challenging process. While organizations quickly invest in technology to facilitate this process, experience shows that the more challenging problem lies with developing the appropriate skills and tools within organizations so that they can learn from important events at all organizational levels. The following volume will introduce some tools, techniques, and case examples for considering some of these issues in greater depth. We hope you find this complex but valuable topic as important as we do.

REFERENCES

Argyris, C. and D. Schon. 1978. *Organizational Learning: Theory, Method and Practice.* Reading, MA: Addison-Wesley.

Argyris, C. 1982. *Reasoning, Learning and Action.* San Francisco, CA: Jossey-Bass.

———. 1993. *Knowledge for Action: A Guide to Overcoming Barriers to Organizational Change.* San Francisco, CA: Jossey-Bass.

Barney, J. 1991. Firm Resources and Sustained Competitive Advantage. *Journal of Management* 17(1): 99–120.

Brown, J. S. and P. Duguid. 1991. Organizational Learning and Communities-of-Practice: Toward a Unified View of Working, Learning and Innovation. *Organization Science* 2(1): 40–57.

Cohen, W. and D. Levinthal. 1990. Absorptive Capacity: A New Perspective on Learning and Innovation. *Administrative Science Quarterly* 35: 128–152.

Cyert, R. M. and J. G. March. 1963. *A Behavioral Theory of the Firm.* Englewood Cliffs, NJ: Prentice-Hall.

Daft, R. and K. Weick. 1984. Toward a Model of Organizations as Interpretive Systems. *Academy of Management Review* 9(2): 284–295.

Daudelin, M. 1996. Learning From Experience Through Reflection. *Organizational Dynamics* 24(3): 36–48.

Davenport, T. and L. Prusak. 1998. *Working Knowledge.* Boston: Harvard Business School Press.

Davenport, T. 1997. *Information Ecology.* New York: Oxford University Press.

De Geuss, A. 1988. Planning As Learning. *Harvard Business Review* (March/April): 70–74.

Dibella, A. J. and E. C. Nevis. 1998. *How Organizations Learn.* San Francisco: Jossey-Bass.

Dougherty, D. 1992. Interpretive Barriers to Successful Product Innovation in Large Firms. *Organization Science* 3(2): 179–202.

Dutton, J. 1993. Interpretations on Automatic: A Different View of Strategic Issue Diagnosis. *Journal of Management Studies* 30(3): 339–357.

Edmondson, A. 1996. Learning From Mistakes Is Easier Said than Done: Group and Organizational Influences on the Detection and Correction of Human Error. *Journal of Applied Behavioral Science* 32(1): 5–28.

Fiol, C. M. and M. A. Lyles. 1985. Organizational Learning. *Academy of Management Review* 10(4): 803–813.

Fisher, K. and M. Fisher. 1998. *The Distributed Mind: Achieving High Performance Through the Collective Intelligence of Knowledge Work Teams.* New York, NY: AMACOM.

Goleman, D. 1995. *Emotional Intelligence.* New York, NY: Bantam Books.

———. 1998. *Emotional Intelligence in the Work Place.* New York, NY: Bantam Books.

Hirschorn, L. 1991. *Managing in the New Team Environment*. Reading, MA: Addison-Wesley.

Kahn, W. 1988. Psychological Conditions of Engagement & Disengagement at Work. *Academy of Management Journal* 33: 692–724.

Kim, D. 1993. The Link Between Individual and Organizational Learning. *Sloan Management Review* (Fall): 37–50.

Kolb, D. 1984. *Experiential Learning: Experience as the Source of Learning and Development*. Englewood Cliffs, NJ: Prentice Hall.

Lakoff, G. 1987. *Women, Fire and Dangerous Things*. Chicago, IL: University of Chicago Press.

Lave, J. and E. Wenger. 1991. *Situated Learning: Legitimate Peripheral Participation*. Cambridge: Cambridge University Press.

Louis, M. R. and R. I. Sutton. 1991. Switching Cognitive Gears: From Habits of Mind to Active Thinking. *Human Relations* 44(1): 55–76.

Mankin, D., S. Cohen, and T. Bikson. 1996. *Teams and Technology: Fulfilling the Promise of the New Organization*. Boston, MA: HBS Press.

March, J. and J. Olsen. 1975. The Uncertainty of the Past: Organizational Learning Under Ambiguity. *European Journal of Political Research* 3: 147–171.

March, J., L. Sproull, and M. Tamuz. 1991. Learning from Samples of One or Fewer. *Organization Science* 2(1): 1–13.

McGill, M. and J. Slocum. 1993. Unlearning the Organization. *Organizational Dynamics* (Autumn): 67–79.

McGill, M., J. Slocum, and D. Lei. 1992. Management Practices in Learning Organizations. *Organizational Dynamics* (Summer): 5–17.

Mohrman, S., S. Cohen, and A. Mohrman. 1995. *Designing Team-Based Organizations: New Forms for Knowledge Work*. San Francisco, CA: Jossey-Bass pp. 63, 82–87, 181–185 & 231.

Moingeon, B. and A. Edmondson (Eds.) (1996). *Organizational Learning an Competitive Advantage*. Thousand Oaks, CA: Sage Publications.

Nevis, E. C., A. J. DiBella, and J. M. Gould. 1995. Understanding Organizations as Learning Systems. *Sloan Management Review* (Winter): 73–85.

Nonaka, I. and H. Takeuchi. 1995. *The Knowledge-Creating Company*. London: Oxford University Press.

Orr, J. E. 1990. Sharing Knowledge, Celebrating Identity. In D. S. Middleton and D. Edwards (eds) *Collective Remembering* (pp. 169–189). Newbury Park, CA: Sage.

Pentland, B. T. 1992. Organizing Moves in Software Support Hot Lines. *Administrative Science Quarterly* 37(4): 527–548.

Prahalad, C. K. and G. Hamel. 1990. The Core Competence of the Corporation. *Harvard Business Review* (May–June): 79–91.

Ruggles, R. 1998. The State of the Notion: Knowledge Management in Practice, *California Management Review* 40(3): 80–89.

Schon, D. A. 1990. *Educating the Reflective Practitioner*. San Francisco, CA: Jossey-Bass.

Senge, P. M. 1990. *The Fifth Discipline: The Art and Practice of the Learning Organization*. New York, NY: DoubleDay Currency.

Slocum, J., M. McGill, and D. Lei. 1994. The New Learning Strategy: Anytime, Anything, Anywhere. *Organizational Dynamics* 23(2): 33–47.

Stata, R. 1989. Organizational Learning: The Key to Management Innovation. *Sloan Management Review* (Spring): 63–74.

Stewart, T. 1997. *Intellectual capital: The new wealth of organizations.* New York, NY: Doubleday.

Szulanski, G. 1996. Exploring Internal Stickiness: Impediments to the Transfer of Best Practices within the Firm. *Strategic Management Journal* 17(Winter Special Issue): 27–43.

Ulrich, D., M. Von Glinlow, and T. Jick. 1993. High-Impact Learning: Building and Diffusing a Learning Capability. *Organizational Dynamics* 22: 52–66.

Walsh, J. P., and G. R. Ungson. 1991. Organizational Memory. *Academy of Management Review* 16(1): 57–91.

Weick, K. 1995. *Sensemaking in organizations.* Thousand Oaks, CA: Sage Publications.

Wenger, E. 1998. *Communities of Practice.* Oxford: Oxford University Press.

Wernerfelt, B. 1984. A Resource Based View of the Firm. *Strategic Management Journal* 5: 171–181.

Wheatley, M. 1994. *Leadership and the New Science: Learning about Organization from an Orderly Universe.* Berret Koehler.

Wick, C. W. , and L. S. Leo'n. 1993. *The Learning Edge.* New York, NY: McGraw Hill.

PART I

Knowledge-Based Strategy to Guide Learning

Chapter 1

The Core Competence of the Corporation[*]

C. K. Prahalad and Gary Hamel

The most powerful way to prevail in global competition is still invisible to many companies. During the 1980s, top executives were judged on their ability to restructure, declutter, and delayer their corporations. In the 1990s, they'll be judged on their ability to identify, cultivate, and exploit the core competencies that make growth possible—indeed, they'll have to rethink the concept of the corporation itself.

Consider the last ten years of GTE and NEC. In the early 1980s, GTE was well positioned to become a major player in the evolving information technology industry. It was active in telecommunications. Its operations spanned a variety of businesses including telephones, switching and transmission systems, digital PABX, semiconductors, packet switching, satellites, defense systems, and lighting products. And GTE's Entertainment Products Group, which produced Sylvania color TVs, had a position in related display technologies. In 1980, GTE's sales were $9.98 billion, and net cash flow was $1.73 billion. NEC, in contrast, was much smaller at $3.8 billion in sales. It had a comparable technological base and computer businesses, but it had no experience as an operating telecommunications company.

Yet look at the positions of GTE and NEC in 1988. GTE's 1988 sales were $16.46 billion, and NEC's sales were considerably higher at $21.89 billion. GTE has, in effect, become a telephone operating company with a position in defense and lighting products. GTE's other businesses are small in global terms. GTE has divested Sylvania TV and Telenet, put switching, transmission, and digital PABX

[*] Reprinted by permission of *Harvard Business Review*, May–June 1990, pp. 79–91. Copyright (1990 by the resident and Fellows of Harvard Business College, all rights reserved.

C. K. Prahalad is professor of corporate strategy and international business at the University of Michigan. Gary Hamel is lecturer in business policy and management at the London Business School. Their most recent *Harvard Business Review* article, "Strategic Intent" (May–June 1989), won the 1989 McKinsey Award for excellence. This article is based on research funded by the Gatsby Charitable Foundation.

into joint ventures, and closed down semiconductors. As a result, the international position of GTE has eroded. Non-U.S. revenue as a percent of total revenue dropped from 20% to 15% between 1980 and 1988.

NEC has emerged as the world leader in semiconductors and as a first-tier player in telecommunications products and computers. It has consolidated its position in mainframe computers. It has moved beyond public switching and transmission to include such lifestyle products as mobile telephones, facsimile machines, and laptop computers—bridging the gap between telecommunications and office automation. NEC is the only company in the world to be in the top five in revenue in telecommunications, semiconductors, and mainframes. Why did these two companies, starting with comparable business portfolios, perform so differently? Largely because NEC conceived of itself in terms of "core competencies," and GTE did not.

RETHINKING THE CORPORATION

Once, the diversified corporation could simply point its business units at particular end product markets and admonish them to become world leaders. But with market boundaries changing ever more quickly, targets are elusive and capture is at best temporary. A few companies have proven themselves adept at inventing new markets, quickly entering emerging markets, and dramatically shifting patterns of customer choice in established markets. These are the ones to emulate. The critical task for management is to create an organization capable of infusing products with irresistible functionality or, better yet, creating products that customers need but have not yet even imagined.

This is a deceptively difficult task. Ultimately it requires radical change in the management of major companies. It means, first of all, that top managements of Western companies must assume responsibility for competitive decline. Everyone knows about high interest rates, Japanese protectionism, outdated antitrust laws, obstreperous unions, and impatient investors. What is harder to see, or harder to acknowledge, is how little added momentum companies actually get from political or macroeconomic "relief." Both the theory and practice of Western management have created a drag on our forward motion. It is the principles of management that are in need of reform.

NEC versus GTE, again, is instinctive and only one of many such comparative cases we analyzed to understand the changing basis for global leadership. Early in the 1970s, NEC articulated a strategic intent to exploit the convergence of computing and communications, what it called "C&C."[1] Success, top management reckoned, would hinge on acquiring *competencies*, particularly in semiconductors. Management adopted an appropriate "strategic architecture," summarized by C&C, and then communicated its intent to the whole organization and the outside world during the mid-1970s.

---

[1] For a fuller discussion, see our article, "Strategic Intent" *HBR*, May–June 1989, p. 63.

NEC constituted a "C&C Committee" of top managers to oversee the development of core products and core competencies. NEC put in place coordination groups and committees that cut across the interests of individual businesses. Consistent with its strategic architecture, NEC shifted enormous resources to strengthen its position in components and central processors. By using collaborative arrangements to multiply internal resources, NEC was able to accumulate a broad array of core competencies.

NEC carefully identified three interrelated streams of technological and market evolution. Top management determined that computing would evolve from large mainframes to distributed processing, components from simple ICs to VLSI, and communications from mechanical cross-bar exchange to complex digital systems we now call ISDN. As things evolved further, NEC reasoned, the computing, communications, and components businesses would so overlap that it would be very hard to distinguish among them, and that there would be enormous opportunities for any company that had built the competencies needed to serve all three markets.

NEC top management determined that semiconductors would be the company's most important "core product." It entered into myriad strategic alliances—over 100 as of 1987—aimed at building competencies rapidly and at low cost. In mainframe computers, its most noted relationship was with Honeywell and Bull. Almost all the collaborative arrangements in the semi-conductor-component field were oriented toward technology access. As they entered collaborative arrangements, NEC's operating managers understood the rationale for these alliances and the goal of internalizing partner skills. NEC's director of research summed up its competence acquisition during the 1970s and 1980s this way: "From an investment standpoint, it was much quicker and cheaper to use foreign technology. There wasn't a need for us to develop new ideas."

No such clarity of strategic intent and strategic architecture appeared to exist at GTE. Although senior executives discussed the implications of the evolving information technology industry, no commonly accepted view of which competencies would be required to compete in that industry were communicated widely. While significant staff work was done to identify key technologies, senior line managers continued to act as if they were managing independent business units. Decentralization made it difficult to focus on core competencies. Instead, individual businesses became increasingly dependent on outsiders for critical skills, and collaboration became a route to staged exits. Today with a new management team in place, GTE has repositioned itself to apply its competencies to emerging markets in telecommunications services.

THE ROOTS OF COMPETITIVE ADVANTAGE

The distinction we observed in the way NEC and GTE conceived of themselves—a portfolio of competencies versus a portfolio of businesses—was repeated across many industries. From 1980 to 1988, Canon grew by 264%,

Honda by 200%. Compare that with Xerox and Chrysler. And if Western managers were once anxious about the low cost and high quality of Japanese imports, they are now overwhelmed by the pace at which Japanese rivals are inventing new markets, creating new products, and enhancing them. Canon has given us personal copiers; Honda has moved from motorcycles to four-wheel off-road buggies. Sony developed the 8mm camcorder, Yamaha, the digital piano. Komatsu developed an underwater remote-controlled bulldozer, while Casio's latest gambit is a small-screen color LCD television. Who would have anticipated the evolution of these vanguard markets?

In more established markets, the Japanese challenge has been just as disquieting. Japanese companies are generating a blizzard of features and functional enhancements that bring technological sophistication to everyday products. Japanese car producers have been pioneering four-wheel steering, four-valve-per-cylinder engines, in-car navigation systems, and sophisticated electronic engine-management systems. On the strength of its product features, Canon is now a player in facsimile transmission machines, desktop laser printers, even semiconductor manufacturing equipment.

In the short run, a company's competitiveness derives from the price/performance attributes of current products. But the survivors of the first wave of global competition, Western and Japanese alike, are all converging on similar and formidable standards for product cost and quality—minimum hurdles for continued competition, but less and less important as sources of differential advantage. In the long run, competitiveness derives from an ability to build, at lower cost and more speedily than competitors, the core competencies that spawn unanticipated products. The real sources of advantage are to be found in management's ability to consolidate corporatewide technologies and production skills into competencies that empower individual businesses to adapt quickly to changing opportunities.

Senior executives who claim that they cannot build core competencies either because they feel the autonomy of business units is sacrosanct or because their feet are held to the quarterly budget fire should think again. The problem in many Western companies is not that their senior executives are any less capable than those in Japan nor that Japanese companies possess greater technical capabilities. Instead, it is their adherence to a concept of the corporation that unnecessarily limits the ability of individual businesses to fully exploit the deep reservoir of technological capability that many American and European companies possess.

The diversified corporation is a large tree. The trunk and major limbs are core products, the smaller branches are business units; the leaves, flowers, and fruit are end products. The root system that provides nourishment, sustenance, and stability is the core competence. You can miss the strength of competitors by looking only at their end products, in the same way you miss the strength of a tree if you look only at its leaves. (See the chart "Competencies: The Roots of Competitiveness.")

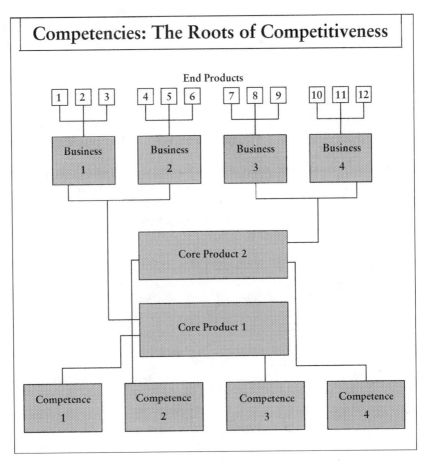

The corporation, like a tree, grows from its roots. Core products are nourished by competencies and engender business units, whose fruit are end products.

FIGURE 1.1 Competencies: The Roots of Competitiveness

Core competencies are the collective learning in the organization, especially how to coordinate diverse production skills and integrate multiple streams of technologies. Consider Sony's capacity to miniaturize or Philips's optical-media expertise. The theoretical knowledge to put a radio on a chip does not in itself assure a company the skill to produce a miniature radio no bigger than a business card. To bring off this feat, Casio must harmonize know-how in miniaturization, microprocessor design, material science, and ultrathin precision casing—the same skills it applies in its miniature card calculators, pocket TVs, and digital watches.

If core competence is about harmonizing streams of technology, it is also about the organization of work and the delivery of value. Among Sony's competencies is miniaturization. To bring miniaturization to its products, Sony must ensure that technologists, engineers, and marketers have a shared understanding of customer needs and of technological possibilities. The force of core competence is felt as decisively in services as in manufacturing. Citicorp was ahead of others investing in an operating system that allowed it to participate in world markets 24 hours a day. Its competence in systems has provided the company the means to differentiate itself from many financial service institutions.

Core competence is communication, involvement, and a deep commitment to working across organizational boundaries. It involves many levels of people and all functions. World-class research in, for example, lasers or ceramics can take place in corporate laboratories without having an impact on any of the businesses of the company The skills that together constitute core competence must coalesce around individuals whose efforts are not so narrowly focused that they cannot recognize the opportunities for blending their functional expertise with those of others in new and interesting ways.

Core competence does not diminish with use. Unlike physical assets, which do deteriorate over time, competencies are enhanced as they are applied and shared. But competencies still need to be nurtured and protected; knowledge fades if it is not used. Competencies are the glue that binds existing businesses. They are also the engine for new business development. Patterns of diversification and market entry may be guided by them, not just by the attractiveness of markets.

Consider 3M's competence with sticky tape. In dreaming up businesses as diverse as "Post-it" notes, magnetic tape, photographic film, pressure-sensitive tapes, and coated abrasives, the company has brought to bear widely shared competencies in substrates, coatings, and adhesives and devised various ways to combine them. Indeed, 3M has invested consistently in them. What seems to be an extremely diversified portfolio of businesses belies a few shared core competencies.

In contrast, there are major companies that have had the potential to build core competencies but failed to do so because top management was unable to conceive of the company as anything other than a collection of discrete businesses. GE sold much of its consumer electronics business to Thomson of France, arguing that it was becoming increasingly difficult to maintain its competitiveness in this sector. That was undoubtedly so, but it is ironic that it sold several key businesses to competitors who were already competence leaders—Black & Decker in small electrical motors, and Thomson, which was eager to build its competence in microelectronics and had learned from the Japanese that a position in consumer electronics was vital to this challenge.

Management trapped in the strategic business unit (SBU) mind-set almost inevitably finds its individual businesses dependent on external sources for critical components, such as motors or compressors. But these are not just components. They are core products that contribute to the competitiveness of a wide range of end products. They are the physical embodiments of core competencies.

HOW NOT TO THINK OF COMPETENCE

Since companies are in a race to build the competencies that determine global leadership, successful companies have stopped imagining themselves as bundles of businesses making products. Canon, Honda, Casio, or NEC may seem to preside over portfolios of businesses unrelated in terms of customers, distribution channels, and merchandising strategy. Indeed, they have portfolios that may seem idiosyncratic at times: NEC is the only global company to be among leaders in computing, telecommunications, and semiconductors *and* to have a thriving consumer electronics business.

But looks are deceiving. In NEC, digital technology, especially VLSI and systems integration skills, is fundamental. In the core competencies underlying them, disparate businesses become coherent. It is Honda's core competence in engines and power trains that gives it a distinctive advantage in car, motorcycle, lawn mower, and generator businesses. Canon's core competencies in optics, imaging, and microprocessor controls have enabled it to enter, even dominate, markets as seemingly diverse as copiers, laser printers, cameras, and image scanners. Philips worked for more than 15 years to perfect its optical-media (laser disc) competence, as did JVC in building a leading position in video recording. Other examples of core competencies might include mechantronics (the ability to marry mechanical and electronic engineering), video displays, bioengineering, and microelectronics. In the early stages of its competence building, Philips could not have imagined all the products that would be spawned by its optical-media competence, nor could JVC have anticipated miniature camcorders when it first began exploring videotape technologies.

Unlike the battle for global brand dominance, which is visible in the world's broadcast and print media and is aimed at building global "share of mind," the battle to build world-class competencies is invisible to people who aren't deliberately looking for it. Top management often tracks the cost and quality of competitors' products, yet how many managers untangle the web of alliances their Japanese competitors have contracted to acquire competencies at low cost? In how many Western boardrooms is there an explicit, shared understanding of the competencies the company must build for world leadership? Indeed, how many senior executives discuss the crucial distinction between competitive strategy at the level of a business and competitive strategy at the level of an entire company?

Let us be clear. Cultivating core competence does *not* mean outspending rivals on research and development. In 1983, when Canon surpassed Xerox in worldwide unit market share in the copier business, its R&D budget in reprographics was but a small fraction of Xerox's. Over the past 20 years, NEC has spent less on R&D as a percentage of sales than almost all of its American and European competitors.

Nor does core competence mean shared costs, as when two or more SBUs use a common facility—a plant, service facility or sales force—or share a common component. The gains of sharing may be substantial, but the search for shared costs is typically a post hoc effort to rationalize production across existing businesses, not a premeditated effort to build the competencies out of which the businesses themselves grow.

Building core competencies is more ambitious and different than integrating vertically moreover. Managers deciding whether to make or buy will start with end products and look upstream to the efficiencies of the supply chain and downstream toward distribution and customers. They do not take inventory of skills and look forward to applying them in nontraditional ways. (Of course, decisions about competencies *do* provide a logic for vertical integration. Canon is not particularly integrated in its copier business, except in those aspects of the vertical chain that support the competencies it regards as critical.)

IDENTIFYING CORE COMPETENCIES—AND LOSING THEM

At least three tests can be applied to identify core competencies in a company. First, a core competence provides potential access to a wide variety of markets. Competence in display systems, for example, enables a company to participate in such diverse businesses as calculators, miniature TV sets, monitors for laptop computers, and automotive dashboards—which is why Casio's entry into the handheld TV market was predictable. Second, a core competence should make a significant contribution to the perceived customer benefits of the end product. Clearly, Honda's engine expertise fills this bill.

Finally, a core competence should be difficult for competitors to imitate. And it *will* be difficult if it is a complex harmonization of individual technologies and production skills. A rival might acquire some of the technologies that comprise the core competence, but it will find it more difficult to duplicate the more or less comprehensive pattern of internal coordination and learning. JVC's decision in the early 1960s to pursue the development of a videotape competence passed the three tests outlined here. RCA's decision in the late 1970s to develop a stylus-based video turntable system did not.

Few companies are likely to build world leadership in more than five or six fundamental competencies. A company that compiles a list of 20 to 30 capabilities has probably not produced a list of core competencies. Still, it is probably a good discipline to generate a list of this sort and to see aggregate capabilities as building blocks. This tends to prompt the search for licensing deals and alliances through which the company may acquire, at low cost, the missing pieces.

Most Western companies hardly think about competitiveness in these terms at all. It is time to take a tough-minded look at the risks they are running. Companies that judge competitiveness, their own and their competitors', primarily in terms of the price/performance of end products are courting the erosion of core competencies—or making too little effort to enhance them. The embedded skills that give rise to the next generation of competitive products cannot be "rented in" by outsourcing and OEM-supply relationships. In our view, too many companies have unwittingly surrendered core competencies when they cut internal investment in what they mistakenly thought were just "cost centers" in favor of outside suppliers.

Consider Chrysler. Unlike Honda, it has tended to view engines and power trains as simply one more component. Chrysler is becoming increasingly dependent on Mitsubishi and Hyundai: between 1985 and 1987, the number of outsourced engines went from 252,000 to 382,000. It is difficult to imagine Honda yielding manufacturing responsibility, much less design, of so critical a part of a car's function to an outside company—which is why Honda has made such an enormous commitment to Formula One auto racing. Honda has been able to pool its engine-related technologies; it has parlayed these into a corporatewide competency from which it develops world-beating products, despite R&D budgets smaller than those of GM and Toyota.

Of course, it is perfectly possible for a company to have a competitive product line up but be a laggard in developing core competencies—at least for a while. If a company wanted to enter the copier business today, it would find a dozen Japanese companies more than willing to supply copiers on the basis of an OEM private label. But when fundamental technologies changed or if its supplier decided to enter the market directly and become a competitor, that company's product line, along with all of its investments in marketing and distribution, could be vulnerable. Outsourcing can provide a shortcut to a more competitive product, but it typically contributes little to building the people-embodied skills that are needed to sustain product leadership.

Nor is it possible for a company to have an intelligent alliance or sourcing strategy if it has not made a choice about where it will build competence leadership. Clearly, Japanese companies have benefited from alliances. They've used them to learn from Western partners who were not fully committed to preserving core competencies of their own. As we've argued in these pages before, learning within an alliance takes a positive commitment of resources—travel, a pool of dedicated people, test-bed facilities, time to internalize and test what has been learned.[2] A company may not make this effort if it doesn't have clear goals for competence building.

Another way of losing is forgoing opportunities to establish competencies that are evolving in existing businesses. In the 1970s and 1980s, many American and European companies—like GE, Motorola, GTE, Thorn, and GEC—chose to exit the color television business, which they regarded as mature. If by "mature" they meant that they had run out of new product ideas at precisely the moment global rivals had targeted the TV business for entry, then yes, the industry was mature. But it certainly wasn't mature in the sense that all opportunities to enhance and apply video-based competencies had been exhausted.

In ridding themselves of their television businesses, these companies failed to distinguish between divesting the business and destroying their video

---

2   "Collaborate with Your Competitors and Win," *HBR* January–February 1989, p. 133, with Yves L. Doz.

media-based competencies. They not only got out of the TV business but they also closed the door on a whole stream of future opportunities reliant on video-based competencies. The television industry, considered by many U.S. companies in the 1970s to be unattractive, is today the focus of a fierce public policy debate about the inability of U.S. corporations to benefit from the $20-billion-a-year opportunity that HDTV will represent in the mid- to late 1990s. Ironically, the U.S. government is being asked to fund a massive research project—in effect, to compensate U.S. companies for their failure to preserve critical core competencies when they had the chance.

In contrast, one can see a company like Sony reducing its emphasis on VCRs (where it has not been very successful and where Korean companies now threaten), without reducing its commitment to video-related competencies. Sony's Betamax led to a debacle. But it emerged with its videotape recording competencies intact and is currently challenging Matsushita in the 8mm camcorder market.

There are two clear lessons here. First, the costs of losing a core competence can be only partly calculated in advance. The baby may be thrown out with the bath water in divestment decisions. Second, since core competencies are built through a process of continuous improvement and enhancement that may span a decade or longer, a company that has failed to invest in core competence building will find it very difficult to enter an emerging market, unless, of course, it will be content simply to serve as a distribution channel.

American semiconductor companies like Motorola learned this painful lesson when they elected to forgo direct participation in the 256k generation of DRAM chips. Having skipped this round, Motorola, like most of its American competitors, needed a large infusion of technical help from Japanese partners to rejoin the battle in the 1-megabyte generation. When it comes to core competencies, it is difficult to get off the train, walk to the next station, and then reboard.

FROM CORE COMPETENCIES TO CORE PRODUCTS

The tangible link between identified core competencies and end products is what we call the core products—the physical embodiments of one or more core competencies. Honda's engines, for example, are core products, linchpins between design and development skills that ultimately lead to a proliferation of end products. Core products are the components or subassemblies that actually contribute to the value of the end products. Thinking in terms of core products forces a company to distinguish between the brand share it achieves in end product markets (for example, 40% of the U.S. refrigerator market) and the manufacturing share it achieves in any particular core product (for example, 5% of the world share of compressor output).

Canon is reputed to have an 84% world manufacturing share in desktop laser printer "engines," even though its brand share in the laser printer business is minuscule. Similarly Matsushita has a world manufacturing share of about

45% in key VCR components, far in excess of its brand share (Panasonic, JVC, and others) of 20%. And Matsushita has a commanding core product share in compressors worldwide, estimated at 40%, even though its brand share in both the air-conditioning and refrigerator businesses is quite small.

It is essential to make this distinction between core competencies, core products, and end products because global competition is played out by different rules and for different stakes at each level. To build or defend leadership over the long term, a corporation will probably be a winner at each level. At the level of core competence, the goal is to build world leadership in the design and development of a particular class of product functionality—be it compact data storage and retrieval, as with Philips's optical-media competence, or compactness and ease of use, as with Sony's micromotors and microprocessor controls.

To sustain leadership in their chosen core competence areas, these companies *seek to maximize their world manufacturing share in core products*. The manufacture of core products for a wide variety of external (and internal) customers yields the revenue and market feedback that, at least partly, determines the pace at which core competencies can be enhanced and extended. This thinking was behind JVC's decision in the mid-1970s to establish VCR supply relationships with leading national consumer electronics companies in Europe and the United States. In supplying Thomson, Thorn, and Telefunken (all independent companies at that time) as well as U.S. partners, JVC was able to gain the cash and the diversity of market experience that ultimately enabled it to outpace Philips and Sony. (Philips developed videotape competencies in parallel with JVC, but it failed to build a worldwide network of OEM relationships that would have allowed it to accelerate the refinement of its videotape competence through the sale of core products.)

JVC's success has not been lost on Korean companies like Goldstar, Sam Sung, Kia, and Daewoo, who are building core product leadership in areas as diverse as displays, semiconductors, and automotive engines through their OEM-supply contracts with Western companies. Their avowed goal is to capture investment initiative away from potential competitors, often U.S. companies. In doing so, they accelerate their competence-building efforts while "hollowing out" their competitors. By focusing on competence and embedding it in core products, Asian competitors have built up advantages in component markets first and have then leveraged off their superior products to move downstream to build brand share. And they are not likely to remain the low-cost suppliers forever. As their reputation for brand leadership is consolidated, they may well gain price leadership. Honda has proven this with its Acura line, and other Japanese car makers are following suit.

Control over core products is critical for other reasons. A dominant position in core products allows a company to shape the evolution of applications and end markets. Such compact audio disc-related core products as data drives and lasers have enabled Sony and Philips to influence the evolution of the computer-peripheral business in optical-media storage. As a company multiplies the number of application arenas for its core products, it can consistently reduce the

Two Concepts of the Corporation: SBU or Core Competence

	SBU	Core Competence
Basis for competition	Competitiveness of today's products	Interfirm competition to build competencies
Corporate structure	Portfolio of businesses related in product-market terms	Portfolio of competencies, core products, and businesses
Status of the business unit	Autonomy is sacrosanct; the SBU "owns" all resources other than cash	SBU is a potential reservoir of core competencies
Resource allocation	Discrete businesses are the unit of analysis; capital is allocated business by business	Businesses and competencies are the unit of analysis: top management allocates capital and talent
Value added of top management	Optimizing corporate returns through capital allocation trade-offs among businesses	Enunciating strategic architecture and building competencies to secure the future

BOX 1.1 Two Concepts of the Corporation: SBU or Core Competence

cost, time, and risk in new product development. In short, well-targeted core products can lead to economies of scale *and* scope.

THE TYRANNY OF THE SBU

The new terms of competitive engagement cannot be understood using analytical tools devised to manage the diversified corporation of 20 years ago, when competition was primarily domestic (GE versus Westinghouse, General Motors versus Ford) and all the key players were speaking the language of the same business schools and consultancies. Old prescriptions have potentially toxic side effects. The need for new principles is most obvious in companies organized exclusively according to the logic of SBUs. The implications of the two alternate concepts of the corporation are summarized in "Two Concepts of the Corporation: SBU or Core Competence."

Obviously diversified corporations have a portfolio of products and a portfolio of businesses. But we believe in a view of the company as a portfolio of competencies as well. U.S. companies do not lack the technical resources to build competencies, but their top management often lacks the vision to build them and the administrative means for assembling resources spread across multiple businesses. A shift in commitment will inevitably influence patterns of diversification, skill deployment, resource allocation priorities, and approaches to alliances and outsourcing.

We have described the three different planes on which battles for global leadership are waged: core competence, core products, and end products. A corporation has to know whether it is winning or losing on each plane. By sheer weight of investment, a company might be able to beat its rivals to blue-sky technologies yet still lose the race to build core competence leadership. If a company is winning the race to build core competencies (as opposed to building leadership in a few technologies), it will almost certainly outpace rivals in new business development. If a company is winning the race to capture world manufacturing share in core products, it will probably outpace rivals in improving product features and the price/performance ratio.

Determining whether one is winning or losing end product battles is more difficult because measures of product market share do not necessarily reflect various companies' underlying competitiveness. Indeed, companies that attempt to build market share by relying on the competitiveness of others, rather than investing in core competencies and world core-product leadership, may be treading on quicksand. In the race for global brand dominance, companies like 3M, Black & Decker, Canon, Honda, NEC, and Citicorp have built global brand umbrellas by proliferating products out of their core competencies. This has allowed their individual businesses to build image, customer loyalty and access to distribution channels.

When you think about this reconceptualization of the corporation, the primacy of the SBU—an organizational dogma for a generation—is now clearly an anachronism. Where the SBU is an article of faith, resistance to the seductions of decentralization can seem heretical. In many companies, the SBU prism means that only one plane of the global competitive battle, the battle to put competitive products on the shelf *today*, is visible to top management. What are the costs of this distortion?

Underinvestment in Developing Core Competencies and Core Products

When the organization is conceived of as a multiplicity of SBUs, no single business may feel responsible for maintaining a viable position in core products nor be able to justify the investment required to build world leadership in some core competence. In the absence of a more comprehensive view imposed by corporate management, SBU managers will tend to underinvest. Recently companies such as Kodak and Philips have recognized this as a potential problem and have begun searching for new organizational forms that will allow them to develop and manufacture core products for both internal and external customers.

SBU managers have traditionally conceived of competitors in the same way they've seen themselves. On the whole, they've failed to note the emphasis Asian competitors were placing on building leadership in core products or to understand the critical linkage between world manufacturing leadership and the ability to sustain development pace in core competence. They've failed to pursue OEM-supply opportunities or to look across their various product divisions in an attempt to identify opportunities for coordinated initiatives.

Imprisoned Resources

As an SBU evolves, it often develops unique competencies. Typically the people who embody this competence are seen as the sole property of the business in which they grew up. The manager of another SBU who asks to borrow talented people is likely to get a cold rebuff. SBU managers are not only unwilling to lend their competence carriers but they may actually hide talent to prevent its redeployment in the pursuit of new opportunities. This may be compared to residents of an underdeveloped country hiding most of their cash under their mattresses. The benefits of competencies, like the benefits of the money supply depend on the velocity of their circulation as well as on the size of the stock the company holds.

Western companies have traditionally had an advantage in the stock of skills they possess. But have they been able to reconfigure them quickly to respond to new opportunities? Canon, NEC, and Honda have had a lesser stock of the people and technologies that compose core competencies but could move them much quicker from one business unit to another. Corporate R&D spending at Canon is not fully indicative of the size of Canon's core competence stock and tells the casual observer nothing about the velocity with which Canon is able to move core competencies to exploit opportunities.

When competencies become imprisoned, the people who carry the competencies do not get assigned to the most exciting opportunities, and their skills begin to atrophy. Only by fully leveraging core competencies can small companies like Canon afford to compete with industry giants like Xerox. How strange that SBU managers, who are perfectly willing to compete for cash in the capital budgeting process, are unwilling to compete for people—the company's most precious asset. We find it ironic that top management devotes so much attention to the capital budgeting process yet typically has no comparable mechanism for allocating the human skills that embody core competencies. Top managers are seldom able to look four or five levels down into the organization, identify the people who embody critical competencies, and move them across organizational boundaries.

Vickers Learns the Value of Strategic Architecture

The idea that top management should develop a corporate strategy for acquiring and deploying core competencies is relatively new in most U.S. companies. There are a few exceptions. An early convert was Trinova (previously Libbey Owens Ford), a Toledo-based corporation, which enjoys a worldwide position in power and motion controls and engineered plastics. One of its major divisions is Vickers, a premier supplier of hydraulics components like valves, pumps, actuators, and filtration devices to aerospace, marine, defense, automotive, earth-moving, and industrial markets.

Vickers saw the potential for a transformation of its traditional business with the application of electronics disciplines in combination with its traditional technologies. The goal was "to ensure that change in technology does not displace Vickers from its customers." This, to be sure, was initially a defensive move: Vickers recognized that unless it acquired new skills, it could not protect existing markets or capitalize on new growth opportunities. Managers at Vickers attempted to conceptualize the likely evolution of (a) technologies relevant to the power and motion control business, (b) functionalities that would satisfy emerging customer needs, and (c) new competencies needed to creatively manage the marriage of technology and customer needs.

Despite pressure for short-term earnings, top management looked to a 10- to 15-year time horizon in developing a map of emerging customer needs, changing technologies, and the core competencies that would be necessary to bridge the gap between the two. Its slogan was "Into the 21st Century." (A simplified version of the overall architecture developed is shown here.)

Vickers is currently in fluid-power components. The architecture identifies two additional competencies, electric-power components and electronic controls. A systems integration capability that would unite hardware, software, and service was also targeted for development.

The strategic architecture, as illustrated by the Vickers example, is not a forecast of specific products or specific technologies but a broad map of the evolving linkages between customer functionality requirements, potential technologies, and core competencies. It assumes that products and systems cannot be defined with certainty for the future but that preempting competitors in the development of new markets requires an early start to building core competencies. The strategic architecture developed by Vickers, while describing the future in competence terms, also provides the basis for making "here and now" decisions about product priorities, acquisitions, alliances, and recruitment.

Since 1986, Vickers has made more than ten clearly targeted acquisitions, each one focused on a specific component or technology gap identified in the overall architecture. The architecture is also the basis for internal development of new competencies. Vickers has undertaken, in parallel, a reorganization to enable the integration of electronics and electrical capabilities with mechanical-based competencies. We believe that it will take another two to three years before Vickers reaps the total benefits from developing the strategic architecture, communicating it widely to all its employees, customers, and investors, and building administrative systems consistent with the architecture.

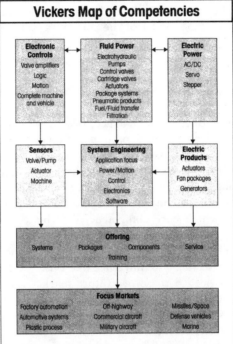

Vickers Map of Competencies

Electronic Controls	Fluid Power	Electric Power
Valve amplifiers	Electrohydraulic	AC/DC
Logic	Pumps	Servo
Motion	Control valves	Stepper
Complete machine and vehicle	Cartridge valves	
	Actuators	
	Package systems	
	Pneumatic products	
	Fuel/Fluid transfer	
	Filtration	

Sensors	System Engineering	Electric Products
Valve/Pump	Application focus	Actuators
Actuator	Power/Motion	Fan packages
Machine	Control	Generators
	Electronics	
	Software	

Offering

Systems	Packages	Components	Service
	Training		

Focus Markets

Factory automation	Off-highway	Missiles/Space
Automotive systems	Commercial aircraft	Defense vehicles
Plastic process	Military aircraft	Marine

BOX 1.2 Vickers Learns the Value of Strategic Architecture

Bounded Innovation

If core competencies are not recognized, individual SBUs will pursue only those innovation opportunities that are close at hand—marginal product-line extensions or geographic expansions. Hybrid opportunities like fax machines, laptop computers, hand-held televisions, or portable music keyboards will emerge only when managers take off their SBU blinkers. Remember, Canon appeared to be in the camera business at the time it was preparing to become a world leader in copiers. Conceiving of the corporation in terms of core competencies widens the domain of innovation.

DEVELOPING STRATEGIC ARCHITECTURE

The fragmentation of core competencies becomes inevitable when a diversified company's information systems, patterns of communication, career paths, managerial rewards, and processes of strategy development do not transcend SBU lines. We believe that senior management should spend a significant amount of its time developing a corporatewide strategic architecture that establishes objectives for competence building. A strategic architecture is a road map of the future that identifies which core competencies to build and their constituent technologies.

By providing an impetus for learning from alliances and a focus for internal development efforts, a strategic architecture like NEC's C&C can dramatically reduce the investment needed to secure future market leadership. How can a company make partnerships intelligently without a clear understanding of the core competencies it is trying to build and those it is attempting to prevent from being unintentionally transferred?

Of course, all of this begs the question of what a strategic architecture should look like. The answer will be different for every company. But it is helpful to think again of that tree, of the corporation organized around core products and, ultimately, core competencies. To sink sufficiently strong roots, a company must answer some fundamental questions: How long could we preserve our competitiveness in this business if we did not control this particular core competence? How central is this core competence to perceived customer benefits? What future opportunities would be foreclosed if we were to lose this particular competence?

The architecture provides a logic for product and market diversification, moreover. An SBU manager would be asked: Does the new market opportunity add to the overall goal of becoming the best player in the world? Does it exploit or add to the core competence? At Vickers, for example, diversification options have been judged in the context of becoming the best power and motion control company in the world (see the insert "Vickers Learns the Value of Strategic Architecture").

The strategic architecture should make resource allocation priorities transparent to the entire organization. It provides a template for allocation decisions by top management. It helps lower level managers understand the logic of allocation priorities and disciplines senior management to maintain consistency. In short, it yields a definition of the company and the markets it serves. 3M, Vickers, NEC, Canon, and Honda all qualify on this score. Honda *knew* it was exploiting what it had learned from motorcycles—how to make high-revving, smooth-running, lightweight engines—when it entered the car business. The task of creating a strategic architecture forces the organization to identify and commit to the technical and production linkages across SBUs that will provide a distinct competitive advantage.

It is consistency of resource allocation and the development of an administrative infrastructure appropriate to it that breathes life into a strategic architecture and creates a managerial culture, teamwork, a capacity to change, and a willingness to share resources, to protect proprietary skills, and to think long term. That is also the reason the specific architecture cannot be copied easily or overnight by competitors. Strategic architecture is a tool for communicating with customers and other external constituents. It reveals the broad direction without giving away every step.

REDEPLOYING TO EXPLOIT COMPETENCIES

If the company's core competencies are its critical resource and if top management must ensure that competence carriers are not held hostage by some particular business, then it follows that SBUs should bid for core competencies in the same way they bid for capital. We've made this point glancingly. It is important enough to consider more deeply.

Once top management (with the help of divisional and SBU managers) has identified overarching competencies, it must ask businesses to identify the projects and people closely connected with them. Corporate officers should direct an audit of the location, number, and quality of the people who embody competence.

This sends an important signal to middle managers: core competencies are *corporate* resources and may be reallocated by corporate management. An individual business doesn't own anybody. SBUs are entitled to the services of individual employees so long as SBU management can demonstrate that the opportunity it is pursuing yields the highest possible pay-off on the investment in their skills. This message is further underlined if each year in the strategic planning or budgeting process unit managers must justify their hold on the people who carry the company's core competencies.

Elements of Canon's core competence in optics are spread across businesses as diverse as cameras, copiers, and semiconductor lithographic equipment and are shown in "Core Competencies at Canon." When Canon identified an opportunity in digital laser printers, it gave SBU managers the right to raid other SBUs to pull together the required pool of talent. When Canon's reprographics products division undertook to develop microprocessor-controlled copiers, it turned to the photo products group, which had developed the world's first microprocessor-controlled camera.

Also, reward systems that focus only on product-line results and career paths that seldom cross SBU boundaries engender patterns of behavior among unit managers that are destructively competitive. At NEC, divisional managers come together to identify next-generation competencies. Together they decide how much investment needs to be made to build up each future competency and the contribution in capital and staff support that each division will need to make. There is also a sense of equitable exchange. One division may make a disproportionate contribution or may benefit less from the progress made, but such short-term inequalities will balance out over the long term.

Incidentally the positive contribution of the SBU manager should be made visible across the company. An SBU manager is unlikely to surrender key people if only the other business (or the general manager of that business who may be a competitor for promotion) is going to benefit from the redeployment. Cooperative SBU managers should be celebrated as team players. Where priorities are clear, transfers are less likely to be seen as idiosyncratic and politically motivated.

Transfers for the sake of building core competence must be recorded and appreciated in the corporate memory. It is reasonable to expect a business that has surrendered core skills on behalf of corporate opportunities in other areas to lose, for a time, some of its competitiveness. If these losses in performance bring immediate censure, SBUs will be unlikely to assent to skills transfers next time.

Finally there are ways to wean key employees off the idea that they belong in perpetuity to any particular business. Early in their careers, people may be exposed to a variety of businesses through a carefully planned rotation program. At Canon, critical people move regularly between the camera business and the copier business and between the copier business and the professional optical-products business. In mid-career, periodic assignments to cross-divisional project teams may be necessary both for diffusing core competencies and for loosening the bonds that might tie an individual to one business even when brighter opportunities beckon elsewhere. Those who embody critical core competencies should know that their careers are tracked and guided by corporate human resource professionals. In the early 1980s at Canon, all engineers under 30 were invited to apply for membership on a seven-person committee that was to spend two years plotting Canon's future direction, including its strategic architecture.

Competence carriers should be regularly brought together from across the corporation to trade notes and ideas. The goal is to build a strong feeling of community among these people. To a great extent, their loyalty should be to the integrity of the core competence area they represent and not just to particular businesses. In traveling regularly, talking frequently to customers, and meeting with peers, competence carriers may be encouraged to discover new market opportunities.

Core Competencies at Canon

	Precision Mechanics	Fine Optics	Micro-electronics
Basic camera	■	■	
Compact fashion camera	■	■	
Electronic camera	■	■	
EOS autofocus camera	■	■	■
Video still camera	■	■	■
Laser beam printer	■	■	■
Color video printer	■		■
Bubble jet printer	■		■
Basic fax	■		■
Laser fax	■		■
Calculator			■
Plain paper copier	■	■	■
Battery PPC	■	■	■
Color copier	■	■	■
Laser copier	■	■	■
Color laser copier	■	■	■
NAVI	■	■	■
Still video system	■	■	■
Laser imager	■	■	■
Cell analyzer	■	■	■
Mask aligners	■		■
Stepper aligners	■		■
Excimer laser aligners	■	■	■

Every Canon product is the result of at least one core competency.

BOX 1.3 Core Competencies at Canon

Core competencies are the wellspring of new business development. They should constitute the focus for strategy at the corporate level. Managers have to win manufacturing leadership in core products and capture global share through brand-building programs aimed at exploiting economics of scope. Only if the company is conceived of as a hierarchy of core competencies, core products, and market-focused business units will it be fit to fight.

Nor can top management be just another layer of accounting consolidation, which it often is in a regime of radical decentralization. Top management must add value by enunciating the strategic architecture that guides the competence acquisition process. We believe an obsession with competence building will characterize the global winners of the 1990s. With the decade underway, the time for rethinking the concept of the corporation is already overdue.

Chapter 2

A Competence Perspective on Strategic Learning and Knowledge Management[*]

Ron Sanchez, Aimé Heene

The growing prominence of accelerating change in the environments of organizations has brought processes for managing change within firms into the forefront of concerns in strategic management. As competition between firms increasingly takes on the character of a contest to identify, create, and leverage new competences (Hamel and Heene, 1994; Heene and Sanchez, 1996; Sanchez, Heene and Thomas, 1996a), effecting significant organizational change increasingly requires changing both the knowledge base within a firm and the way the firm uses its existing knowledge to compete more effectively. Consequently, improving a firm's strategic flexibility (Sanchez, 1993, 1995; Sanchez and Heene, 1996) to create new competences in response to environmental change is likely to require rethinking the ways a firm can create and acquire new knowledge and may require entirely new concepts for applying new knowledge to greatest strategic effect.

The topic of organizational learning and knowledge has received much recent attention from a number of perspectives, including economic and organization theory (Boisot, 1995), organization studies (Nonaka and Takeuchi, 1995), technological change (Durand, 1993), social systems (von Krogh and Vicari, 1993), cognition (Walsh, 1995), and international comparative studies (Hedlund and Nonaka, 1993), among others. In this discussion, we introduce a perspective on organizational learning and knowledge that is now being developed within the movement to build a theory of organizational competence and competence-based competition. A key interest of this perspective is understanding how better approaches to learning and knowledge utilization within organizations can improve the competence building and leveraging processes of firms. Thus, the emphasis in the competence perspective is on *strategic* forms of learning and knowledge management which can improve the performance of firms in competence-based competition.

We begin by proposing concepts of *strategic learning* and *strategic knowledge* based on ideas now being developed within the competence perspective. We suggest related definitions for strategic learning and strategically relevant knowledge. In so doing, we also suggest some important distinctions between forms of knowledge and processes of learning that occur in individuals and those that occur in organizations. We also discuss some fundamental ways in which knowledge assets differ from other kinds of strategic assets, and drawing on Boisot (1995) and Sanchez (1996a), we suggest some implications of this conceptualization of strategic knowledge assets for strategy theory, research, and practice. Important aspects of the topics we discuss are developed more fully in the chapters in this volume, and we briefly review their contributions. We conclude by proposing an agenda for further research to improve our understanding of strategically significant learning and knowledge management processes.

STRATEGICALLY RELEVANT KNOWLEDGE AND LEARNING

What is meant by *knowledge*? What is *learning*? How are knowledge and learning interrelated conceptually and organizationally?

These fundamental questions have occupied researchers in cognitive studies for many years, but today are being approached from a variety of new perspectives. Our objective in this discussion is not to review these multiple initiatives to understand knowledge and learning, but rather to introduce a competence perspective on knowledge and learning to facilitate connecting the ongoing work in competence with work in other perspectives.

Knowledge is defined by Sanchez, Heene and Thomas (1996b: 9) as "the set of beliefs held by an *individual* about causal relationships among phenomena" (emphasis added). Causal relationships in this definition are cause-and-effect relationships between imaginable events or actions and likely consequences of those events or actions.[1] *Organizational knowledge* is then defined as the shared set of beliefs about causal relationships held by individuals within a group (Sanchez et al., 1996b: 9). The intent of these definitions is threefold: First, to stipulate that strategically relevant knowledge is never certain, but rather only

---

[1] Knowledge therefore includes beliefs that some events or actions will have no significant consequences in a context of current interest. Human minds, like organizations, tend to merge beliefs about non-consequential events or actions into the background of consciousness and to focus limited cognitive processing capacities (Simon, 1957) on understanding and managing events and actions believed to be consequential in a context of current interest. Thus, the development of "cognitive blind spots" (van der Vorst, 1996) is inherent in creating and using knowledge in competitive environments, and managing the blind spots in firms therefore becomes an important aspect of managing strategic learning.

exists in the form of *beliefs*.[2] In other words, knowledge is not absolute or deterministic, but consists of more or less firmly held beliefs based on probabilistic assessments of possible causal relationships between phenomena. Second, to recognize that knowledge originates with and exists within individual humans, but that organizations may also have knowledge that may exist in various forms understood by more than one individual within an organization. We shall address below the potential strategic importance of individual and organizational forms of knowledge. Third, to refocus the concept of knowledge on conscious mental processes (beliefs) rather than lower-level neural processes at the level of sensory-motor coordination.[3]

Knowledge is fundamental to organizational *competence*, which Sanchez, Heene and Thomas define as an ability to sustain the coordinated deployment of assets and capabilities in a way that promises to help a firm to achieve its goals (1996b: 8). Having competence implies an organizational intention to achieve some desired result (goal) through specific actions. Since an intention to accomplish some goal through taking action(s) requires that individuals and groups within a firm have some beliefs as to how a firm's capabilities and skills can be used to "cause" certain desired effects, knowledge and the application of knowledge through action are at the foundation of the concepts of skills, capabilities, and (ultimately) organizational competence. Sanchez, Heene and Thomas (1996b) make a further distinction between *skills*, which are defined as the "micro-level" knowledge-in-action of one or a few individuals, and *capabilities* of firms, which are defined as "macro-level" organizational knowledge-in-action expressed through "repeatable patterns of action in the use of assets" (1996b: 7). In this framework, *skill* may be seen as "a special form of *capability*, with the connotation of a rather specific capability useful in a specialized situation or related to the use of a specialized asset" (1996b: 7). For example, a firm may have a capability in efficient manufacturing that consists of a number of

---

[2] We recognize that by defining knowledge as *beliefs* held by individuals or organizations rather than by some absolute standard of "certain knowledge", we are implying that different individuals or organizations might have specific instances of "knowledge" that are inconsistent or even contradictory. However, our interest is in understanding how knowledge and learning can improve the strategic management of organizations in a dynamically uncertain world. In this context, the important perspective is the *ex ante* perspective of managers in organizations who must make decisions under conditions of significant causal ambiguity. Thus, invoking a concept of certain knowledge would be inappropriate to this context. Indeed, the concept of causal ambiguity presumes that nothing can be "known" in a form other than belief based on assessments of probabilities (Lippman and Rumelt, 1982; Sanchez and Heene, 1996a).

[3] Here we allude to Polyani's (1962) famous skater who "knows" more than she can tell about how she skates. We suggest that whatever the skater cannot tell (albeit with some mental effort), she really does *not* "know", at least not within the concept of knowledge proposed by Sanchez, Heene and Thomas (1996b) and adopted by us here. We revisit Polyani's skater when we discuss the hazards of mapping knowledge concepts from one context of analysis directly onto another context.

interrelated skills in routing flows of work-in-progress, maintaining machine settings, monitoring conformance to specifications, and other specific tasks involved in manufacturing.

Learning is a process which changes the state of knowledge of an individual or organization. A change in state of knowledge may take the form of the adoption of a new belief about new causal relationships, the modification of an existing belief, the abandonment of a previously held belief, or a change in the degree of confidence with which an individual or individuals within an organization hold a belief or set of beliefs.

Within the conception of the firm as an *open system* (Sanchez and Heene, 1996a) in which there are asset stocks and flows (Dierickx and Cool, 1989), knowledge is a stock of beliefs held by individuals or groups of individuals within an organization, and learning represents flows that lead to a change in the stocks of beliefs within the organization.

Knowledge stocks may vary not only by the "content" of knowledge an individual or organization has (i.e. by the causal relationship that is the object of belief), but also by the degree to which knowledge held by an individual or organization can be put to some use—i.e., by the process capabilities of the organization in acting on its beliefs. Here we borrow the concept of *mastery* from education theory to suggest basic levels of action response which an acquired belief can facilitate. Education theory suggests that knowledge may be usefully characterized at four levels of "mastery": reproduction, explanation, application, and integration (Heene, 1993). As Sanchez (1996a) notes,

> . . . *reproduction* is like recall; an acquirer of articulated knowledge can only write it down, but is not able to impute a meaning to the articulated knowledge. *Explanation* indicates an understanding of the articulated knowledge in the sense that the acquirer can explain the knowledge in terms of some imputed meaning. *Application* implies an ability to apply some articulated knowledge correctly when asked to do so. *Integration* indicates attainment of mastery of some knowledge in the sense that the acquirer understands the uses to which the knowledge can be applied and can selectively choose to apply that knowledge in situations where it is beneficial to do so.

These levels of knowledge mastery suggest that knowledge within an organization may exist at different levels of usefulness. In other words, an individual or organization may have varying abilities to apply different forms of knowledge to carry out actions that help a firm accomplish its goals. Thus, different levels of knowledge mastery within firms may lead to different competence levels across firms and subsequently to different competitive outcomes in competence-based competition.

Learning may therefore change not only what kind of knowledge a firm has, but also the level of mastery at which the firm knows and can act on what it knows. Increasing the level of mastery of individual and organizational knowledge-in-action both leads to and benefits from an increase in the degree of confidence with which an individual or individuals within an organization hold a belief or set of beliefs. As a firm develops different levels of mastery of organizational knowledge and different ways of using its organizational knowledge in different contexts, it will develop various artifacts and representations of its knowledge. At the most basic level, firms will develop or adopt language to express shared beliefs. Some language may be provided by established technical or professional vocabularies, but some words will be coined or used in idiosyncratic ways within firms as a languaging process (van Krogh, Roos and Slocum, 1994) begins to *articulate* and connect beliefs of individuals and create a framework for organizational knowledge. As knowledge is articulated by individuals and groups, the organization may try to codify this knowledge (Sanchez, 1996a; Wright, 1996). *Codification* employs various means in an attempt to provide a structure to knowledge—ranging from schema to make the subject of various knowledge recognizable within an organization, to various expressions (e.g. manuals, engineering drawings) of specific knowledge intended to make the substance of that knowledge comprehensible to various individuals in the organization. Codification schemes therefore become vital mechanisms for improving the *apprehensibility* of knowledge (Sanchez, 1996a) and thus for transferring knowledge between groups within an organization and indeed between organizations.

A firm's processes for articulating, codifying, and transferring knowledge within the organization and to other organizations are important determinants of its ability to leverage its existing knowledge effectively—and thus of its ability to leverage its competences to greatest strategic effect. Similarly, a firm's processes for identifying, acquiring, codifying, and transferring new knowledge are central to its ability to build new organizational competences. Thus, strategically important organizational learning consists both of processes for creating new knowledge within individuals and groups within a firm (Nonaka and Takeuchi, 1995) and processes to leverage knowledge effectively within and across organizations (Sanchez, 1996a, 1996b; Sanchez and Mahoney, 1995).

INDIVIDUAL VERSUS ORGANIZATIONAL KNOWLEDGE AND LEARNING

Early work in cognition focused on studying knowledge and learning in individuals. With the increased recognition of the importance of organizational knowledge and learning to the effective performance of firms in dynamic environments, much attention is now being focused within the management literatures on the study of organizational forms of knowledge and learning. Not surprisingly, there has been a noticeable tendency in much of this research to use concepts of knowledge and learning developed in cognitive studies of individuals to represent knowledge and learning in organizations. We believe in many instances the simple mapping of knowledge and learning concepts from one context of analysis to another is theoretically unwarranted and has produced some misleading notions about organizational knowledge and learning processes.

We briefly revisit the example of Polyani's (1962) skater to make this point. Polyani uses the example of the skater (who can skate beautifully but who cannot explain how she manages to skate the way she does) to propose that "we know more than we can say" (1962). This example has been invoked by many writers to suggest that important knowledge within individuals and within organizations can be "tacit"—i.e. *incapable* of articulation. We believe that Polyani's use of the term "know" in his famous phrase is semantically unfortunate and, indeed, symptomatic of our need today for more carefully developed concepts and vocabulary for understanding knowledge. If our vocabulary is imprecise, the concepts we attempt to build with that vocabulary will be vague and of limited power to generate insights. We suggest that it is conceptually inadequate to use a single term like "knowing" to describe processes as different as what the skater does, what a manager or accountant does, and what a research and development organization does. We propose that there is no existent theoretical justification warranting extension of a concept of a skater's knowledge, that exists but cannot be articulated, to a manager engaged in work of a higher mental order or to the work of an organization. Similar problems of theoretical warrant exist for other concepts borrowed from studies of individual cognition and applied without adequate consideration to organizational knowledge and learning—indeed to more complex contexts of individual knowledge and learning.

HOW KNOWLEDGE ASSETS DIFFER FROM OTHER KINDS OF ASSETS

Knowledge assets differ fundamentally from other kinds of economic assets. Boisot (1995: 11) identifies two strategically important idiosyncratic properties of knowledge as an economic asset: the value of information (as an expression of knowledge) to one party in a potential exchange can only be ascertained if the information is disclosed by the party holding the information, but disclosure transfers the information to the other party and thereby diminishes its value to the original holder. Both properties contribute to market failures in information exchange, and "it is the failure of markets on information grounds that gives rise in the real world to alternative institutional arrangements such as firms for the vernance of [such] economic transactions" (1995: 18). Difficulties in appraising the value of knowledge and difficulties in obtaining the full potential value of acquired knowledge are discussed by Sanchez (1996a), and these may also contribute to market failures in the exchange and use of knowledge in various forms.

We suggest that these market-failure-inducing properties of knowledge assets have significant strategic implications beyond those commonly recognized in the strategy literature to date. Thus far, a common view within the strategy literature has been to regard individual and organizational knowledge as an asset to be zealously guarded within a firm, lest it be revealed to competitors and its strategic value lost thereby. Much emphasis, for example, has been placed on creating "tacit" individual and organizational knowledge as strategic assets, on the premise that tacit knowledge would be more difficult for competitors to discover an articulated forms of knowledge. We suggest that this strategy for creating and managing knowledge assets overlooks some key concerns: not only will it be difficult for competitors to acquire and use knowledge that is tacit, but it will be difficult for other individuals and groups within a firm to access and use tacit knowledge. Not articulating and codifying knowledge limits its transferability within an organization and us limits the benefits a firm might obtain if it could leverage its knowledge quickly and widely. Keeping knowledge in tacit forms may therefore incur high opportunity costs which must be weighed against the risk of diminished strategic value if codified knowledge were to be discovered and used by competitors.

Sanchez (1996) has suggested that at least three categories of knowledge may exist within firms: know-how (practical knowledge), know-why (theoretical knowledge), and know-what (strategic knowledge). Recognition of the different strategic value of these kinds of knowledge assets in different competitive contexts may enable managers to codify and share some kinds of knowledge with suppliers and other firms to improve a firm's ability to benefit from leveraging its knowledge widely and quickly. At the same time, the most strategically valuable or sensitive kinds of knowledge may be protected to prevent their leakage beyond the firm. Such theoretical development of new concepts of organizational knowledge may lead to better concepts for managing knowledge strategically. Thus, there appears to be an especially promising and direct link between the potential for theory building in organizational knowledge and improved understanding of how knowledge assets can be managed to obtain greatest strategic benefit.

CONTRIBUTIONS OF CURRENT RESEARCH

The chapters in this volume explore various aspects of learning processes within organizations (Løwendahl and Haanes, 1996; Hall, 1996; Boisot, Griffiths and Moles, 1996; and Wright, 1996), learning processes across organizational boundaries (Klavans and Deeds, 1996; Sivula, van den Bosch and Elfring, 1996; Quélin, 1996), and the strategic management of knowledge within and across firm boundaries (Sanchez, 1996b; Post, 1996; Lang, 1996). We briefly review the contribution of each of the articles to better strategic learning and knowledge management.

Strategic Learning Within Organizations

Using the concept of competence as a framework for studying organizational learning, Løwendahl and Haanes (1996) propose that the most useful unit of analysis for learning processes may be the various value-creating *activities* within a firm. Drawing on action theory and theories of collective action, they suggest that firms be viewed as *activity systems* in which learning takes place through participation in activities and in which "incoherence, dilemma, and conflict are seen to offer important avenues for learning". Applying this framework to a case study of Alcatel Telecom Norway, they suggest several characteristics of activities as units of analysis that show the dynamic, interconnected, and permeable nature of competence building and leveraging (Sanchez and Heene, 1996b).

The decision-making process of managers that determines what intangible assets a firm should develop is studied by Hall (1996). He reports a technique that managers have used to identify both current portfolios of intangible assets within their firms and the composition of future portfolios which could improve the competitive advantages of a firm. Hall introduces concepts from complexity theory to suggest ways in which organizational dynamics of learning can be improved within a firm. Extending the discussion of control loops within firms as open systems (Sanchez and Heene, 1996a), he suggests that negative feedback "command-and-control" processes in firms limit the ability of managers to identify strategically valuable new intangible resources, and he discusses ways to assure positive feedback that can help managers to identify opportunities to create valuable new intangible assets.

The way in which relevant knowledge becomes structured within and between firms is studied by Boisot, Griffiths and Moles (1996). Introducing a "culture space" as a conceptual tool, they develop an information-based interpretation of competence which clarifies ways in which the processing of information within firms governs the development and use of new competences. They also suggest a *paradox of value* that arises when using information in ways that increase the efficiency of a firm's use of a competence may also lead to loss of control of the competence.

The way in which learning processes may take on specific kinds of characteristics or *biases* within firms is discussed by Wright (1996). He suggests that the nature of the work firms perform will lead to systemic biases in the kinds of knowledge development systems firms adopt. His studies of firms in the semiconductor industry suggest that in that industry, some firms develop a "theorizing and codifying" form of learning bias, while others develop learning-by-doing systems that lead to "tangible knowledge integration". Each of these knowledge development systems leads to the development of specific kinds of knowledge and thus the creation of specific kinds of competences within firms.

Strategic Learning Between Organizations

The building of new competences in the biotechnology industry is studied by Klavans and Deeds (1996) to gain further insights into different ways that firms can go about acquiring new knowledge. Their study assesses the impact of different organizational approaches to learning on the ability of a firm to create value in a knowledge-intensive competitive environment, using the value of initial public offerings of shares in biotechnology firms to evaluate different kinds of learning that may be used in building new competences: basic scientific discovery, technology development (conversion of scientific knowledge into products and processes), and absorptive capacity (the ability to recognize valuable information outside the firm, obtain it, and redeploy existing resources to use it effectively). Their study suggests that in the context of the biotechnology industry in the United States, both technology development and absorptive capacity modes of knowledge creation can be effective in creating new competences of significant strategic value.

Close interactions between business service firms and clients in knowledge-intensive industries (e.g. in consulting engineering services) may create many opportunities for service-providing firms to expand their knowledge bases and improve their competences. Sivula, van den Bosch and Elfring (1996) analyze knowledge transfer processes in service provider-client relationships to develop a model for better knowledge management of vertical alliances within an industry.

A firm's current knowledge creating capabilities constrain its ability to build competences, and thus a firm's potential for building new competences is path dependent. Quélin (1996) suggests that developing means for integrating external knowledge into the firm may open important new avenues for overcoming path dependency and allow more rapid acquisition of new competences through strategic alliances. He discusses mechanisms which can improve the acquisition and integration of external knowledge in three types of strategic alliances: alliances to access existing competences, alliances to combine complementary assets, and alliances to create new capabilities.

Strategic Knowledge Management

Effective strategic management of a firm's knowledge assets requires recognition of the potential strategic value of each of the firm's different stocks of knowledge. Sanchez (1996) proposes a framework for analyzing a firm's knowledge assets that suggests several approaches to leveraging and controlling a firm's strategic knowledge assets. After a critical appraisal of the strategic value of "tacit" knowledge within organizations, he suggests that knowledge within firms has different *contents*—which are characterized as *know-how, know-why,* and *know-what*—that are used in different strategic *contexts*. He proposes a framework for developing knowledge management strategies based on analysis of the contents of a firm's knowledge and the context in which it will be used.

Modular product architectures may create an important framework for managing knowledge within a firm and within networks of firms (Sanchez, 1995, 1996b; Sanchez and Mahoney, 1995). Post (1996) explains the use of modularity by Baan Company, a rapidly growing Dutch software firm, as an architecture for creating software applications programs for business. Explaining how the concept of modularity was developed through the strategic logic and management processes of Baan Company, Post shows how modular product architectures create knowledge structures that enable flexible expansion, modification, and redeployment of the firm's software capabilities and products. The flexibility derived from its modular knowledge architecture has become a strategic means for improving the competence leveraging and building of Baan Company.

Sanchez and Mahoney (1995) have argued that adopting modularity in product design as a knowledge management strategy may also enable the adoption of modular organization designs. Lang (1996) investigates the relationship between modular product design and modular organization structures through a study of ARM Ltd, a developer of RISC-chip technology that has used modular product design to improve its flexibility and adaptability in a highly dynamic product market. Using a modular product architecture to structure a network of licensing relationships, ARM Ltd has developed complementary capabilities in alliance management and technology transfer that give it considerable ability to build and leverage new competences.

CONCLUSION

We conclude by reiterating that organizational knowledge and learning cannot be understood adequately from a strategic perspective simply by projecting onto organizations concepts borrowed from studies of individual knowledge and learning. As the chapters in this volume suggest, however, new and strategically useful insights into organizational knowledge and learning may be developed by studying real organizations from a variety of competence-based perspectives. As more firms in industries with rapidly changing knowledge bases become interested in developing new processes for creating and leveraging knowledge, we suggest that there is both unique need and opportunity for researchers to develop more grounded and interactive theory-building relationships with organizations (Mahoney and Sanchez, 1996). We suggest that the potential gains from developing a more involved and interactive mode of research into strategic learning and knowledge management are significant, but that realizing those gains will challenge both strategy researchers and strategic managers to pursue new modes of learning about learning.

REFERENCES

Boisot, Max, H. (1995). *The Information Space*, London: Routledge.

Boisot, Max, H., Dorothy Griffiths and Veronica Moles (1996). "The dilemma of competence: Differentiation versus integration in the pursuit of learning", in Ron Sanchez and Aimé Heene, editors, *Strategic Learning and Knowledge Management*, Chichester: John Wiley & Sons.

Dierickx, Ingmar and Karel Cool (1989). "Asset stock accumulation and sustainability of competitive advantage", *Management Science*, 35, pp. 1504–1511.

Durand, Thomas (1993). "The dynamics of cognitive technological maps", pp. 165–189, in Peter Lorange et al., editors, *Implementing Strategic Processes: Change, Learning, and Co-operation*, Oxford: Blackwell.

Hall, Richard (1996). "Complex systems, complex learning, and competence building", in Ron Sanchez and Aimé Heene, editors, *Strategic Learning and Knowledge Management*, Chichester: John Wiley & Sons.

Hamel, Gary and Aimé Heene (1994). "Conclusions: Which theory of strategic management do we need for tomorrow?", pp. 315–320, in *Competence-Based Competition*, Gary Hamel and Aimé Heene, editors, New York: John Wiley.

Hedlund, Gunnar and Ikujiro Nonaka (1993). "Models of knowledge management in the West and Japan", pp. 117–144, in Peter Lorange et al., editors, *Implementing Strategic Processes: Change, Learning, and Co-operation*, Oxford: Blackwell.

Heene, Aimé (1993). "Classifications of competence and their impact on defining, measuring, and developing 'core competence'", paper presented at Second International Workshop on Competence-Based Competition, EIASM, Brussels, Belgium, November 1993.

Heene, Aimé and Ron Sanchez (1996). *Competence-Based Strategic Management*, Chichester: John Wiley & Sons.

Klavans, Dick and David L. Deeds (1996). "Competence building in biotechnology start-ups: The role of scientific discovery, technical development, and absorptive capacity", in Ron Sanchez and Aimé Heene, editors, *Strategic Learning and Knowledge Management*, Chichester: John Wiley & Sons.

Lang, John W. (1996). "Leveraging knowledge across firm boundaries: Achieving strategic flexibility through modularization and alliances", in Ron Sanchez and Aimé Heene, editors, *Strategic Learning and Knowledge Management*, Chichester: John Wiley & Sons.

Løwendahl, Bente and Knut Haanes (1996). "The unit of activity: A new way to understand competence building and leveraging", in Ron Sanchez and Aimé Heene, editors, *Strategic Learning and Knowledge Management*, Chichester: John Wiley & Sons.

Mahoney, Joseph, T. and Ron Sanchez (1996). "Competence theory building: Reconnecting management theory and management practice", in Aimé Heene and Ron Sanchez, editors, *Competence-Based Strategic Management*, Chichester: John Wiley & Sons.

Nonaka, Ikujiro and Hirotaka Takeuchi (1995). *The Knowledge-Creating Company*, Oxford: Oxford University Press. Polyani, M. (1962). *Personal Knowledge*, Chicago: University of Chicago Press.

Post, Henk, A. (1996). "Modularity in product design, development, and organization: A case study of the Baan Company", in Ron Sanchez and Aimé Heene, editors, *Strategic Learning and Knowledge Management*, Chichester: John Wiley & Sons.

Quélin, Bertrand (1996). "Appropriability and the creation of new capabilities through strategic alliances", in Ron Sanchez and Aimé Heene, editors, *Strategic Learning and Knowledge Management*, Chichester: John Wiley & Sons.

Sanchez, Ron (1993). "Strategic flexibility, firm organization, and managerial work in dynamic markets: A strategic options perspective", *Advances in Strategic Management*, 9, pp. 251–291.

Sanchez, Ron (1995). "Strategic flexibility in product competition", *Strategic Management Journal*, 16 (summer), pp. 135–159.

Sanchez, Ron (1996a). "Managing articulated knowledge in competence-based competition", in Ron Sanchez and Aimé Heene, editors, *Strategic Learning and Knowledge Management*, Chichester: John Wiley & Sons.

Sanchez, Ron (1996b). "Strategic product creation: Managing new interactions of technology, markets, and organizations", *European Management Journal*, 14(2).

Sanchez, Ron and Aimé Heene (1996a). "A systems view of the firm in competence-based competition", in *Dynamics of Competence-Based Competition: Theory and Practice in the New Strategic Management*, Ron Sanchez, Aimé Heene and Howard Thomas, editors, Oxford: Elsevier.

Sanchez, Ron and Aimé Heene (1996b). "Competence-based strategic management: Concepts and issues for theory, research, and practice", in Aimé Heene and Ron Sanchez, editors, *Competence-Based Strategic Management*, Chichester: John Wiley & Sons.

Sanchez, Ron, Aimé Heene and Howard Thomas (1996a). *Dynamics of Competence-Based Competition: Theory and Practice in the New Strategic Management*, Ron Sanchez, Aimé Heene and Howard Thomas, editors, Oxford: Elsevier.

Sanchez, Ron, Aimé Heene and Howard Thomas (1996b). "Towards the theory and practice of competence-based competition", in *Dynamics of Competence-Based Competition: Theory and Practice in the New Strategic Management*, Ron Sanchez, Aimé Heene and Howard Thomas, editors, Oxford: Elsevier.

Sanchez, Ron and Joseph T. Mahoney (1995). "Modularity, flexibility, and knowledge management in product and organization design", University of Illinois Working Paper #95–0121, Champaign IL 61820.

Simon, Herbert (1957). *Models of Man*, New York: John Wiley & Sons.

Sivula, Petteri, Frans A.J. van den Bosch and Tom Elfring (1996). "Competence building by incorporating clients into the development of a business service firm's knowledge base", in Ron Sanchez and Aimé Heene, editors, *Strategic Learning and Knowledge Management*, Chichester: John Wiley & Sons.

van der Vorst, Roland (1996). "The blind spots of competence identification: A systems theoretic perspective", in Aimé Heene and Ron Sanchez, editors, *Competence-Based Strategic Management*, Chichester: John Wiley & Sons.

von Krogh, Georg, Johan Roos and Ken Slocum (1994). "An essay on corporate epistemology", *Strategic Management Journal*, 15 (Special Issue), pp. 53–71.

von Krogh, Georg and Salvatore Vicari (1993). "An autopoesis approach to experimental strategic learning", pp. 394–410, in Peter Lorange et al., editors, *Implementing Strategic Processes: Change, Learning, and Co-operation*, Oxford: Blackwell.

Walsh, James, P. (1995). "Managerial and organizational cognition: Notes from a trip down memory lane", *Organization Science*, 6(3), pp. 280–321.

Wright, Russell, W. (1996). "Tangible integration versus intellectual codification skills: A comparison of learning processes in developing logic and memory semiconductors", in Ron Sanchez and Aimé Heene, editors, *Strategic Learning and Knowledge Management*, Chichester: John Wiley & Sons.

PART II

Organizational Level Learning

Chapter 3

Absorptive Capacity: A New Perspective on Learning and Innovation[*]

Wesley M. Cohen
Carnegie Mellon University

Daniel A. Levinthal
University of Pennsylvania

In this paper, we argue that the ability of a firm to recognize the value of new, external information, assimilate it, and apply it to commercial ends is critical to its innovative capabilities. We label this capability a firm's absorptive capacity and suggest that it is largely a function of the firm's level of prior related knowledge. The discussion focuses first on the cognitive basis for an individual's absorptive capacity including, in particular, prior related knowledge and diversity of background. We then characterize the factors that influence absorptive capacity at the organizational level, how an organization's absorptive capacity differs from that of its individual members, and the role of diversity of expertise within an organization. We argue that the development of absorptive capacity, and, in turn, innovative performance are history- or path-dependent and argue how lack of investment in an area of expertise early on may foreclose the future development of a technical capability in that area. We formulate a model of firm investment in research and development (R&D), in which R&D contributes to a firm's absorptive capacity, and test predictions relating a firm's investment in R&D to the knowledge underlying technical change within an industry. Discussion focuses on the implications of absorptive capacity for the analysis of other related innovative activities, including basic research, the adoption

[*] Reprinted with permission © 1990 by Cornell University.

and diffusion of innovations, and decisions to participate in cooperative R&D ventures.[**]

INTRODUCTION

Outside sources of knowledge are often critical to the innovation process, whatever the organizational level at which the innovating unit is defined. While the example of Japan illustrates the point saliently at the national level (e.g., Westney and Sakakibara, 1986; Mansfield, 1988; Rosenberg and Steinmueller, 1988), it is also true of entire industries, as pointed out by Brock (1975) in the case of computers and by Peck (1962) in the case of aluminum. At the organizational level, March and Simon (1958: 188) suggested most innovations result from borrowing rather than invention. This observation is supported by extensive research on the sources of innovation (e.g., Mueller, 1962; Hamberg, 1963; Myers and Marquis, 1969; Johnston and Gibbons, 1975; von Hippel, 1988). Finally, the importance to innovative performance of information originating from other internal units in the firm, outside the formal innovating unit (i.e., the R&D lab), such as marketing and manufacturing, is well understood (e.g., Mansfield, 1968).

The ability to exploit external knowledge is thus a critical component of innovative capabilities. We argue that the ability to evaluate and utilize outside knowledge is largely a function of the level of prior related knowledge. At the most elemental level, this prior knowledge includes basic skills or even a shared language but may also include knowledge of the most recent scientific or technological developments in a given field. Thus, prior related knowledge confers an ability to recognize the value of new information, assimilate it, and apply it to commercial ends. These abilities collectively constitute what we call a firm's "absorptive capacity."

At the level of the firm—the innovating unit that is the focus here—absorptive capacity is generated in a variety of ways. Research shows that firms that conduct their own R&D are better able to use externally available information (e.g., Tilton, 1971; Allen, 1977; Mowery, 1983). This implies that absorptive capacity may be created as a byproduct of a firm's R&D investment. Other work suggests that absorptive capacity may also be developed as a byproduct of a firm's manufacturing operations. Abernathy (1978) and Rosenberg (1982) have noted that through direct involvement in manufacturing, a firm is better able to

[**] We appreciate the comments of Kathleen Carley, Robyn Dawes, Mark Fichman, Tom Finholt, Sara Kiesler, Richard Nelson, Linda Pike, and three anonymous referees. The representations and conclusions presented herein are those of the authors. They have not been adopted in whole or in part by the Federal Trade Commission, its Bureau of Economics, or any other entity within the commission. The FTC's Disclosure Avoidance Officer has certified that the data included in this paper do not identify individual company line-of-business data.

recognize and exploit new information relevant to a particular product market. Production experience provides the firm with the background necessary both to recognize the value of and implement methods to reorganize or automate particular manufacturing processes. Firms also invest in absorptive capacity directly, as when they send personnel for advanced technical training. The concept of absorptive capacity can best be developed through an examination of the cognitive structures that underlie learning.

Cognitive Structures

The premise of the notion of absorptive capacity is that the organization needs prior related knowledge to assimilate and use new knowledge. Studies in the area of cognitive and behavioral sciences at the individual level both justify and enrich this observation. Research on memory development suggests that accumulated prior knowledge increases both the ability to put new knowledge into memory, what we would refer to as the acquisition of knowledge, and the ability to recall and use it. With respect to the acquisition of knowledge, Bower and Hilgard (1981: 424) suggested that memory development is self-reinforcing in that the more objects, patterns and concepts that are stored in memory, the more readily is new information about these constructs acquired and the more facile is the individual in using them in new settings.

Some psychologists suggest that prior knowledge enhances learning because memory—or the storage of knowledge—is developed by associative learning in which events are recorded into memory by establishing linkages with pre-existing concepts. Thus, Bower and Hilgard (1981) suggested that the breadth of categories into which prior knowledge is organized, the differentiation of those categories, and the linkages across them permit individuals to make sense of and, in turn, acquire new knowledge. In the context of learning a language, Lindsay and Norman (1977: 517) suggested the problem in learning words is not a result of lack of exposure to them but that "to understand complex phrases, much more is needed than exposure to the words: a large body of knowledge must first be accumulated. After all, a word is simply a label for a set of structures within the memory system, so the structures must exist before the word can be considered learned." Lindsay and Norman further suggested that knowledge may be nominally acquired but not well utilized subsequently because the individual did not already possess the appropriate contextual knowledge necessary to make the new knowledge fully intelligible.

The notion that prior knowledge facilitates the learning of new related knowledge can be extended to include the case in which the knowledge in question may itself be a set of learning skills. There may be a transfer of learning skills across bodies of knowledge that are organized and expressed in similar ways. As a consequence, experience or performance on one learning task may influence and improve performance on some subsequent learning task (Ellis, 1965). This progressive improvement in the performance of learning tasks is a form of knowledge transfer that has been referred to as "learning to learn" (Ellis, 1965; Estes, 1970). Estes (1970: 16), however, suggested that the term "learning to learn" is a misnomer in that prior experience with a learning task does not necessarily improve performance because an individual knows how to learn (i.e., form new associations) better, but that an individual may simply have accumulated more prior knowledge so that he or she needs to learn less to attain a given level of performance. Notwithstanding what it is about prior learning experience that may affect subsequent performance, both explanations of the relationship between early learning and subsequent performance emphasize the importance of prior knowledge for learning.

The effect of prior learning experience on subsequent learning tasks can be observed in a variety of tasks. For instance, Ellis (1965: 4) suggested that "students who have thoroughly mastered the principles of algebra find it easier to grasp advanced work in mathematics such as calculus." Further illustration is provided by Anderson, Farrell, and Sauers (1984), who compared students learning LISP as a first programming language with students learning LISP after having learned Pascal. The Pascal students learned LISP much more effectively, in part because they better appreciated the semantics of various programming concepts.

The literature also suggests that problem-solving skills develop similarly. In this case, problem-solving methods and heuristics typically constitute the prior knowledge that permits individuals to acquire related problem-solving capabilities. In their work on the development of computer programming skills, Pirolli and Anderson (1985) found that almost all students developed new programs by analogy-to-example programs and that their success was determined by how well they understood why these examples worked.

We argue that problem solving and learning capabilities are so similar that there is little reason to differentiate their modes of development, although exactly what is learned may differ: learning capabilities involve the development of the capacity to assimilate existing knowledge, while problem-solving skills represent a capacity to create new knowledge. Supporting the point that there is little difference between the two, Bradshaw, Langley, and Simon (1983) and Simon (1985) suggested that the sort of necessary preconditions for successful learning that we have identified do not differ from the pre-conditions required for problem solving and, in turn, for the creative process. Moreover, they argued that the processes themselves do not differ much. The prior possession of relevant knowledge and skill is what gives rise to creativity, permitting the sorts of associations and linkages that may have never been considered before. Likewise, Ellis (1965: 35) suggested that Harlow's (1959) findings on the development of learning sets provide a possible explanation for the behavioral phenomenon of "insight" that typically refers to the rapid solution of a problem. Thus, the psychology literature suggests that creative capacity and what we call absorptive capacity are quite similar.

To develop an effective absorptive capacity, whether it be for general knowledge or problem-solving or learning skills, it is insufficient merely to expose an individual briefly to the relevant prior knowledge. Intensity of effort is critical. With regard to storing knowledge in memory, Lindsay and Norman (1977: 355) noted that the more deeply the material is processed—the more effort used, the more processing makes use of associations between the items to be learned and knowledge already in the memory—the better will be the later retrieval of the item. Similarly, learning-set theory (Harlow, 1949, 1959) implies that important aspects of learning how to solve problems are built up over many practice trials on related problems. Indeed, Harlow (1959) suggested that if practice with a particular type of problem is discontinued before it is reliably learned, then little transfer will occur to the next series of problems. Therefore, he concluded that considerable time and effort should be spent on early problems before moving on to more complex problems.

Two related ideas are implicit in the notion that the ability to assimilate information is a function of the richness of the pre-existing knowledge structure: learning is cumulative, and learning performance is greatest when the object of learning is related to what is already known. As a result, learning is more difficult in novel domains, and, more generally, an individual's expertise—what he or she knows well—will change only incrementally. The above discussion also suggests that diversity of knowledge plays an important role. In a setting in which there is uncertainty about the knowledge domains from which potentially useful information may emerge, a diverse background provides a more robust basis for learning because it increases the prospect that incoming information will relate to what is already known. In addition to strengthening assimilative powers, knowledge diversity also facilitates the innovative process by enabling the individual to make novel associations and linkages.

From Individual to Organizational Absorptive Capacity

An organization's absorptive capacity will depend on the absorptive capacities of its individual members. To this extent, the development of an organization's absorptive capacity will build on prior investment in the development of its constituent, individual absorptive capacities, and, like individuals' absorptive capacities, organizational absorptive capacity will tend to develop cumulatively. A firm's absorptive capacity is not, however, simply the sum of the absorptive capacities of its employees, and it is therefore useful to consider what aspects of absorptive capacity are distinctly organizational. Absorptive capacity refers not only to the acquisition or assimilation of information by an organization but also to the organization's ability to exploit it. Therefore, an organization's absorptive capacity does not simply depend on the organization's direct interface with the external environment. It also depends on transfers of knowledge across and within subunits that may be quite removed from the original point of entry. Thus, to understand the sources of a firm's absorptive capacity, we focus on the structure of communication between the external environment and the organization, as well as among the subunits of the organization, and also on the character and distribution of expertise within the organization.

Communication systems may rely on specialized actors to transfer information from the environment or may involve less structured patterns. The problem of designing communication structures cannot be disentangled from the distribution of expertise in the organization. The firm's absorptive capacity depends on the individuals who stand at the interface of either the firm and the external environment or at the interface between subunits within the firm. That interface function may be diffused across individuals or be quite centralized. When the expertise of most individuals within the organization differs considerably from that of external actors who can provide useful information, some members of the group are likely to assume relatively centralized "gatekeeping" or "boundary-spanning" roles (Allen, 1977; Tushman, 1977). For technical information that is difficult for internal staff to assimilate, a gatekeeper both monitors the environment and translates the technical information into a form understandable to the research group. In contrast, if external information is closely related to ongoing activity, then external information is readily assimilated and gatekeepers or boundary-spanners are not so necessary for translating information. Even in this setting, however, gatekeepers may emerge to the extent that such role specialization relieves others from having to monitor the environment.

A difficulty may emerge under conditions of rapid and uncertain technical change, however, when this interface function is centralized. When information flows are somewhat random and it is not clear where in the firm or subunit a piece of outside knowledge is best applied, a centralized gatekeeper may not provide an effective link to the environment. Under such circumstances, it is best for the organization to expose a fairly broad range of prospective "receptors" to the environment. Such an organization would exhibit the organic structure of Burns and Stalker (1961: 6), which is more adaptable "when problems and requirements for action arise which cannot be broken down and distributed among specialist roles within a clearly defined hierarchy."

Even when a gatekeeper is important, his or her individual absorptive capacity does not constitute the absorptive capacity of his or her unit within the firm. The ease or difficulty of the internal communication process and, in turn, the level of organizational absorptive capacity are not only a function of the gatekeeper's capabilities but also of the expertise of those individuals to whom the gatekeeper is transmitting the information. Therefore, relying on a small set of technological gatekeepers may not be sufficient; the group as a whole must have some level of relevant background knowledge, and when knowledge structures are highly differentiated, the requisite level of background may be rather high.

The background knowledge required by the group as a whole for effective communication with the gatekeeper highlights the more general point that shared knowledge and expertise is essential for communication. At the most basic level, the relevant knowledge that permits effective communication both within and across subunits consists of shared language and symbols (Dearborn and Simon, 1958; Katz and Kahn, 1966; Allen and Cohen, 1969; Tushman,

1978; Zenger and Lawrence, 1989). With regard to the absorptive capacity of the firm as a whole, there may, however, be a trade-off in the efficiency of internal communication against the ability of the subunit to assimilate and exploit information originating from other subunits or the environment. This can be seen as a trade-off between inward-looking versus outward-looking absorptive capacities. While both of these components are necessary for effective organizational learning, excessive dominance by one or the other will be dysfunctional. If all actors in the organization share the same specialized language, they will be effective in communicating with one another, but they may not be able to tap into diverse external knowledge sources. In the limit, an internal language, coding scheme, or, more generally, any particular body of expertise could become sufficiently overlapping and specialized that it impedes the incorporation of outside knowledge and results in the pathology of the not-invented-here (NIH) syndrome. This may explain Katz and Allen's (1982) findings that the level of external communication and communication with other project groups declines with project-group tenure.

This trade-off between outward- and inward-looking components of absorptive capacity focuses our attention on how the relationship between knowledge sharing and knowledge diversity across individuals affects the development of organizational absorptive capacity. While some overlap of knowledge across individuals is necessary for internal communication, there are benefits to diversity of knowledge structures across individuals that parallel the benefits to diversity of knowledge within individuals. As Simon (1985) pointed out, diverse knowledge structures coexisting in the same mind elicit the sort of learning and problem solving that yields innovation. Assuming a sufficient level of knowledge overlap to ensure effective communication, interactions across individuals who each possess diverse and different knowledge structures will augment the organization's capacity for making novel linkages and associations—innovating—beyond what any one individual can achieve. Utterback (1971), summarizing research on task performance and innovation, noted that diversity in the work setting "stimulates the generation of new ideas." Thus, as with Nelson and Winter's (1982) view of organizational capabilities, an organization's absorptive capacity is not resident in any single individual but depends on the links across a mosaic of individual capabilities.

Beyond diverse knowledge structures, the sort of knowledge that individuals should possess to enhance organizational absorptive capacity is also important. Critical knowledge does not simply include substantive, technical knowledge; it also includes awareness of where useful complementary expertise resides within and outside the organization. This sort of knowledge can be knowledge of who knows what, who can help with what problem, or who can exploit new information. With regard to external relationships, von Hippel (1988) has shown the importance for innovation of close relationships with both buyers and suppliers. To the extent that an organization develops a broad and active network of internal and external relationships, individuals' awareness of others' capabilities and knowledge will be strengthened. As a result, individual absorptive capacities are leveraged all the more, and the organization's absorptive capacity is strengthened.

The observation that the ideal knowledge structure for an organizational subunit should reflect only partially overlapping knowledge complemented by nonoverlapping diverse knowledge suggests an organizational trade-off between diversity and commonality of knowledge across individuals. While common knowledge improves communication, commonality should not be carried so far that diversity across individuals is substantially diminished. Likewise, division of labor promoting gains from specialization should not be pushed so far that communication is undermined. The difficulties posed by excessive specialization suggest some liabilities of pursuing production efficiencies via learning by doing under conditions of rapid technical change in which absorptive capacity is important. In learning by doing, the firm becomes more practiced and hence more capable at activities in which it is already engaged. Learning by doing does not contribute to the diversity that is critical to learning about or creating something that is relatively new. Moreover, the notion of "remembering by doing" (Nelson and Winter, 1982) suggests that the focus on one class of activity entailed by learning by doing may effectively diminish the diversity of background that an individual or organization may have at one time possessed and, consequently, undercut organizational absorptive capacity and innovative performance.

It has become generally accepted that complementary functions within the organization ought to be tightly intermeshed, recognizing that some amount of redundancy in expertise may be desirable to create what can be called cross-function absorptive capacities. Cross-function interfaces that affect organizational absorptive capacity and innovative performance include, for example, the relationships between corporate and divisional R&D labs or, more generally, the relationships among the R&D, design, manufacturing, and marketing functions (e.g., Mansfield, 1968: 86–88). Close linkages between design and manufacturing are often credited for the relative success of Japanese firms in moving products rapidly from the design stage through development and manufacturing (Westney and Sakakibara, 1986). Clark and Fujimoto (1987) argued that overlapping product development cycles facilitate communication and coordination across organizational subunits. They found that the speed of product development is strongly influenced by the links between problem-solving cycles and that successful linking requires "direct personal contacts across functions, liaison roles at each unit, cross-functional task forces, cross-functional project teams, and a system of 'product manager as integrator'" (Clark and Fujimoto, 1987: 24). In contrast, a process in which one unit simply hands off the design to another unit is likely to suffer greater difficulties.

Some management practices also appear to reflect the belief that an excessive degree of overlap in functions may reduce the firm's absorptive capacity and that diversity of backgrounds is useful. The Japanese practice of rotating their R&D personnel through marketing and manufacturing operations, for example, while creating knowledge overlap, also enhances the diversity of background of their personnel. Often involving the assignment of technical personnel to other functions for several years, this practice also suggests that some intensity of experience in each of the complementary knowledge domains is necessary to put an effective absorptive capacity in place; breadth of knowledge cannot be superficial to be effective.

The discussion thus far has focused on internal mechanisms that influence the organization's absorptive capacity. A question remains as to whether absorptive capacity needs to be internally developed or to what extent a firm may simply buy it via, for example, hiring new personnel, contracting for consulting services, or even through corporate acquisitions. We suggest that the effectiveness of such options is somewhat limited when the absorptive capacity in question is to be integrated with the firm's other activities. A critical component of the requisite absorptive capacity for certain types of information, such as those associated with product and process innovation, is often firm-specific and therefore cannot be bought and quickly integrated into the firm. This is reflected in Lee and Allen's (1982) findings that considerable time lags are associated with the integration of new technical staff, particularly those concerned with process and product development. To integrate certain classes of complex and sophisticated technological knowledge successfully into the firm's activities, the firm requires an existing internal staff of technologists and scientists who are both competent in their fields and are familiar with the firm's idiosyncratic needs, organizational procedures, routines, complementary capabilities, and extramural relationships. As implied by the discussion above, such diversity of knowledge structures must coexist to some degree in the same minds. Moreover, as Nelson and Winter's (1982) analysis suggests, much of the detailed knowledge of organizational routines and objectives that permit a firm and its R&D labs to function is tacit. As a consequence, such critical complementary knowledge is acquired only through experience within the firm. Illustrating our general argument, Vyssotsky (1977), justifying the placement of Bell Labs within AT&T, argued: "For research and development to yield effective results for Bell System, it has to be done by . . . creative people who understand as much as they possibly can about the technical state of the art, and about Bell System and what System's problems are. The R&D people must be free to think up new approaches, and they must also be closely coupled to the problems and challenges where innovation is needed. This combination, if one is lucky, will result in insights which help the Bell System. That's why we have Bell Labs in Bell System, instead of having all our R&D done by outside organizations."

Path Dependence and Absorptive Capacity

Our discussion of the character of absorptive capacity and its role in assimilating and exploiting knowledge suggests a simple generalization that applies at both the individual and organizational levels: prior knowledge permits the assimilation and exploitation of new knowledge. Some portion of that prior knowledge should be very closely related to the new knowledge to facilitate assimilation, and some fraction of that knowledge must be fairly diverse, although still related, to permit effective, creative utilization of the new knowledge. This simple notion that prior knowledge underlies absorptive capacity has important implications for the development of absorptive capacity over time and, in turn, the innovative performance of organizations. The basic role of prior knowledge suggests two features of absorptive capacity that will affect innovative performance in an evolving, uncertain environment (Cohen and Levinthal, 1989b). Accumulating absorptive capacity in one period will permit its more efficient accumulation in the next. By having already developed some absorptive capacity in a particular area, a firm may more readily accumulate what additional knowledge it needs in the subsequent periods in order to exploit any critical external knowledge that may become available. Second, the possession of related expertise will permit the firm to better understand and therefore evaluate the import of intermediate technological advances that provide signals as to the eventual merit of a new technological development. Thus, in an uncertain environment, absorptive capacity affects expectation formation, permitting the firm to predict more accurately the nature and commercial potential of technological advances. These revised expectations, in turn, condition the incentive to invest in absorptive capacity subsequently. These two features of absorptive capacity—cumulativeness and its effect on expectation formation—imply that its development is domain-specific and is path- or history-dependent.

The cumulativeness of absorptive capacity and its effect on expectation formation suggest an extreme case of path dependence in which once a firm ceases investing in its absorptive capacity in a quickly moving field, it may never assimilate and exploit new information in that field, regardless of the value of that information. There are two reasons for the emergence of this condition, which we term "lockout" (Cohen and Levinthal, 1989b). First, if the firm does not develop its absorptive capacity in some initial period, then its beliefs about the technological opportunities present in a given field will tend not to change over time because the firm may not be aware of the significance of signals that would otherwise revise its expectations. As a result, the firm does not invest in absorptive capacity and, when new opportunities subsequently emerge, the firm may not appreciate them. Compounding this effect, to the extent that prior knowledge facilitates the subsequent development of absorptive capacity, the lack of early investment in absorptive capacity makes it more costly to develop a given level of it in a subsequent period. Consequently, a low initial investment in absorptive capacity diminishes the attractiveness of investing in subsequent periods even if the firm becomes aware of technological opportunities.[1] This possibility of firms being "locked-out" of subsequent technological developments has

---

[1] A similar result emerges from models of adaptive learning. Levitt and March (1988: 322) noted that "a competency trap can occur when favorable performance with an inferior procedure leads an organization to accumulate more experience with it, thus keeping experience with a superior procedure inadequate to make it rewarding to use."

recently become a matter of concern with respect to industrial policy. For instance, Reich (1987: 64) declaims Monsanto's exit from "float-zone" silicon manufacturing because he believes that the decision may be an irreversible exit from a technology, in that ". . . each new generation of technology builds on that which came before, once off the technological escalator it's difficult to get back on."

Thus, the cumulative quality of absorptive capacity and its role in conditioning the updating of expectations are forces that tend to confine firms to operating in a particular technological domain. If firms do not invest in developing absorptive capacity in a particular area of expertise early on, it may not be in their interest to develop that capacity subsequently, even after major advances in the field. Thus, the pattern of inertia that Nelson and Winter (1982) highlighted as a central feature of firm behavior may emerge as an implication of rational behavior in a model in which absorptive capacity is cumulative and contributes to expectation formation. The not-invented-here syndrome, in which firms resist accepting innovative ideas from the environment, may also at times reflect what we call lockout. Such ideas may be too distant from the firm's existing knowledge base—its absorptive capacity—to be either appreciated or accessed. In this particular setting, NIH may be pathological behavior only in retrospect. The firm need not have acted irrationally in the development of the capabilities that yields the NIH syndrome as its apparent outcome.

A form of self-reinforcing behavior similar to lockout may also result from the influence of absorptive capacity on organizations' goals or aspiration levels. This argument builds on the behavioral view of organizational innovation that has been molded in large part by the work of March and Simon (1958). In March and Simon's framework, innovative activity is instigated due to a failure to reach some aspiration level. Departing from their model, we suggest that a firm's aspiration level in a technologically progressive environment is not simply determined by past performance or the performance of reference organizations. It also depends on the firm's absorptive capacity. The greater the organization's expertise and associated absorptive capacity, the more sensitive it is likely to be to emerging technological opportunities and the more likely its aspiration level will be defined in terms of the opportunities present in the technical environment rather than strictly in terms of performance measures. Thus, organizations with higher levels of absorptive capacity will tend to be more proactive, exploiting opportunities present in the environment, independent of current performance. Alternatively, organizations that have a modest absorptive capacity will tend to be reactive, searching for new alternatives in response to failure on some performance criterion that is not defined in terms of technical change per se (e.g., profitability, market share, etc.).

A systematic and enduring neglect of technical opportunities may result from the effect of absorptive capacity on the organization's aspiration level when innovative activity (e.g., R&D) contributes to absorptive capacity, which is often the case in technologically progressive environments. The reason is that the firm's aspiration level then depends on the very innovative activity that is triggered by a failure to meet the aspiration level itself. If the firm engages in little innovative activity, and is therefore relatively insensitive to the opportunities in the external environment, it will have a low aspiration level with regard to the exploitation of new technology, which in turn implies that it will continue to devote little effort to innovation. This creates a self-reinforcing cycle. Likewise, if an organization has a high aspiration level, influenced by externally generated technical opportunities, it will conduct more innovative activity and thereby increase its awareness of outside opportunities. Consequently, its aspiration level will remain high. This argument implies that reactive and proactive modes of firm behavior should remain rather stable over time. Thus, some organizations (like Hewlett-Packard and Sony) have the requisite technical knowledge to respond proactively to the opportunities present in the environment. These firms do not wait for failure on some performance dimension but aggressively seek out new opportunities to exploit and develop their technological capabilities.[2]

The concept of dynamically self-reinforcing behavior that may lead to the neglect of new technological developments provides some insight into the difficulties firms face when the technological basis of an industry changes—what Schumpeter (1942) called "the process of creative destruction." For instance, the change from electromechanical devices to electronic ones in the calculator industry resulted in the exit of a number of firms and a radical change in the market structure (Majumdar, 1982). This is an example of what Tushman and Anderson (1986) termed competence-destroying technical change. A firm without a prior technological base in a particular field may not be able to acquire one readily if absorptive capacity is cumulative. In addition, a firm may be blind to new developments in fields in which it is not investing if its updating capability is low. Accordingly, our argument implies that firms may not realize that they should be developing their absorptive capacity due to an irony associated with its valuation: the firm needs to have some absorptive capacity already to value it appropriately.

Absorptive Capacity and R&D Investment

The prior discussion does not address the question of whether we can empirically evaluate the importance of absorptive capacity for innovation. There is a key insight that permits empirical tests of the implications of absorptive capacity for innovative activity. Since technical change within an industry—typically incremental in character (Rosenberg and Steinmueller, 1988)—is often closely related to a firm's ongoing R&D activity, a firm's ability to exploit

---

[2] This argument that such reactive and proactive behavior may coexist in an industry over the long run assumes that there is slack in the selection environment and that technologically progressive behavior is not essential to survival. One can, alternatively, identify a number of industries, such as semiconductors, in which it appears that only firms that aggressively exploit technical opportunities survive.

external knowledge is often generated as a byproduct of its R&D. We may therefore consider a firm's R&D as satisfying two functions: we assume that R&D not only generates new knowledge but also contributes to the firm's absorptive capacity.[3] If absorptive capacity is important, and R&D contributes to it, then whatever conditions the firm's incentives to learn (i.e., to build absorptive capacity) should also influence R&D spending. We may therefore consider the responsiveness of R&D activity to learning incentives as an indication of the empirical importance of absorptive capacity. The empirical challenge then is to understand the impact of the characteristics of the learning environment on R&D spending.

We construct a simple static model of firm R&D intensity, which is defined as R&D divided by sales. Normalization of R&D by firm sales controls for the effect of firm size, which affects the return per unit of R&D effort. This model is developed in the broader context of what applied economists have come to believe to be the three classes of industry-level determinants of R&D intensity: demand, appropriability, and technological opportunity conditions (Cohen and Levin, 1989). Demand is often characterized by the level of sales and the price elasticity of demand. The latter indicates the degree to which a firm's revenue will increase due to a reduction in price. For example, in the case of a process innovation that reduces the cost of production and, in turn, the product price, the price elasticity of demand reflects the associated change in total revenue that influences the economic return to innovative effort. Appropriability conditions refer to the degree to which firms capture the profits associated with their innovative activity and are often considered to reflect the degree to which valuable knowledge spills out into the public domain. The emphasis here is on valuable knowledge, because if a competitor's knowledge spills out but the competitor has already exploited a first-mover advantage in the marketplace, this knowledge is no longer valuable to the firm and does not constitute a spillover by our definition. The level of spillovers, in turn, depends on the strength of patents within an industry, the efficacy of secrecy, and/or first-mover advantages. Technological opportunity represents how costly it is for the firm to achieve some normalized unit of technical advance in a given industry. As typically conceived, there are two dimensions of technological opportunity (Cohen and Levin, 1989). The first, incorporated in our model, refers simply to the quantity of extraindustry technological knowledge, such as that originating from government or university labs, that effectively complements and therefore leverages the firm's own knowledge output. The second dimension of technological opportunity is the degree to which a unit of new knowledge improves the technological performance of the firm's manufacturing processes or products and, in turn, the firm's profits. For example, given the vitality of the underlying science and technology, an advance

---

[3]   We refer readers interested in the details of the theoretical and subsequent empirical analysis and results to Cohen and Levinthal (1989a), from which the following discussion is drawn.

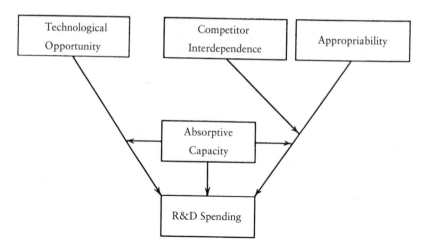

FIGURE 3.1 Model of Absorptive Capacity and R&D Incentives

in knowledge promises to yield much larger product-performance payoffs in the semiconductor industry than in steel.[4]

The basic model of how absorptive capacity affects the determination of R&D expenditures is represented diagramatically in Figure 3.1. We postulate that learning incentives will have a direct effect on R&D spending. We also suggest that where the effect of other determinants, such as technological opportunity and appropriability, depend on the firm's or rivals' assimilation of knowledge, absorptive capacity—and therefore learning incentives—will mediate those effects. Finally, we suggest that the effect of appropriability conditions (i.e., spillovers) will be conditioned by competitor interdependence. In this context, we define interdependence as the extent to which a rival's technical advances diminish the firm's profits.

There are two factors that will affect a firm's incentives to learn, and, therefore, its incentives to invest in absorptive capacity via its R&D expenditures. First, there is the quantity of knowledge to be assimilated and exploited: the more there is, the greater the incentive. Second, there is the difficulty (or, conversely, the ease) of learning. Some types of information are more difficult to assimilate and use than others. We interpret this to mean that per unit of knowledge, the cost of its absorption may vary depending on the characteristics of that knowledge. As learning is more difficult, more prior knowledge has to have been accumulated via R&D for effective learning to occur. As a result, this is a more costly learning environment. In such a setting, R&D is more important to

---

[4]   This second dimension is incorporated in the model developed in Cohen and Levinthal (1989a). We do not incorporate this second dimension in the present model because all the qualitative theoretical and empirical results associated with this second dimension of technological opportunity are the same as those associated with the first considered here.

building absorptive capacity and the more R&D effort the firm will need to have expended to achieve some level of absorptive capacity. Thus, for a given level of a firm's own R&D, the level of absorptive capacity is diminished in environments in which it is more difficult to learn. In addition, we are suggesting that a more difficult learning environment increases the marginal effect of R&D on absorptive capacity. In contrast, in environments in which learning is less demanding, a firm's own R&D has little impact on its absorptive capacity. In the extreme case in which external knowledge can be assimilated without any specialized expertise, a firm's own R&D would have no effect on its absorptive capacity.

We have argued that the ease of learning is in turn determined by the characteristics of the underlying scientific and technological knowledge. Although it is difficult to specify a priori all the relevant characteristics of knowledge affecting the ease of learning, they would include the complexity of the knowledge to be assimilated and the degree to which the outside knowledge is targeted to the needs and concerns of the firm. When outside knowledge is less targeted to the firm's particular needs and concerns, a firm's own R&D becomes more important in permitting it to recognize the value of the knowledge, assimilate, and exploit it. Sources that produce less targeted knowledge would include university labs involved in basic research, while more targeted knowledge may be generated by contract research labs, or input suppliers. In addition, the degree to which a field is cumulative, or the field's pace of advance, should also affect how critical R&D is to the development of absorptive capacity. The more that findings in a field build on prior findings, the more necessary is an understanding of prior research to the assimilation of subsequent findings. The pace of advance of a field affects the importance of R&D to developing absorptive capacity because the faster the pace of knowledge generation, the larger the staff required to keep abreast of new developments. Finally, following Nelson and Winter (1982), the less explicit and codified the relevant knowledge, the more difficult it is to assimilate.

To structure the analysis, we assumed that firms purposefully invest in R&D to generate profit and take into account R&D's dual role in both directly generating new knowledge and contributing to absorptive capacity. Knowledge is assumed to be useful to the firm in that increments to a firm's own knowledge increase the firm's profits while increments to rivals' knowledge diminish them. We posit a simple model of the generation of a firm's technological knowledge that takes into account the major sources of technological knowledge utilized by a firm: the firm's own R&D knowledge that originates with its competitors' R&D, spillovers, and that which originates outside the industry. Figure 3.2 provides a stylized representation of this model in which, first, the firm generates new knowledge directly through its own R&D, and second, extramural knowledge, drawn from competitors as well as extraindustry sources such as government and university labs, also contribute to the firm's knowledge. A central feature of the model is that the firm's absorptive capacity determines the extent to which this extramural knowledge is utilized, and this absorptive capacity itself

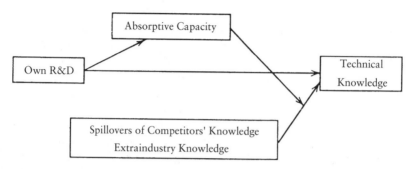

FIGURE 3.2 Model of Sources of a Firm's Technical Knowledge

depends on the firm's own R&D. Because of this mediating function, absorptive capacity influences the effects of appropriability and technological opportunity conditions on R&D spending. Thus, the effects of appropriability and technological opportunity are not independent of R&D itself.

A key assumption in the model is that exploitation of competitors' research findings is realized through the interaction of the firm's absorptive capacity with competitors' spillovers. This interaction signifies that a firm is unable to assimilate externally available knowledge passively. Rather, to utilize the accessible R&D output of its competitors, the firm invests in its absorptive capacity by conducting R&D. Figure 3.2 also illustrates that, like its assimilation of competitors' R&D output, a firm's assimilation of extraindustry knowledge—the dimension of technological opportunity considered here—is constrained by its absorptive capacity. According to our model, therefore, the factors that affect learning incentives (i.e., the ease of learning and the quantity of available knowledge) influence the effects of appropriability and technological opportunity conditions on R&D.

Direct Effect of Ease of Learning

As shown formally in Cohen and Levinthal (1989a), this model implies that as the ease of learning diminishes, learning becomes more dependent on a firm's own R&D, and R&D spending increases because of two effects. First, the marginal impact of R&D on absorptive capacity is greater in more difficult learning environments. As the learning environment becomes more difficult, however, there is a second, more subtle effect. Since, ceteris paribus, a more difficult learning environment lowers firms' absorptive capacities, R&D activity becomes more of a private good in the sense that competitors are now less able to tap into the firm's R&D findings that spill out.

Technological Opportunity

We predict that an increase in technological opportunity—the amount of available relevant external technical knowledge—will elicit more R&D in more difficult learning environments. Greater technological opportunity signifies greater amounts of external information, which increase the firm's incentive to build absorptive capacity, and a more challenging learning environment increases the level of R&D necessary to build absorptive capacity.

Appropriability

We predict that spillovers will provide, in part, a positive incentive to conduct R&D due to the interaction of spillovers with an endogenous absorptive capacity. Traditionally, spillovers have been considered only a deterrent to R&D activity (e.g., Nelson, 1959; Arrow, 1962; Spence, 1984). In the standard view, a firm's incentive to invest in R&D is diminished to the extent that any findings from such activities are exploited by competitors and thereby diminish the innovator's own profits. In our framework, however, this negative appropriability incentive associated with spillovers is counterbalanced by a positive absorptive-capacity-building incentive. The more of its competitors' spillovers there are out there, the more incentive the firm has to invest in its own R&D, which permits it to exploit those spillovers.

We have shown elsewhere (Cohen and Levinthal, 1989a) that when this absorption incentive is large, as when learning is difficult, spillovers may actually encourage R&D. The relative magnitude of the absorption incentive is greater when firms within an industry are less interdependent in the sense that rivals' technical advances have less of an effect on the firm's own profits. With less interdependence, the degree to which rivals gain from the firm's R&D spillovers at the firm's expense diminishes relative to the benefit of being able to exploit the rivals' spillovers. Either a more competitive market structure or a higher price elasticity of demand for the firm's product can diminish interdependence in an industry.

METHODS

Data and Measures

To test the predictions of our framework for R&D activity, we used cross-sectional survey data on technological opportunity and appropriability conditions in the American manufacturing sector collected from R&D lab managers by Levin et al. (1983, 1987), and the Federal Trade Commission's Line of Business Program data on business unit sales, transfers, and R&D expenditures. The dependent variable, R&D intensity, was defined as company-financed business-unit research and development expenditures, expressed as a percentage of business unit sales and transfers over the period 1975 through 1977. The data on interindustry differences in technological opportunity and approriability are industry (line of business) mean scores computed as an average over all respondents within a given industry. The sample consists of 1,719 business units representing 318 firms in 151 lines of business.

The data pose two estimation issues. First, some 24 percent of the firms performed no R&D in at least one year. If the independent variables reflect both the probability of conducting R&D, as well as the amount of R&D spending, then a Tobit analysis would be appropriate. Alternatively, a firm may require some initial level of absorptive capacity before it is influenced by the characteristics of the learning environment. In this case, the variables reflecting the ease of learning only affect the amount of R&D conducted by firms engaging in R&D activity and not the probability of engaging in R&D activity. In light of the uncertainty over the appropriate estimation technique, we explored the robustness of the results by analyzing a Tobit and an OLS (or GLS) specification. The second estimation issue is the presence of heteroscedasticity. We found the assumption of homoscedasticity to be violated, with the logarithm of the error variance being a linear function of the exogenous variables and the number of respondents to Levin et al.'s (1983, 1987) survey. Unless otherwise noted, the results we report in this section reflect robust effects that hold across three different estimation methods, including ordinary least squares (OLS), generalized least squares (GLS) in which we adjust for heteroscedasticity, and Tobit, which was used when we included the observations for which R&D expenditures were zero.

We tested our predictions in the context of an empirical model of business unit R&D intensity in which technological opportunity, appropriability, and demand conditions are considered as the principal industry-level determinants of firms' R&D spending. While data constraints do not permit observation of the direct effect of the ease of learning or its determinants on firms' R&D spending, we were able to examine how these variables condition the influence on R&D of technological opportunity and appropriability conditions.

Technological opportunity was assessed with variables measuring the "relevance" or "importance" for technological progress in each line of business of what are considered to be two critical sources of technological opportunity—the science base of the industry and extraindustry sources of knowledge (Cohen and Levin, 1989). These measures are drawn from Levin et al.'s survey, in which R&D managers indicated on a 7-point Likert scale the relevance eleven basic and applied fields of science and the importance of external sources of knowledge to technological progress in a line of business. The basic fields of science include biology, chemistry, mathematics, and physics, and the applied fields of science include agricultural science, applied math/operations research, computer science, geology, materials science, medical science, and metallurgy.[5] The five extraindustry sources of knowledge considered here included equipment suppliers (EQUIPTECH), materials suppliers (MATERIALTECH), downstream users of the industry's products (USERTECH), government laboratories and agencies

---

[5] Although geology was classed as a basic science by Levin et al., we classed it as an applied science because of its inductive methodology and intensive use by firms in the extractive sector.

(GOVTECH), and universities (UNIVTECH). We interpreted the measures of the relevance or importance of each field or knowledge source to index the relative quantity of knowledge generated by that field or source that is potentially useful. We then distinguished across the eleven scientific fields and the five extraindustry knowledge source variables on the basis of the ease of learning associated with each. We suggested above that one important determinant of the ease of learning is the degree to which outside knowledge is targeted to a firm's needs and concerns. One can readily distinguish among both the eleven fields and the five extraindustry knowledge sources on that basis. The knowledge associated with the basic sciences is typically less targeted than that associated with the applied sciences. We also distinguished among the extraindustry knowledge sources on the same basis. A priori, we ranked university labs, government labs, materials suppliers, and equipment suppliers as providing increasingly more targeted knowledge to firms. We did not rank the relative effect of knowledge originating from users because, as suggested by von Hippel (1978), users will often provide a product idea to potential suppliers, but the informativeness of the "solution concept" is quite variable. Therefore, the targeted quality of the information is variable as well.

To represent intraindustry spillovers of R&D, we employed measures from Levin et al.'s survey of the effectiveness of six mechanisms used by firms to capture and protect the competitive advantages of new processes and new products: patents to prevent duplication, patents to secure royalty income, secrecy, lead time, moving quickly down the learning curve, and complementary sales and service efforts. We employed the maximum value of the effectiveness scores attained by these mechanisms as our measure of appropriability or spillovers, and label this variable APPROPRIABILITY; a high level of APPROPRIABILITY reflects a low level of spillovers.

In our theory, we predicted an interaction effect by which, as the ease of learning diminishes, or firms become less interdependent, the effect of spillovers on R&D spending should become more positive (or less negative). In the absence of any direct measure of the ease of learning, we distinguished categorically between those industries in which basic science was more relevant to technical progress than the relatively more targeted applied sciences and assumed that learning was generally less difficult in industries that fell into the latter category. Thus, we created a dummy variable, DUMBAS, that equals one when the average value of the relevance scores associated with the basic fields exceeds that associated with the applied fields and that equals zero otherwise. We specified the dummy variable, DUMAPP, analogously. To capture the interdependence of firms, we employed measures of industries' competitiveness as represented by each industry's four-firm, concentration ratio (C4) and industry-level estimates of the price elasticity of demand (PELAS).

To further control for industry demand conditions, we used industry estimates developed by Levin (1981) of price elasticity (PELAS) and income elasticity (INCELAS) and a demand time-shift parameter (DGROWTH). Finally, we included another control variable that may also reflect technological opportunity, industry maturity. We used a somewhat crude measure of industry maturity, NEWPLANT, that measures the percentage of an industry's property, plant, and equipment installed within the preceding five years.

RESULTS

Technological Opportunity

Our theory suggests that when the targeted quality of knowledge is less (i.e., learning is more difficult), an increase in the relevance (i.e., quantity) of knowledge should have a more positive effect on R&D intensity. Therefore, the coefficient estimates of the variables measuring the relevance of the four basic scientific fields should exceed those of the variables measuring the relevance of the seven applied scientific fields. Confirming the prediction, Table 3.1 indicates that the estimated coefficients for the applied sciences are, with the exception of computer science, lower than that for the basic sciences. The similarity of the estimate of the effect of the relevance of computer science, an applied science, to those of some of the basic sciences suggests that the assumption may not be correct that only one determinant of the ease of learning, the targeted quality of the field, varies systematically across the fields of applied and basic science. Another determinant of the ease of learning postulated above is a field's pace of advance, where faster pace should require more R&D to permit assimilation, and the pace of advance in computer science has been relatively rapid over the past two decades.

To further test the prediction that the coefficient values of the less targeted, basic science field variables would exceed those of the applied fields, we estimated a specification, otherwise identical to the first, in which we constrained the coefficients of the basic sciences to be the same and the coefficients of the applied sciences to be the same. This shows the effect on R&D spending as the overall technological opportunity associated with basic science and applied science, respectively, change. The constrained coefficient estimates of the effect of the technological opportunity associated with the basic and applied sciences are significantly different (at the $p < 0.01$ level) across all estimation methods, with the former equal to 0.189 and the latter equal to −0.080 in the GLS estimation. Therefore, relative to the effect of an increase in the technological opportunity associated with applied science, an increase in that associated with basic science elicits more R&D.

Our predicted ranking of the coefficient magnitudes associated with the extraindustry sources of knowledge, reflecting increasingly targeted knowledge from these sources, is largely confirmed. The coefficient estimate for the importance of knowledge originating from universities exceeds that for government labs, which, in turn, is greater than that for materials suppliers, which exceeds that for equipment suppliers. The difference between coefficient values is

TABLE 3.1 Analysis of R&D Intensity*

| | Regression Coefficient | | |
Variable	OLS (N = 1302)	GLS (N = 1302)	Tobit (N = 1719)
Intercept	−5.184••	−2.355•	−4.086••
	(1.522)	(1.037)	(1.461)
APPROPRIABILITY x C4	0.213	0.342••	0.368••
	(0.128)	(0.103)	(0.130)
APPROPRIABILITY x PELAS	−0.192	−0.200•	−0.176
	(0.106)	(0.091)	(0.103)
APPROPRIABILITY x DUMAPP	0.448•	0.248	0.211
	(0.202)	(0.143)	(0.194)
APPROPRIABILITY x DUMBAS	0.302	0.174	0.094
	(0.208)	(0.144)	(0.206)
USERTECH	0.470••	0.397••	0.612••
	(0.104)	(0.069)	(0.107)
UNIVTECH	0.374••	0.318••	0.395••
	(0.131)	(0.091)	(0.147)
GOVTECH	0.221•	0.069	0.137
	(0.106)	(0.079)	(0.107)
MATERIALTECH	−0.258••	−0.074	−0.303••
	(0.098)	(0.070)	(0.100)
EQUIPTECH	−0.401••	−0.484••	−0.574••
	(0.111)	(0.077)	(0.117)
Biology	0.314••	0.185••	0.276•
	(0.102)	(0.071)	(0.114)
Chemistry	0.289••	0.081	0.191•
	(0.084)	(0.062)	(0.088)
Math	0.184	0.151	0.123
	(0.131)	(0.097)	(0.143)
Physics	0.373••	0.323••	0.310•
	(0.117)	(0.091)	(0.128)
Agricultural Science	−0.441••	−0.273••	−0.308••
	(0.088)	(0.064)	(0.099)
Applied Math/Operations Research	−0.237	−0.117	−0.366•
	(0.148)	(0.102)	(0.152)
Computer Science	0.294•	0.116	0.433••
	(0.124)	(0.090)	(0.122)
Geology	−0.363••	−0.240••	−0.365••
	(0.084)	(0.061)	(0.097)
Materials Science	−0.110	−0.150	0.116
	(0.125)	(0.095)	(0.118)
Medical Science	−0.179	−0.133	−0.133
	(0.093)	(0.070)	(0.103)

TABLE 3.1 *Continued*

Metallurgy	$-0.315^{••}$	$-0.195^{••}$	$-0.393^{••}$
	(0.077)	(0.053)	(0.089)
NEWPLANT	$0.057^{••}$	$0.049^{••}$	$0.045^{••}$
	(0.008)	(0.006)	(0.007)
PELAS	0.936	$1.082^{•}$	0.892
	(0.611)	(0.527)	(0.573)
INCELAS	$1.077^{••}$	$0.587^{••}$	$1.112^{••}$
	(0.170)	(0.131)	(0.188)
DGROWTH	0.068	-0.074	0.004
	(0.090)	(0.053)	(0.105)
R^2	0.287		

$^{•}p < 0.05$; $^{••}p < 0.01$.
* Reproduced from Cohen and Levinthal (1989a: 590–591, 569–596). Standard errors are in parentheses.

statistically significant in the case of government sources versus materials suppliers for both the OLS and Tobit results ($p < 0.01$) and in the case of materials suppliers versus equipment suppliers in the GLS results ($p < 0.01$). While we had no prediction regarding the coefficient value for USERTECH, the consistently high value of the coefficient estimate may reflect some element of demand conditions. Consistent with this, we have observed the variable USERTECH to be significantly correlated with measures of the importance of product differentiation (cf. Cohen and Levinthal, 1989a).

Appropriability

The results largely support the prediction that the ease of learning conditions the effect of knowledge spillovers. The effect on R&D intensity of increasing appropriability (i.e., diminishing spillovers) was significantly greater ($p < 0.05$) in those industries in which the applied sciences are more relevant to innovation than the basic sciences. This result suggests that the positive absorption incentive associated with spillovers is greater in industries in which the difficulty of learning is greater. Second, there is a significant positive effect ($p < 0.01$) of the interaction between market concentration and the appropriability level. As market concentration increases (indexing a diminution in competitiveness), the positive effect of a given appropriability level on R&D intensity increases, as predicted. Likewise, the effect of the interaction of the price elasticity of demand and the level of appropriability is negative (but only significant at $p < 0.05$ in the GLS estimate), providing additional support for the proposition that the positive effect of spillovers will increase in industries in which firms are less interdependent. The results suggest that the learning environment affects the impact of spillovers on R&D spending and that the importance of the positive absorptive-capacity-building incentive relative to that of the negative appropriability incentive is conditioned by the degree of competitor interdependence.

While we have shown that the learning environment modifies the effect of appropriability conditions, the question remains whether spillovers may, on balance, actually encourage R&D in some industries. To explore this possibility, we examined the effect of spillovers in the four two-digit SIC code level industries for which our sample contains enough lines of business to permit separate industry regressions. These include SICs 20 (food processing), 28 (chemicals), 35 (machinery), and 36 (electrical equipment). Due to the reduction in the degrees of freedom for industry-level variables, we simplified the estimating equation to consider only the direct effect of APPROPRIABILITY, and the science field variables were summarized as the maximum relevance scores attained by the basic and applied fields, respectively. In SICs 28 and 36, the effect of the APPROPRIABILITY variable was negative and significant at conventional levels, implying that R&D intensity rises with spillovers. In the Tobit results, the sign was also positive for SICs 28 and 36, but the coefficient estimates were not quite significant at the 0.05 confidence level. Thus, in SICs 28 (chemicals) and 36 (electrical equipment), R&D intensity rose with spillovers when we controlled for other industry-level variables conventionally thought to drive R&D spending, including technological opportunity and demand conditions. Although the analyses showing a positive effect of spillovers in these two industry groups do not represent a direct test of our model, the results suggest, particularly when considered with the interaction results, that the positive absorption incentive associated with spillovers may be sufficiently strong in some cases to more than offset the negative appropriability incentive.

IMPLICATIONS FOR INNOVATIVE ACTIVITY

Drawing on our prior work (Cohen and Levinthal, 1987, 1989a), we offer some implications of absorptive capacity for the analysis of other innovative activities, including basic research, the adoption and diffusion of innovations, and decisions to participate in cooperative R&D ventures, that follow from the preceding analyses.

The observation that R&D creates a capacity to assimilate and exploit new knowledge provides a ready explanation of why some firms may invest in basic research even when the preponderance of findings spill out into the public domain. Specifically, firms may conduct basic research less for particular results than to be able to provide themselves with the general background knowledge that would permit them to exploit rapidly useful scientific and technological knowledge through their own innovations or to be able to respond quickly—become a fast second—when competitors come up with a major advance (see also Rosenberg, 1990). In terms of our discussion of the cognitive and organizational aspects of absorptive capacity, we may think of basic research as broadening the firm's knowledge base to create critical overlap with new knowledge and providing it with the deeper understanding that is useful for exploiting new technical developments that build on rapidly advancing science and technology.

This perspective on the role of basic research offers a rather different view of the determinants of basic research than that which has dominated thinking in this area for the thirty years since Nelson's (1959) seminal article. Nelson hypothesized that more diversified firms will invest more heavily in basic research because, assuming imperfect markets for information, they will be better able to exploit its wide-ranging and unpredictable results. Nelson thus saw product-market diversification as one of the key determinants of basic research.[6] Emphasizing the role of basic research in firm learning, our perspective redirects attention from what happens to the knowledge outputs from the innovation process to the nature of the knowledge inputs themselves. Considering that absorptive capacity tends to be specific to a field or knowledge domain means that the type of knowledge that the firm believes it may have to exploit will affect the sort of research the firm conducts. From this vantage point, we would conjecture that as a firm's technological progress becomes more closely tied to advances in basic science (as has been the case in pharmaceuticals), a firm will increase its basic research, whatever its degree of product-market diversification. We also suggest, with reference to all firm research, not just basic research, that as the fields underlying technical advance within an industry become more diverse, we may expect firms to increase their R&D as they develop absorptive capacities in each of the relevant fields. For example, as automobile manufacturing comes to draw more heavily on newer fields such as microelectronics and ceramics, we expect that manufacturers will expand their basic and applied research efforts to better evaluate and exploit new findings in these areas.

The findings on the role of absorptive capacity and the ways in which it may be developed also have implications for the analysis of the adoption and diffusion of innovations. Our perspective implies that the ease of learning, and thus technology adoption, is affected by the degree to which an innovation is related to the pre-existing knowledge base of prospective users. For example, personal computers diffused more rapidly at the outset among consumers and firms who had prior experience on mainframes or minicomputers. Likewise, software engineering practices seem to be adopted more readily by programmers with previous Pascal rather than Fortran experience because the structure of Pascal more closely reflects some of the underlying principles of software engineering (Smith et al., 1989). Our argument also suggests that an innovation that is fully incorporated in capital equipment will diffuse more rapidly than more disembodied innovations that require some complementary expertise on the part of potential users. This is one of the anticipated benefits of making computers more "user friendly."

[6] Markets for information often fail because they inherently represent a situation of information asymmetry in which the less informed party cannot properly value the information he or she wishes to purchase, and the more informed party, acting self-interestedly, attempts to exploit that inability (Williamson. 1975).

The importance of absorptive capacity also helps explain some recent findings regarding firms' cooperative research ventures. First, Link (1987) has observed that cooperative research ventures are actually found more typically in industries that employ more mature technologies rather than in industries in which technology is moving ahead quickly—as seems to be suggested by the popular press. Second, it has been observed that cooperative ventures that have been initiated to pursue basic research, as well as more applied research objectives, have been subject over the years to increasing pressure to focus on more short-term research objectives (Mowery and Rosenberg, 1989). The simple notion that it is important to consider the costs of assimilating and exploiting knowledge from such ventures provides at least a partial explanation for these phenomena. Many cooperative ventures are initiated in areas in which the cost to access the output of the venture is low, or they often gravitate toward such areas over time. Conversely, those who are attempting to encourage cooperative research ventures in quickly advancing fields should recognize that the direct participation in the venture should represent only a portion of the resources that it will take to benefit from the venture. Participating firms also must be prepared to invest internally in the absorptive capacity that will permit effective exploitation of the venture's knowledge output.

CONCLUSION

Our empirical analysis of R&D investment suggested that firms are in fact sensitive to the characteristics of the learning environment in which they operate. Thus, absorptive capacity appears to be part of a firm's decision calculus in allocating resources for innovative activity. Despite these findings, because absorptive capacity is intangible and its benefits are indirect, one can have little confidence that the appropriate level, to say nothing of the optimal level, of investment in absorptive capacity is reached. Thus, while we have proposed a model to explain R&D investment, in which R&D both generates innovation and facilitates learning, the development of this model may ultimately be as valuable for the prescriptive analysis of organizational policies as its application may be as a positive model of firm behavior.

An important question from a prescriptive perspective is When is a firm most likely to underinvest in absorptive capacity to its own long-run detriment? Absorptive capacity is more likely to be developed and maintained as a byproduct of routine activity when the knowledge domain that the firm wishes to exploit is closely related to its current knowledge base. When, however, a firm wishes to acquire and use knowledge that is unrelated to its ongoing activity, then the firm must dedicate effort exclusively to creating absorptive capacity (i.e., absorptive capacity is not a byproduct). In this case, absorptive capacity may not even occur to the firm as an investment alternative. Even if it does, due to the intangible nature of absorptive capacity, a firm may be reluctant to sacrifice current output as well as gains from specialization to permit its technical personnel to acquire the requisite breadth of knowledge that would permit absorption of knowledge from new domains. Thus, while the current discussion addresses key features of organizational structure that determine a firm's absorptive capacity and provides evidence that investment is responsive to the need to develop this capability, more research is necessary to understand the decision processes that determine organizations' investments in absorptive capacity.

REFERENCES

Abernathy, William, J. 1978 *The Productivity Dilemma*. Baltimore: Johns Hopkins University Press.

Allen, Thomas, J. 1977 *Managing the Flow of Technology*. Cambridge, MA: MIT Press.

Allen, Thomas, J., and Stephen D. Cohen 1969 "Information flows in R&D labs." *Administrative Science Quarterly*, 20: 12–19.

Anderson, John R., Robert Farrell, and Ron Sauers 1984 "Learning to program in LISP." *Cognitive Science*, 8: 87–129.

Arrow, Kenneth, J. 1962 "Economic welfare and the allocation of resources for invention." In R. R. Nelson (ed.), *The Rate and Direction of Inventive Activity*: 609–625. Princeton, NJ: Princeton University Press.

Bower, Gordon, H., and Ernest R. Hilgard 1981 *Theories of Learning*. Englewood Cliffs, NJ: Prentice-Hall.

Bradshaw, Gary, F., Patrick W. Langley, and Herbert A. Simon 1983 "Studying scientific discovery by computer simulation." *Science*, 222: 971–975.

Brock, Gerald, W. 1975 *The U.S. Computer Industry*. Cambridge, MA: Ballinger.

Burns, Tom, and George M. Stalker 1961 *The Management of Innovation*. London: Tavistock.

Clark, Kim, B., and Takahiro Fujimoto 1987 "Overlapping problem solving in product development." Technical Report, Harvard Business School.

Cohen, Wesley, M., and Richard C. Levin 1989 "Empirical studies of innovation and market structure." In R. C. Schmalensee and R. Willig (eds.), *Handbook of Industrial Organization*: 1059–1107. Amsterdam: Elsevier.

Cohen, Wesley, M., and Daniel A. Levinthal 1987 "Participation in cooperative research ventures and the cost of learning." Technical Report, Dept. of Social and Decision Sciences, Carnegie Mellon University.

——— 1989a "Innovation and learning: The two faces of R&D." *Economic Journal*, 99: 569–596.

——— 1989b "Fortune favors the prepared firm." Technical Report, Dept. of Social and Decision Sciences, Carnegie Mellon University.

Dearborn, R., and Herbert A. Simon 1958 "Selective perception in executives." *Sociometry*, 21: 140–144.

Ellis, Henry Carlton 1965 *The Transfer of Learning*. New York: MacMillan.

Estes, William Kaye 1970 *Learning Theory and Mental Development*. New York: Academic Press.

Hamberg, Daniel 1963 "Invention in the industrial research laboratory." *Journal of Political Economy*, 71: 95–115.

Harlow, H. F. 1949 "The formation of learning sets." *Psychological Review*. 56: 51–65.

———1959 "Learning set and error factor theory." In S. Koch (ed.), *Psychology: A Study of Science*, 2: 492–537. New York: McGraw-Hill.

Johnston, R., and M. Gibbons 1975 "Characteristics of information usage in technological innovation." *IEEE Transactions on Engineering Management*, 27–34, EM–22.

Katz, Daniel, and Robert L. Kahn 1966 *The Social Psychology of Organizations*. New York: Wiley.

Katz, Ralph 1982 "The effects of group longevity on project communication and performance." *Administrative Science Quarterly*. 27: 81–104.

Katz, Ralph, and Thomas J. Allen 1982 "Investigating the not invented here (NIH) syndrome: A look at the performance, tenure, and communication patterns of 50 R&D project groups." *R&D Management*, 12: 7–12.

Lee, Denis, M. S., and Thomas J. Allen 1982 "Integrating new technical staff: Implications for acquiring new technology." *Management Science*, 28: 1405–1420.

Levin, Richard C. 1981 "Toward an empirical model of Schumpeterian competition." Technical Report, Dept. of Economics, Yale University.

Levin, Richard, C., Alvin K. Klevorick, Richard R. Nelson, and Sidney G. Winter 1983 "Questionnaire on industrial research and development." Dept. of Economics, Yale University.

——— 1987 "Appropriating the returns from industrial R&D." *Brookings Papers on Economic Activity*, 783–820.

Levitt, Barbara, and James G. March 1988 "Organizational learning." *Annual Review of Sociology*, 14: 319–340.

Lindsay, Peter H., and Donald A. Norman 1977 *Human Information Processing*. Orlando, FL: Academic Press.

Link, Albert, N. 1987 "Cooperative research activity in U.S. Manufacturing." Technical Report, University of North Carolina, Greensboro, Final report submitted to the National Science Foundation under grant PRA 85–212664.

Majumdar, Bodiul Alam 1982 *Innovations, Product Developments and Technology Transfers: An Empirical Study of Dynamic Competitive Advantage, The Case of Electronic Calculators*. Lanham, MD: University Press of America.

Mansfield, Edwin 1968 *Economics of Technological Change*. New York: Norton.

——— 1988 "The speed and cost of industrial innovation in Japan and the United States: External vs. internal technology." *Management Science*, 34(10): 1157–1168.

March, James G., and Herbert A. Simon 1958 *Organizations*. New York: Wiley.

Mowery, David, C. 1983 "The relationship between intrafirm and contractual forms of industrial research in American manufacturing, 1900–1940." *Explorations in Economic History*, 20: 351–374.

Mowery, David C., and Nathan Rosenberg 1989 *Technology and the Pursuit of Economic Growth*. New York: Cambridge University Press.

Mueller, Willard, F. 1962 "The origins of the basic inventions underlying DuPont's major product and process innovations, 1920 to 1950." In R. R. Nelson (ed.), *The Rate and Direction of Inventive Activity*: 323–358. Princeton: Princeton University Press.

Myers, Sumner, and Donald C. Marquis 1969 "Successful industrial innovations." Washington, DC: National Science Foundation, NSF 69–17.

Nelson, Richard, R. 1959 "The simple economics of basic research." *Journal of Political Economy*, 67: 297–306.

Nelson, Richard R., and Sidney Winter 1982 *An Evolutionary Theory of Economic Change*. Cambridge, MA: Harvard University Press.

Peck, Merton, J. 1962 "Inventions in the postwar American aluminum industry." In R. R. Nelson (ed.), *The Rate and Direction of Inventive Activity*: 279–298. Princeton: Princeton University Press.

Pirolli, Peter L., and John R. Anderson 1985 "The role of learning from example in the acquisition of recursive programming skill." *Canadian Journal of Psychology*, 39: 240–272.

Reich, Robert, B. 1987 "The rise of techno-nationalism" *Atlantic*, May: 63–69.

Rosenberg, Nathan 1982 *Inside the Black Box: Technology and Economics*. New York: Cambridge University Press.

———— 1990 "Why do firms do basic research (with their own money)?" *Research Policy* (in press).

Rosenberg, Nathan, and W. Edward Steinmueller 1988 "Why are Americans such poor imitators?" *American Economic Review*, 78(2): 229–234.

Schumpeter, Joseph A. 1942 *Capitalism, Socialism and Democracy*. New York: Harper and Row.

Simon, Herbert A. 1985 "What we know about the creative process." In R. L. Kuhn (ed.), *Frontiers in Creative and Innovative Management*: 3–20. Cambridge, MA: Ballinger.

Smith, Gordon, Wesley, M. Cohen, William Hefley, and Daniel A. Levinthal 1989 "Understanding the adoption of Ada: A field study report." Technical Report, Software Engineering Institute, Carnegie Mellon University.

Spence, A. Michael 1984 "Cost reduction, competition, and industry performance." *Econometrica*, 52: 101–122.

Tilton, John E. 1971 *International Diffusion of Technology: The Case of Semiconductors*. Washington, DC: Brookings Institution.

Tushman, Michael, L. 1977 "Special boundary roles in the innovation process." *Administrative Science Quarterly*, 22: 587–605.

———— 1978 "Technical communication in R&D laboratories: The impact of project work characteristics." *Administrative Science Quarterly*, 21: 624–644.

Tushman, Michael L., and Philip Anderson 1986 "Technological discontinuities and organizational environments." *Administrative Science Quarterly*, 31: 439–465.

Utterback, James M. 1971 "The process of technological innovation within the firm." *Academy of Management Journal*, 12: 75–88.

von Hippel, Eric 1978 "Successful industrial products from customer ideas." *Journal of Marketing*, 42: 39–49.

———— 1988 *The Sources of Innovation*. New York: Oxford University Press.

Vyssotsky, V. A. 1977 "The innovation process at Bell Labs." Technical Report, Bell Laboratories.

Westney, D. Eleanor, and Kiyonori Sakakibara 1986 "The role of Japan-based R&D in global technology strategy." In M. Hurowitch (ed.), *Technology in the Modern Corporation*: 217–232, London: Pergamon.

Williamson, Oliver, E. 1975 *Markets and Hierarchies: Analysis and Antitrust Implications*. New York: Free Press.

Zenger, Todd R., and Barbara S. Lawrence 1989 "Organizational demography: The differential effects of age and tenure distributions on technical communication." *Academy of Management Journal*, 32: 353–376.

Chapter 4

Feeding Organizational Memory: Improving on Knowledge Management's Promise to Business Performance[1]

Rob Cross
Boston University

Lloyd Baird
Boston University

Knowledge management has recently emerged as a means of improving business performance. However, many early initiatives have focused almost exclusively on information technology applications and so missed the myriad ways in which knowledge can become embedded in an organization. The pay off for knowledge management lies with getting newly created knowledge to a truly organizational level where others can put such knowledge to use. In this process, we have found that organizations better able to embed lessons from key experiences into a variety of organizational structures and processes are better able to improve business performance. By moving beyond the simple use of information technology to capture lessons and reusable work products, these efforts ensure that important lessons are put to use in work activities of a broad base of employees as quickly and efficiently as possible. The following chapter outlines an approach for executives to

[1] Boston University Working Paper. Please Address Correspondence to: Rob Cross; Boston University School of Management; Organizational Behavior Department; 595 Commonwealth Avenue; Boston, MA 02215; rcross@bu.edu

both identify what knowledge is strategically worth expenditure of effort to learn and how to feed organization memory by embedding learning in relationships, process and products.

FEEDING ORGANIZATIONAL MEMORY: AN EXPERIENCE WORTH LEARNING FROM

The product roll out seemed a disaster along many fronts for the pharmaceutical organization. Following a wave approach, the organization had first introduced its new product in several European countries concurrently. This process had been troublesome enough, but seemed to pale in comparison to some of the challenges experienced in the effort in the United States. Despite hiring numerous consultants proclaiming knowledge of everything from local markets to trade legalities to manufacturing expertise, it seemed that the roll out experienced every snag that happened with the first wave. At every juncture, the problems that the current roll out was facing by and large seemed to have been experienced with the earlier European roll out. Why, in this second effort, was the roll out contending with (and losing precious time and money attempting to cope with) problems that had already been largely solved in another forum? While problems were not identical, they were similar enough for this organization to benefit from the prior experience of others. The problem was that while mechanisms such as Total Quality Management (TCM) and continuous improvement methodologies helped the company learn in its manufacturing processes, no approach had been established to capture what was learned and embed it in the product roll out process. And the cost for not learning was significant— not only was the organization paying outside expertise for things already learned in other segments of the company, but also making the same mistakes and losing precious time, money, and revenue.

No doubt the members of the different roll out teams learned a great deal about themselves, the product role out process, and how they would do things differently in the next effort. Experience, particularly difficult experience, is a salient and powerful mentor. Yet if strategic initiatives only educate those involved in the projects, an organization misses substantial opportunity to improve business performance. If the pharmaceutical company had been more systematic about learning from its first roll out and transferring that knowledge to successive efforts, performance would no doubt have been substantially improved. Not only within the teams but across the organization. Learning from important efforts and driving that learning into business operations quickly can yield significant and quantifiable benefits. It is in this vein of thought that the capture and sharing of lessons and reusable work products has become one of the central tenets of knowledge management's promise to improve business performance (Stewart 1997; Davenport and Prusak 1998; O'Dell and Grayson 1998; Ruggles 1998). A recent review of 31 knowledge management projects in 24 companies concluded that "the energy in knowledge management has been spent on treating knowledge as an 'it,' an entity separate from the people who create and use it" (Davenport, De Long, and Beers 1998, 45). Rather than focus on organizational or cultural initiatives crucial to knowledge creation and sharing, many organizations have turned to building databases housing lessons and reusable work products. Given physical and cognitive limitations of any one individual holding specialized knowledge, these repositories reduce bottlenecks for individuals seeking information. Further, they provide one means of reducing the amount of organizational "forgetting" as a function of turnover. However, as so poignantly demonstrated by reengineering, technology alone can only accomplish so much in the pursuit of improving business performance (Hammer and Champy 1993; Hammer and Stanton 1995). Truly improving business performance demands more than sophisticated technologies—it requires attending to the seemingly irrational needs of employees and the often idiosyncratic way that information is used and problems solved in organizations. We are at a point in knowledge management's life cycle that interest is beginning to shift from the simple accumulation of knowledge to ensuring that captured knowledge is effectively put to use by as broad a population as possible. With the advent of the file cabinet, photocopier, and database, we have proven effective in collecting far more information (and sometimes knowledge) than we can ever put to use. Ensuring that this wealth of information is used has proven a more daunting challenge.

To truly improve efficiency and effectiveness in knowledge-intensive work, we must attend to the ways that people seek out answers to ambiguous problems and use knowledge in organizational settings. Ultimately, this requires a move from simply putting more knowledge into databases to leveraging the many ways that knowledge can migrate into an organization and impact business performance. Distributed technologies such as Lotus Notes or intranet sites can effectively disseminate certain forms of information and create virtual forums for connecting experts. However, they are only one of a variety of ways that learning from a significant organizational experience can be captured and driven into an organization's operations. For example, knowledge gained from an experience can be embedded in an organization by altering work processes or a product's architecture. This is an extremely efficient form of knowledge transfer because it does not require mental work on the part of other employees already overloaded in today's information rich environment. By embedding learnings we not only reduce the information load that people must cope with, but also increase the consistency with which knowledge throughout an organization is employed.

For the past two and a half years, we have worked closely with two consortia of organizations that were actively implementing knowledge management within their organizations. These were all *Fortune* 100 companies and came from such diverse industries as automobile manufacturing, petroleum, pharmaceuticals, electric utilities, consumer products, financial services, and even government agencies. Despite the diversity of both industries and knowledge management initiatives, we found two common themes across the more successful programs. First, the more successful efforts focused their knowledge capturing and sharing activities on knowledge that had a true impact on business performance. Second, these efforts did not leave to chance the possibility that employees would stumble across and understand relevant knowledge embedded in a database. Rather, they actively sought to weave such lessons into the way work was done in as many ways as possible.

The following article outlines a way to increase organizational improvement from important experiences by considering knowledge capture and sharing from more than a technical perspective. By first identifying important organizational initiatives worth learning from, and then assessing the many ways that knowledge from such an experience migrates into an organization and is used in future initiatives, we believe executives will get the results sought from knowledge management.

ORGANIZATIONAL LEARNING AS MEMORY DEVELOPMENT: A NEW LOOK AT AN OLD TOPIC

Due largely to the popularization of Peter Senge's work, many agree that an organization's ability to learn faster than its competition is a significant source of competitive advantage (Stata 1989; Senge 1990; Ulrich, Von Glinlow, and Jick 1993; McGill and Slocum 1993; Slocum, McGill, and Lei 1994; Nevis, Dibella, and Gould 1995). But what does it mean to say an organization can learn? Can one truly learn outside of its individuals? How would we know if it did? These and other philosophical questions have concerned both researchers and practitioners for some time (Cyert and March 1963; Argyris and Schon 1996; Hedberg 1981; Daft and Weick 1984; Fiol and Lyles 1985; Levitt and March 1988; Kim 1993; Dibella and Nevis 1998). Rather than digress into a philosophic quagmire on what it means to learn outside of the individual, one constructive way to think about this vague topic is by considering learning as a process of developing organizational memory. When we say an organization can learn, we are focused on the way in which knowledge becomes embedded in networks of relationships, information technology, business processes, performance management systems, or product/service offerings. These are important structures that in various ways act as a form of memory that employees rely on to perform their work.

Early theoretical conceptions of organizational memory were very broad and included aspects such as culture, structure, and the physical layout of specific organizational settings (Walsh and Ungson 1991). While powerful contours of organizational life, these aspects of an organization changed only slowly over long periods of time. As a result, past work on organizational memory provided us with little insight as to how to maximize organizational level benefits of learning from key organizational initiatives.

To better understand how knowledge developed from experience migrates into an organization, we interviewed project teams in professional services, financial services, and manufacturing organizations. All teams had recently completed significant projects for their respective organizations and were asked (1) what did you learn from the experience and (2) where did this knowledge go within the organization after the project. By analyzing responses to the second question, we found that knowledge from experience tends to enter an organization and be held in several "bins": individuals, relationships, information repositories, work processes, support systems, and product or service offerings.

Individuals

Most would agree that an important form of knowledge in organizational settings resides within the individual employees that enter and exit the workplace each day. Various human resource programs for the past decade or so have increasingly found ways to help employees learn and develop from important work experiences. For example, work in the genre of action learning has provided one set of tools to further leverage experience as a way of learning via structured collective or individual processes of reflection (Kolb 1984; Daudelin 1996). However, while these interventions can be effective for individual learning, they give us little insight as to how knowledge developed from one experience becomes a form of organizational memory brought to bear on future initiatives.

We found individual learning in organizations to be path dependent and inform organizational memory based largely on where individuals next took their experiential knowledge. Two implications emerged from our research. First, a principal mechanism of learning is via social interaction as other organizational members learn most profoundly in interaction with people who themselves are applying knowledge from past endeavors.[2] Second, the learning of individuals can be stunted (at least temporarily) as they are employed in future projects based on what they already know (not based on what they might be able to learn). This left some frustrated, as one team member noted, "You get in a position in one spot and develop an expertise, then the organization looks to exploit this expertise in future projects while your individual development stagnates."

Individuals are a rich form of organizational memory as their knowledge can be dynamically shared and applied in future projects. However, it is also a form of memory that is at best only loosely held in organizations, as when people leave, what they know leaves. Many claim that today's knowledge workers are a new breed of employee best thought of as "volunteers" that are mobile and able

---

[2]   This is consistent with recent work on situated learning and communities of practice (Lave and Wenger 1991; Brown and Duguid 1991; Orr 1996; Wenger 1998) and shows the extent to which such learning can extend beyond the boundary of any given community in a path dependent fashion.

to apply their knowledge elsewhere should they perceive a better opportunity (Quinn 1992; Handy 1994; Arthur, Claman, and DeFillippi 1995; Sveiby 1997). Turnover in knowledge work is often fairly high and so loss of this form of organizational memory is frequent. More importantly, as put by one manager, "it is the better people with the better knowledge that frequently find the better opportunities."

Networks and Relationships

In a broad sense, people are employed in organizations to solve problems—whether the problem is diagnosing someone's health, crafting a financial instrument, developing a new drug, or making a legal argument. We have traditionally held people we consider experts (e.g. doctors or scientists) accountable for knowledge in their domain and expect them to have mastered all past thinking and also to keep abreast of new knowledge as it emerges. However, in today's information intensive environment, only rarely will any one person have enough knowledge to solve increasingly complex problems. Witness today's medical profession where despite an unparalleled formal education, doctors are frequently "taught" by their patients who have more time to review the massive amounts of data related to their specific issue. Rather than trying to master increasingly vast domains of knowledge, a more important personal competency today is being able to find and apply relevant information efficiently and effectively.

Usually, when we think of where people turn for information we think of databases or other sources of information such as policy and procedure manuals. However, a significant yet often overlooked component of an individual's information environment is composed of the relationships to which one is able to turn to for various informational needs. One study has demonstrated that people are roughly five times as likely to turn to friends or colleagues for answers than other sources of information (Allen 1984). In our own research, we found that more frequently than not, people only enter knowledge bases when directed to a specific lesson or reusable work product by a trusted colleague. Further, people tended to initiate such discussions with colleagues whom they had worked with before and so developed both confidence in their abilities and trust that these individuals would be helpful.

Important relationships build up from experience as a result of working with members of a project team or functional department liaison. Two important features of these relationships make them useful in future organizational initiatives and thus a component of organizational memory. First, time spent interacting on work tasks helps establish a sense of reciprocity and trust with certain colleagues. This social capital is what allows employees to turn to colleagues for help on future initiatives and actually get useful assistance or advice. Second, by working closely together, colleagues build up an understanding of each member's unique knowledge and skills. It is this understanding that allows one to tap other organizational members at appropriate times in future efforts.

Information Stores

The heart of knowledge management has been distributed technology such as Lotus Notes or intranet sites. To date most initiatives have focused on identifying important knowledge in various pockets of an organization and building a technical infrastructure to support knowledge capture, dissemination, and collaboration. Less structured forms of knowledge are often supported by and accumulated within discussion databases where participants record experiences and react to others' comments. Pragmatically, such databases allow physically distributed employees to connect with and learn from relevant others in the context of evolving problems. More structured knowledge repositories often contain internal and external forms of knowledge such as lessons, reports, and work products. In the ideal, these technologies allow an organization to bring its collective intellect to bear on any given problem irrespective of boundaries of time or space.

However, as outlined above, we found that these databases at best perform a complementary role to personal networks when people are seeking answers to problems. As a result, no matter how robust the search functionality or customized the knowledge base, an individual's network of relationships tapped prior to entry into these databases often determines what knowledge is accessed and how it is used. It seems that technology might play a more restricted role in helping to resolve organizational problems than we often think. This is not to downplay the importance of these knowledge repositories as a form of memory. The ability to reuse work products and learn from lessons of others both improves the quality of solutions as well as the efficiency with which they are generated. It is, however, to make salient the point that technology itself is only one form of memory that your employees likely tap in solving organizational problems—and its use is somewhat narrow.

Work Processes and Support Systems

Learning from an important event can become a component of organizational memory by virtue of alterations to processes, procedures, or support systems. As TQM has shown, embedding lessons of experience into either an organization's core work processes or support systems (e.g. incentives, evaluation processes, communication mechanisms) yields a relatively long term impact on the behavior of employees. A prime example of an organization effective in incorporating knowledge into its practices is McDonalds. As outlined by McGill and Slocum, McDonalds has "engineered in knowledge, designing machines that make it virtually impossible to overcook the hamburgers, underserve the amount of fries, or short change the customer" (1993, 69).

However, while this form of memory has a significant ongoing behavioral impact on many organizational members, it is also a difficult form of memory to develop for important learning events that are not repetitive (e.g. innovative approaches to consulting engagements). We found that many organizations had well established mechanisms for embedding learning in processes that they engaged in frequently. However, only a few consciously attempted to learn from less structured events such as new product development or innovative financial transactions. This is problematic as these are the events from which an organization can often learn the most—particularly in an increasingly turbulent business environment that does not allow long product life cycles. Considering changes to aspects of an organization's infrastructure as a means of knowledge transfer is powerful in that this is a form of transfer that does not place as much of a demand on employee's attention as lessons stored in a distributed database.

Product or Service Offering

An organization's key product or service offerings also constitute an important form of organizational memory. In several organizations, we found that lessons learned in one setting were embedded in products or service offerings in the form of product/service line extensions or entirely new service lines. These offerings then became a powerful form of ongoing memory for the organization that tended to shape skills and organizational capabilities developed in the future.

This can be demonstrated by comparing a consulting firm specializing in organizational development with one specializing in strategic planning. Organizational design (OD) often relies heavily on facilitation skills and OD knowledge, whereas a firm specializing in strategic planning tends to develop excellence in analytical skills, industry knowledge, and to some extent creative problem solving. Firms in our study indicated that a primary form of learning was working with clients and customers. Skills and knowledge demanded of service offerings influenced both training strategies and experiential knowledge developed on the job. Further, as a result of differing key offerings, certain ways of organizing, communication channels, information filters, and problem solving strategies developed that tended to focus employees on certain forms of information, knowledge, and skills, and not on others.

In addition to shaping what an organization becomes good at over time, product or service offerings also can result in blind spots. To a greater or lesser extent, organizations are designed to support delivery of core offerings to valued market segments. It is often extremely hard to overcome the inertia created by an organization largely designed to support the delivery and continuous improvement of a given core offering. Consider the story of IBM who dominated the main frame market, but fell roughly five years behind competitors in bringing the technically more simple personal computer to market. The trajectory of improvements in features and functionality that are dictated by an organization's best customers often result in a blindspot to emerging service offerings in new markets (Christensen 1997).

INCREASING LEARNING FROM KEY CYCLES OF EXPERIENCE

The question now becomes how an organization can focus its efforts to improve learning from strategic initiatives by filling these "bins." This is largely a two-step process. The first step entails identification of knowledge worth the expenditure of effort to capture and weave into an organization's business. Too often this process is overlooked with the result being an accumulation of far more information than anyone within an organization can employ. The second step entails developing mechanisms that ensure learning from these experiences is woven tightly into an organization's operations. This requires identification of the forms of memory important for a given business and development of various solutions for maximizing learning from relevant experience. Problematically, these solution sets often cross the functional domains of Human Resources, Operations, and Information Technology. Coordinating such efforts requires a unique commitment to learning and knowledge management. As a result, while no organization we studied excelled in all aspects of embedding learning into organizational memory, we do have exemplars in every category.

Focusing Knowledge Capture and Learning Initiatives

The first question an organization must grapple with is what experience is worth learning from. Many treatments of individual and organizational learning have considered the topic from a nearly utopian perspective—claiming learning imperative to organizations and implicitly taking a perspective that we should learn and capture knowledge from all experiences (Senge 1990; Wheatley 1994). While these approaches hold enormous potential they are often impractical. If nothing else, history continues to remind us that management interventions must be at least aimed in the direction of business problems to be sustainable over time. The key questions become: Learning about what? And how will learning influence organizational performance?

Identification of key experiences from which an organization can learn (i.e. core work processes, new product development, etc.) helps focus knowledge capture efforts in those areas that will most build organizational memory with a payoff in performance. Trying to learn from all situations is generally a losing proposition because important learning events are often sporadic or unique. Further, experiences worth learning from are often critical business initiatives that pressure participants to survive the present rather than increase organizational memory beneficial in future initiatives. If anything, employees will tend to pick those events to learn from that provide the least to learn—ones where they are already confident of answers and so do not have to take interpersonal risks or engage in the hard work of learning.

Translating experiences into knowledge actionable for organizational members requires planning and resources to define and pursue learning worth expenditure of effort (March, Sproull, and Tamuz 1991; Moingeon and Edmondson 1996; Sanchez and Heene 1997). More successful efforts tend to build a business case for knowledge collection efforts, and this business case relies fundamentally on the improvement of business performance. It is one thing to talk of the merit of knowledge abstractly, it is another to ensure that your organization is identifying and applying knowledge to resolve business problems. In general, we have found three steps important in this approach.

First, it is important to link any sort of learning or knowledge capture effort with either business line or organizational strategy (Baird and Henderson 1999). This goal driven approach can be applied at various organizational levels and is principally concerned with identifying a limited set of capabilities that an organization must have in order to distinguish themselves from their competitors in the eyes of their customers. For example, within British Petroleum (BP), finding oil has been identified as a core capability. They spend approximately $250K per day for each well being drilled, so the faster they find oil and begin to recoup that cost, the better off they are financially. As a result, transferring knowledge on new management practices, technologies, or geological understanding across drilling efforts has a significant business performance link.

Second, with these broad strategic imperatives identified, it is then important to focus on a critical few performance drivers. Once your organization or department has honed in on the capabilities critical to business success, the next step is to drill down a level of detail to focus on the few critical processes that enable you to excel on a capability. In the case of BP, they asked, "What are the critical factors that allow one drilling team to consistently outperform another?" They found that one critical factor was the definition of stretch goals for the drilling team and sustaining commitment to those goals. Shared knowledge around goal setting, the development of a recommit process, and other actions surfaced as high performing teams shared the mechanisms they used to keep their stretch goals real for all team members.

Finally, with strategically relevant knowledge identified, it becomes important to establish a collection plan and accountabilities. Identifying important knowledge is one problem. Ensuring that it is collected and driven back into business operations is another issue entirely that is too often overlooked. The trick is to design a collection plan that is simple, quickly integrated into the work process, and that produces value for those actually doing the capturing. Effective collection plans begin with very specific questions that an organization must answer to ensure that learning is focused on critical issues and not a process of collecting more information than anyone finds useful.

In addition, this step entails clearly defining responsibility for getting some of the work done. The task is to provide a clear and unambiguous message that the object is not just to share knowledge, but to improve performance. Some organizations have found that establishing a more formal performance contract helps keep this action orientation. The key components include definition of the stakeholders for the initiative, establishment of leadership roles, definition of expected outcome, benefits, and a general timeline on which to establish these results. In the end, the contract simply gets down on paper the areas of focus, the critical few questions to be answered, who is going to be doing the collection, how, and what the expected results are.

Feeding Organizational Memory

With important experiences identified, the next step is to identify ways that your own organization is maximizing its learning potential from these key cycles of experience. Outlined in the right hand side of Figure 4.1 are some pointers to help assess how your organization is doing in relation to these aspects of memory, as well as some ideas on how to improve in these efforts. As will quickly become apparent, the process of maximizing higher level learning from experience requires a myriad of tools employed at both the team and organizational level.

Individuals

Given the power of individuals as forms of dynamic memory within organizations, executives should ensure that employees are learning from experience in ways that benefit the organization as well as the immediate project. This raises the question as to how staffing decisions are made within your organization—are they based exclusively on current demands or are they at least influenced by a longer term view toward ensuring that knowledge and skills relevant for future competitiveness are being developed? Work experiences can be extremely powerful mechanisms to ensure effective development and also provide the employee with an increased sense of challenge so crucial today. A common tenet of career development programs has long been to place individuals in positions that will maximize their learning processes.

Sound staffing practices can identify and place people in effective development opportunities, but ensuring that people learn from their experiences requires focused attention. Key to any form of experiential learning program is taking time to reflect on experience and define what is learned (Kolb 1984; Schon, 1990). While we all learn by reflecting on events in haphazard fashions (i.e. in the car on the way to work), more effective organizations have found a way to structure the reflection process to ensure that individuals learn the most from an experience. The U.S. Army was the first large organization to implement After Action Reviews (AARs). AARs are simply a structured way for individuals and groups to learn from important experiences. This structured process allows groups to take a break in the action and ask: What was the intent? What is actually happening? What have I/we learned? Organizations such as Chrysler, Ford, and Analog Devices are employing AARs as interventions to continually learn from and improve in new product development experiences. In all of these organizations, the AAR has proven to be an effective way to get employees to capture learning from their work experience. Experience alone is not a kind mentor.

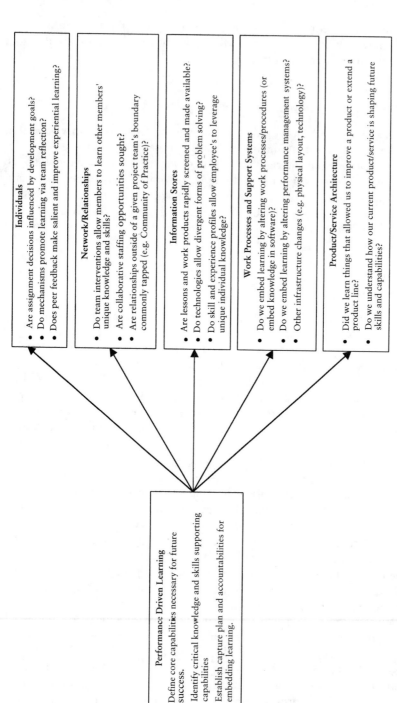

FIGURE 4.1 Feeding Organizational Memory

However, experience that is reflected upon and learned from is a great teacher. And the more you can provide structure for the learning, the more likely people are to feed their own and their organization's memory. Finally, peer feedback mechanisms improve one's own learning by leveraging the perspective of others.

Networks and Relationships

Most work of any significance in organizational settings is accomplished within teams (Hirschorn 1991; Katzenbach and Smith 1993; Mohrman, Cohen, and Mohrman 1995; Mankin, Cohen, and Bikson 1996; Fisher and Fisher 1998). As a result, strong relationships that one can tap in future initiatives are often developed in project teams or other working groups assigned an organizational task. While easy to overlook, these relationships provide a crucial component of an organization's memory. In the words of one manager in our study, ". . . just because [team member] knows something that I may need to know does not mean that he is going to share it with me in a way that is helpful. Not because he is hoarding the information, but because he is busy and doesn't have the time to share what he knows at the level of detail that I may need. The only reason that he will take the time to tell me what I need to know is because we have worked together, fought through a tough project, and developed a relationship that we each know we can rely on."

There are two features of such relationships that make them helpful. First, a sense of reciprocity and trust that builds up over time. It is this social bond that allows a relationship to be functional in future initiatives. Second, an understanding of others' unique knowledge and skills builds up over time such that an individual becomes increasingly precise regarding how others' knowledge may be helpful in relation to a given problem. Both features of a relationship are necessary for them to be instrumental to future efforts. Problematically, most of our team interventions focus largely on shared vision and process skills that help to create a harmonious environment, but do little to educate team members of each others' unique skills and abilities. This often does not help the team perform its tasks or develop an understanding of team members' unique knowledge and skills so they might be tapped in future initiatives.

This is a larger problem than one may think on first blush. Studies consistently show that when work groups form to engage in a task, they experience what is called the unshared knowledge problem (Stasser 1992 and 1995). Rather than engaging in discussions that help them to learn the unique backgrounds of individual members, they tend to focus on some domain that people have in common. Of course this is a natural human process. By finding common areas of interest, acquaintances, or past experience, we are able to start a conversation with people we do not know. However, the result is that groups formed quickly often never get to an understanding of their teammates' unique skills and abilities until extremely late in a given effort (if at all). In more staid times, working relationships developed as a product of interaction over longer time periods. This is not so in today's turbulent business environment. As we are working in an environment where we are increasingly forming and disbanding teams on a project basis to accomplish work, we must pay more attention to the way that these teams develop knowledge of each other.

Rather than engage in experiential learning activities focused exclusively on team process skills, such as ropes courses, it is more effective to focus on task-based activities that serve to develop both team process and awareness of others' knowledge in relation to the task at hand. Such interventions help build harmony while at the same time establishing awareness of others' knowledge. At British Petroleum they have implemented peer reviews as a way to tap into others' skills. Before engaging in any significant task, the individual or group invites peers to provide input. Because the focus is performance, those who can best comment are most likely to be invited. Through this peer review process not only is performance on the task at hand improved, but people become much more aware of the unique skills and abilities others can bring to projects.

In addition, many proponents of team learning seem to ignore the fact that generally the great bulk of time spent on projects is not in team meetings but on various tasks. Looking for opportunities to carve out assignments such that two or more members can collaborate can often be another effective means of building relationships and improving the quality of ideas entering the team discussions. Several consulting organizations that we spoke with indicated that they had begun to focus on staffing two or more people on projects when possible. This flies in the face of conventional wisdom as, given startup and marketing costs, it is far more efficient to staff one person for six months on an effort than two people for three months. However, recognizing the importance of relationships from both a morale and future network perspective, many of these firms are making what may initially appear a poor economic decision by recognizing the substantial long term payoff.

Finally, networks of important relationships are also furthered by organizational initiatives broader than a given team project. One social structure within organizations attracting the attention of both academics and practitioners today is the community of practice (Lave and Wenger 1991; Brown and Duguid 1991; Orr 1996; Wenger 1998). While often an elusive concept, communities are being either found or established to facilitate collaboration in such diverse settings as professional services, research and development, and manufacturing. In many cases, these communities are effective forums for individuals with specialized knowledge to collaborate and learn from each other. In others, they provide means of developing strategic capabilities or technologies and facilitating change processes.

Communities of practice can be particularly effective for organizations that have transitioned from functional to cross-functional team structures. For example, the exploration division of Shell Oil transitioned to a team-based structure recently to overcome inefficiencies caused by cross-functional handoffs. However, when they did this, they found they were losing the depth of knowledge that accrues in a functional structure. By forming communities of practice, they were able to help reintegrate the knowledge of these specialists for the relatively low cost of providing time, meeting rooms, and an intranet site. Not only did these groups of specialists truly enjoy getting together with people who thought like them, but the organization benefited in quantifiable ways as problems were solved more effectively.

However, effective communities of practice pose significant organizational challenges that we are only beginning to work through. For example, while technology can help support communities of practice, both research and consulting experiences have shown that the social bond of these groups is the more important determinant of success. Development of this bond takes significant effort and time, as most organizations' performance management systems value either team or individual performance and so do not easily accommodate or value what can emerge from communities. To obtain the benefits anticipated from communities of practice, organizations must invest both time and some hard resources to identify, nurture, and maintain these groups. They have to learn how to learn from their experiences.

Information Stores

With rapid technical advancements in computing power, speed, memory, and connectivity, it is increasingly possible to share knowledge developed from experience with others across boundaries of time and space. Organizations more effective in leveraging information technology to support organizational memory have developed an ability to do two things. First, they have developed technology, policies, and procedures within their organization to ensure that lessons and reusable work products are screened by panels of experts (to ensure quality of data) and entered rapidly into distributed technologies such that others can benefit from the knowledge. Second, these organizations have increasingly begun to leverage both knowledge repositories and means of virtually connecting employees to engage in dialogue. Such virtual forums allow members of an organization to tap relevant expertise across boundaries of time and space, and yield the potential of being able to bring the collective intellect of an organization to bear on specific problems.

Professional services firms and, in particular, consulting organizations have been one of the earliest movers in employing distributed technologies to house lessons, reusable work products, and methodologies. In the early 1990s, Arthur Andersen began producing Global Best Practices CD-ROM disks and distributing them to their consultants. These CDs contained a wealth of information regarding best practices in various industries that consultants could use at their client site engagements. Over the years, Arthur Andersen has evolved to the use of an intranet site called KnowledgeSpace that provides various forms of knowledge to consultants. This site provides knowledge important to the work of Arthur Andersen consultants including methodologies and tools, best practice examples, prior exemplar engagements, and standard marketing presentations for a wide range of service and industry focused offerings. In addition, the site hosts a variety of on-line communities that allow experts engaged with a specific concern to connect as well as the ability to start a conference center to support virtual teamwork.

An important principle of any technology designed to improve business performance is that it must support the way work is accomplished within a given community. Consultants are rarely in their own office, instead they spend by far the bulk of their time in client settings. This raises difficult problems for knowledge repositories that are housed on an intranet site—access and the ability to download tools or presentations can be particularly cumbersome. Ernst and Young recognized the importance of supporting their consultants in the environment where they work by developing knowledge repositories called PowerPacks that can be downloaded to individual computers.[3] These are highly filtered databases containing leading client deliverables, best practices, skill profiles for experts in any given practice, and important articles or conference references.

The important feature of these PowerPacks is that they are tailored to how the consultant works and consistently support this work in a variety of ways. Access to knowledge is instant and not hampered by speed issues associated with intranet site access. Display and organization of these databases is customized by those communities using the knowledge which makes it more relevant to the work of individual consultants. Knowledge contained in these PowerPacks is also highly filtered as all materials have been carefully screened and evaluated for their applicability.

Establishing ways for experts to be tapped and brought to bear on a problem is also very important. An assumption behind the creation of knowledge repositories is that the problems that people bump into in their consulting engagements are sufficiently similar over time that solutions generated in one area are appropriate in others. Often this does not hold, as problems may be very novel or complex in the eye of a beholder. In such scenarios, an organization needs to be able to tap relevant experts who can mold their knowledge to the problem at hand as quickly and efficiently as possible.

Many organizations have recently begun to leverage on-line communities of practice and other divergent forums to allow individuals to engage relevant experts with a problem. These divergent forums can be effective by allowing employees to pose "Does anybody know?" kinds of questions to a group of relevant experts. These forums are very effective in bringing the collective intellect of a community to bear on a given problem if an organization has found some way to reward sharing behavior. However, there are often problem scenarios in knowledge-based work where there is no clearly defined question or problem— as in the beginning of a project. In these settings, individuals need to have the ability to contact specific people within organizations. In response to this need, many organizations we spoke with were developing corporate yellow pages or

---

[3] PowerPack is copyrighted by Ernst & Young.

skill profiles of employees (this need is also a primary driver of Lotus' new Community Space Product).

Work Processes and Support Systems

Many organizations have very sophisticated means of improving repeatable work processes based on continuous improvement and TQM practices. However, in a world of rapid change, these work processes begin to shift so quickly as to make TQM difficult. As a result, organizations should put in place mechanisms to ensure that learning from important experiences is not forgotten as soon as a project is disbanded or significant changes occur. Given the frenetic pace of organizational life, it becomes far too likely that important lessons will not be fed back into the organization unless specific efforts are made on the part of executives to ensure that this happens. After all, team members we are asking for recommendations are swamped and generally do not have incentives to make recommendations to improve other teams, but rather to get their own work done as quickly as possible. Effective programs along this front should be established with an eye toward altering ineffective work processes.

At Chrysler, for example, product development teams capture lessons learned and translate them into suggested modifications to the product development process. As a result, when team members leave or new product development processes are initiated, the knowledge remains and continues to impact performance because learning is embedded within the process. In addition, companies must also look to adapt aspects of their infrastructure to ensure that ongoing behavior within organizational settings is influenced appropriately (e.g. information systems, performance management systems, etc.). Far too often organizations look to change work processes without recognizing the impact support systems have on the way work is done.

In recognizing the importance of this process, Xerox has developed the Eureka system to capture lessons learned on how to fix and service copiers. When a field service agent finds a better way of working, he or she is encouraged to submit the tip for evaluation and validation by a Tiger Team (a recognized panel of experts within the organization). Once a tip is found to work, it is added to the repository of knowledge and eventually works through a process that results in modification of standard operating procedures. The driver for the whole system is that the person's name is attached to the tip. Those who get the most tips accepted are those considered for promotion to the Tiger Team—a position highly valued as a result of peer recognition. The name recognition and promotion potential are absolutely critical support systems that drive the work process redesign.

Product or Service Architecture

Recently, proponents of the resource-based view of the firm have demonstrated the extent to which competitive ability hinges on skills and knowledge embedded within an organization (Wernerfelt 1984; Barney 1991; Prahalad and Hamel 1990). As we move further and further into the knowledge economy, it becomes increasingly important to be more cognizant about how the services and products you offer today shape what you know, as well as what you are likely to learn as you move forward. Being aware of this allows an organization to focus on key areas that will continue to enhance critical capabilities rather than migrate into poor technical skills or undesirable markets.

This was profoundly demonstrated by one professional services firm in our study. This organization was developing (and continues to do so) a service line in telecommunications consulting. In one significant consulting project, the consulting team discovered a unique means of identifying and valuing certain inefficiencies in billing and collection processes (a core process within any telecommunications organization). This unique approach allowed the client organization to pinpoint and invest in improvement efforts with a great deal more efficiency than had been done before. The problem identification and solution process was so successful that it was immediately sold to another high profile telecommunications organization, and the people involved in doing the initial work were staffed on the subsequent engagement. As word of the success of these engagements spread to other offices, several partners and managers specializing in telecommunications began calling to get some ideas on how to employ this similar approach. Unfortunately, no time was ever made to document this potential service offering and the three people employed in the initial engagement left the firm for a variety of reasons. The end result was that this organization essentially lost an ability to sell a unique kind of engagement. While presentations captured the outcome of the engagement, there was no memory of the process used, tools developed, or key selling points. Without this memory, other people in the organization (who were very busy themselves) chose not to even try to deliver this offering to clients, preferring to fall back on tried and true methods of process mapping.

A consumer product organization participating in our study provides one approach that recognizes the extent to which a product offering constitutes a form of ongoing organizational memory. The organization conducts significant project debriefs after each new product development effort. While project debriefs have been around for some time, this company takes its analysis one step further. First, these reviews are heavily focused on identifying relevant learnings that should shape the next development effort, but for some reason were not able to be included in the initiative just completed (e.g. certain scientific or engineering advancements that were not discovered in time). Second, this organization also conducts a fairly extensive analysis of the skills and organizational infrastructure that such new product initiatives might demand and plots these needs against the skills perceived to be of future significance to the organization from a competitive perspective. Conducting both of these assessments helps ensure that important learnings are not relearned in the next effort and that there is some understanding of the skills and capabilities that the organization will be cultivating by pursuing certain product extensions and not others.

CONCLUSION

Learning is increasingly important in organizations today. Many organizations have recently focused on knowledge management in an effort to improve business performance by reusing work products and other lessons of experience. However, rather than improving business performance, most are finding that they are accumulating enormous stores of information that are overwhelming and often not used. Our work leads us to believe that if organizations want to see business improvements they must look to embed knowledge into various organizational structures and processes.

By considering organizational learning as alteration to memory, organizations can learn more effectively in appropriate strategic directions. Contrary to most knowledge management proponents, capturing and sharing knowledge via distributed technologies is not the only (and perhaps not even the most important) form of learning an organization should concern itself with today. By focusing on memory "bins" relevant to your organization, programs can be built that ensure knowledge is not only abstracted from an experience, but also effectively and efficiently driven into business performance.

REFERENCES

Allen, T. 1984. *Managing the Flow of Technology*. Cambridge, MA: MIT Press.

Argyris, C. and Schon, D. 1996. *Organizational Learning II: Theory, Method and Practice*. Reading, MA: Addison-Wesley.

Arthur, M. B., P. H. Claman, and R. J. DeFillippi. 1995. Intelligent Enterprise, Intelligent Careers. *Academy of Management Executive* 9(4): 7–22.

Baird, L. and J. Henderson. 1999. The Knowledge Engine: A Leaders Guide to Creating and Leveraging Knowledge Assets. Boston University Working Paper.

Barney, J. 1991. Firm Resources and Sustained Competitive Advantage. *Journal of Management* 17(1): 99–120.

Brown, J. S. and P. Duguid. 1991. Organizational Learning and Communities-of-Practice: Toward a Unified View of Working, Learning and Innovation. *Organization Science* 2(1): 40–57.

Christensen, C. 1997. *The Innovator's Dilemma: When Technologies Cause Great Firms to Fail*. Boston, MA: Harvard Business School Press.

Cyert, R. M. and J. G. March. 1963. *A Behavioral Theory of the Firm*. Englewood Cliffs, NJ: Prentice-Hall.

Daft, R. and K. Weick. 1984. Toward a Model of Organizations as Interpretive Systems. *Academy of Management Review* 9(2): 284–295.

Daudelin, M. W. 1996. Learning From Experience Through Reflection. *Organizational Dynamics* 24(3): 36–48.

Davenport, T., D. Delong, and M. Beers. 1998. Successful Knowledge Management Projects. *Sloan Management Review* (Winter): 43–57.

Davenport, T. and L. Prusak. 1998. *Working Knowledge.* Boston: Harvard Business School Press.

Dibella, A. J. and E. C. Nevis. 1998. *How Organizations Learn.* San Francisco: Jossey Bass.

Edmondson, A. 1996. Learning From Mistakes Is Easier Said Than Done: Group and Organizational Influences on the Detection and Correction of Human Error. *Journal of Applied Behavioral Science* 32(1): 5–28.

Fisher, K. and M. Fisher. 1998. *The Distributed Mind: Achieving High Performance Through the Collective Intelligence of Knowledge Work Teams.* New York, NY: AMACOM.

Fiol, C. M. and M. A. Lyles. 1985. Organizational Learning. *Academy of Management Review* 10(4): 803–813.

Hammer, M. and J. Champy. 1993. *Reengineering the Corporation: A Manifesto for Business Revolution.* New York, NY: HarperBusiness.

Hammer, M. and S. Stanton. 1995. *The Reengineering Revolution: A Handbook.* New York, NY: HarperBusiness.

Handy, C. 1994. *The Age of Paradox.* Boston, MA: Harvard Business School Press.

Hedberg, B. 1981. How Organizations Learn and Unlearn. In P. C. Nystrom and W. H. Starbuck (eds.), *Handbook of Organizational Design.* New York, NY: Oxford University Press.

Hirschorn, L. 1991. *Managing in the New Team Environment.* Reading, MA: Addison-Wesley.

Katzenbach, J. and D. Smith. 1993. *The Wisdom of Teams: Creating the High-Performance Organization.* New York, NY: HarperBusiness. Pages: 11–19 and 98–104.

Kim, D. 1993. The Link Between Individual and Organizational Learning. *Sloan Management Review* (Fall): 37–50.

Kolb, D. 1984. *Experiential Learning: Experience as the Source of Learning and Development* New York, NY: Prentice Hall.

Levitt, B. and J. G. March. 1988. Organizational Learning. *Annual Review of Sociology* 14: 319–340.

Lave, J. and E. Wenger. 1991. *Situated Learning: Legitimate Peripheral Participation.* Cambridge, UK: Cambridge University Press.

Mankin, D., S. Cohen, and T. Bikson. 1996. *Teams and Technology: Fulfilling the Promise of the New Organization.* Boston, MA: HBS Press.

March, J., L. Sproull, and M. Tamuz, 1991. Learning from Samples of One or Fewer. *Organization Science* 2(1): 1–13.

McGill, M. and J. Slocum. 1993. Unlearning the Organization. *Organizational Dynamics* (Autumn): 67–79.

McGill, M., J. Slocum, and D. Lei. 1992. Management Practices in Learning Organizations. *Organizational Dynamics* (Summer): 5–17.

Mohrman, S., S. Cohen, and A. Mohrman. 1995. *Designing Team-Based Organizations: New Forms for Knowledge Work*. San Francisco, CA: Jossey-Bass. Pages: 63, 82–87, 181–185 and 231.

Moingeon, B. and A. Edmondson, eds. 1996. *Organizational Learning as Competitive Advantage*. Thousand Oaks, CA: Sage Publications.

Nevis, E., A. DiBella, and J. Gould. 1995. Understanding Organizations as Learning Systems. *Sloan Management Review* (Winter): 73–85.

Nonaka, I. and H. Takeuchi. 1995. *The Knowledge-Creating Company*. London: Oxford University Press.

O'Dell, C. and C. J. Grayson. 1998. *If Only We Knew What We Know*. New York, NY: Free Press.

Orr, J. E. 1996. *Talking About Machines: An Ethnography of a Modern Job*. Ithaca, NY: Cornell University Press.

Prahalad, C. K. and G. Hamel. 1990. The Core Competence of the Corporation. *Harvard Business Review* (May-June): 79–91.

Quinn, J. B. 1992. *Intelligent Enterprise*. New York, NY: Free Press.

Ruggles, R. 1998. The State of the Notion: Knowledge Management in Practice, *California Management Review* 40(3): 80–89.

Sanchez, R. and A. Heene. 1997. *Strategic Learning & Knowledge Management*. Chicester: John Wiley.

Schon, D. A. 1990. *Educating the Reflective Practitioner*. San Francisco, CA: Jossey-Bass.

Senge, P. M. 1990. *The Fifth Discipline: The Art and Practice of the Learning Organization*. New York, NY: DoubleDay Currency.

Slocum, J., M. McGill, and D. Lei. 1994. The New Learning Strategy: Anytime, Anything, Anywhere. *Organizational Dynamics* 23(2): 33–47.

Stasser, G. 1992. Discovery of Hidden Profiles by Decision-Making Groups: Solving a Problem Versus Making a Judgement. *Journal of Personality and Social Psychology* 63(3): 426–434.

———1995. Expert Roles and Information Exchange During Discussion: The Importance of Knowing Who Knows What. *Journal of Experimental Social Psychology* 31: 244–265.

Stata, R. 1989. Organizational Learning: The Key to Management Innovation. *Sloan Management Review* (Spring): 63–74.

Stewart, T. 1997. *Intellectual capital: The new wealth of organizations*. New York, NY: Doubleday.

Sveiby, K. 1997. *The New Organizational Wealth: Managing and Measuring Knowledge-Based Assets*. San Francisco, CA: Berret-Koehler.

Ulrich, D., M. Von Glinlow, and T. Jick. 1993. High-Impact Learning: Building and Diffusing a Learning Capability. *Organizational Dynamics* 22: 52–66.

Walsh, J. P. and G. R. Ungson. 1991. Organizational Memory. *Academy of Management Review* 16(1): 57–91.

Wenger, E. 1998. *Communities of Practice*. Oxford: Oxford University Press.

Wernerfelt, B. 1984. A Resource Based View of the Firm. *Strategic Management Journal* 5: 171-181.

Wheatley, M. 1994. *Leadership and the New Science: Learning about Organization from an Orderly Universe*. Berret Koehler.

Chapter 5

The Factory as a Learning Laboratory

Dorothy Leonard-Barton[*]
Associate Professor at the Harvard Business School.

What is the next production frontier? The author argues that it is operating factories as "learning laboratories." These are complex organizational ecosystems that integrate problem solving, internal knowledge, innovation and experimentation, and external information. Chaparral Steel is the model example, and the experiences of its managers and employees are used throughout the article to show how the learning laboratory works.

Just after 2:00 A.M. on 26 March 1991, the night crew at the Chaparral Steel minimill in Midlothian, Texas, cast the first production run of "near net-shape" steel beams in the United States. General Manager Lou Colatriano grinned with tired satisfaction and headed home for his first break in forty-four hours. From a sketch on a paper napkin to the first red-hot slab of metal that emerged from a patented mold to streak down the new mill line, the elapsed time was twenty-seven months. That included design, mold development, modeling, pilot runs, and construction, and it represented expertise from five companies on three continents. "One of our core competencies," explained CEO Gordon Forward, "is the rapid realization of new technology into products. We are a learning organization."

Every manufacturing company in the United States would like to be able to make that statement. Yet a steel mill seems an unlikely place to look for lessons on the quick commercial realization of inventions. In fact, so does any factory, as innovation is generally associated with research laboratories and development organizations. Moreover, we usually assume that the pressure to get product out the door conflicts with learning. But as speed to market becomes an increasingly

* Reprinted with permission.

important criterion of competitive success, we need to rethink our concept of what a factory is. Factories *can* be learning laboratories.

For decades, U.S. factories were passive service organizations to the rest of the company, churning out products designed without benefit of manufacturing input and burying product and process defects under mountains of inventory. The past decade has seen a transformation of many of these operations into low-inventory organizations dedicated to total quality and to active participation in new product development. What is the next frontier for production? In this article I suggest that it is running operations as learning laboratories.

WHAT IS A LEARNING LABORATORY?

A learning laboratory is an organization dedicated to knowledge creation, collection, and control. Contribution to knowledge is a key criterion for all activities, albeit not the only one. In a learning laboratory, tremendous amounts of knowledge and skill are embedded in physical equipment and processes and embodied in people. More important, however, are the nontechnical aspects, the managerial practices and underlying values that constantly renew and support the knowledge bases.

In this article I put Chaparral Steel under the microscope as an example of a highly successful learning laboratory; its leadership has put tremendous effort into creating a consistent learning system. Many of Chaparral's practices are found piecemeal (often experimentally) in other U.S. organizations. As my references suggest, scholars studying best practices among Japanese manufacturers have made strikingly parallel observations, and Chaparral's policies are consistent with prescriptions by organizational learning theorists. Whether you are managing a fabrication shop or claims processing in an insurance office, Chaparral's management system offers a potentially useful model.

TAKING AN ORGANIC SYSTEM VIEW

Chaparral is the tenth largest U.S. steel producer. Its high-quality standards have been rewarded by the market, and it consistently sets records for productivity, compared to both U.S. and Asian competitors (see the sidebar, "The Evidence on Chaparral Steel"). Clearly, whatever it is doing works.

A close look at the company reveals an organic learning system so tightly integrated that Forward says he can tour competitors through the plant, show them almost "*everything*, and we will be giving away *nothing* because they can't take it home with them." His confidence derives from the fact that the learning laboratory cannot be constructed piecemeal. It is comprehensible only as an organic whole; close scrutiny is required to appreciate its delicacy. To complicate matters, such a corporate ecosystem is in continuous flux, constantly regenerating itself. Even if a competitor identifies important elements of the system, emulation will require time. By then, Chaparral managers trust they will have moved on to the next innovation. The Chaparral system has evolved in response to a turbulent competitive environment, as Forward observes: "We have to go like hell all the time. If the price of what we sell goes up too high . . . all of a sudden lots of folks will be jumping in. And they can get into business in eighteen months or so. . . . We constantly chip away the ground we stand on. We have to keep out front all the time."[1]

A learning laboratory does not occur spontaneously but is designed, created, and maintained through constant managerial attention to communicating the underlying values, checking the management systems smallest details for consistency, and adapting any inharmonious elements. Thus managers designing a learning laboratory need to adopt holistic, systems thinking. They will have to acknowledge the practical utility and bottom-line impact of corporate values. They may have to confront chronic underestimation of the interdependence between incentive and education systems and corporate strategy. Moreover, such systems thinking must permeate the organization's every level. Everyone in the firm must appreciate the self-reinforcing nature of knowledge-creating activities. Only by comprehending the whole system can one understand why, when a fragment of the learning laboratory is pulled out to be examined (a particular project, a specific learning activity), it comes out vinelike, trailing roots back to deeply held values and widely observed management practices. It is this intense interconnectedness that makes such systems difficult to imitate and fragile—but effective.[2]

Learning requires creation and control of both external and internal knowledge for both current and future operations. Therefore, four distinguishing activities are critical to a learning laboratory: (1) problem solving (in current operations); (2) internal knowledge integration (across functions and projects); (3) innovation and experimentation (to build for the future); and (4)

---

[1] G. Forward interviewed by A. M. Kantrow, "Wide-Open Management at Chaparral Steel," *Harvard Business Review*, May-June 1986, pp. 96–102. Organization theorists would see Chaparral's culture as an appropriate response to such an environment. Scholars theorize that learning will not happen without a certain amount of stress and that complex, uncertain environments require decentralized, laterally linked organizations. See: C. M. Fiol and M. A. Lyles, "Organizational Learning," *Academy of Management Review* 10 (1985): 803–813; and R. Duncan and A. Weiss, "Organizational Learning: Implications for Organizational Design," *Research in Organizational Behavior* 1 (1979): 75–123.

[2] Senge argues persuasively that successful leaders are systems thinkers, able to see "interrelationships, not things, and processes, not snapshots." See: P. Senge, "The Leader's New Work: Building Learning Organizations," *Sloan Management Review*, Fall 1990, pp. 7–23. Other theorists similarly note how interrelated are strategy, structure, and culture in creating learning environments. See: Fiol and Lyles (1985).

The Evidence on Chaparral Steel

Chaparral has been setting records in steel production almost since its inception in 1975. In October 1982, it set a world record by producing 67,666 tons in one month—then the highest monthly tonnage produced from a single electric furnace/continuous casting combination. By 1984, the company was listed in *Fortune's* May 28 cover story on the ten best-managed factories in the United States.

Chaparral's pace of improved performance continues unabated. Compared to a Japanese average output of 600 tons per worker-year and a U.S. output of 350 tons, Chaparral put out 1,100 tons of steel per worker-year in 1989. Its 1990 productivity figures of 1.5 worker-hours per rolled ton of steel compared to an overall U.S. average of 5.3 (including integrated steel mills), a Japanese average of 5.6, and a German average of 5.7. Chaparral is currently the largest supplier of steel rod for the oil industry and the largest supplier of rod for mobile home frames in the United States.

The company has won significant international recognition for quality as well. In spring 1989, Chaparral was awarded the right to use the Japanese Industrial Standard certification on its general structural steel products. It was the first U.S. steel company and only the second company outside Japan given that privilege. Out of approximately fourteen U.S. companies producing hot-rolled carbon bars and shapes, the company claims to be the only one certified by the AIME (American Institute of Mining, Metallurgical, and Petroleum Engineers) for nuclear applications. Similarly, it is one of two companies, out of fifteen, whose steel is certified by the American Builders of Ships and that therefore do not have to seek certification for each individual job.

Chaparral has a reputation for quality at the low-cost end of its product line as well. A customer's study comparing scrap rates of Chaparral steel to that of the only other company from which the customer purchased, revealed a difference ranging from four to twenty-five times as low for common carbon bar and three to five times for the much more expensive alloys.

BOX 5.1 The Evidence on Chaparral Steel

integration of external information flows (see Figure 5.1).[3] Each activity is the operational expression of an underlying value and is strongly supported by a compatible managerial system of procedures and incentives. Thus each activity,

[3] I assume that learning occurs if "through its processing of information, the range of [an organization's] potential behaviors is changed." See: G. Huber, "Organizational Learning: The Contributing Processes and the Literatures," *Organizational Science* 2 (1991): 89. That is, beyond contributing to an accumulation of formal knowledge bases, learning creates "capacities . . . for intelligent action." See: G. Morgan and R. Ramirez, "Action Learning: A Holographic Metaphor for Guiding Social Change," *Human Relations* 37 (1983): 21. A growing literature on the topic emphasizes that organizational learning is more than an aggregation of individual learning. See, for instance: B. Hedberg,

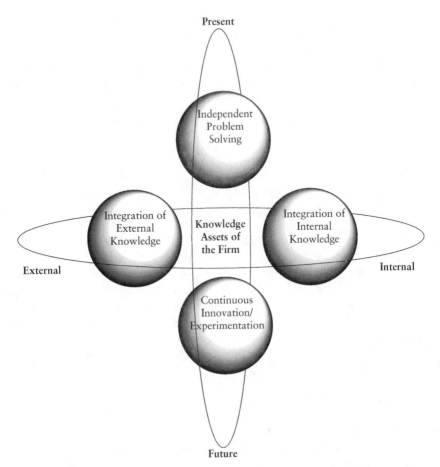

FIGURE 5.1 Knowledge Creation and Control Activities in a Learning Laboratory

value, and managerial system functions as an internally consistent subsystem. Although I will describe each subsystem separately, the four are mutually aligned and interrelated; that is, values and managerial systems underlying one

"How Organizations Learn and Unlearn," in *Handbook of Organizational Design*, eds. P. Nystrom and W. Starbuck (New York: Oxford University Press, 1981), pp. 3–27. While the four critical activities proposed here have not been previously combined into a framework, each has been identified as characteristic of a learning organization. On problem identification and solving, see: E. Hutchins, "Organizing Work by Adaptation," *Organization Science* 2 (1991): 14–39. On integration of internal information, see: Duncan and Weiss (1979). On experimentation, see: R. Bohn, "Learning by Experimentation in Manufacturing," (Cambridge, Massachusetts: Harvard Business School, Working Paper No. 88–001, 1988). On acquisition and use of external information, see: Huber (1991), pp. 88–115.

subsystem also support the other three. An in-depth look at the four subsystems at Chaparral suggests some of the principles that distinguish a learning laboratory.[4]

Before exploring these subsystems, however, we need a brief explanation of Chaparral's near net-shape project, an innovative foray directly into the traditional territory of "Big Steel" that illustrates the company's knowledge creation and control subsystems.

THE NEAR NET-SHAPE PROJECT

One way to push equipment performance and ensure learning is to set goals for each project considerably beyond current production capabilities.[5] Chaparral managers set a very ambitious goal for the near net-shape project: to produce large (eighteen- and twenty-four-inch wide) structural steel I-beams for the same per-pound cost as the simple round reinforcing bars ("re-bars"), the company's first product. "We knew what it took to make rebar," explains General Manager Duff Hunt. "The challenge was to produce a more difficult product for the same cost. . . . We decided on the twenty-four-inch because we wanted to explore the most technically challenging product. Because there may, be some idiosyncrasies about the process that we need to learn, we also chose a second size . . . based on the amount of North American consumption." Reaching this cost objective (half of Big Steel's) required drastically reducing the energy costs (roughly 25 percent of total) of rolling the steel into the required end shape. The nearer to the final ("net") shape the molten steel could be cast, the less rolling required.

The only known processes for casting steel to its near net shape were far too capital and labor intensive for Chaparral, which views large investments in either capital or labor as a threat to future flexibility. The steel-making molds and processes developed for the near net-shape project therefore embody knowledge beyond anything available on the market and, in fact, beyond anything the leading vendors of steel-making molds thought possible. The approximately four-foot copper alloy tube through which the molten steel passes to emerge in

---

[4] Chaparral managers have verified the accuracy of the descriptions of activities and events offered here, but they are not responsible for the characterization of learning laboratories in general or for the way I have analyzed their organizational culture.

[5] Other researchers also imply the utility of stretch goals as stimuli for learning. Such goals may be thought of as "performance gaps" deliberately induced to motivate knowledge generation. See: Duncan and Weiss (1979). Itami suggests that "overextensions" and "dynamic imbalances" created to challenge the organization characterize the most successful Japanese manufacturing companies. See: H. Itami and T. Roehl. *Mobilizing Invisible Assets* (Cambridge, Massachusetts: Harvard University Press, 1987). Moreover, the goal for this particular project fits Senge's prescription of a blend of extrinsic and intrinsic visions, in that both outside competition and improvement over prior performances are invoked: Senge (1990).

nearly I-beam shape is deceptively simple in appearance. However, the mold is patented, which suggests that the combined expertise of Chaparral designers and Italian and German mold fabricators endowed it with cutting-edge knowledge. The mold is contoured so the hot metal won't bind as it shrinks going through, and the fabrication methods produce an absolutely smooth finish on the sides, to lessen chances of rending the thin skin surrounding the molten steel as it emerges. It is difficult to imagine how Chaparral could have succeeded in this knowledge-intensive project had the company not been run as a learning laboratory.

THE LEARNING LABORATORY SYSTEM

Some of the activities, values, and managerial practices described below characterize any high-quality organization. Others are very unusual—at least in the United States. Since they operate as a system, we have to look at the whole operation to understand why emulating just some parts may never produce true learning laboratories.

Subsystem One: Owning the Problem and Solving It

The first critical learning subsystem is the triad of (1) the independent problem solving required for continuous improvement of current processes, (2) egalitarianism as an underlying value, and (3) shared rewards as the reinforcing incentives system (see Figure 5.2). Empowered individuals, who command respect in the organization and who feel ownership in the system, have the self-confidence, freedom, and motivation to continuously solve problems. The

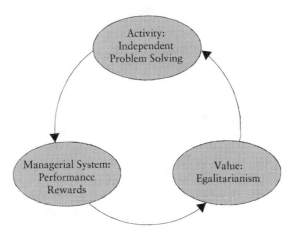

FIGURE 5.2 Subsystem One: Owning the Problem and Solving It

principle involved here turns the old production saw of "if it ain't broke, don't fix it" on its head and maintains: "if it ain't being fixed continuously, it's broke."

Activity: A Independent Problem Solving

Learning starts with empowered individuals who can identify and solve problems independently because they have a clear sense of operating objectives. The often-articulated vision at Chaparral is to lead the world in the low-cost, safe production of high-quality steel. This resembles the mission of many other companies that are not learning organizations. For a learning lab, the test of a vision is the extent to which it permeates the whole organization, guiding every micro and macro decision. Unless the vision can be directly translated into operational principles, that is, into guidelines for running the factory lines, it may have little effect on actual shop-floor behavior. Chaparral's goal of leading the world requires innovation beyond the current cutting edge of production techniques. Maintaining a cost advantage requires constant improvements in productivity. The vision dictates that those improvements cannot come at the expense of quality or employee safety. Therefore the goal for every hour, the criterion for every person's activity, is crystal clear: make ever more steel—increasingly better than anyone else. "We never stray far from the market," says Hunt.

In a learning environment, progress has to be everyone's business—not just that of a few specialists. At Chaparral, who owns a production problem and responsibility for its solution? An incident during the first few weeks of operating the near net-shape caster, when cooling hoses were bursting, provides some insight. "When something like that comes up, and there seems no immediate solution," explains a senior operator, "you go see what the problem is. You don't say, 'That's not my area,' or 'I don't know that much about it.' You just show up." In this case, a group of operators, a welder, some foremen, and a buyer spontaneously gathered to discuss the problem and just as spontaneously scattered to seek solutions. "Everybody telephoned some person they thought might know how to fix the problem—vendors, experts—and within three to four hours we were getting calls back," says the senior operator. "Service people were showing up, and we worked the problem out. If it had been just one guy, probably a foreman, and everyone walked out, . . . it would have taken him ten times longer to find a solution."

Because the performance goal is very clear, supervisors do not need to micromanage the line, and the organization runs lean. For instance, two months after the first run of the near net-shape casting, the pulpit controls operator is carefully checking the timing on the line with a stopwatch. The red-hot beams pass through the rolling mill stand once, then stop, reverse, and go through again. Meanwhile, the flow of steel behind the beam being rolled is diverted. Every second of unnecessary diversion costs money because the diverted steel will have to be reheated to be rolled. Therefore the operator wants to achieve split-second timing. Asked who suggested he perform this function (which is often given to a process engineer elsewhere), he is surprised at the question: "No one."

He considers it obvious that improvement is always a part of his job: "We're still learning, but we will get it. You just take it upon yourself to roll as much steel as you can whether you are the pulpit operator, the roller, the furnace operator. . . . We want to do the best we possibly can. Everybody here has the attitude to pick up the pace."

One of the greatest advantages of this attitude, as a maintenance foreman points out, is that "ideas come from just about everybody. The operators working on the equipment have a lot of input because they see the exact problems when they happen." Moreover, potential improvements are immediately enacted with no wait for management approval or standardization of "best practices." If it works, it is the *de facto* standard. If it improves performance, everyone will imitate it. "Whoever can come up with an idea on how to fix it, from the millwrights or myself right on up to the top, . . . does it right then," explains a foreman. At Chaparral, there is no formal requirement, as at some Japanese companies, for a certain number of improvement suggestions from each employee. Everyone is involved in some process improvement projects, and, as the foreman explains, "We are all out here to make it run. Probably 90 percent of the problems never even make it to the morning meetings [held among everyone on the shift to discuss problems]. They are fixed in the field."[6]

The downside to this intrapreneurial attitude is that although managers set the goals, no one has the authority to tell another employee *how* to accomplish a task. Process engineers and supervisors who know a better procedure often have difficulty convincing operators on the line—much less their peers. "You can't tell them how to do it," Administration Vice President Dennis Beach admits somewhat ruefully, "and they don't do it the way you would." The engineers concur. They are not called upon enough, in their opinions. However, the benefits from general ownership of all problems are that it is not possible to "pass the buck" and no one expects a steady-state manufacturing process—ever.

Value: Egalitarianism and Respect for the Individual

A learning environment is premised on egalitarianism, the assumption that all individuals have potential to contribute to the joint enterprise (if they are willing to develop competence). Forward has observed, "We figured that if we could tap the egos of everyone in the company, we could move mountains."[7] Outward

---

[6] Morgan and Ramirez (1983) suggest that a "holographic" organization (which epitomizes a learning organization for them) is designed so that "the nature of 'one's job' at any one time is defined by *problems facing the whole*" (emphasis in original, p. 4). Similarly, from his study of knowledge creation in some of Japan's top firms, Nonaka concludes that "every single member of the organization should be able to suggest problems . . . and . . . solutions." See: I. Nonaka, "Managing Innovation as an Organizational Knowledge Creation Process" (Rome: Technology Strategies in the Nineties Conference Paper, 21 May 1992), p. 44.

[7] Quoted by B. Dumaine, "Chaparral Steel: Unleash Workers and Cut Costs," *Fortune*, 18 May 1992, p. 88.

symbols of values are important because they convey meaningful messages to all employees. At Chaparral there are no assigned parking places, no different colored hard hats or uniforms reflecting title or position, and the company dining room is a local diner. More unusual, a scant two levels separate the CEO from operators in the rolling mill; a visitor is surprised when an operator stops Forward on a walk through the plant to discuss a new product's problems. A millwright notes: "If you have tact, you can tell anybody from Mr. Forward on down exactly what is on your mind. There is no problem in expressing your opinion here." Repeated requests to interview a particularly knowledgeable project manager are politely rebuffed with a shrug and an explanation from a vice president: "Sorry, he just doesn't want to. I can't *make* him." However, respect for the individual does not mean equality of responsibility, lack of discipline, or even consensual decision making. Chaparral managers believe that a supervisor should be a leader, trained to make good decisions—including hiring and firing.

Managerial System: Performance Rewards

Positive thinking and slogans alone cannot create genuine employee investment in innovation and in identifying and solving problems.[8] Chaparral has taken unusual steps to ensure that performance and incentive systems back up management's belief in egalitarianism. In 1986–1987, when employment leveled off, and management confronted potential stagnation, the pay structure was overhauled to reward accumulation of skills as well as performance. Even more radical (especially for a steel mill) was the switch from hourly wages to salary for everyone. There are no time clocks at Chaparral. Forward explains, "When I am ill, I get a day off. Why shouldn't everyone else?" He is fond of saying that the management system was designed for the 97 percent who are "conscientious people who want to put in a full day's work." The 3 percent who abused the system were let go. Beach summarizes the philosophy: "We manage by adultery. We treat everyone like an adult." Moreover, the pain and pleasure of work are spread around. For instance, in contrast to many factories, operators are not assigned to shifts according to seniority. Everyone rotates into night shift, a practice that fosters knowledge accumulation twenty-four hours a day and guards against a possible disproportionate accumulation of skills and knowledge in the most favored hours. The reward for seniority is thus not greater comfort, but more challenges. How do senior employees feel about that? "During the summer in Texas," one foreman rationalizes with a grin, "you'd *rather* work at night."

Steel-making is hot, dirty, demanding work; the pace of innovation and the constant pressure to produce more, better, and more safely in this organization

---

[8] Argyris and Schon point out that "espoused theory" does not always influence behavior; "theory in practice" does. See: C. Argyris and D. Schon, *Organizational Learning* (Reading, Massachusetts: Addison-Wesley, 1978). See also: S. Kerr, "On the Folly of Rewarding A, While Hoping for B," *Academy of Management Journal*, December 1975, pp. 769–783.

exacerbate the brutal conditions imposed by the technology. What keeps the workforce from burning out? One factor is the incentive systems that have evolved.[9]

Bonus schemes are linked to company profits—for everyone. "We think janitors and secretaries are important in our success, too, and they should share in the rewards," observes Forward. An operator comments, "The more money the company makes, the more money I make. The profit-sharing system creates built-in pride." Further, 93 percent of the employees are stockholders and together own 3 percent of the stock. In 1988, each employee received one share for every year worked at the company; 62 percent buy additional shares every month through payroll deductions. Although the monetary implications are small, this policy is consistent with the rest of the rewards structure, and some employees find it symbolically important. A furnace controls operator comments, "I feel like this company partly belongs to me. Owning part of the company makes you care. I take better care not to waste anything because I feel like I am paying for it."

These could be just words, of course. Scholars studying the relationship between such incentive systems and productivity have not reached consensus about the benefits of employee shareholding (partly because share-holding agreements vary widely). However, there is strong support for the notion that profit sharing generally does raise productivity.'[10] At Chaparral, the dual incentives of employee profit sharing and shareholding seem a natural complement to the rest of the learning laboratory system.

Subsystem Two: Garnering and Integrating Knowledge

The second subsystem revolves around knowledge accrual (see Figure 5.3). In the learning laboratory, knowledge is highly and visibly valued. Management invests in educating the whole person, not just the technical side, and knowledge flows freely across boundaries. The principle is this: every day, in every project, add to the knowledge resources.

---

[9] Von Glinow argues that the most effective organizational reward system to attract and retain highly skilled people is an "integrated culture" that combines a concern for people with very strong performance expectations. Chaparral's system appears to fit her description. See: M. A. Von Glinow, "Reward Strategics for Attracting, Evaluating, and Retaining Professionals," *Human Resource Management* 24 (1985): 191–206.

[10] In a macro-analysis of sixteen studies using forty-two different data samples that estimated the effect of profit sharing on productivity, the authors conclude that "these studies taken together provide the strongest evidence that profit sharing and productivity are positively related." See: M L. Weitzman and D. L. Kruse, "Profit Sharing and Productivity," in *Paying for Productivity* (Washington, D. C.: The Brookings Institution, 1990), p. 139.

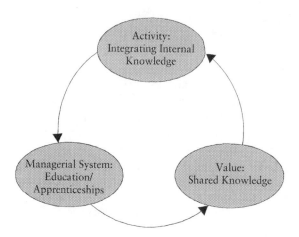

FIGURE 5.3 Subsystem Two: Garnering and Integrating Knowledge

Activity: Integrating Internal Knowledge

In a learning laboratory, one would expect to see visible embodiment of knowledge creation and control in highly innovative physical systems. Chaparral boasts of such cutting-edge equipment as an automobile shredder that they believe is the fastest and most efficient in the world, a horizontal (instead of vertical) caster, and some of the most advanced digital furnace controls anywhere. Because of the constant push to improve production, Chaparral managers have to design what they need, rather than purchase the best available equipment off-the-shelf. Why design in-house? "To keep the knowledge here," a mill manager explains. Moreover, managers assume that the performance of *any* purchased equipment can be improved. Some improvements are novel enough to be patented. Rolling mill equipment that its vendor believed was limited to eight-inch slabs is turning out fourteen-inch, and the vendor has tried to buy back the redesign. The two electric arc furnaces, designed originally to melt annual rates of 250,000 and 500,000 tons of scrap metal, respectively, now produce over 600,000 and 1 million tons, respectively.

The physical processes following the molding step are also knowledge intensive. Only one other steel mill in the world does the hot-link rolling employed in the near net-shape casting project, whereby hot cast steel is sent directly into the rolling mills. Using this technique was a big risk because no one knew exactly what the properties of the thinner cast steel would be. The hot link meant less subsequent rolling than usual and hence less "working" of the steel to obtain the desired crystalline structure. The risk paid off when the combination near net-shape casting and hot link turned out to produce steel with exceptionally good metallurgical characteristics. Chaparral processes seem clear outgrowths of skill, yet how does such expertise and knowledge accumulate?

Just as continuous processing has great advantages for manufacturing over most batch processing, so the unimpeded flow of information aids learning more than fragmented, batch-processed information.[11] Most organizations are physically structured to emphasize vertical (hierarchical) and horizontal (functional) boundaries. In contrast, Chaparral management emphasizes homogenizing the level of knowledge throughout; few pockets of information are isolated by position, function, or working shift.[12]

Information flow at Chaparral is obviously aided by its size, deliberately held to under a thousand employees. An individual garnering knowledge on a trip, at a conference, or from an experiment can readily transmit it, as all employees are located in the same place and know each other. The company was also designed to facilitate knowledge flows by encouraging as many accidental meetings as possible. The plant layout accommodates the hands-on style of management favored at Chaparral; even Forward's office is just steps away from the furnaces and mills. The locker room is located here also, so that at least once a day employees cycle through the one-story headquarters building.[13] Consequently, meetings are as likely to be held in the halls as in the conference rooms. Since many decisions go unrecorded and memos are anathema, it is important that people see each other frequently.

Hierarchical boundaries are minimal. This is a do-it-yourself company with no acknowledged staff positions and only a few positions that seem stafflike, such as personnel. There are fifty graduate engineers and technicians, all with line duties. In fact, everyone has line responsibilities, most of them tied directly to steel production, and decision making is pushed down to the lowest possible supervisory level, "where the knowledge is." Lead operators are selected for their knowledge-transmitting as well as knowledge-creating skills, because much knowledge flows horizontally among peers. Work is structured with the objective of disseminating knowledge. For instance, in commissioning the new mill that receives the near net-shape product (that is, ramping it up to problem-free production), only two teams of operators are being trained. Each team works a

[11] This advantage was confirmed in a study by: K. Clark and T. Fujimoto. "Overlapping Problem Solving in Product Development," in *Managing International Manufacturing*, ed. K. Ferdows (North Holland: Elsevier Science Publishers, 1989). Huber (1991) suggests a reason for the advantage: "When information is widely distributed in an organization, so that more and more varied sources for it exist, retrieval efforts are more likely to succeed and individuals and units art more likely to be able to learn. Therefore information distribution leads *to more broadly based* organizational learning" (pp. 100–101). Fiol and Lyles (1985) similarly cite research showing that learning is enhanced by decentralized structures that diffuse decision influence.

[12] Nonaka (1992), after describing very similar policies at Kao Corporation, observes: "Asymmetrical distribution of information destroys the equality of relationships and leads to unilateral command instead of mutual interaction" (p. 48).

[13] For an understanding of the impact on communication patterns of physical proximity and centrally located common facilities, see: T. Allen, *Managing the Flow of Technology* (Cambridge, Massachusetts: The MIT Press, 1977), ch. 8.

twelve-hour shift (with paid overtime). After the initial eight weeks of this grueling schedule, these operators will be dispersed among the rest of the crews to diffuse the knowledge they have created and assimilated about the new process's idiosyncrasies.

Chaparral has also proven that traditional horizontal boundaries can be redrawn and expectations altered. The quality control department is responsible for reacting to quality problems identified by operators on the line—not by separate inspectors. Production workers do 40 percent of maintenance tasks. A maintenance foreman notes that "at Chaparral, we get involved with the whole process. We are not just tied to one area."

Although the company has a marketing department, everyone is considered a salesperson. Every employee from CEO to receptionist has a business card to use with customers. Security guards do data entry while on night duty and are trained paramedics as well. Such multifunctional experience is encouraged not only to make the organization more flexible but because management believes it discourages territorial possessiveness over information.

No research and development (R&D) department exists separate from production. Forward maintains that "everybody is in research and development. The plant is our laboratory." This statement has implications beyond the obvious that there is no research function. Some of the problem solving and experimentation that are done in the midst of production involve research. However, interfacing with the possessors of the latest scientific knowledge is not restricted to an elite group of specialists. Knowledge accumulation in a learning lab cannot be the responsibility of a few special people. Forward describes the large, separate research centers in some companies as "lovely, really nice. But the first time I went into one of them I thought I was entering Forest Lawn [Cemetery]. After you spend some time there, you realize you *are* in Forest Lawn. Not because there are no good ideas there, but because the good ideas are dying there all the time."[14]

At Chaparral, even operators participate in R&D activities. When the world's leading supplier was constructing the patented mold for the near net-shape project, the three-person team that shuttled back and forth to the site in Germany, learning about the fabrication process and serving as a source of information about the intended production process, included an operator. As described later in Subsystem Four, Chaparral employees at all levels are constantly tapping into the latest, most current knowledge banks around the world.

---

[14] Interview by A. M. Kantrow (1986). A remarkably similar philosophy was observed in four Japanese companies, where "employees are trained from the first day on the job that 'R&D is everybody's business.'" See: M. Basadur, "Managing Creativity: A Japanese Model," *The Executive* 6 (1992): 29–42. Itami (1987) similarly propose "'excessive' experimentation in production" since "experimentation and learning do not take place only in the lab" (p. 95).

Value: Shared Knowledge

Since performance drives everything in this company, and individual incentives are tied to performance, employees seem engaged in a marathon relay race, where winning as a company team takes precedence over individual ownership of ideas, and knowledge is liberally shared. There are acknowledged experts, such as the director of operations who is an "equipment whiz," and the mold expert who was largely responsible for the near-net shape design, and the organization does not lack for large egos. However, Vice President of Operations Dave Fournie says that "you don't *have* to have credit for particular ideas to be thought good at your job. Lots of innovations take more than one good idea. They go through a gestation period, and lots of people figure out how to make sense of it. The point is to focus on the good of the *whole*. That's why we don't have suggestion boxes, where you hide ideas so someone else won't steal them."

Chaparral employees are often unable to identify the source of production innovation. Production Manager Paul Wilson explains, "It is hard to say who fathers an idea. It doesn't make any difference. Everyone shares in the pride of doing, and if the experiment fails, everyone shares in the failure. In other places, a few people do a lot of innovating. Here a lot of people do little bits that add up." A millwright makes similar observations: "No one is looked down upon. If I am supposed to know more than somebody else but that other person catches [an oversight], well that's fine—he just bailed me out. I am more than likely going to help him out a different time."

Managerial System: Apprenticeships and Education

An organization that values knowledge must provide mechanisms for continuous learning. Chaparral management has sent some employees to school to obtain advanced degrees, but it also invests heavily in an unusual formal apprenticeship program for everyone in the plant, which it developed with the Bureau of Apprenticeship and Training in the U.S. Department of Labor. (Most apprenticeships are run by unions.) As Forward notes, "Expertise must be in the hands of the people that make the product."

The roughly three-and-a-half-year program allows apprentices to progress to the level of senior operator/craftsman by successfully completing 7,280 hours of on-the-job training and designated formal schooling. The foremen of individual crews schedule the on-the-job training and evaluate the candidate's systematic progression through various tasks in the factory. For example, 2,200 hours in steel-pouring operations is one qualification in the ladle metallurgy apprenticeship. In addition, all apprentices complete study programs in safety, operating processes across the entire company, mathematics as related to operations, metallurgy, and basic mechanical maintenance "in an effort to give all operators a solid basic understanding of the equipment used and the operating processes." Scheduling this study, which requires four hours of unpaid work a week, is left up to the individuals, who have five options: home study with manuals and videos; in-plant study in instructor-monitored study rooms; formal classes;

personalized tutoring by instructors; and study in work areas as operations permit. (Operators may also get credit for prior experience by proving knowledge on the job.) Courses include basic engineering knowledge such as conduction in liquids and gases, as well as very specific skills such as ladder logic programming for understanding programmable controllers and lubricant storage and handling. Perhaps more surprising are such sessions as "working with other people" under "troubleshooting skills."

The most unusual aspect is the instructors. Selected foremen rotate in from the factory floor to teach. "It creates a lot of credibility for the education program on the factory floor," explains one instructor. "What's more," he adds wryly, "I have to live with what I teach. So I'd better do a good job."

Chaparral also invests in outside courses of all types, tending to train its own people rather than hiring those with a particular skill. A maintenance foreman attended a special engineering course because "no one knew anything about vibration analysis so I was asked to go study it." External education includes nontechnical courses as well. In few factories would a furnace controls operator attend a Dale Carnegie-type course to help him enhance the interpersonal skills critical to smooth teamwork. Line managers are expected to be technical experts, constantly up-to-date with cutting-edge technology—whether that be some aspect of metallurgy or human resources. Therefore every manager attends conferences and cultivates a professional network of information sources. The manager of the scrap shredding operations, for instance, has just attended a conference on recycling—in the future, Chaparral's expertise in recycling may be an important corporate capability.[15]

Subsystem Three: Challenging the Status Quo

The third subsystem in a learning laboratory involves constantly pushing knowledge frontiers (see Figure 5.4). The company must select employees for their desire to challenge their own and others' thinking. They must see risk as positive, because it comes with the experimentation critical to innovation. The company must select suppliers for their superior capabilities—and for their willingness to be pushed beyond the bounds of their current knowledge. The principle involved is this: always reach beyond your grasp.

Activity: Continuous Experimentation

Learning requires constant pushing beyond the known, and Chaparral employees are skilled experimenters. A visitor was surprised to find that extensive overhead slides explaining the formal Taguchi experimental designs that

---

[15] Descriptions of Japanese best practices reveal similar strong emphasis on both on-the-job training and formal education. See, for example: J. Sullivan and I. Nonaka, "The Application of Organizational Learning Theory to Japanese and American Management," *Journal of International Business Studies* 17 (1986): 127–147.

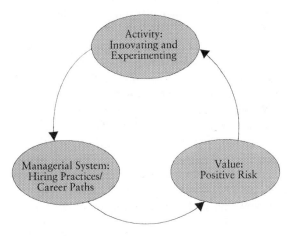

FIGURE 5.4 Subsystem Three: Challenging the Status Quo

were guiding the development of the horizontal caster had been prepared for the board of directors. This extremely technical presentation was to help directors understand the methodical knowledge-creation process, enable them to identify critical decision points, and thereby better equip them to evaluate the risk. Another example of knowledge-creating experimentation more often found in research laboratories than factories is the one-sixth scale model of the near net-shape caster, which uses water to approximate the flow of steel. Standing alongside the rolling mill, close to a water source, this model allowed testing of several types of baffles and lengths of mold. Resulting observations guided much of the eventual mold design decisions.

Innumerable large and small experiments are more of the "cut-and-try" variety. "We aren't always as systematic about our learning as we could be," Forward admits. Many creative simulations are conducted right on the production line. The advantage is that the more closely the experimental environment approximates the final production environment, the more immediately relevant is the information generated. The disadvantage is the obvious potential to disrupt production—which is why most factories prefer to isolate experimentation. In one of many projects leading to the near net-shape casting, a prototype of metal splashboards was first constructed out of plywood. By continuously soaking the wood in water, the crews were able to keep it from being consumed by molten steel just long enough to prove the concept. "We were the local hardware store's favorite plywood customers for a while," one employee recalled. Similarly, during the design of the near net-shape caster, several prototype molds of almost pure copper were used to determine if casting a dog-bone-shaped slab was possible. The soft molds held together just long enough to show this new casting process's feasibility.[16]

The operating rule is this: if you have an idea, try it. Line managers authorize tens of thousands of dollars for experiments without higher authority. Hunt explains, "We use products to do research. We can close the feedback loop between researchers and users by using new methods and new materials within our own facility." Wilson agrees: "In other companies, the word is—don't rock the boat. Here we rock the hell out of the boat. We don't know the factory's limits. We want it to change, to evolve."

Not every suggestion is instantly accepted. When a maintenance operator at a conference spied new digital furnace pulpit controls, he then had to convince his supervisor to invest. For almost two years, the supervisor remained uninterested in visiting the Mexican vendor and a site using the controls. Yet the operator persisted. Finally, his supervisor understood the potential of these state-of-the-art controls and agreed to their installation and customization to Chaparral operators' specifications.

During the development of the near net-shape beams, Chaparral frequently disconcerted development partners by its innovation speed. One innovation followed so hard on the heels of the previous one that they almost overlapped. When the German mold developers finished a prototype on schedule and called to ask how they should ship it, they were astonished to be told, "Don't ship it at all; cut it up and make it look like this." The designers had already learned enough from the prototyping process to improve the design. A new mold would be required. What surprised partners was that Chaparral did not appear to begrudge the "wasted" $40,000 per mold, since the knowledge engendered by each prototype enabled the next step in innovation.

Value: Positive Risk

In a research laboratory, risk is accepted as the norm, since the cutting edge is always fraught with uncertainty. In contrast, risk is usually anathema in a production environment. Managers of a learning factory must tolerate, even welcome, a certain amount of risk as a concomitant of knowledge acquisition. Chaparral managers avoid riskless projects because a "sure thing" holds no promise of competitive advantage—no opportunity to outlearn competitors. Says Forward, "We look at risk differently from other people. We always ask what is the risk of doing *nothing*. We don't bet the company, but if we're not taking some calculated risks, if we stop growing, we may die."

This positive attitude toward risk permeates the company. If everyone experiments, learns, and innovates, then neither success nor failure can be

---

[16] For an interesting contrast in stimulating learning, see the carefully constructed routines in the "learning bureaucracy": P. Adler, "The 'Learning Bureaucracy': New United Motor Manufacturing, Inc.," in *Research in Organizational Behavior*, eds. B. M. Staw and L. L. Cummings (Greenwich, Connecticut: JAI Press, forthcoming).

heavily personalized. If individuals are singled out for praise, then they have an incentive to protect ideas as intellectual property rather than seek embellishment from friendly critics and codevelopers. If individuals are singled out for blame, then the risk of failure may overwhelm the impulse to innovate. What happens when you try something and it doesn't work? What is the penalty? "Everybody makes mistakes," a Chaparral foreman responds. "You don't have to cover up a mistake here. You just fix it and keep on going." The philosophy appears to apply even when the failed experiment is very expensive. In 1986, when Fournie was medium section mill superintendent, he championed the installation of a $1.5 million arc saw for cutting finished beams. Not only did the magnetic fields attract any small unattached pieces of metal for yards around, including pens and watches, but the engineers were never able to refine the equipment to the point of effective operation. Since promoted to vice president of operations, Fournie is somewhat amused to find that visitors "can't believe you can make a mistake like that and not get crucified." He tries to take the same attitude toward those who work for him: "You don't start them out on $1.5 million projects, but you have to give them freedom to make mistakes. The reward for having ideas is getting to carry them out. You give them bigger and bigger chunks and evaluate." Operators on the line have a consistent view of the atmosphere for innovation: "You have an idea—good, bad, indifferent—just spit it out and we'll talk about it. Someone may laugh [at it] but you'll laugh back next week."

A potential hazard of this positive attitude toward risk is that no one wants to admit a mission is impossible. "Once we say we will do something," Fournie explains, "we hang on and try like nobody's ever tried before. Tenacity makes lots of projects work here that don't work other places—but when it just can't be done, it's hard to call the project off." One of his key criteria for determining if people are ready for promotion is whether they know when to ask for help, when to admit that they are in over their heads: "It's a tough call . . . the hardest decision to learn to make." He speaks from experience. He not only set up the arc saw project; he killed it.

Managerial System: Hiring Practices and Career Paths

The most important managerial system in a learning laboratory is selecting and retaining the right employees. Because employees must be innovators, constantly challenging the status quo, they are selected as much for their potential, their attitude toward learning, and their enthusiasm as for a specific background. Although top managers and a few specialized "gurus" at Chaparral have extensive steel experience, when Chaparral was first set up, management decided not to look for workers with industry experience. Beach explains: "We were looking for bright, enthusiastic, articulate people, and we preferred people who had not been exposed to other companies' bad habits." The company therefore hired (and continues to hire) from the immediate geographic area, seeking ranchers and farmers with mechanical ability but no steel experience. Chaparral looks for "a twinkle in the eye, a zest for life," for "basically conscientious people who can put in a strong day's work and enjoy what they're doing." This love of work is critical in an organization that deliberately runs somewhat understaffed to avoid laying people off during market downturns. A learning laboratory is not a good match for someone who works solely for a paycheck or who equates promotion with increasingly easy work.

Chaparral's original applicants went through six weeks of intensive training with daily evaluations and faced stiff competition. Top performers were given their choice of jobs and an immediate 20 percent pay raise. Highly selective hiring procedures continue to reflect concern that new employees fit into the Chaparral culture, that at least one supervisor be personally committed to their training and progress, and that the team have a stake in their success. Although personnel does some preliminary screening, current applicants undergo one or more days of demanding interviews with at least five employees, including two foremen, before they join Chaparral. Only one out of ten applicants selected for interviews can expect to be hired, and the final decision belongs to the foreman with direct responsibility. These very cautious, resource-intensive selection practices may account in part for the extremely dedicated workforce, which boasts an absentee rate about one-fourth that represented by the National Association of Manufacturers.

Since people are the key resource in a knowledge-intensive organization, keeping them is critical.[17] Beach explains: "From the very beginning, we designed this organization with Maslow's hierarchy of needs in mind [i.e., that once people's basic needs for food, shelter, and belonging are satisfied, they will aspire to a fourth level of need, self-esteem, and finally, the fifth, self-actualization.] I know it's not stylish, but we really believe in that hierarchy, so we constantly look at what will help people become self-actualized, at their ego needs. . . . People like a challenge and a well-defined goal out there."[18]

---

[17] Clearly a tradeoff exists between stability in the workforce and the diversity needed to stimulate innovation. March proposes that "a modest level of turnover, by introducing less socialized people, increases exploration and thereby improves aggregate knowledge." See: J. March, "Exploration and Exploitation in Organizational Learning," *Organization Science* 2 (1991): 79. However, others point to the "insistence on selection of company members at an early point in life and avoidance of the introduction of new people at higher management levels" as an important influence on an information-sharing culture: I. Nonaka and J. Johansson, "Japanese Management: What about the 'Hard' Skills?" *Academy of Management Review* 10 (1985): 184. Simon observes that turnover can become a "barrier to innovation" because of the increased cost of socialization: H. Simon, "Bounded Rationality and Organizational Learning," *Organization Science* 2 (1991): 125–134. Chaparral's management takes pride in its low turnover rate.

[18] Interestingly, Hanover Insurance CEO William O'Brien made a similar reference to Maslow's hierarchy: "Our traditional hierarchical organizations are designed to provide for the first three levels [of the hierarchy] but not the fourth and fifth. . . . Our organizations do not offer people sufficient opportunities for growth." Quoted in Senge (1990): 20.

A strong aid in motivating continuous innovation is a clear path for advancement, not just in salary but in position. Asked what he looks for in a job, a millwright responds: "As long as I am moving forward, I can think for myself, and I feel that I am contributing, I will be happy." Chaparral managers believe that skilled, innovative people will leave an organization if they see no possibility for personal growth. During the 1986–1987 reorganization to address possible stagnation, some maintenance and shipping operations were reorganized into autonomous, self-directed teams with rotating leadership. Management regards this change as an organizational experiment that may provide a model for other parts of the company.

The company invests in crosstraining at a number of levels. Management has learned the necessity of training in advance of the need because of problems experienced early in the company's history, when operators who were automatically moved up into lead and then supervisory positions as vacancies opened proved underprepared. In response, Chaparral management established such idiosyncratic practices as "vice-ing." In other companies, when a foreman or supervisor is absent, usually the foreman from a prior shift stays on in that position. When a similar absence occurs at Chaparral, the prior foreman works the extra hours, at his usual pay level, but in a *subordinate* role. The most senior operator or craftsman is then temporarily promoted to "vice foreman" to cover the supervisory position. Thus the company retains operating experience in the form of the prior shift foreman and simultaneously trains the senior operator for future work as a foreman. A supervisor explains, "You get a little pay increase and a whole lot more responsibility. I got a chance to see whether I really wanted to be a foreman or not, and it gives you a little respect for the boss's job."

Managers are similarly prepared for the future. Recently the production managers for the three mills were given the title of general manager and asked to learn each other's jobs and to cover for each other. This crosstraining is intended to prepare them for general management of an entire operation, when Chaparral starts up another site.[19]

Subsystem Four: Creating a Virtual Research Organization through Networking

A learning laboratory obviously needs access to the latest knowledge, embodied in the best minds and best equipment available. However, not all companies can afford an internal research organization. Moreover, no company can cover all the technological advances, worldwide, that may affect its future.

---

[19] Such experience and knowledge sharing even at managerial levels is noted as a characteristic of Japanese organizations, which are "able to cover for an absent individual quite easily, because other individuals have a relatively greater understanding of the requisite information": Nonaka and Johansson (1985): 185. See also the discussion of designing organizations with redundant skills: Morgan and Ramirez (1983): 5.

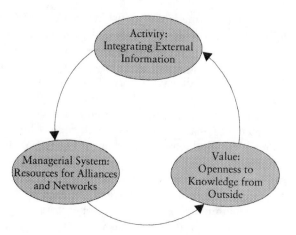

FIGURE 5.5   Subsystem Four: Creating a Virtual Organization

Therefore the principle behind the fourth and final subsystem is this: create a virtual research organization through extensive networking and alliances—for learning and for economic reasons (see Figure 5.5).

Activity: Integrating External Knowledge

At Chaparral, employees constantly scan the world for technical expertise that others have already invested in. Managers never hesitate to invent when necessary but only after assuring themselves through extensive searches that no available system will suit their needs. While building the horizontal caster, they made repeated trips to the few other world sites that had somewhat similar equipment. Chaparral also constantly benchmarks its capabilities, not just against immediate competitors but also against best-of-class companies, even those from totally different industries. Three on-site laboratories support production through chemical and physical product analysis, but the company has created a virtual research organization through extensive networking and alliances. Information obtained externally is rapidly incorporated through development projects, flowing through the created network almost as readily as it does inside the walls of the learning laboratory, because in both cases people working directly in production transmit the knowledge.

The network was heavily used in the near net-shape project. At its outset, a team of managers and foremen visited Japan and determined that one firm had the most advanced "profile" casting process in the world. Yet it was inflexible, would cost "more than the entire company," and was more labor intensive than desired. Chaparral therefore enlisted the help of German and Italian suppliers. At first extremely skeptical of this small company from the middle of Texas and hence unwilling to try to make the radical mold design, the German supplier began to believe that seemingly impossible goals could be achieved only when it saw how far Chaparral had progressed with the help of the Italians. Chaparral employees visited the German vendor every few weeks, and ultimately Chaparral's expertise combined with the German's cutting-edge knowledge to produce a patented mold that neither company could have made alone.

Concerned that the relatively thin cast steel emerging from this mold might have undesirable metallurgical qualities, Chaparral reached again into its network for testing. Since it had not yet built its own rolling mill, and none existed anywhere that could receive the novel shape, managers identified a production laboratory in Mexico with very flexible equipment. Chaparral's superintendent of steel-melt technology went to Mexico to direct the simulation of the future mill design, using Mexican equipment and workers. To their delight, Chaparral managers discovered that the samples demonstrated superior characteristics.

The development and testing laboratories in the German and Mexican firms served as virtual extensions of the corporation, for they possessed special equipment and skills that complemented Chaparral's design capabilities. However, knowing such sources of expertise exist would be useless if the factory were not able to tap them, to jointly create more knowledge, and then to absorb that knowledge into the production system.

Chaparral's collegial knowledge network seems more characteristic of a research laboratory than of a factory. Possibly because of Forward's early career as a research metallurgist, the company aggressively pursues the latest knowledge. Chaparral sought the coveted Japanese certification for steel, not because managers thought they would ever sell much steel in Japan, but because they believed the Japanese would go through the company's process carefully—and Chaparral would learn much from the exercise. Forward takes a distinctly nontraditional view of environmental scanning for a factory: "By the time you hear about a technology in a paper at a conference, it is too late." This philosophy explains why Chaparral invests in unorthodox knowledge-gathering mechanisms, for instance, by cosponsoring a research conference with the Colorado School of Mining about a new alloy under investigation. Forward himself treks back regularly to his alma mater, MIT, to consult with university experts.[20]

Very occasionally, this method of R&D has failed the company. The most notable example is the previously mentioned electric arc saw. No one in the plant or in its network of experts, including the vendor, was able to solve the technical difficulties. The mill manager left the saw in place for almost a year to allow time for everyone to attempt solutions and to accept failure, while he sought an alternative technology. It is not clear that an in-house R&D facility would have helped in this case because the required invention lay in the unfamiliar realm of electromagnetic fields. Managers at Chaparral believe that through their virtual

---

[20] Again the parallel with Japanese practice, at least as described in literature, is striking. Nonaka and Johansson describe how Japanese firms consult with outside experts, not as troubleshooters, but as educators on the general topic. It is up to the company's own personnel to translate that newly acquired intelligence into application. See: Nonaka and Johansson (1985).

R&D organization, they can actually tap a larger variety of knowledge bases than they would be able to support internally, given their size. Still, they will have to continue investing in internal expertise in order to integrate the externally obtained knowledge.

Value: Openness to Knowledge from Outside

Knowledge garnered through such networks can flourish only in an environment that rejects the "not invented here" mentality. At Chaparral, "not *reinvented* here" is the operative slogan. There is no value in recreating something— only in building on the best existing knowledge. People in a learning laboratory value the capability to absorb and use knowledge as much as to create it. They understand that all invention is a process of synthesis. As its practices suggest, a key Chaparral value is global outreach—openness to innovation, whatever its origin. Knowledge is valued not so much for the pedigree of its source but for its usefulness.

Managerial System: Resources for Alliances and Networks

To support information gathering and reinforce global outreach, the company invests heavily in employee travel (and regards the expenses as just that— investments), often sending a team, including foremen and technical staff as well as vice presidents and operators, to investigate a new technology or to benchmark against competitors. Newly acquired knowledge need not filter down through the ranks, because the people who absorbed it are the ones who will apply it. In 1990, seventy-eight people from production, several of them operators, visited a customer site at least once. They also visit other minimills. Asked why he visited a sister plant, an operator states: "To see if I could pick up any new ideas to use here." And did he? "Yes, several." And he points out some small operational changes. Forward elaborates: "We send the people who can best tell us what's going on—whoever they are." Chaparral managers also invest in long-term relationships with suppliers to extend the network. In 1985, while seeking Japanese suppliers, they identified a high-quality company that was not doing much development. As a general manager explains, although it was clear that initially the supplier "would learn more than we" from the alliance, Chaparral spent the money to send employees over to "hand hold" so as to develop a capability that would be useful in the future.

This constant dispersal of mixed employee teams to customers, competitors, and suppliers throughout the world serves a dual purpose. The visits are regarded as learning sabbaticals that keep life "exciting" for employees. They are a source of information for the company as a whole. "We want them to . . . come back with new ideas about how to make improvements or new ways to understand the problem."[21]

---

[21] Kantrow (1986): 101.

CONCLUSION

The factory, in fact any backroom operation, is not usually regarded as an arena for experimentation and learning. Chaparral Steel challenges this concept of operations. Factories *can* function as learning laboratories (see Table 5.1). The most important characteristic of such organizations is that they are totally integrated systems. They are difficult to imitate because every employee, from CEO to line operator, is technically capable and interested in learning. Moreover, the whole organization is designed around the creation and control of knowledge. The four subsystems described above are not only internally linked but tremendously dependent upon each other. Continuous education depends upon the careful selection of willing learners. Sending workers throughout the world to garner ideas is cost effective only if they are empowered to apply what they've learned. The organization is unlikely to be open to outside knowledge if it does not place a strong value on sharing knowledge or does not give rewards for bettering the whole company's performance. Thus continuous learning depends upon the sense of ownership derived from the incentive systems, upon the pride of accomplishment derived from special educational systems, upon values embedded in policies and managerial practices, as well as upon specific technical skills. The line operator appears to take the same perspective on the conduct of daily activities as the CEO. Chaparral is tremendously consistent.

Paradoxically, the system's interdependence is also a potential weakness, as competencies often are.[22] A learning laboratory may have trouble recreating

TABLE 5.1 Comparison of Traditional Factory with Factory as Learning Lab

	Traditional Factory	*Learning Lab*
1. Research and development function	Separate and distant from production.	Merged with production (everyone does development).
2. Experimentation on factory floor	Rare, feared.	Constant, welcomed.
3. Innovation	Exclusive province of engineers.	Everyone's business (but their own methods).
4. Equipment and processes	If it works, don't fix it.	Design your own; constantly improve.
5. New technology	Reject: not invented here.	Never reinvent here.

[22] I have argued that core capabilities almost inevitably have a flip side, core rigidities, that hamper nontraditional projects and can hobble an organization in moving to new competencies. See: D. Leonard-Barton, "Core Capabilities and Core Rigidities in New Product Development," *Strategic Management Journal* 13 (1992): 111–126.

itself. Any organization is likely to be somewhat limited by its "congenital knowledge" and by the stamp placed upon it by its founders.[23] A significant challenge for Chaparral is how to grow. Forward has noted that "to stand still is to fall behind," and the company's credo to provide growth for its skilled people requires some forward momentum. Therefore, it must either grow larger where it is or clone itself in a new location. How will it transplant the deep worker knowledge, the motivation, the commitment, and the informal systems of knowledge sharing?

For other companies interested in creating factories as learning laboratories, the questions are: Can it be done in a plant within a large corporation, where many of the managerial systems have already been set corporatewide and therefore are not at the plant manager's discretion? Can an existing plant be transformed when plant managers may not have the luxury of selecting people as freely as Chaparral did? Can a company less geographically isolated hope to reap returns on investing in its employees' intellectual advancement, or will they be lured away by other companies?

Similar questions were raised a decade ago when U.S. manufacturers first began to understand how Japanese companies were competing on the basis of quality. Initially overwhelmed by the difference in activities, values, and managerial systems implied by the total quality approach, many U.S. managers were pessimistic about their ability to change their operations to the extent needed and reluctant to invest in employee education. Yet today, many U.S.-based factories achieve quality levels never even aspired to in 1980.[24]

For many of these improvements, the Japanese were our teachers, having learned from Deming and Juran.[25] According to some researchers, Japanese managers may also be ahead of their U.S. counterparts in creating learning laboratories, since "Japanese companies are usually adept at organizational learning."[26] As the references at the end of this article suggest, many of Chaparral's managerial practices and values also characterize best practices in Japan, such as

---

[23] Huber (1991) discusses this limitation. See also: J. Kimberly, "Issues in the Creation of Organizations: Initiation, Innovation, and Institutionalization," *Academy of Management Journal* 22 (1979): 437–457.

[24] This includes Japanese transplants such as New United Motor Manufacturing, Inc., whose employees are mostly rehires from the same United Auto Workers workforce that had one of the industry's worst labor records. See: R. Rehder, "The Japanese Transplant: A New Management Model for Detroit," *Business Horizons*, January-February 1988, pp. 52–61.

[25] See the profiles of these two men in: O. Port, "Dueling Pioneers," *Business Week*, 25 October 1991, p. 17.

[26] Nonaka and Johansson (1985). In fact, some management practices now being imported into the United States were advocated by younger U.S. contemporaries of Deming such as Chris Argyris, whose early books were translated into Japanese within a year of their publication in the United States. See: C. Argyris, *Personality and Organization* (New York: Harper Brothers, 1957) and *Integrating the Individual* (New York: John Wiley & Sons, 1964).

investing extensively in formal and informal education; searching worldwide for the best technology and methods and absorbing that knowledge into home operations; and valuing employee empowerment, problem solving, and risk taking.[27] Apparently, such learning systems are not uniquely Japanese.

Of course, creating a learning laboratory in a "greenfield" site is easier than in an existing plant. As not all U.S. factories can start up from scratch, creating a learning laboratory implies big changes. But do we really have any choice? No financial formulas, corporate reshuffling of departments, or exhortations by corporate management to integrate across functions will foster the creativity and productivity needed for international competition.

Experts on change management suggest that three critical elements are required for altering current practices: (1) dissatisfaction with the status quo; (2) a clear model of what the changed organization will look like, and (3) a process for reaching that model, that vision of the future.[28] Examples such as Chaparral can aid all three. One way of stimulating dissatisfaction with current practices and hence motivation to change is to observe other companies where an alternative management style appears to be yielding superior results. By benchmarking against such companies, managers can derive principles to incorporate into their own particular visions. Chaparral offers a model of a factory as a learning laboratory, and if the specifics are not transferable, the principles underlying the Chaparral vision are.

The precise process for implementing these principles will differ markedly from company to company. It is possible to interrupt a factory's current systems by introducing new equipment, new learning skills and activities, new knowledge-creating management systems, or new values. But interrupting a current system is only the first step. As the Chaparral example demonstrates, learning skills, management procedures, and values are interrelated. Values unsupported by management systems are vapid; management systems that run counter to values are likely to be sabotaged; learning activities unsupported by values and management practices will be short-lived. If a learning capability is to be developed, the whole system must eventually be addressed.

---

[27] See, for example, R. Rehder and H. Finston, "How Is Detroit Responding to Japanese and Swedish Organization and Management Systems?" *Industrial Management* 33 (1991): 6–8, 17–21; R. T. Pascale, *Managing on the Edge* (New York: Simon Schuster, 1990), ch. 9; and G. Shibata, D. Tse, I. Vertinsky, and D. Wehrung, "Do Norms of Decision-Making Styles, Organizational Design, and Management Affect Performance of Japanese Firms? An Exploratory Study of Medium and Large Firms," *Managerial and Decision Economics* 12 (1991): 135–146.

[28] See, for example, M. Beer, *Organization Change and Development* (Santa Monica, California: Goodyear Publishing Company, 1980), ch. 3.

The author is grateful to the employees of Chaparral Steel for their patience, to Gil Preuss for help in field work, and to colleagues Chris Argyris, David Garvin, and Steven Wheelwright and two anonymous reviewers for comments on earlier drafts. The study was supported by the Division of Research, Harvard Business School.

Chapter 6

Understanding Organizations as Learning Systems

Edwin C. Nevis, Anthony J. DiBella and
Janet M. Gould*

*How can you tell if your company is, indeed, a Learning organization?
What is a learning organization anyway? And how can you improve the
learning systems in your company? The authors provide a framework
for examining a company, based on its "learning orientations," a set of
critical dimensions to organizational learning, and "facilitating factors,"
the processes that affect how easy or hard it is for learning to occur.
They illustrate their model with examples from four firms they studied—Motorola, Mutual Investment Corporation, Electricité de France,
and Fiat—and conclude that all organizations have systems that support
learning.*

With the decline of some well-established firms, the diminishing competitive power of many companies in a burgeoning world market, and the need for
organizational renewal and transformation, interest in organizational learning
has grown. Senior managers in many organizations are convinced of the importance of improving learning in their organizations. This growth in awareness has
raised many unanswered questions: What is a learning organization? What determines the characteristics of a good learning organization (or are all learning
organizations good by definition)? How can organizations improve their learning? In the literature in this area, authors have used different definitions or

* Reprinted with permission. Edwin C. Nevis is director of special studies at the Organizational Learning Center, MIT Sloan School of Management. Anthony DiBella is a visiting
assistant professor at the Carroll School of Management, Boston College. Janet M. Gould
is associate director at the Organizational Learning Center.

119

models of organizational learning or have not defined their terms.[1] Executives have frequently greeted us with comments like these:

- "How would I know a learning organization if I stumbled over it?"
- "You academics have some great ideas, but what do I do with a mature, large organization on Monday morning?"
- "I'm not sure what a good learning organization is, but you should not study us because we are a bad learning organization."

Our research is dedicated to helping organizations become better learning systems. We define organizational learning as the capacity or processes within an organization to maintain or improve performance based on experience. Learning is a systems-level phenomenon because it stays within the organization, even if individuals change. One of our assumptions is that organizations learn as they produce. Learning is as much a task as the production and delivery of goods and services. We do not imply that organizations should sacrifice the speed and quality of production in order to learn, but, rather, that production systems be viewed as learning systems. While companies do not usually regard learning as a function of production, our research on successful firms indicates that three learning-related factors are important for their success:

1. Well-developed core competencies that serve as launch points for new products and services. (Canon has made significant investments over time in developing knowledge in eight core competencies applied in the creation of more than thirty products.)
2. An attitude that supports continuous improvement in the business's value-added chain. (Wal-Mart conducts ongoing experiments in its stores.)
3. The ability to fundamentally renew or revitalize. (Motorola has a long history of renewing itself through its products by periodically exiting old lines and entering new ones.)

These factors identify some of the qualities of an effective learning organization that diligently pursues a constantly enhanced knowledge base. This knowledge allows for the development of competencies and incremental or transformational change. In these instances, there is assimilation and utilization of knowledge and some kind of integrated learning system to support such "actionable learning." Indeed, an organization's ability to survive and grow is based on advantages that stem from core competencies that represent collective learning.[2]

---

[1] C. Argyris, "Double Loop Learning in Organizations," *Harvard Business Review,* September-October 1977, pp. 115–124; K. Weick, *The Social Psychology of Organizing* (Reading, Massachusetts: Addison-Wesley, 1979); B. Leaviit and J. G. March, "Organizational Learning," *Annual Review of Sociology* 14 (1988): 319–340; P. M. Senge, *The Fifth Discipline* (New York: Doubleday, 1990); and E. H. Schein, "How Can Organizations Learn Faeter? The Challenge of Entering the Green Room," *Sloan Management Review,* Winter 1993, pp. 85–92.
[2] C. K. Prahalad and G. Hamel, "The Core Competence of the Corporation," *Harvard Business Review,* May-June 1990, pp. 79–91.

As a corollary to this assumption, we assume that all organizations engage in some form of collective learning as part of their development.[3] The creation of culture and the socialization of members in the culture rely on learning processes to ensure an institutionalized reality.[4] In this sense, it may be redundant to talk of "learning organizations." On the other hand, all learning is not the same; some learning is dysfunctional, and some insights or skills that might lead to useful new actions are often hard to attain. The current concern with the learning organization focuses on the gaps in organizational learning capacity and does not negate the usefulness of those learning processes that organizations may do well, even though they have a learning disability. Thus Argyris and Schön emphasize double-loop learning (generative) as an important, often missing, level of learning in contrast with single-loop learning (corrective), which they have found to be more common.[5] Similarly, Senge makes a highly persuasive case for generative learning, "as contrasted with adaptive learning," which he sees as more prevalent.[6] The focus for these theorists is on the learning required to make transformational changes—changes in basic assumptions—that organizations need in today's fast-moving, often chaotic environment. Their approach does not negate the value of everyday incremental "fixes"; it provides a more complete model for observing and developing organizational learning. After periods of significant discontinuous change, incremental, adaptive learning may be just the thing to help consolidate transformational or generative learning.

Another assumption we make is that the value chain of any organization is a domain of integrated learning. To think of the value chain as an integrated learning system is to think of the work in each major step, beginning with strategic decisions through to customer service, as a subsystem for learning experiments. Structures and processes to achieve outcomes can be seen simultaneously as operational tasks and learning exercises; this holds for discrete functions and for cross-functional activities, such as new product development. The organization encompasses each value-added stage as a step in doing business, not as a fixed classification scheme. Most organizations do not think this way, but it is useful for handling complexity. With this "chunking," we are able to study learning better and to see how integration is achieved at the macro-organizational level. This viewpoint is consistent with a definition of organizations as *complex arrangements of people, in which teaming takes place.*

[3] J. Child and A. Kieser, "Development of Organizations over Time," in N. C. Nystrom and W. H. Starbuck, eds., *Handbook of Organizational Design* (Oxford: Oxford University Press, 1981), pp. 28–64; and E. H. Schein, *Organizational Culture and Leadership* (San Francisco: Jossey-Bass, 1992).
[4] J. Van Maanen and E. H. Schein, "Toward a Theory of Organizational Socialization," *Research in Organizational Behavior* 1 (1979): 1–37.
[5] C. Argyris and D. A. Schön, *Organizational Learning: A Theory of Action Perspective* (Reading, Massachusetts: Addison-Wesley, 1978).
[6] Senge (1990).

While we have not looked at organizations' full value-added chains, we selected our research sites so that we could examine learning in different organizational subsets. In addition, we gathered data indicating preferences or biases in investments in learning at different points of the chain and to understand how learning builds, maintains, improves, or shifts core competencies. Do organizations see certain stages of the chain where significant investment is more desirable than at others?

Our last assumption is that the learning process has identifiable stages. Following Huber, whose comprehensive review of the literature presented four steps in an organizational learning process, we arrived at a three-stage model:

1. Knowledge acquisition—The development or creation of skills, insights, relationships.
2. Knowledge sharing—The dissemination of what has been learned.
3. Knowledge utilization—The integration of learning so it is broadly available and can be generalized to new situations.[7]

Most studies of organizational learning have been concerned with the acquisition of knowledge and, to a lesser extent, with the sharing or dissemination of the acquired knowledge (knowledge transfer). Less is known about the assimilation process, the stage in which knowledge becomes institutionally available, as opposed to being the property of select individuals or groups. Huber refers to the assimilation and utilization process as "organizational memory." While this is an important aspect of knowledge utilization, it is limited and works better when discussing information, as distinct from knowledge. True knowledge is more than information; it includes the meaning or interpretation of the information, and a lot of intangibles such as the tacit knowledge of experienced people that is not well articulated but often determines collective organizational competence. Studies of organizational learning must be concerned with all three stages in the process.

Early in our research, it became clear that organizational learning does not always occur in the linear fashion implied by any stage model. Learning may take place in planned or informal, often unintended, ways. Moreover, knowledge and skill acquisition takes place in the sharing and utilization stages. It is not something that occurs simply by organizing an "acquisition effort." With this in mind, we shifted our emphasis to look for a more fluid and chaotic learning environment, seeking less-defined, more subtle embodiments.

---

[7] Huber identifies four constructs linked to organizational learning that he labels knowledge aquisition, information distribution, information interpretation, and organizational memory. Implicit in this formulation is that learning progresses through a series of stages. Our framework makes this sequence explicit and connects it to organizational action. Huber does not make this connection since to him learning alters the range of potential, rather than actual, behaviors. See: G. Huber, "Organizational Learning: The Contributing Processes and Literature, *Organization Science* 2 (1991): 88–115.

The first phase of our research was based on intensive field observations in four companies, Motorola Corporation, Mutual Investment Corporation (MIC), Electricité de France (EDF), and Fiat Auto Company.[8] We wanted to have both service and manufacturing settings in U.S. and European environments. We chose two sites where we had access to very senior management and two where we were able to study lower levels. We selected Motorola as an example of a good learning organization; we were able to observe organizational learning during its fourteen-year quality improvement effort.

We did not attempt to study entire firms or to concentrate on any single work units in these four organizations. For example, at Motorola, we began by studying two senior management teams of twenty to twenty-five executives each from all parts of the corporation. Each team focuses on a critical issue defined by the CEO and COO, to whom the groups report. The teams' structures were designed as executive education interventions and vehicles for "real-time" problem solving. Our objective was to see how these teams reflected and utilized organizational learning at Motorola.

From our interview data, we identified what organizational members claimed they had learned and why. We wrote case descriptions of the learning processes in their organizations, which we shared with the organizations to ensure their accuracy. Using a grounded analysis, we identified categories that reflected learning orientations and then constructed a two-part model of the critical factors that describe organizations as learning systems.[9] We have since tested this model in data-gathering workshops with personnel from more than twenty *Fortune* "500" companies. Our testing led us to revise some of the model's components, while retaining its overall framework.

CORE THEMES

Next we discuss the core themes that emerged from our research and provided a basis for our model.

---

[8] At Motorola, we observed and interviewed fifty senior managers, visited the paging products operations, and had access to about twenty-five internal documents. At Mutual Investment Corporation (a pseudonym for a large financial services company based in the United States), we observed and interviewed corporation employees in the investment funds group and the marketing groups. At Electricité de France, we observed and interviewed employees in the nuclear power operations. At Fiat, we observed and interviewed employees in the Direzione Technica (engineering division) in Torino, Italy.

[9] A. Strauss, *Qualitative Analysis for Social Scientists* (Cambridge: Cambridge University Press, 1987).

All Organizations Are Learning Systems

All the sites we studied function as learning systems. All have formal and informal processes and structures for the acquisition, sharing, and utilization of knowledge and skills. Members communicated broadly and assimilated values, norms, procedures, and outcome data, starting with early socialization and continuing through group communications, both formal and informal. We talked with staff people in some firms who claimed that their companies were not good learning organizations, but, in each, we were able to identify one or more core competencies that could exist only if there were learning investments in those areas. Some type of structure or process would have to support the informed experience and formal educational interventions required for knowledge acquisition, sharing, and utilization. We found this in both our field sites and other firms. For example, one firm that considers itself to be a poor learning organization because of its difficulty in changing some dysfunction has a reputation in its industry for superior field marketing. It is clear that this group has well-developed recruiting, socialization, training and development, and rotating assignment policies that support its cadre of respected marketing people. Obviously, some learning has been assimilated at a fairly deep level.

Learning Conforms to Culture

The nature of learning and the way in which it occurs are determined by the organization's culture or subcultures. For example, the entrepreneurial style of MIC's investment funds group results in a learning approach in which information is made available to fund managers and analysts, but its use is at the managers' discretion. In addition, there is a good deal of leeway in how fund managers make their investments; some are intuitive, some rely heavily on past performance, and a few use sophisticated computer programs. Thus the fund managers' use or application of learning is largely informal, not dictated by formal, firmwide programs. Meanwhile, the culture of MIC's marketing groups is more collaborative; learning is derived more from interaction within and between cross-functional work groups and from improved communication.

In contrast, there is no question that a great deal of organizational learning about quality has occurred at Motorola, but its emphasis on engineering and technical concerns resulted in an earlier, complete embrace of total quality by product manufacturing groups. In a culture that heavily rewards product group performance, total quality in products and processes that require integrated, intergroup action lags behind, particularly in the marketing of systems that cut across divisions.

Style Varies between Learning Systems

There are a variety of ways in which organizations create and maximize their learning. Basic assumptions about the culture lead to learning values and investments that produce a different learning style from a culture with another pattern of values and investments. These style variations are based on a series of learning orientations (dimensions of learning) that members of the organization may not see. We have identified seven learning orientations, which we see as bipolar variables.

For example, each of two distinct groups at both Motorola and MIC had different approaches to the way it accrued and utilized knowledge and skills. One Motorola group had great concern for specifying the metrics to define and measure the targeted learning. The other group was less concerned with very specific measures but, instead, stressed broad objectives. In the two groups at MIC, the methods for sharing and utilizing knowledge were very different; one was informal, and the other more formal and collaborative. From these variations, we concluded that the pattern of the learning orientations largely makes up an organizational learning system. The pattern may not tell us how *well* learning is promoted but tells a lot about what is learned and where it occurs.

Generic Processes Facilitate Learning

How well an organization maximizes learning within its chosen style does not occur haphazardly. Our data suggest that talking about "the learning organization" is partially effective; some policies, structures, and processes do seem to make a difference. The difference is in how easy or hard it is for useful learning to happen, and in how effective the organization is in "working its style." By analyzing why learning took place in the companies we studied, we identified ten facilitating factors that induced or supported learning. While we did not observe all the factors at each site, we saw most of them and at other sites as well. Thus we view them as generic factors that any organization can benefit from, regardless of its learning style. For example, scanning, in which benchmarking plays an important role, was so central to learning at Motorola that it is now an integral ongoing aspect of every important initiative in the company. Although MIC tends to create knowledge and skill internally, it maintains an ongoing vigilance toward its external environment. On the negative side, the absence of solid, ongoing external scanning in other organizations is an important factor in their economic difficulties.

A MODEL OF ORGANIZATIONS AS LEARNING SYSTEMS

Our two-part model describes organizations as learning systems (see Figure 6.1). First, *learning orientations* are the values and practices that reflect

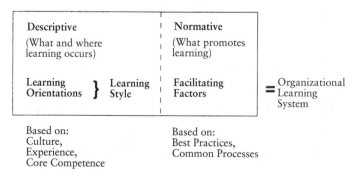

FIGURE 6.1 A Model of Organizations as Learning Systems

where learning takes place and the nature of what is learned. These orientations form a pattern that defines a given organization's "learning style." In this sense, they are descriptive factors that help us to understand without making value judgments. Second, *facilitating factors* are the structures and processes that affect how easy or hard it is for learning to occur and the amount of effective learning that takes place. These are standards based on best practice in dealing with generic issues. (See the sidebar for definitions of the learning orientations and facilitating factors we identified.)

Both parts of the model are required to understand an organization as a learning system; one without the other provides an incomplete picture. In addition, separating the parts enables organizations to see that they do indeed function as learning systems of some kind, and that their task is to understand better what they do well or poorly. (The idea of assessing what exists is more useful than the pejorative notion that there is only one good way to be a learning organization.) Finally, a refined, detailed list of factors related to organizational learning may help companies select areas for learning improvement that do not demand drastic culture change but, rather, can lead to incremental change over time.

Learning Orientations

In the next section, we expand on the definitions of the seven learning orientations and provide examples of each.

1. Knowledge Source

To what extent does the organization develop new knowledge internally or seek inspiration in external ideas? This distinction is seen as the difference between innovation and adaptation—or imitation. In the United States, there is a tendency to value innovativeness more highly and look down on "copiers."

Definitions of the Orientations and Factors

Seven Learning Orientations

1. Knowledge Source: Internal—External. Preference for developing knowledge internally versus preference for acquiring knowledge developed externally.

2. Product-Process Focus: What?—How? Emphasis on accumulation of knowledge about what products/service are versus how organization develops, makes, and delivers its products/services.

3. Documentation Mode: Personal—Public. Knowledge is something individuals possess versus publicly available know-how.

4. Dissemination Mode: Formal—Informal. Formal, prescribed, organization-wide methods of sharing learning versus informal methods, such as role modeling and casual daily interaction.

5. Learning Focus: Incremental—Transformative. Incremental or corrective learning versus transformative or radical learning.

6. Value-Chain Focus: Design—Deliver. Emphasis on learning investments in engineering/production activities ("design and make" functions) versus sales/service activities

Ten Facilitating Factors

1. Scanning Imperative. Information gathering about conditions and practices outside the unit; awareness of the environment; curiosity about the external environment in contrast to the internal environment.

2. Performance Gap. Shared perception of a gap between actual and desired state of performance; performance shortfalls seen as opportunities for learning.

3. Concern for Measurement. Considerable effort spent on defining and measuring key factors when venturing into new areas; striving for specific, quantifiable measures; discussion of metrics as a learning activity.

4. Experimental Mind-set. Support for trying new things; curiosity about how things work; ability to "play" with things; "failures" are accepted, not punished; changes in work processes, policies, and structures are a continuous series of learning opportunities.

5. Climate of Openness. Accessibility of information; open communications within the organization; problems/errors/lessons are shared, not hidden; debate and conflict are acceptable ways to solve problems.

7. Operational Variety. Variety of methods, and systems; appreciation of diversity; pluralistic rather than singular definition of valued competencies.

8. Multiple Advocates. New ideas and methods advanced by employees at all levels; more than one champion.

9. Involved Leadership. Leaders articulate vision, are engaged in its implementation; frequently interact with members; become actively involved in educational programs.

10. Systems Perspective. Interdependence of organizational units; problems and solutions seen in terms of systemic relationships among processes; connection between the unit's needs and goals and the company's.

BOX 6.1 Definitions of the Orientations and Factors

("market and deliver" functions). 7. **Skill Development Focus: Individual—Group.** Development of individuals' skills versus team or group skills.	6. **Continuous Education.** Ongoing commitment to education at all levels of the organization; clear support for all members' growth and development.

BOX 6.1 *Continued*

American critiques of Japanese businesses often mention that the Japanese are good imitators but not good innovators. In our opinion, both of these approaches have great merit as opposing styles rather than as normative or negative behaviors.

Although our data show a tendency in organizations to prefer one mode over the other, the distinction is not clear-cut. While MIC does scan its environment, it prefers to innovate in responding to customer needs and problems and has been a leader in developing new financial products and services. EDF modeled its nuclear power plants on U.S. technology. Motorola appears to be equally vigorous in innovation and in reflective imitation; it has been innovative in developing new products and adroit at adapting others' processes, such as benchmarking and TQM procedures. Among firms not in this study, American Airlines, Wal-Mart, Merck, and Rubbermaid appear to be innovative in producing knowledge. And American Home Products is a good example of a highly successful, reflective imitator, as are AT&T's Universal Credit Card, Tyco Toys (a Lego "copier"), and Lexus and Infiniti automobiles.

2. Product-Process Focus

Does the organization prefer to accumulate knowledge about product and service outcomes or about the basic processes underlying various products? Many observers have stated that one reason Japanese companies are so competitive is that they make considerably more investments in process technologies in comparison to U.S. companies. The difference is between interest in "getting product out the door" and curiosity about the steps in the processes. All organizations give some attention to each side; the issue is to organize for learning in both domains.

Motorola makes learning investments on both sides. The executives: we observed spent roughly equal amounts of time in collaborative learning about processes and outcomes. They paid less attention to "people processes" than to "hard" or technical processes, but many of them accepted the importance of process issues. MIC, EDF, and Fiat have traditionally focused almost exclusively on product issues but are now making greater learning investments in process issues.

3. Documentation Mode

Do attitudes vary as to what constitutes knowledge and where knowledge resides? At one pole, knowledge is seen in personal terms, as something an individual possesses by virtue of education or experience. This kind of knowledge is lost when a longtime employee leaves an organization; processes and insights evaporate because they were not shared or made a part of collective memory. At the other pole, knowledge is defined in more objective, social terms, as being a consensually supported result of information processing. This attitude emphasizes organizational memory or a publicly documented body of knowledge.

MIC's investment funds group focuses on a personal documentation style, eschewing policy statements and procedure manuals. In keeping with its entrepreneurial orientation, MIC makes it possible for individuals to learn a great deal, but there is little pressure to codify this. Though engaged in a business that values "hard data," the group supports subjective, tacit knowledge in decision-making processes. And at Fiat's Direzione Technica, where the individual has historically been the repository of knowledge, efforts are being made to establish a *memoria technica,* or engineering knowledge bank. Motorola shows evidence of both approaches but works hard to make knowledge explicit and broadly available.

4. Dissemination Mode

Has the organization established an atmosphere in which learning evolves or in which a more structured, controlled approach induces learning? In the more structured approach, the company decides that valuable insights or methods should be shared and used by others across the organization. It uses written communication and formal educational methods or certifies learning through writing the procedures down. In the more informal approach, learning is spread through encounters between role models and gatekeepers who compellingly reinforce learning. In another approach, learning occurs when members of an occupational group or work team share their experiences in ongoing dialogue.[10]

MIC's investment funds group clearly prefers informal dissemination in which learning develops and is shared in loosely organized interactions. This method occurs in other MIC areas, although the marketing groups are becoming more structured in their dissemination. Motorola supports both approaches, though it invests heavily in structured, firmwide programs when senior management wants a basic value or method institutionalized. It considered quality so critical that it now includes vendors and customers in its dissemination. (Recently, some vendors were told that they had to compete for the Malcolm Baldrige Quality Award in order to be on the company's approved vendor list.) EDF prefers formal modes, emphasizing documented procedures that all share.

---

[10] For a discussion of "communities of practice" see: J. S. Brown and P. Puguid, "Organizational Learning and Communities of Practice," *Organization Science* 2 (1991): 40–57.

Fiat's Direzione Technical formally spreads knowledge by accumulating it in specialist departments and then disseminating it to cross-functional design teams.

5. Learning Focus

Is learning concentrated on methods and tools to improve what is already being done or on testing the assumptions underlying what is being done? Argyris and Schön call the former "single-loop learning" and the latter "double-loop learning."[11] They have rightfully argued that organizational performance problems are more likely due to a lack of awareness and inability to articulate and check underlying assumptions than to a function of poor efficiency. In our opinion, these learning capabilities reinforce each other. Organizations may have a preference for one mode over the other, but a sound learning system can benefit from good work in both areas.

Our research sites displayed a range of behavior. EDF is primarily focused on incremental issues and does not question its basic assumptions. It prides itself on being the world's major nuclear power utility and devotes significant resources to being the most efficient, safe operator through small improvements rather than transformations. Though similar, Fiat's Direzione Technica is beginning to question assumptions about its new product development process. Since 1987, MIC has been in a transformational mode, particularly in the way that its marketing groups have focused on a questioning learning style. Motorola is fairly well balanced in its orientation; the founding family has historically accepted the concept of organizational renewal, which has led to far-reaching changes in the company's product lines through the years and to an inquisitive style. On the other hand, its strong dedication to efficiency learning often precludes questioning basic assumptions.

6. Value-Chain Focus

Which core competencies and learning investments does the organization value and support? By learning investments, we mean all allocations of personnel and money to develop knowledge and skill over time, including training and education, pilot projects, developmental assignments, available resources, and so on. If a particular organization is "engineering focused" or "marketing driven," it is biased in favor of substantial learning investments in those areas. We divided the value chain into two categories: internally directed activities of a "design and make" nature, and those more externally focused of a "sell and deliver" nature. The former include R&D, engineering, and manufacturing. The latter are sales, distribution, and service activities. Although this does some disservice to the value chain concept, the breakdown easily accounts for our observations.

At MIC, the investment funds group focuses on the design and make side. While this is balanced by learning investments on the deliver side in the MIC marketing groups, there is a strong boundary between these groups, and the fund

---

[11] Argyris and Schön (1978).

management side is regarded as the organization's core. Motorola's total quality effort clearly recognizes the importance of value-added at both sides, but "design and make" is significantly ahead of "deliver" in learning investments in quality. Fiat's Direzione Technica is clearly oriented toward design and make, although its new system of simultaneous engineering is balancing its approach with increased sensitivity to the deliver side. EDF nuclear operations focuses squarely on efficient production. While not in our study, Digital Equipment Corporation's learning investments traditionally were much more heavily focused on "design and make" than on "deliver."

7. Skill Development Focus

Does the organization develop both individual and group skills? We believe it helps to view this as a stylistic choice, as opposed to seeing it in normative terms. In this way, an organization can assess how it is doing and improve either one. It can also develop better ways of integrating individual learning programs with team needs by taking a harder look at the value of group development.

MIC designed the investment funds group to promote individual learning, which seems to fit with its culture and reward system. Heavy investment in team learning would probably improve its performance. On the other hand, MIC's marketing groups, more supportive of collective learning, are now investing in team development as one way to improve its total effectiveness. Fiat's Direzione Technica has been oriented toward more individual development, but, with its new reliance on cross-functional work teams, group development is increasingly more important. Recently, Motorola has become more team oriented and is making heavier investments in collaborative learning. It designed the two executive groups we observed to foster collective learning on two strategic issues affecting the entire company. EDF develops both individual and group skills, especially in control-room teams. All EDF employees follow individual training programs for certification or promotion. Control-room teams also learn, in groups, by using plant simulators. Some other firms that emphasize team learning are Federal Express, which invests heavily in teams for its quality effort, and Herman Miller, which stresses participative management and the Scanlon plan.

We view the seven learning orientations as a matrix. An organizational unit can be described by the pattern of its orientations in the matrix, which in turn provides a way to identify its learning style. Given the characteristics of the sites we studied and other sites we are familiar with, we believe it is possible to identify learning styles that represent a distinct pattern of orientations. Such styles may reflect the industry, size, or age of an organization, or the nature of its technology.

Facilitating Factors

The second part of our model is the facilitating factors that expedite learning. The ten factors are defined in the sidebar.

1. Scanning Imperative

Does the organization understand or comprehend the environment in which it functions? In recent years, researchers have emphasized the importance of environmental scanning and agreed that many organizations were in trouble because of limited or poor scanning efforts. Thus many firms have increased their scanning capacity. Five years into Motorola's quality program, a significant scanning effort showed it what others, particularly the Japanese, were doing. In reaction, Motorola substantially changed its approach and won the first Baldrige Award four years later. By contrast, the mainframe computer manufacturers (Cray, Unisys, IBM) and the U.S. auto companies in the 1970s failed to respond to developing changes that sound investigative work would have made painfully visible. Recent changes at Fiat result from a concerted scanning effort in which fifty senior managers visited the manufacturing facilities of world-class auto and other durable goods companies.

2. Performance Gap

First, how do managers, familiar with looking at the differences between targeted outcomes and actual performance, analyze variances? When feedback shows a gap, particularly if it implies failure, their analysis often leads to experimenting and developing new insights and skills. One reason that well-established, long-successful organizations are often not good learning systems is that they experience lengthy periods in which feedback is almost entirely positive; the lack of disconfirming evidence is a barrier to learning.

Secondly, is there a potential new vision that is not simply a quantitative extension of the old or goes well beyond the performance level seen as achievable in the old vision? One or more firm members may visualize something not previously noted. Awareness of a performance gap is important because it often leads the organization to recognize that learning needs to occur or that something already known may not be working. Even if a group cannot articulate exactly what that need might be, its awareness of ignorance can motivate learning, as occurred at Motorola after its 1984 benchmarking. Currently, this "humility" is driving Fiat's Direzione Technica to make a major study of what it needs to know.

In our findings, EDF provides perhaps the best instance of a performance gap leading to adaptive learning. Due to the nature of the nuclear power business, performance variations became the catalyst for a learning effort to again achieve the prescribed standard. We also found that future-oriented CEOs encouraged performance-gap considerations related to generative learning at Motorola and MIC (patent company).

3. Concern for Measurement

Does the organization develop and use metrics that support learning? Are measures internally or externally focused, specific, and custom-built or standard measures? The importance of metrics in total quality programs has been well documented and is used in target-setting programs such as management by objectives.[12] Our interest is in how the discourse about measurements, and the search for the most appropriate ones, is a critical aspect of learning, almost as much as learning that evolves from responding to the feedback that metrics provide.

Motorola executives believe that concern for measurement was one of the most critical reasons for their quality program's success. At three or four critical junctures, reexamination of measurement issues helped propel a move to a new level of learning. They are applying this factor to new initiatives, a major concern of the executive groups we observed. At EDF, the value of metrics is clearly associated with the performance gap. Its nuclear power plants are authorized to operate at certain specifications that, if not met, may suggest or predict an unplanned event leading to shutdown. Each occasion becomes an opportunity for learning to take place.

4. Experimental Mind-set

Does the organization emphasize experimentation on an ongoing basis? If learning comes through experience, it follows that the more one can plan guided experiences, the more one will learn. Until managers see organizing for production at any stage of the value chain as a learning experiment as well as a production activity, learning will come slowly. Managers need to learn to act like applied research scientists at the same time they deliver goods and services.[13]

We did not see significant evidence of experimental mind-sets at our research sites, with some notable exceptions at Motorola. At its paging products operation, we observed the current production line for one product, a blueprint and preparation for the new setup to replace the line, and a "white room" laboratory in which research is now underway for the line that will replace the one currently being installed. Motorola University constantly tries new learning approaches; the two executive groups we observed at Motorola were also part of an experiment in executive education.

We have seen evidence of experimental mind-sets in reports about other firms. For example, on any given day, Wal-Mart conducts about 250 tests in its stores, concentrated on sales promotion, display, and customer service. Although a traditional firm in many ways, 3M's attitude toward new product development and operational unit size suggests a strong experimental mind-set.

---

[12] W. H. Schmidt and J. P. Finnegan, *The Race Without a Finish Line: America's Quest for Total Quality* (San Francisco: Jossey-Bass, 1992).

[13] For the idea of the factory as a learning laboratory, see: D. Leonard-Barton, "The Factory as a Learning Laboratory," *Sloan Management Review,* Fall 1992, pp. 39–52.

5. Climate of Openness

Are the boundaries around information flow permeable so people can make their own observations? Much informal learning is a function of daily, often unplanned interactions among people. In addition, the opportunity to meet with other groups and see higher levels of management in operation promotes learning.[14] People need freedom to express their views through legitimate disagreement and debate. Another critical aspect is the extent to which errors are shared and not hidden.[15]

Perhaps the most dramatic example of openness in our findings is EDF, where abnormalities or deviations are publicly reported throughout the entire system of fifty-seven nuclear power plants. The company treats such incidents as researchable events to see if the problem exists anywhere else and follows up with a learning-driven investigation to eliminate it. It then disseminates this knowledge throughout the company. While this openness may be explained by the critical nature of problems in a nuclear power plant, we can only speculate as to what would be gained if any organization functioned as though a mistake is potentially disastrous and also an opportunity to learn.

6. Continuous Education

Is there a commitment to lifelong education at all levels of the organization? This includes formal programs but goes well beyond that to more pervasive support of any kind of developmental experience. The mere presence of traditional training and development activities is not sufficient; it must be accompanied by a palpable sense that one is never finished learning and practicing (something akin to the Samurai tradition). The extent to which this commitment permeates the entire organization, and not just the training and development groups, is another indicator. In many ways, this factor is another way of expressing what Senge calls "personal mastery."

MIC does an excellent job of exposing its young analysts to developmental experiences. Its chairman also seeks knowledge in many areas, not just direct financial matters. Motorola has a policy in which every employee has some educational experience every year; it has joint ventures with several community colleges around the country; joint programs with the state of Illinois for software competence development and training of school superintendents, and on-the-job and classroom experiences for managers up to the senior level. The company spends 3.6 percent of its revenues on education and plans to double this amount.[16] Among firms not in our study, General Electric, Unilever, and Digital

---

[14] This skill has been referred to as "legitimate peripheral participation." See: J. Lave and E. Wenger, *Situated Learning: Legitimate Peripheral Participation* (Palo Alto, California: Institute for Research on Learning, IRL Report 90–0013, 1990).

[15] C. Argyris, *Strategy, Change, and Defensive Routines* (Boston: Putman, 1985).

[16] See "Companies That Train Best," *Fortune*, 8 February 1993, pp. 44–48; and "Motorola: Training for the Millenium," *Business Week*, 28 March 1994, pp. 158–163.

Equipment Corporation have valued continuous education at all levels for many years.

7. Operational Variety

Is there more than one way to accomplish work goals? An organization that supports variation in strategy, policy, process, structure, and personnel is more adaptable when unforeseen problems arise. It provides more options and, perhaps even more important, allows for rich stimulation and interpretation for all its members. This factor helps enhance future learning in a way not possible with a singular approach.

We did not see a great deal of variety at our sites. EDF, perhaps due to the importance of total control over operations, shows little variation. Fiat's Direzione Technica follows similar response routines, although the change to a new structure should lead to greater variation because of its independent design teams. An exception is MIC investment funds group, where we identified at least three different methods that fund managers used in making investment decisions. Senior management, although a bit skeptical about one of the methods, seemed willing to support all three as legitimate approaches.

8. Multiple Advocates

Along with involved leadership, is there more than one "champion" who sets the stage for learning? This is particularly necessary in learning that is related to changing a basic value or a long-cherished method. The greater the number of advocates who promote a new idea, the more rapidly and extensively the learning will take place. Moreover, in an effective system, any member should be able to act as an awareness-enhancing agent or an advocate for new competence development. In this way, both top-down and bottom-up initiatives are possible.

One of the authors participated in two significant change efforts that failed, largely because there was only one champion in each case. One highly frustrated CEO said, "It doesn't do me or the company any good if I'm the only champion of this new way of doing business." At Motorola, we found that a major factor in the quality effort's success was the early identification, empowerment, and encouragement of a significant number of advocates. In a current initiative we observed, Motorola is enlisting a minimum of 300 champions in strategic parts of the company. Digital Equipment Corporation has had learning initiators throughout the company since its early days. Digital's problem has been in assimilating and integrating the lessons of its myriad educational and experimental efforts, rather than in creating an environment that enables broad-scale initiation. MIC's investment funds group encourages many individuals to initiate their own learning but not to proselytize.

9. Involved Leadership

Is leadership at every organizational level engaged in hands-on implementation of the vision? This includes eliminating management layers, being visible in the bowels of the organization, and being an active, early participant in any learning effort. Only through direct involvement that reflects coordination, vision, and integration can leaders obtain important data and provide powerful role models.

At Motorola, CEO Bob Galvin not only drove the quality vision, he was a student in the first seminars on quality and made it the first item on the agenda at monthly meetings with his division executives. Much-admired Wal-Mart CEO David Glass spends two or three days each week at stores and warehouses; employees can call him at home and are often transferred to his hotel when he is in the field. Mike Walsh of Tenneco (formerly of Union Pacific Railroad) meets with groups of employees at all levels in what Tom Peters calls "conversation."[17]

10. Systems Perspective

Do the key actors think broadly about the interdependency of organizational variables? This involves the degree to which managers can look at their internal systems as a source of their difficulties, as opposed to blaming external factors. Research in the field of systems dynamics has demonstrated how managers elicit unintended consequences by taking action in one area without seeing its dynamic relationship to its effects.[18]

Despite its importance, this factor was relatively lacking at our research sites. MIC and Motorola are structured so that there are strong boundaries between groups and functions. Both have changed their perspectives recently, MIC as a consequence of unexpected internal problems related to the October 1987 stock market crash, and Motorola after experiencing difficulties in selling large-scale systems (as opposed to discrete products). In a 1992 survey of 3,000 Motorola employees that asked them to evaluate their unit based on Senge's five factors, they rated systems thinking the lowest and the one that required the most work to improve organizational learning. In contrast, Fiat's Direzione Technica took a systems approach to understanding the consequences of its structure on new product development. As a result, it changed the structure to establish mechanisms for simultaneous engineering. To reduce the new products' time to market, functions now work in parallel rather than sequentially.

GENERAL DIRECTIONS FOR ENHANCING LEARNING

We have divided the seven learning orientations and ten facilitating factors into three stages—knowledge acquisition, dissemination, and utilization.

---

[17] T. Peters, *Liberation Management* (New York: Knopf, 1992).

[18] Jay W. Forrester is considered to be the founder of the field of systems thinking.

Figure 6.2 shows the orientations and factors within this framework. Within our two-part model, there are two general directions for enhancing learning in an organizational unit. One is to embrace the existing style and improve its effectiveness. This strategy develops a fundamental part of the culture to its fullest extent. For example, a firm that is a reflective imitator more than an innovator could adopt this strategy with heightened awareness of its value. A company that has benefited from heavy learning investments on the "make" side of the value chain would see the value of those investments and decide to build further on them. This approach builds on the notion that full acceptance of what has been accomplished is validating and energizing for those involved. It is similar to the

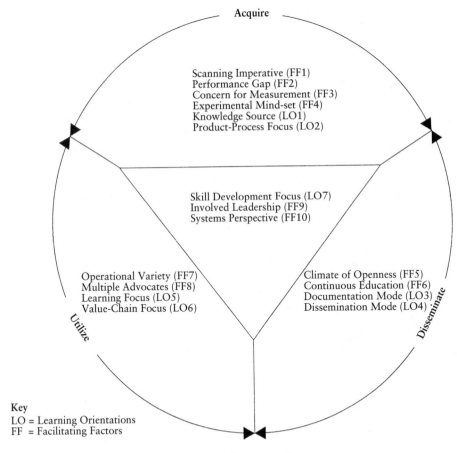

FIGURE 6.2 Elements of an Organizational Learning System

appreciative inquiry numerous organizational change consultants advocate.[19] The task is to select two or three facilitating factors to improve on.

The second direction is to change learning orientations. The organizational group would make more learning investments at a different part of the value chain, try to be an innovator if it is now more of an imitator, and so on. These are different changes from those involved in enhancing the facilitative factors, and the tactics will be different. Some changes will be seen as an attack on the organization's basic values, and it may be possible to avoid this by moving toward balance between the two poles, so members of the organization will support the existing style and advocate the "new look" as a supplementary measure.

Supporting the Learning Orientations

In the second phase of our research, in which we worked closely with personnel from more than thirty *Fortune* "500" companies to identify their learning orientations, we validated our notion that organizations learn in varied ways. The singular "learning organization" should be a pluralistic model.

Looking at "what is" in a descriptive rather than normative way has another advantage in that you see better what you are *not* by examining better what you *are*. In the gestalt approach to dealing with resistance to organizational change, it has been well documented that change comes more readily if the targets of change first become more aware of and more accepting of their resistance.[20] In other words, it is important to gain full knowledge and appreciation of your organizational assumptions about learning whether you want to build on them or alter them.

This model may also be used to identify the complementarity of styles between coordinating organizations and to recognize that circumstances may dictate conditions and orientations in particular settings. For example, EDF's nuclear operations are constrained from transforming real-time operations due to the potentially dire consequences (e.g., the Chernobyl disaster) of operating under novel assumptions. However, at EDF, testing system assumptions is characteristic of its R&D division, which uses new technologies in the design of new plants. Thus changing one's style needs to be considered from a systems perspective; it may also be associated with the stage of organizational development.[21]

---

[19] S. Srivastra and D. L. Cooperrider and Associates, *Appreciative Management and Leadership* (San Francisco: Jossey-Bass, 1990).

[20] E. Nevis, *Organizational Consulting: A Gestalt Approach* (Cleveland: Gestalt Institute of Cleveland Press, 1987).

[21] W. R. Torbert, *Managing the Corporate Dream* (New York: Dow Jones-Irwin, 1987).

Strategies for Improving Organizational Learning Capability

When starting to improve its learning capabilities, an organization may decide to focus on any stage of the learning cycle—knowledge acquisition, dissemination, or utilization. While it may be possible or necessary to look at all three phases simultaneously, focusing on a single area is more manageable. The next task is to select an option for focus:

1. Improve on learning orientations. There are two reasons for selecting this option. First, the organization may decide to shift its position on one or more learning orientations. Second, the current pattern of learning orientations has resulted in identifiable strong competencies, so improving or expanding them may be the best way to enhance the unit's learning capabilities. This focus assumes that facilitating factors meet an acceptable standard and that more can be accomplished by adding to the strong base established by the learning orientations.

2. Improve on facilitating factors. In this option, the organization accepts its pattern of learning orientations as adequate or appropriate to its culture and decides that improving the systems and structures of the facilitating factors is the most useful course. This option assumes that maximizing the facilitating factors would add more to the organization's learning capabilities than enhancing or changing the current learning orientations.

3. Change both learning orientations and facilitating factors. An organization should select this option when it sees the other variables as inadequate. This option assumes that large-scale change is necessary and that changing one group of variables without changing the other will be only partially successful.

Each organizational unit or firm must make the decision to pursue one strategy or another for itself. While there are no rules for making this decision, the three options are incrementally more difficult to implement (i.e., one is the easiest to implement; three is the hardest). From the first to the third options, the resistance to change within the organization increases significantly. It is one thing to develop a plan for improving what is already done reasonably well; it is another to engage in nothing less than near-total transformation. It is one thing to stay within accepted, assimilated paradigms; it is another to replace institutionalized models.

Whatever the organization's choice, we offer three guidelines for developing and implementing a chosen strategy:

1. Before deciding to become something new, study and evaluate what you are now. Without full awareness and appreciation of current assumptions about management, organization, and learning, it is not possible to grasp what is being done well and what might be improved or changed.

2. Though the systemic issues and relationships in organizational life require that change be approached from multiple directions and at several points, organizations can change in major ways if people experience success with more modest, focused, and specific changes. As with many skills, there is a learning curve for the skill of managing and surviving transitions.

Large-scale change requires that many initiatives be put into place in a carefully designed, integrated sequence.

3. Organizations must consider cultural factors in choosing and implementing any strategy, particularly when considering how it does specific things. For example, in a highly individualistic society like the United States or the United Kingdom, skill development focuses on individual skills; in comparison, more communitarian societies such as Japan or Korea have traditionally focused on group skill development. Moving from one pole to the other is a major cultural change; to simply improve on the existing orientation is much easier.

To help managers better understand the learning capabilities in their own organizations, we have developed and are testing an "organizational learning inventory." This diagnostic tool will enable an organization's members to produce a learning profile based on our model. The profile can guide managers to their choices for improving learning capability. Through further research, we intend to show how learning profiles vary within and across different companies and industries.

ACKNOWLEDGMENTS

The research in this paper was supported by a grant from the International Consortium for Executive Development Research, Lexington, Massachusetts, and by the MIT Organizational Learning Center. The authors would like to thank Joseph Reelin, Edgar Schein, Peter Senge, and Sandra Waddock for their helpful comments on an earlier version of this paper.

PART III

Community

Chapter 7

Organizational Learning and Communities-of-Practice: Toward A Unified View of Working, Learning, and Innovation[*]

John Seely Brown and Paul Duguid[**]
Xerox Palo Alto Research Center and Institute for Research on Learning

Recent ethnographic studies of workplace practices indicate that the ways people actually work usually differ fundamentally from the ways organizations describe that work in manuals, training programs, organizational charts, and job descriptions. Nevertheless, organizations tend to rely on the latter in their attempts to understand and improve work practice. We examine one such study. We then relate its conclusions to compatible investigations of learning and of innovation to argue that conventional descriptions of jobs mask not only the ways people work, but also significant learning and innovation generated in the informal communities-of-practice in which they work. By reassessing work, learning, and innovation in the context of actual communities and actual practices, we suggest that the connections between these three become apparent. With a unified view of working, learning, and innovating, it should be possible to reconceive of and redesign organizations to improve all three.

(LEARNING; INNOVATION; GROUPS; DOWNSKILLING; ORGANIZATIONAL CULTURES NONCANONICAL PRACTICE)

---

[*] Accepted by Lee S. Sproull and Michael D. Cohen.
[**] Reprinted with permission.

INTRODUCTION

Working, learning, and innovating are closely related forms of human activity that are conventionally thought to conflict with each other. Work practice is generally viewed as conservative and resistant to change; learning is generally viewed as distinct from working and problematic in the face of change; and innovation is generally viewed as the disruptive but necessary imposition of change on the other two. To see that working, learning, and innovating are interrelated and compatible and thus potentially complementary, not conflicting forces requires a distinct conceptual shift. By bringing together recent research into working, learning, and innovating, we attempt to indicate the nature and explore the significance of such a shift.

The source of the oppositions perceived between working, learning, and innovating lies primarily in the gulf between precepts and practice. Formal descriptions of work (e.g., "office procedures") and of learning (e.g., "subject matter") are abstracted from actual practice. They inevitably and intentionally omit the details. In a society that attaches particular value to "abstract knowledge," the details of practice have come to be seen as nonessential, unimportant, and easily developed once the relevant abstractions have been grasped. Thus education, training, and technology design generally focus on abstract representations to the detriment, if not exclusion of actual practice. We, by contrast, suggest that practice is central to understanding work. Abstractions *detached from practice* distort or obscure intricacies of that practice. Without a clear understanding of those intricacies and the role they play, the practice itself cannot be well understood, engendered (through training), or enhanced (through innovation).

We begin by looking at the variance between a major organization's formal descriptions of work both in its training programs and manuals and the actual work practices performed by its members. Orr's (1990a, 1990b, 1987a, 1987b) detailed ethnographic studies of service technicians illustrate how an organization's view of work can overlook and even oppose what and who it takes to get a job done. Based on Orr's specific insights, we make the more general claim that reliance on espoused practice (which we refer to as *canonical practice*) can blind an organization's core to the actual, and usually valuable practices of its members (including *noncanonical practices,* such as "work arounds"). It is the actual practices, however, that determine the success or failure of organizations.

Next, we turn to learning and, in particular, to Lave and Wenger's (1990) practice-based theory of learning as "legitimate peripheral participation" in "communities-of-practice." Much conventional learning theory, including that implicit in most training courses, tends to endorse the valuation of abstract knowledge over actual practice and as a result to separate learning from working and, more significantly, learners from workers. Together Lave and Wenger's analysis and Orr's empirical investigation indicate that this knowledge-practice separation is unsound, both in theory and in practice. We argue that the composite concept of "learning-in-working" best represents the fluid evolution of learning through practice.

From this practice-based standpoint, we view learning as the bridge between working and innovating. We use Daft and Weick's (1984) interpretive account of "enacting" organizations to place innovation in the context of changes in a community's "way of seeing" or interpretive view. Both Orr's and Lave and Wenger's research emphasize that to understand working and learning, it is necessary to focus on the formation and change of the communities in which work takes place. Taking all three theories together, we argue that, through their constant adapting to changing membership and changing circumstances, evolving communities-of-practice are significant sites of innovating.

1. WORKING

A. Canonical Practice

Orr's (1990a, 1990b, 1987a, 1987b) ethnography of service technicians (reps) in training and at work in a large corporation paints a clear picture of the divergence between espoused practice and actual practice, of the ways this divergence develops, and of the trouble it can cause. His work provides a "thick" (see Geertz 1973), detailed description of the way work actually progresses. Orr contrasts his findings with the way the same work is thinly described in the corporation's manuals, training courses, and job descriptions.[1]

The importance of such an approach to work in progress is emphasized by Bourdieu (1973), who distinguishes the *modus operandi* from the *opus operatum*—that is, the way a task, as it unfolds over time, looks to someone at work on it, while many of the options and dilemmas remain unresolved, as opposed to the way it looks with hindsight as a finished task. (Ryle (1954) makes a similar point.) The *opus operatum*, the finished view, tends to see the action in terms of the task alone and cannot see the way in which the process of doing the task is actually structured by the constantly changing conditions of work and the world. Bourdieu makes a useful analogy with reference to a journey as actually carried out on the ground and as seen on a map ("an abstract space, devoid of any landmarks or any privileged centre" (p. 2)). The latter, like the *opus operatum*, inevitably smooths over the myriad decisions made with regard to changing conditions: road works, diversions, Memorial Day parades, earthquakes, personal fatigue, conflicting opinions, wrong-headed instructions, relations of authority, inaccuracies on the map, and the like. The map, though potentially useful, *by itself* provides little insight into how *ad hoc* decisions presented by changing conditions can be resolved (and, of course, each resolved decision changes the conditions once more). As a journey becomes more complex, the map increasingly conceals what is actually needed to make the journey. Thick

---

[1] For a historical overview of anthropology of the workplace, see Burawoy (1979).

description, by contrast, ascends from the abstraction to the concrete circumstances of actual practice, reconnecting the map and the mapped.

Orr's study shows how an organization's maps can dramatically distort its view of the routes its members take. This "misrecognition," as Bourdieu calls it, can be traced to many places, including pedagogic theory and practice. Often it has its more immediate cause in the strategy to downskill positions. Many organizations are willing to assume that complex tasks can be successfully mapped onto a set of simple, Tayloristic, canonical steps that can be followed without need of significant understanding or insight (and thus without need of significant investment in training or skilled technicians). But as Bourdieu, Suchman (1987a), and Orr show, actual practice inevitably involves tricky interpolations between abstract accounts and situated demands. Orr's reps' skills, for instance, are most evident in the improvised strategies they deploy to cope with the clash between prescriptive documentation and the sophisticated, yet unpredictable machines they work with. Nonetheless, in the corporation's eyes practices that deviate from the canonical are, by definition, deviant practices. Through a reliance on canonical descriptions (to the extent of overlooking even their own noncanonical improvisations), managers develop a conceptual outlook that cannot comprehend the importance of noncanonical practices. People are typically viewed as performing their jobs according to formal job descriptions, despite the fact that daily evidence points to the contrary (Suchman 1987b). They are held accountable to the map, not to road conditions.[2]

In Orr's case, the canonical map comes in the form of "directive" documentation aimed at "single point failures" of machines. Indeed, the documentation is less like a map than a single predetermined route with no alternatives: it provides a decision tree for diagnosis and repair that assumes both predictable machines and an unproblematic process of making diagnoses and repairs through blindly following diagnostic instructions. Both assumptions are mistaken. Abstractions of repair work fall short of the complexity of the actual practices from which they were abstracted. The account of actual practice we describe below is anything but the blind following of instructions.

The inadequacies of this corporation's directive approach actually make a rep's work more difficult to accomplish and thus perversely demands more, not fewer, improvisational skills. An ostensible downskilling and actual upskilling therefore proceed simultaneously. Although the documentation becomes more prescriptive and ostensibly more simple, in actuality the task becomes more improvisational and more complex. The reps develop sophisticated noncanonical practices to bridge the gulf between their corporation's canonical approach and successful work practices, laden with the dilemmas, inconsistencies, and

---

[2] Not all the blame should be laid on the managers' desk. As several anthropologists, including Suchman (1987a) and Bourdieu (1977) point out, "informants" often describe their jobs in canonical terms though they carry them out in noncanonical ways. Lave (1988) argues that informants, like most people in our society tend to privilege abstract knowledge. Thus they describe their actions in its terms.

unpredictability of everyday life. The directive documentation does not "deprive the workers of the skills they have;" rather, "it merely reduces the amount of information given them" (Orr 1990a, 26). The burden of making up the difference between what is provided and what is needed then rests with the reps, who in bridging the gap actually protect the organization from its own shortsightedness. If the reps adhered to the canonical approach, their corporation's services would be in chaos.

Because this corporation's training programs follow a similar downskilling approach, the reps regard them as generally unhelpful. As a result, a wedge is driven between the corporation and its reps: the corporation assumes the reps are untrainable, uncooperative, and unskilled; whereas the reps view the overly simplistic training programs as a reflection of the corporation's low estimation of their worth and skills. In fact, their valuation is a testament to the depth of the rep's insight. They recognize the superficiality of the training because they are conscious of the full complexity of the technology and what it takes to keep it running. The corporation, on the other hand, blinkered by its implicit faith in formal training and canonical practice and its misinterpretation of the rep's behavior, is unable to appreciate either aspect of their insight.

In essence, Orr shows that in order to do their job the reps must—and do—learn to make better sense of the machines they work with than their employer either expects or allows. Thus they develop their understanding of the machine not in the training programs, but in the very conditions from which the programs separate them—the authentic activity of their daily work. For the reps (and for the corporation, though it is unaware of it), learning-in-working is an occupational necessity.

B. Noncanonical Practice

Orr's analyses of actual practice provide various examples of how the reps diverge from canonical descriptions. For example, on one service call (Orr 1990b, 1987b) a rep confronted a machine that produced copious raw information in the form of error codes and obligingly crashed when tested. But the error codes and the nature of the crashes did not tally. Such a case immediately fell outside the directive training and documentation provided by the organization, which tie errors to error codes. Unfortunately, the problem also fell outside the rep's accumulated, improvised experience. He summoned his technical specialist, whose job combines "trouble-shooting consultant, supervisor, and occasional instructor." The specialist was equally baffled. Yet, though the canonical approach to repair was exhausted, with their combined range of noncanonical practices, the rep and technical specialist still had options to pursue.

One option—indeed the only option left by canonical practice now that its strategies for repair had been quickly exhausted—was to abandon repair altogether and to replace the malfunctioning machine. But both the rep and the specialist realized that the resulting loss of face for the company, loss of the customer's faith in the reps, loss of their own credit within their organization, and loss of money to the corporation made this their last resort. Loss of face or faith has considerable ramifications beyond mere embarrassment. A rep's ability to enlist the future support of customers and colleagues is jeopardized. There is evidently strong social pressure from a variety of sources to solve problems without exchanging machines. The reps' work is not simply about maintaining machines; it is also and equally importantly, about maintaining social relations: "A large part of service work might better be described as repair and maintenance of the social setting" (Orr 1990b, 169). The training and documentation, of course, are about maintaining machines.

Solving the problem *in situ* required constructing a coherent account of the malfunction out of the incoherence of the data and documentation. To do this, the rep and the specialist embarked on a long story-telling procedure. The machine, with its erratic behavior, mixed with information from the user and memories from the technicians, provided essential ingredients that the two aimed to account for in a composite story. The process of forming a story was, centrally, one of diagnosis. This process, it should be noted, *begins* as well as ends in a communal understanding of the machine that is wholly unavailable from the canonical documents.

While they explored the machine or waited for it to crash, the rep and specialist (with contributions from the ethnographer) recalled and discussed other occasions on which they had encountered some of the present symptoms. Each story presented an exchangeable account that could be examined and reflected upon to provoke old memories and new insights. Yet more tests and more stories were thereby generated.

> The key element of diagnosis is the situated production of understanding through narration, in that the integration of the various facts of the situation is accomplished through a verbal consideration of those facts with a primary criterion of coherence. The process is situated, in Suchman's terms, in that both the damaged machine and the social context of the user site are essential resources for both the definition of the problem and its resolution. . . . They are faced with a failing machine displaying diagnostic information which has previously proved worthless and in which no one has any particular confidence this time. They do not know where they are going to find the information they need to understand and solve this problem. In their search for inspiration, they tell stories (Orr 1990b, 178–179).

The story-telling process continued throughout the morning, over lunch, and back in front of the machine, throughout the afternoon, forming a long but purposeful progression from incoherence to coherence: "The final trouble-shooting session was a five hour effort. . . . This session yielded a dozen anecdotes told during the trouble shooting, taking a variety of forms and serving a variety of purposes" (Orr 1990b, 10).

Ultimately, these stories generated sufficient interplay among memories, tests, the machine's responses, and the ensuing insights to lead to diagnosis and repair. The final diagnosis developed from what Orr calls an "antiphonal recitation" in which the two told different versions of the same story: "They are talking about personal encounters with the same problem, but the two versions are significantly different" (Orr 1987b, 177). Through story-telling, these separate experiences converged, leading to a shared diagnosis of certain previously encountered but unresolved symptoms. The two (and the ethnographer) had constructed a communal interpretation of hitherto uninterpretable data and individual experience. Rep and specialist were now in a position to modify previous stories and build a more insightful one. They both increased their own understanding and added to their community's collective knowledge. Such stories are passed around, becoming part of the repertoire available to all reps. Orr reports hearing a concise, assimilated version of this particular false error code passed among reps over a game of cribbage in the lunch room three months later (Orr 1990b, 181ff.). A story, once in the possession of the community, can then be used—and further modified—in similar diagnostic sessions.

C. Central Features of Work Practice

In this section, we analyze Orr's thick description of the rep's practice through the overlapping categories, "narration," "collaboration," and "social construction"—categories that get to the heart of what the reps do and yet which, significantly, have no place in the organization's abstracted, canonical accounts of their work.

Narration

The first aspect of the reps' practice worth highlighting is the extensive narration used. This way of working is quite distinct from following the branches of decision tree. Stories and their telling can reflect the complex social web within which work takes place and the relationship of the narrative, narrator, and audience to the specific events of practice. The stories have a flexible generality that makes them both adaptable and particular. They function, rather like the common law, as a usefully underconstrained means to interpret each new situation in the light of accumulated wisdom and constantly changing circumstances.

The practice of creating and exchanging of stories has two important aspects. First of all, telling stories helps to diagnose the state of a troublesome machine. Reps begin by extracting a history from the users of the machine, the users' story, and with this and the machine as their starting point, they construct their own account. If they cannot tell an adequate story on their own, then they seek help—either by summoning a specialist, as in the case above, or by discussing the problem with colleagues over coffee or lunch. If necessary, they work together at the machine, articulating hunches, insights, misconceptions, and the like, to dissect and augment their developing understanding. Story telling allows them to keep track of the sequences of behavior and of their theories, and thereby to work towards a coherent account of the current state of the machine.

The reps try to impose coherence on an apparently random sequence of events in order that they can decide what to do next. Unlike the documentation, which tells reps *what* to do but not *why,* the reps' stories help them develop causal accounts of machines, which are essential when documentation breaks down. (As we have suggested, documentation, like machines, will always break down, however well it is designed.) What the reps do in their story telling is develop a causal map out of their experience to replace the impoverished directive route that they have been furnished by the corporation. In the absence of such support, the reps Orr studied cater to their own needs as well as they can. Their narratives yield a story of the machine fundamentally different from the prescriptive account provided by the documentation, a story that is built in response to the particulars of breakdown.

Despite the assumptions behind the downskilling process, to do their job in any significant sense, reps need these complex causal stories and they produce and circulate them as part of their regular noncanonical work practice. An important part of the reps' skill, though not recognized by the corporation, comprises the ability to create, to trade, and to understand highly elliptical, highly referential, and to the initiated, highly informative war stories. Zuboff (1988) in her analysis of the skills people develop working on complex systems describes similar cases of story telling and argues that it is a necessary practice for dealing with "smart" but unpredictable machines. The irony, as Orr points out, is that for purposes of diagnosis the reps have no smart machines, just inadequate documentation and "their own very traditional skills."

It is worth stressing at this point that we are not arguing that communities simply can and thus should work without assistance from trainers and the corporation in general. Indeed, we suggest in our conclusion that situations inevitably occur when group improvisation simply cannot bridge the gap between what the corporation supplies and what a particular community actually needs. What we are claiming is that corporations must provide support that corresponds to the real needs of the community rather than just to the abstract expectations of the corporation. And what those needs are can only be understood by understanding the details and sophistications of actual practice. In Orr's account, what the reps needed was the means to understand the machine causally and to relate this causal map to the inevitable intricacies of practice. To discern such needs, however, will require that corporations develop a less formal and more practice-based approach to communities and their work.

The second characteristic of story telling is that the stories also act as repositories of accumulated wisdom. In particular, community narratives protect the reps' ability to work from the ravages of modern idealizations of work and related downskilling practices. In Orr's example, the canonical decision trees, privileging the decontextualized over the situated, effectively sweep away the clutter of practice. But it is in the face of just this clutter that the reps' skills are needed. Improvisational skills that allow the reps to circumvent the inadequacies of both the machines and the documentation are not only developed but also preserved in community story telling.

Jordan's (1989) work similarly draws attention to the central, dual role of informal stories. She studied the clash between midwifery as it is prescribed by officials from Mexico City and as it is practiced in rural Yucatan. The officials ignore important details and realities of practice. For instance, the officials instruct the midwives in practices that demand sterile instruments though the midwives work in villages that lack adequate means for sterilization. The midwives' noncanonical practices, however, circumvent the possibility of surgical operations being carried out with unsterile instruments. These effective practices survive, despite the government's worryingly decontextualized attempts to replace them with canonical practices, through story telling. Jordan notes that the two aspects of story telling, diagnosis and preservation, are inseparable. Orr also suggests that "The use of story-telling both to preserve knowledge and to consider it in subsequent diagnoses coincides with the narrative character of diagnosis" (Orr 1990b, 178). We have pulled them apart for the purpose of analysis only.

Collaboration

Based as it is on shared narratives, a second important aspect of the reps' work is that it is obviously communal and thereby *collaborative*. In Orr's example, the rep and specialist went through a collective, not individual process. Not only is the learning in this case inseparable from working, but also individual learning is inseparable from collective learning. The insight accumulated is not a private substance, but socially constructed and distributed. Thus, faced with a difficult problem reps like to work together and to discuss problems in groups. In the case of this particular problem, the individual rep tried what he knew, failed, and there met his limits. With the specialist he was able to trade stories, develop insights, and construct new options. Each had a story about the condition of the machine, but it was in telling it antiphonally that the significance emerged.

While it might seem trivial, it is important to emphasize the collaborative work within the reps' community, for in the corporation's eyes their work is viewed individually. Their documentation and training implicitly maintain that the work is individual and the central relationship of the rep is that between an individual and the corporation:

> The activities defined by management are those which one worker will do, and work as the relationship of employment is discussed in terms of a single worker's relationship to the corporation. I suspect the incidence of workers alone in relations of employment is quite low, and the existence of coworkers must contribute to those activities done in the name of work. . . . The fact that work is commonly done by a group of workers together is only sometimes acknowledged in the literature, and the usual presence of such a community has not entered into the definition of work (Orr 1990a, 15).

In fact, as Orr's studies show, not only do reps work with specialists, as in the example given here, but throughout the day they meet for coffee or for meals and trade stories back and forth.

Social Construction

A third important aspect of Orr's account of practice, and one which is interfused with the previous two and separated here only to help in clarification, involves *social construction*. This has two parts. First and most evident in Orr's example, the reps constructed a shared understanding out of bountiful conflicting and confusing data. This constructed understanding reflects the reps' view of the world. They developed a *rep's* model of the machine, not a trainer's, which had already proved unsatisfactory, nor even an engineer's, which was not available to them (and might well have been unhelpful, though Orr interestingly points out that reps cultivate connections throughout the corporation to help them circumvent the barriers to understanding built by their documentation and training). The reps' view, evident in their stories, interweaves generalities about "this model" with particularities about "this site" and "this machine."

Such an approach is highly situated and highly improvisational. Reps respond to whatever the situation itself—both social and physical—throws at them, a process very similar to Levi-Strauss's (1966) concept of *bricolage*: the ability to "make do with 'whatever is to hand'" (p. 17). What reps need for *bricolage* are not the partial, rigid models of the sort directive documentation provides, but help to build, *ad hoc* and collaboratively, robust models that do justice to particular difficulties in which they find themselves. Hutchins, in his analysis of navigation teams in the U.S. Navy (in press, 1991), similarly notes the way in which understanding is constructed within and distributed throughout teams.

The second feature of social construction, as important but less evident than the first, is that in telling these stories an individual rep contributes to the construction and development of his or her own identity as a rep and reciprocally to the construction and development of the community of reps in which he or she works. Individually, in telling stories the rep is becoming a member. Orr notes, "this construction of their identity as technicians occurs both in doing the work and in their stories, and their stories of themselves fixing machines show their world in what they consider the appropriate perspective" (Orr 1990b, 187). Simultaneously and interdependently, the reps are contributing to the construction and evolution of the community that they are joining—what we might call a "community of interpretation," for it is through the continual development of these communities that the shared means for interpreting complex activity get formed, transformed, and transmitted.

The significance of both these points should become apparent in the following sections, first, as we turn to a theory of learning (Lave and Wenger's) that, like Orr's analysis of work, takes formation of identity and community membership as central units of analysis; and second as we argue that innovation can be seen as at base a function of changes in community values and views.

2. LEARNING

The theories of learning implicated in the documentation and training view learning from the abstract stance of pedagogy. Training is thought of as the *transmission* of explicit, abstract knowledge from the head of someone who knows to the head of someone who does not in surroundings that specifically exclude the complexities of practice and the communities of practitioners. The setting for learning is simply assumed not to matter.

Concepts of knowledge or information transfer, however, have been under increasing attack in recent years from a variety of sources (e.g., Reddy 1979). In particular, learning theorists (e.g. Lave 1988; Lave and Wenger 1990) have rejected transfer models, which isolate knowledge from practice, and developed a view of learning as social construction, putting knowledge back into the contexts in which it has meaning (see also Brown, Collins, and Duguid 1989; Brown and Duguid, in press; Pea 1990). From this perspective, learners can in one way or another be seen to construct their understanding out of a wide range of materials that include ambient social and physical circumstances and the histories and social relations of the people involved. Like a magpie with a nest, learning is built out of the materials to hand and in relation to the structuring resources of local conditions. (For the importance of including the structuring resources in any account of learning, see Lave 1988.) What is learned is profoundly connected to the conditions in which it is learned.

Lave and Wenger (1990), with their concept of *legitimate peripheral participation* (LPP), provide one of the most versatile accounts of this constructive view of learning. LPP, it must quickly be asserted, is *not* a method of education. It is an analytical category or tool for understanding learning across different methods, different historical periods, and different social and physical environments. It attempts to account for learning, not teaching or instruction. Thus this approach escapes problems that arise through examinations of learning from pedagogy's viewpoint. It makes the conditions of learning, rather than just abstract subject matter, central to understanding what is learned.

Learning, from the viewpoint of LPP, essentially involves becoming an "insider." Learners do not receive or even construct abstract, "objective," individual knowledge; rather, they learn to function in a community—be it a community of nuclear physicists, cabinet makers, high school classmates, street-corner society, or, as in the case under study, service technicians. They acquire that particular community's subjective viewpoint and learn to speak its language. In short, they are enculturated (Brown, Collins, and Duguid 1989). Learners are acquiring not explicit, formal "expert knowledge," but the embodied ability to behave as community members. For example, learners learn to tell and appreciate community-appropriate stories, discovering in doing so, all the narrative-based resources we outlined above. As Jordan (1989) argues in her analysis of midwifery, "To acquire a store of appropriate stories and, even more importantly, to know what are appropriate occasions for telling them, is then part of what it means to become a midwife" (p. 935).

Workplace learning is best understood, then, in terms of the communities being formed or joined and personal identities being changed. The central issue in learning is *becoming* a practitioner not learning *about* practice. This approach draws attention away from abstract knowledge and cranial processes and situates it in the practices and communities in which knowledge takes on significance. Learning about new devices, such as the machines Orr's technicians worked with, is best understood (and best achieved) in the context of the community in which the devices are used and that community's particular interpretive conventions. Lave and Wenger argue that learning, understanding, and interpretation involve a great deal that is not explicit or explicable, developed and framed in a crucially *communal* context.

Orr's study reveals this sort of learning going on in the process of and inseparable from work. The rep was not just an observer of the technical specialist. He was also an important participant in this process of diagnosis and story telling, whose participation could legitimately grow in from the periphery as a function of his developing understanding not of some extrinsically structured training. His legitimacy here is an important function of the social relations between the different levels of service technician, which are surprisingly egalitarian, perhaps as a result of the inherent incoherence of the problems this sort of technology presents: a specialist cannot hope to exert hierarchical control over knowledge that he or she must first construct cooperatively. "Occupational communities . . . have little hierarchy; the only real status is that of member" (Orr 1990a, 33).

A. Groups and Communities

Having characterized both working and learning in terms of communities, it is worth pausing to establish relations between our own account and recent work on groups in the workplace. Much important work has been done in this area (see, for example, the collections by Hackman (1990) and Goodman and Associates (1988)) and many of the findings support our own view of work activity. There is, however, a significant distinction between our views and this work. Group theory in general focuses on groups as canonical, bounded entities that lie within an organization and that are organized or at least sanctioned by that organization and its view of tasks. (See Hackman 1990, pp. 4–5.). The communities that we discern are, by contrast, often noncanonical and not recognized by the organization. They are more fluid and interpenetrative than bounded, often crossing the restrictive boundaries of the organization to incorporate people from outside. (Orr's reps can in an important sense be said to work in a community that includes both suppliers and customers.) Indeed, the canonical organization becomes a questionable unit of analysis from this perspective. And significantly, communities are emergent. That is to say their shape and membership emerges in the process of activity, as opposed to being created to carry out a task. (Note, by contrast, how much of the literature refers to the *design* or *creation* of new groups (e.g. Goodman and Associates 1988). From our viewpoint, the central questions more involve the *detection* and *support* of emergent or existing communities.)

If this distinction is correct then it has two particularly important corollaries. First, work practice and learning need to be understood not in terms of the groups that are ordained (e.g. "task forces" or "trainees"), but in terms of the communities that emerge. The latter are likely to be noncanonical (though not necessarily so) while the former are likely to be canonical. Looking only at canonical groups, whose configuration often conceals extremely influential interstitial conununities, will not provide a clear picture of how work or learning is actually organized and accomplished. It will only reflect the dominant assumptions of the organizational core.

Second, attempts to introduce "teams" and "work groups" into the workplace to enhance learning or work practice are often based on an assumption that without impetus from above, an organization's members configure themselves as individuals. In fact, as we suggest, people work and learn collaboratively and vital interstitial communities are continually being formed and reformed. The reorganization of the workplace into canonical groups can wittingly or unwittingly disrupt these highly functional noncanonical—and therefore often invisible—communities. Orr argues:

> The process of working and learning together creates a work situation which the workers value, and they resist having it disrupted by their employers through events such as a reorganization of the work. This resistance can surprise employers who think of labor as a commodity to arrange to suit their ends. The problem for the workers is that this community which they have created was not part of the series of discrete employment agreements by which the employer populated the work place, nor is the role of the community in doing the work acknowledged. *The work can only continue free of disruption if the employer can be persuaded to see the community as necessary to accomplishing work* (Orr 1990, 48, emphasis added).

B. Fostering Learning

Given a community-based analysis of learning so congruent with Orr's analysis of working, the question arises, how is it possible to foster learning-in-working? The answer is inevitably complex, not least because all the intricacies of context, which the pedagogic approach has always assumed could be stripped away, now have to be taken back into consideration. On the other hand, the ability of people to learn *in situ,* suggests that as a fundamental principle for supporting learning, attempts to strip away context should be examined with caution. If learners need access to practitioners at work, it is essential to question didactic approaches, with their tendency to separate learners from the target community and the authentic work practices. Learning is fostered by fostering access to and membership of the target community-of-practice, not by explicating abstractions of individual practice. Thus central to the process are the recognition and legitimation of community practices.

Reliance on formal descriptions of work, explicit syllabuses for learning about it, and canonical groups to carry it out immediately set organizations at a disadvantage. This approach, as we have noted, can simply blind management to the practices and communities that actually make things happen. In particular, it can lead to the isolation of learners, who will then be unable to acquire the implicit practices required for work. Marshall (in Lave and Wenger 1990) describes a case of apprenticeship for butchers in which learning was extremely restricted because, among other things, "apprentices . . . could not watch journeymen cut and saw meat" (p. 19). Formal training in cutting and sawing is quite different from the understanding of practice gleaned through informal observation that copresence makes possible and absence obviously excludes. These trainees were simply denied the chance to become legitimate peripheral participants. If training is designed so that learners cannot observe the activity of practitioners, learning is inevitably impoverished.

Legitimacy and peripherality are intertwined in a complex way. Occasionally, learners (like the apprentice butchers) are granted legitimacy but are denied peripherality. Conversely, they can be granted peripherality but denied legitimacy. Martin (1982) gives examples of organizations in which legitimacy is explicitly denied in instances of "open door" management, where members come to realize that, though the door is open, it is wiser not to cross the threshold. If either legitimacy or peripherality is denied, learning will be significantly more difficult.

For learners, then, a position on the periphery of practice is important. It is also easily overlooked and increasingly risks being "designed out," leaving people physically or socially isolated and justifiably uncertain whether, for instance, their errors are inevitable or the result of personal inadequacies. It is a significant challenge for design to ensure that new collaborative technologies, designed as they so often are around formal descriptions of work, do not exclude this sort of implicit, extendable, informal periphery. Learners need legitimate access to the periphery of communication—to computer mail, to formal and informal meetings, to telephone conversations, etc., and, of course, to war stories. They pick up invaluable "know how"—not just information but also manner and technique—from being on the periphery of competent practitioners going about their business. Furthermore, it is important to consider the periphery not only because it is an important site of learning, but also because, as the next section proposes, it can be an important site for innovation.

3. INNOVATING

One of the central benefits of these small, self-constituting communities we have been describing is that they evade the ossifying tendencies of large organizations. Canonical accounts of work are not only hard to apply and hard to learn.

They are also hard to change. Yet the actual behaviors of communities-of-practice are constantly changing both as newcomers replace old timers and as the demands of practice force the community to revise its relationship to its environment. Communities-of-practice like the reps' continue to develop a rich, fluid, noncanonical world view to bridge the gap between their organization's static canonical view and the challenge of changing practice. This process of development is inherently innovative. "Maverick" communities of this sort offer the core of a large organization a means and a model to examine the potential of alternatives views of organizational activity through spontaneously occurring experiments that are simultaneously informed and checked by experience. These, it has been argued (Hedberg, Nystrom and Starbuck 1976; Schein 1990), drive innovation by allowing the parts of an organization to step outside the organization's inevitably limited core world view and simply try something new. Unfortunately, people in the core of large organizations too often regard these noncanonical practices (if they see them at all) as counterproductive.

For a theoretical account of this sort of innovation, we turn to Daft and Weick's (1984) discussion of interpretive innovation. They propose a matrix of four different kinds of organization, each characterized by its relationship to its environment. They name these relationships "undirected viewing," "conditioned viewing," "discovering," and "enacting." Only the last two concern us here. It is important to note that Daft and Weick too see the community and not the individual "inventor" as the central unit of analysis in understanding innovating practice.

The discovering organization is the archetype of the conventional innovative organization, one which responds—often with great efficiency—to changes it detects in its environment. The organization presupposes an essentially prestructured environment and implicitly assumes that there is a correct response to any condition it discovers there. By contrast, the *enacting organization* is proactive and highly interpretive. Not only does it respond to its environment, but also, in a fundamental way, it creates many of the conditions to which it must respond. Daft and Weick describe enacting organizations as follows:

> These organizations construct their own environments. They gather information by trying new behaviors and seeing what happens. They experiment, test, and stimulate, and they ignore precedent, rules, and traditional expectations (Daft and Weick 1984, p. 288).

Innovation, in this view, is not simply a response to empirical observations of the environment. The source of innovation lies on the interface between an organization and its environment. And the process of innovating involves actively constructing a conceptual framework, imposing it on the environment, and reflecting on their interaction. With few changes, this could be a description of the activity of inventive, noncanonical groups, such as Orr's reps, who similarly "ignore precedent, rules, and traditional expectations" and break conventional boundaries. Like story telling, enacting is a process of interpretive sense making and controlled change.

A brief example of enacting can be seen in the introduction of the IBM Mag-I memory typewriter "as a new way of organizing office work" (Pava cited in Barley 1988). In order to make sense and full use of the power of this typewriter, the conditions in which it was to be used had to be reconceived. In the old conception of office work, the potential of the machine could not be realized. In a newly conceived understanding of office practice, however, the machine could prove highly innovative. Though this new conception could not be achieved without the new machine, the new machine could not be fully realized without the conception. The two changes went along together. Neither is wholly either cause or effect. Enacting organizations differ from discovering ones in that in this reciprocal way, instead of waiting for changed practices to emerge and responding, they enable them to emerge and anticipate their effects.

Reregistering the environment is widely recognized as a powerful source of innovation that moves organizations beyond the paradigms in which they begin their analysis and within which, without such a reformation, they must inevitably end it. This is the problem which Deetz and Kersten (1983) describe as closure: "Many organizations fail because . . . closure prohibits adaptation to current social conditions" (p. 166). Putnam (1983) argues that closure-generating structures appear to be "fixtures that exist independent of the processes that create and transform them" (p. 36). Interpretive or enacting organizations, aware as they are that their environment is not a given, can potentially adopt new viewpoints that allow them to see beyond the closure-imposing boundary of a single world view.

The question remains, however, how is this reregistering brought about by organizations that seem inescapably trapped within their own world view? We are claiming that the actual noncanonical practices of interstitial communities are continually developing new interpretations of the world because they have a practical rather than formal connection to that world. (For a theoretical account of the way practice drives change in world view, see Bloch 1977.) To pursue our connection with the work of the reps, closure is the likely result of rigid adherence to the reps' training and documentation and the formal account of work that they encompass. In order to get on with their work, reps overcome closure by reregistering their interpretation of the machine and its ever changing milieu. Rejection of a canonical, predetermined view and the construction through narration of an alternative view, such as Orr describes, involve, at heart, the complex intuitive process of bringing the communicative, community schema into harmony with the environment by reformulating both. The potential of such innovation is, however, lost to an organization that remains blind to noncanonical practice.

An enacting organization must also be capable of reconceiving not only its environment but also its own identity, for in a significant sense the two are mutually constitutive. Again, this reconceptualization is something that people who develop noncanonical practices are continuously doing, forging their own and their community's identity in their own terms so that they can break out of the restrictive hold of the formal descriptions of practice. Enacting organizations similarly regard both their environment and themselves as in some sense unanalyzed and therefore malleable. They do not assume that there is an ineluctable structure, a "right" answer, or a universal view to be discovered; rather, they continually look for innovative ways to impose new structure, ask new questions, develop a new view, become a new organization. By asking different questions, by seeking different *sorts* of explanations, and by looking from different points of view, different answers emerge—indeed different environments and different organizations mutually reconstitute each other dialectically or reciprocally. Daft and Weick (1984) argue, the interpretation can "shape the environment more than the environment shapes the interpretation" (p. 287).

Carlson's attempts to interest people in the idea of dry photocopying—xerography—provide an example of organizational tendencies to resist enacting innovation. Carlson and the Batelle Institute, which backed his research, approached most of the major innovative corporations of the time—RCA, IBM, A. B. Dick, Kodak. All turned down the idea of a dry copier. They did not reject a flawed machine. Indeed, they all agreed that it worked. But they rejected the *concept* of an office copier. They could see no use for it. Even when Haloid bought the patent, the marketing firms they hired consistently reported that the new device had no role in office practice (Dessauer 1971). In some sense it was necessary both for Haloid to reconceive itself (as Xerox) and for Xerox's machine to help bring about a reconceptualization of an area of office practice for the new machine to be put into manufacture and use.

What the evaluations saw was that an expensive machine was not needed to make a record copy of original documents. For the most part, carbon paper already did that admirably and cheaply. What they failed to see was that a copier allowed the proliferation of copies and of copies of copies. The quantitative leap in copies and their importance independent of the original then produced a qualitative leap in the way they were used. They no longer served merely as records of an original. Instead, they participated in the productive interactions of organizations' members in a unprecedented way. (See Latour's (1986) description of the organizational role of "immutable mobiles.") Only in use in the office, enabling and enhancing new forms of work, did the copier forge the conceptual lenses under which its value became inescapable.

It is this process of seeing the world anew that allows organizations reciprocally to see themselves anew and to overcome discontinuities in their environment and their structure. As von Hippel (1988), Barley (1988), and others point out, innovating is not always radical. Incremental improvements occur throughout an innovative organization. Enacting and innovating can be conceived of as at root sense-making, congruence-seeking, identity-building activities of the sort engaged in by the reps. Innovating and learning in daily activity lie at one end of a continuum of innovating practices that stretches to radical innovation cultivated in research laboratories at the far end.

Alternative world views, then, do not lie in the laboratory or strategic planning office alone, condemning everyone else in the organization to submit to a unitary culture. Alternatives are inevitably distributed throughout all the different communities that make up the organization. For it is the organization's communities, at all levels, who are in contact with the environment and involved in interpretive sense making, congruence finding, and adapting. It is from any site of such interactions that new insights can be coproduced. If an organizational core overlooks or curtails the enacting in its midst by ignoring or disrupting its communities-of-practice, it threatens its own survival in two ways. It will not only threaten to destroy the very working and learning practices by which it, knowingly or unknowingly, survives. It will also cut itself off from a major source of potential innovation that inevitably arises in the course of that working and learning.

4. CONCLUSION: ORGANIZATIONS AS COMMUNITIES-OF-COMMUNITIES

The complex of contradictory forces that put an organization's assumptions and core beliefs in direct conflict with members' working, learning, and innovating arises from a thorough misunderstanding of what working, learning, and innovating are. As a result of such misunderstandings, many modem processes and technologies, particularly those designed to downskill, threaten the robust working, learning, and innovating communities and practice of the workplace. Between Braverman's (1974) pessimistic view and Adler's (1987) optimistic one, lies Barley's (1988) complex argument, pointing out that the intent to downskill does not *necessarily* lead to downskilling (as Orr's reps show). But the intent to downskill may first drive noncanonical practice and communities yet further underground so that the insights gained through work are more completely hidden from the organization as a whole. Then later changes or reorganizations, whether or not intended to downskill, may disrupt what they do not notice. The gap between espoused and actual practice may become too large for noncanonical practices to bridge.

To foster working, learning, and innovating, an organization must close that gap. To do so, it needs to reconceive of itself as a community-of-communities, acknowledging in the process the many noncanonical communities in its midst. It must see beyond its canonical abstractions of practice to the rich, full-blooded activities themselves. And it must legitimize and support the myriad enacting activities perpetrated by its different members. This support cannot be intrusive, or it risks merely bringing potential innovators under the restrictive influence of the existing canonical view. Rather, as others have argued (Nystrom and Starbuck 1984; Hedberg 1981; Schein 1990) communities-of-practice must be allowed some latitude to shake themselves free of received wisdom.

A major entailment of this argument may be quite surprising. Conventional wisdom tends to hold that large organizations are particularly poor at innovating and adapting. Tushman and Anderson (1988), for example, argue justifiably that the *typical*, large organization is unlikely to produce discontinuous innovation. But size may not be the single determining feature here. Large, *atypical*, enacting organizations have the potential to be highly innovative and adaptive. Within an organization perceived as a collective of communities, not simply of individuals, in which enacting experiments are legitimate, separate community perspectives can be amplified by interchanges among communities. Out of this friction of competing ideas can come the sort of improvisational sparks necessary for igniting organizational innovation. Thus large organizations, *rejectively structured*, are perhaps particularly well positioned to be highly innovative and to deal with discontinuities. If their internal communities have a reasonable degree of autonomy and independence from the dominant world view, large organizations might actually accelerate innovation. Such organizations are uniquely positioned to generate innovative discontinuities incrementally, thereby diminishing the disruptiveness of the periodic radical reorganization that Nadler calls "frame breaking" (Nadler 1988). This occurs when conventional organizations swing wholesale from one paradigm to another (see also Bartunek 1984). An organization whose core is aware that it is the synergistic aggregate of agile, semiautonomous, self-constituting communities and not a brittle monolith is likely to be capable of extensible "frame bending" well beyond conventional breaking point.

The important interplay of separate communities with independent (though interrelated) world views may in part account for von Hippel's (1988) account of the sources of innovation and other descriptions of the innovative nature of business alliances. Von Hippel argues that sources of innovation can lie outside an organization among its customers and suppliers. Emergent communities of the sort we have outlined that span the boundaries of an organization would then seem a likely conduit of external and innovative views into an organization. Similarly, the alliances Powell describes bring together different organizations with different interpretive schemes so that the composite group they make up has several enacting options to choose from. Because the separate communities enter as independent members of an alliance rather than as members of a rigid hierarchy, the alternative conceptual viewpoints are presumably legitimate and do not get hidden from the core. There is no concealed noncanonical practice where there is no concealing canonical practice.

The means to harness innovative energy in any enacting organization or alliance must ultimately be considered in the design of organizational architecture and the ways communities are linked to each other. This architecture should preserve and enhance the healthy autonomy of communities, while simultaneously building an interconnectedness through which to disseminate the results of separate communities' experiments. In some form or another the stories that support learning-in-working and innovation should be allowed to circulate. The technological potential to support this distribution—e-mail, bulletin boards, and other devices that are capable of supporting narrative exchanges—is available. But narratives, as we have argued, are embedded in the social system in which they arise and are used. They cannot simply be uprooted and repackaged for circulation without becoming prey to exactly those problems that beset the old abstracted canonical accounts. Moreover, information cannot be assumed to circulate freely just because technology to support circulation is available (Feldman and March 1981). Eckert (1989), for instance, argues that information travels differently within different socioeconomic groups. Organizational assumptions that given the "right" medium people will exchange information **freely** overlook the way in which certain socioeconomic groups, organizations, and in particular, corporations, implicitly treat information as a commodity to be hoarded and exchanged. Working-class groups, Eckert contends, do pass information freely and Orr (1990a) notes that the reps are remarkably open with each other about what they know. *Within* these communities, news travels fast; community knowledge is readily available to community members. But these communities must function within corporations that treat information as a commodity and that have superior bargaining power in negotiating the terms of exchange. In such unequal conditions, internal communities cannot reasonably be expected to surrender their knowledge freely.

As we have been arguing throughout, to understand the way information is constructed and travels within an organization, it is first necessary to understand the different communities that are formed within it and the distribution of power among them. Conceptual reorganization to accommodate learning-in-working and innovation, then, must stretch from the level of individual communities-of-practice and the technology and practices used there to the level of the overarching organizational architecture, the community-of-communities.

It has been our unstated assumption that a unified understanding of working, learning, and innovating is potentially highly beneficial, allowing, it seems likely, a synergistic collaboration rather than a conflicting separation among workers, learners, and innovators. But similarly, we have left unstated the companion assumption that attempts to foster such synergy through a conceptual reorganization will produce enormous difficulties from the perspective of the conventional workplace. Work and learning are set out in formal descriptions so that people (and organizations) can be held accountable; groups are organized to define responsibility; organizations are bounded to enhance concepts of competition; peripheries are closed off to maintain secrecy and privacy. Changing the way these things are arranged will produce problems as well as benefits. An examination of both problems and benefits has been left out of this paper, whose single purpose has been to show where constraints and resources lie, rather than the rewards and costs of deploying them. Our argument is simply that for working, learning, and innovating to thrive collectively depends on linking these three, in theory and in practice, more closely, more realistically, and more reflectively than is generally the case at present.

ACKNOWLEDGMENTS

This paper was written at the Institute for Research on Learning with the invaluable help of many of our colleagues, in particular Jean Lave, Julian Orr, and Etienne Wenger, whose work, with that of Daft and Weick, provides the canonical texts on which we based our commentary.

REFERENCES

Adler, P. S. (1987), "Automation and Skill: New Directions," *International Journal of Technology Management* 2 (5/6), 761–771.

Barley, S. R. (1988), "Technology, Power, and the Social Organization of Work: Towards a Pragmatic Theory of Skilling and Deskilling," *Research in the Sociology of Organizations,* 6, 33–80.

Bartunek, J. M. (1984), "Changing Interpretive Schemes and Organizational Restructuring: The Example of a Religious Order," *Administrative Science Quarterly,* 29, 355–372.

Bourdieu, P. (1977), *Outline of a Theory of Practice,* trans R. Nice. Cambridge: Cambridge University Press. (First published in French, 1973.)

Bloch, M. (1977), "The Past and the Present in the Present," *Man[NS],* 12, 278–292.

Braverman, H. (1974), *Labor and Monopoly Capitalism: The Degradation of Work in the Twentieth Century,* New York: Monthly Review Press.

Brown, J. S. and P. Duguid, (in press), "Enacting Design," in P. Adler (Ed.), *Designing Automation for Usability,* New York: Oxford University Press.

Brown, J. S., A. Collins and P. Duguid (1989), "Situated Cognition and the Culture of Learning," *Education Researcher,* 18, 1, 32–42. (Also available in a fuller version as IRL Report 88–0008, Palo Alto, CA: Institute for Research on Learning.)

Burawoy, M. (1979), "The Anthropology of Industrial Work," *Annual Review of Anthropology,* 8, 231–266.

Daft, R. L. and K. E. Weick (1984), "Toward a Model of Organizations as Interpretation Systems," *Academy of Management Review,* 9, 2, 284–295.

Deetz, S. A. and A. Kersten (1983), "Critical Models of Interpretive Research," in L. L. Putnam and M. E. Pacanowsky (Eds.), *Communication and Organizations: An Interpretive Approach,* Beverly Hills, CA: Sage Publications.

Dessauer, J. H. (1971), *My Years with Xerox: The Billions Nobody Wanted,* Garden City, Doubleday. Eckert, P. (1989), *Jocks and Burnouts,* New York: Teachers College Press.

Feldman, M. S. and J. G. March (1981), "Information in Organizations as Signal and Symbol," *Administrative Science Quarterly,* 26, 171–186.

Geertz, C. (1973), *Interpretation of Cultures: Selected Essays,* New York: Basic Books.

Goodman, P. and Associates (1988), *Designing Effective Work Groups,* San Francisco: Jossey-Bass.

Hackman, J. R. (Ed.) (1990), *Groups that Work (and Those that Don't),* San Francisco: Jossey-Bass.

Hedberc, B. (1981), "How Organizations Learn and Unlearn," in P. C. Nystrom and W. H. Starbuck, *Handbook of Organizational Design, Vol. 1: Adapting Organizations to their Environments,* New York: Oxford University Press.

———, P. C. Nystrom and W. H. Starbuck (1976), "Designing Organizations to Match Tomorrow," in P. C. Nystrom and W. H. Starbuck (Eds.), *Prescriptive Models of Organizations,* Amsterdam, Netherlands: North-Holland Publishing Company.

Hutchins, E. (1991), "Organizing Work by Adaptation," *Organization Science, 2, 1,* 14–39.

——— (in press), "Learning to Navigate," in S. Chalkin and J. Lave (Eds.), *Situated Learning,* Cambridge: Cambridge University Press.

Jordan, B. (1989), "Cosmopolitical Obstetrics: Some Insights from the Training of Traditional Midwives," *Social Science and Medicine, 28, 9,* 925–944. (Also available in slightly different form as *Modes of Teaching and Learning: Questions Raised by the Training of Traditional Birth Attendants,* IRL report 88–0004, Palo Alto, CA: Institute for Research on Learning.)

Latour, B. (1986), "Visualization and Cognition: Thinking with Eyes and Hands," *Knowledge and Society, 6,* 1–40.

Lave J. (1988), *Cognition in Practice: Mind, Mathematics, and Culture in Everyday Life,* New York: Cambridge University Press.

——— and E. Wenger (1990), *Situated Learning: Legitimate Peripheral Participation,* IRL report 90–0013, Palo Alto, CA.: Institute for Research on Learning. (Also forthcoming (1990) in a revised version, from Cambridge University Press.)

Levi-Strauss, C. (1966), *The Savage Mind,* Chicago: Chicago University Press.

Martin, J. (1982), "Stories and Scripts in Organizational Settings," in A. H. Hastorf and A. M. Isen (Eds.), *Cognitive and Social Psychology,* Amsterdam: Elsevier.

Nadler, D. (1988), "Organizational Frame Bending: Types of Change in the Complex Organization," in R. H. Kilman, T. J. Covin, and associates (Eds.), *Corporate Transformation: Revitalizing Organizations for a Competitive World,* San Francisco: Jossey-Bass.

Nystrom, P. C. and W. H. Starbuck (1984), "To Avoid Organizational Crises, Unlearn." *Organizational Dynamics,* Spring, 53–65.

Orr, J. (1990a), "Talking about Machines: An Ethnography of a Modern Job," Ph.D. Thesis, Cornell University.

——— (1990b), "Sharing Knowledge, Celebrating Identity: War Stories and Community Memory in a Service Culture," in D. S. Middleton and D. Edwards (Eds.), *Collective Remembering: Memory in Society,* Beverley Hills, CA: Sage Publications.

——— (1987a), "Narratives at Work: Story Telling as Cooperative Diagnostic Activity," *Field Service Manager,* June, 47–60.

——— (1987b), *Talking about Machines: Social Aspects of Expertise,* Report for the Intelligent Systems Laboratory, Xerox Palo Alto Research Center, Palo Alto, CA.

Pea, R. D. (1990), Distributed Cognition, IRL Report 90–0015, Palo Alto, CA: Institute for Research on Learning.

Putnam, L. L. (1983), "The Interpretive Perspective: An Alternative to Functionalism," in L. L Putnam and M. E. Pacanowsky (Eds.), *Communication and Organizations: An Interpretive Approach,* Beverley Hills, CA: Sage Publications.

Reddy, M. J. (1979), "The Conduit Metaphor," in Andrew Ortony (Ed.), *Metaphor and Thought,* Cambridge: Cambridge University Press, 284–324.

Ryle, G. (1954), *Dilemmas: The Tamer Lectures,* Cambridge: Cambridge University Press.

Schein, E. H. (1990), "Organizational Culture," *American Psychologist,* 45, 2, 109–119.

Schön, D. A. (1987), *Educating the Reflective Practitioner,* San Francisco: Jossey-Bass.

—— (1984). *The Reflective Practitioner,* New York: Basic Books.

Schön, D. A. (1971), *Beyond the Stable State,* New York: Norton.

Scribner, S. (1984), "Studying Working Intelligence," in B. Rogoff and J. Lave (Eds). *Everyday Cognition: Its Development in Social Context,* Cambridge, MA: Harvard University Press.

Suchman, L. (1987a), *Plans and Situated Actions: The Problem of Human–Machine Communication,* New York: Cambridge University Press.

(1987b), "Common Sense in Interface Design," *Techni, 1,* 1, 38–40.

Tushman, M. L. and P. Anderson (1988), "Technological Discontinuities and Organization Environments," in A. M. Pettigrew (Ed.), *The Management of Strategic Change,* Oxford: Basil Blackwell.

van Maanen, J. and S. Barley (1984), "Occupational Communities: Culture and Control in Organizations," in B. Straw and L. Cummings (Eds.), *Research in Organizational Behaviour,* London: JAI Press.

von Hippel, E. (1988), *The Sources of Innoration,* New York: Oxford University Press.

Zuboff, S. (1988), *In the Age of the Smart Machine: The Future of Work and Power,* New York: Basic Books.

Chapter 8

Legitimate Peripheral Participation in Communities of Practice[*]

J. Lave and E. Wenger

We now can begin to turn the observations of the previous chapter into objects to be analyzed. In the following sections, we recast the central characteristics of these several historical realizations of apprenticeship in terms of legitimate peripheral participation. First, we discuss the structuring resources that shape the process and content of learning possibilities and apprentices' changing perspectives on what is known and done. Then we argue that "transparency" of the sociopolitical organization of practice, of its content and of the artifacts engaged in practice, is a crucial resource for increasing participation. We next examine the relation of newcomers to the discourse of practice. This leads to a discussion of how identity and motivation are generated as newcomers move toward full participation. Finally, we explore contradictions inherent in learning, and the relations of the resulting conflicts to the development of identity and the transformation of practice.

STRUCTURING RESOURCES FOR LEARNING IN PRACTICE

One of the first things people think of when apprenticeship is mentioned is the master-apprentice relation. But in practice the roles of masters are surprisingly variable across time and place. A specific master-apprentice relation is not even ubiquitously characteristic of apprenticeship learning. Indeed, neither Yucatec midwives nor quartermasters learn in specific master-apprentice relations. Newcomers to A. A. do have special relations with specific old-timers who act as their sponsors, but these relations are not what defines them as newcomers. In contrast, tailors' apprentices most certainly have specific relations with

---

* Reprinted by permission.

their masters, without whom they wouldn't be apprentices. Master tailors must sponsor apprentices before the latter can have legitimate access to participation in the community's productive activities. In short, the form in which such legitimate access is secured for apprentices depends on the characteristics of the division of labor in the social milieu in which the community of practice is located. Thus, the midwife is learning a specialism within her own family of orientation, a form of labor different, but not separated in marked ways, from the widely distributed "ordinary" activities of everyday life; legitimate participation comes diffusely through membership in family and community. Where apprentices learn a specialized occupation, sponsorship into a community of practice—within a community in the more general sense—becomes an issue. Intentional relations, and even contractual relations with a specific master, are common. It should be clear that, in shaping the relation of masters to apprentices, the issue of conferring legitimacy is more important than the issue of providing teaching.

Even in the case of the tailors, where the relation of apprentice to master is specific and explicit, it is not this relationship, but rather the apprentice's relations to other apprentices and even to other masters that organize opportunities to learn; an apprentice's own master is too distant, an object of too much respect, to engage with in awkward attempts at a new activity. In A. A., old-timers who act as "sponsors" reportedly withhold advice and instruction appropriate to later stages; they hold back and wait until the newcomer becomes "ready" for a next step through increasing participation in the community (Alibrandi 1977). In all five cases described in the preceding chapter, in fact, researchers insist that there is very little observable teaching; the more basic phenomenon is learning. The practice of the community creates the potential "curriculum" in the broadest sense—that which may be learned by newcomers with legitimate peripheral access. Learning activity appears to have a characteristic pattern. There are strong goals for learning because learners, as peripheral participants, can develop a view of what the whole enterprise is about, and what there is to be learned. Learning itself is an improvised practice: A learning curriculum unfolds in opportunities for engagement in practice. It is not specified as a set of dictates for proper practice.

In apprenticeship opportunities for learning are, more often than not, given structure by work practices instead of by strongly asymmetrical master-apprentice relations. Under these circumstances learners may have a space of "benign community neglect" in which to configure their own learning relations with other apprentices. There may be a looser coupling between relations among learner on the one hand and the often hierarchical relations between learners and old-timers on the other hand, than where directive pedagogy is the central motive of institutional organization. It seems typical of apprenticeship that apprentices learn mostly in relation with other apprentices. There is anecdotal evidence (Butler personal communication; Hass n.d.) that where the circulation of knowledge among peers and near-peers is possible, it spreads exceedingly rapidly and effectively. The central grounds on which forms of education that differ from schooling are condemned are that changing the person is not the central motive of the enterprise in which learning takes place (see the last section of this chapter). The effectiveness of the circulation of information among peers suggests, to the contrary, that engaging in practice, rather than being its object, may well be a *condition* for the effectiveness of learning.

So far, we have observed that the authority of masters and their involvement in apprenticeship varies dramatically across communities of practice. We have also pointed out that structuring resources for learning come from a variety of sources, not only from pedagogical activity. We argue that a coherent explanation of these observations depends upon *decentering* common notions of mastery and pedagogy. This decentering strategy is, in fact, deeply embedded in our situated approach—for to shift as we have from the notion of an individual learner to the concept of legitimate peripheral participation in communities of practice is precisely to decenter analysis of learning. To take a decentered view of master-apprentice relations leads to an understanding that mastery resides not in the master but in the organization of the community of practice of which the master is part: The master as the locus of authority (in several senses) is, after all, as much a product of the conventional, centered theory of learning as is the individual learner. Similarly, a decentered view of the master as pedagogue moves the focus of analysis away from teaching and onto the intricate structuring of a community's learning resources.

THE PLACE OF KNOWLEDGE: PARTICIPATION, LEARNING CURRICULA, COMMUNITIES OF PRACTICE

The social relations of apprentices within a community change through their direct involvement in activities; in the process, the apprentices' understanding and knowledgeable skills develop. In the recent past, the only means we have had for understanding the processes by which these changes occur have come from conventional speculations about the nature of "informal" learning: That is, apprentices are supposed to acquire the "specifics" of practice through "observation and imitation." But this view is in all probability wrong in every particular, or right in particular circumstances, but for the wrong reasons. We argue instead that the effects of peripheral participation on knowledge-in-practice are not properly understood; and that studies of apprenticeship have presumed too literal a coupling of work processes and learning processes.

To begin with, newcomers' legitimate peripherality provides them with more than an "observational" lookout post: It crucially involves *participation* as a way of learning—of both absorbing and being absorbed in—the "culture of practice." An extended period of legitimate peripherality provides learners with opportunities to make the culture of practice theirs. From a broadly peripheral perspective, apprentices gradually assemble a general idea of what constitutes the practice of the community. This uneven sketch of the enterprise (available if there is legitimate access) might include who is involved; what they do; what everyday life is like; how masters talk, walk, work, and generally conduct their lives; how people who are not part of the community of practice interact with it; what other learners are doing; and what learners need to learn to become full practitioners. It includes an increasing understanding of how, when, and about what old-timers collaborate, collude, and collide, and what they enjoy, dislike, respect, and admire. In particular, it offers exemplars (which are grounds and motivation for learning activity), including masters, finished products, and more advanced apprentices in the process of becoming full practitioners.

Such a general view, however, is not likely to be frozen in initial impressions. Viewpoints from which to understand the practice evolve through changing participation in the division of labor, changing relations to ongoing community practices, and changing social relations in the community. This is as true, in different ways, of reformed alcoholics as they socialize with other A. A. members as it is of quartermasters as they move through different aspects of navigation work. And learners have multiply structured relations with ongoing practice in other ways. Apprenticeship learning is not "work-driven" in the way stereotypes of informal learning have suggested; the ordering of learning and of everyday practice do not coincide. Production activity-segments must be learned in different sequences than those in which a production process commonly unfolds, if peripheral, less intense, less complex, less vital tasks are learned before more central aspects of practice.

Consider, for instance, the tailors' apprentices, whose involvement starts with both initial preparations for the tailors' daily labor and finishing details on completed garments. The apprentices progressively move backward through the production process to cutting jobs. (This kind of progression is quite common across cultures and historical periods.) Under these circumstances, the initial "circumferential" perspective absorbed in partial, peripheral, apparently trivial activities—running errands, delivering messages, or accompanying others—takes on new significance: It provides a first approximation to an armature of the structure of the community of practice. Things learned, and various and changing viewpoints, can be arranged and interrelated in ways that gradually transform that skeletal understanding.

When directive teaching in the form of prescriptions about proper practice generates one circumscribed form of participation (in school), preempting participation in ongoing practice as the legitimate source of learning opportunities, the goal of complying with the requirements specified by teaching engenders a practice different from that intended (Bourdieu 1977). In such cases, even though the pedagogical structure of the circumstances of learning has moved away from the principle of legitimate peripheral participation with respect to the target practice, legitimate peripheral participation is still the core of the learning that takes place. This leads us to distinguish between a *learning curriculum* and a *teaching curriculum*. A learning curriculum consists of situated opportunities (thus including exemplars of various sorts often thought of as "goals") for the improvisational development of new practice (Lave 1989). A learning curriculum is a field of learning resources in everyday practice *viewed from the perspective of learners*. A teaching curriculum, by contrast, is constructed for the instruction of newcomers. When a teaching curriculum supplies—and thereby limits—structuring resources for learning, the meaning of what is learned (and control of access to it, both in its peripheral forms and its subsequently more complex and intensified, though possibly more fragmented, forms) is mediated through an instructor's participation, by an external view of what knowing is about. The learning curriculum in didactic situations, then, evolves out of participation in a specific community of practice engendered by pedagogical relations and by a prescriptive view of the target practice as a subject matter, as well as out of the many and various relations that tie participants to their own and to other institutions.

A learning curriculum is essentially situated. It is not something that can be considered in isolation, manipulated in arbitrary didactic terms, or analyzed apart from the social relations that shape legitimate peripheral participation. A learning curriculum is thus characteristic of a community. In using the term community, we do not imply some primordial culture-sharing entity. We assume that members have different interests, make diverse contributions to activity, and hold varied viewpoints. In our view, participation at multiple levels is entailed in membership in a *community of practice*. Nor does the term community imply necessarily co-presence, a well-defined, identifiable group, or socially visible boundaries. It does imply participation in an activity system about which participants share understandings concerning what they are doing and what that means in their lives and for their communities.

The concept of community underlying the notion of legitimate peripheral participation, and hence of "knowledge" and its "location" in the lived-in world, is both crucial and subtle. The community of practice of midwifery or tailoring involves much more than the technical knowledgeable skill involved in delivering babies or producing clothes. A community of practice is a set of relations among persons, activity, and world, over time and in relation with other tangential and overlapping communities of practice. A community of practice is an intrinsic condition for the existence of knowledge, not least because it provides the interpretive support necessary for making sense of its heritage. Thus, participation in the cultural practice in which any knowledge exists is an epistemological principle of learning. The social structure of this practice, its power relations, and its conditions for legitimacy define possibilities for learning (i.e., for legitimate peripheral participation).

It is possible to delineate the community that is the site of a learning process by analyzing the reproduction cycles of the communities that seem to be involved and their relations. For the quartermasters, the cycle of navigational practice is quite short; a complete reproduction of the practice of quartermastering may take place every five or six years (as a novice enters, gradually becomes a full participant, begins to work with newcomer quartermasters who in their own turn become full participants and reach the point at which they are ready to work with newcomers). The reproduction cycle of the midwives', the tailors', or the butchers' communities is much longer. In A. A., its length is rather variable as individuals go through successive steps at their own pace. Observing the span of developmental cycles is only a beginning to such an analysis (and a rough approximation that sets aside consideration of the transformation and change inherent in ongoing practice—see below), for each such cycle has its own trajectory, benchmarks, blueprints, and careers (Stack 1989).

In addition to the useful analytic questions suggested by a temporal focus on communities of practice, there is a further reason to address the delineation of communities of practice in processual, historical terms. Claims *about* the definition of a community of practice and the community of practice actually in process of reproduction in that location may not coincide—a point worth careful consideration.

For example, in most high schools there is a group of students engaged over a substantial period of time in learning physics. What community of practice is in the process of reproduction? Possibly the students participate only in the reproduction of the high school itself. But assuming that the practice of physics is also being reproduced in some form, there are vast differences between the ways high school physics students participate in and give meaning to their activity and the way professional physicists do. The actual reproducing community of practice, within which schoolchildren learn about physics, is not the community of physicists but the community of schooled adults. Children are introduced into the latter community (and its humble relation with the former community) during their school years. The reproduction cycles of the physicist's community start much later, possibly only in graduate school (Traweek 1988).

In this view, problems of schooling are not, at their most fundamental level, pedagogical. Above all, they have to do with the ways in which the community of adults reproduces itself, with the places that newcomers can or cannot find in such communities, and with relations that can or cannot be established between these newcomers and the cultural and political life of the community.

In summary, rather than learning by replicating the performances of others or by acquiring knowledge transmitted in instruction, we suggest that learning occurs through centripetal participation in the learning curriculum of the ambient community. Because the place of knowledge is within a community of practice, questions of learning must be addressed within the developmental cycles of that community, a recommendation which creates a diagnostic tool for distinguishing among communities of practice.

THE PROBLEM OF ACCESS: TRANSPARENCY AND SEQUESTRATION

The key to legitimate peripherality is access by newcomers to the community of practice and all that membership entails. But though this is essential to the reproduction of any community, it is always problematic at the same time. To become a full member of a community of practice requires access to a wide range of ongoing activity, old-timers, and other members of the community; and to information, resources, and opportunities for participation. The issue is so central to membership in communities of practice that, in a sense, all that we have said so far is about access. Here we discuss the problem more specifically in connection with issues of understanding and control, which along with involvement in productive activity are related aspects of the legitimate peripherality of participants in a practice.

The artifacts employed in ongoing practice, the technology of practice, provide a good arena in which to discuss the problem of access to understanding. In general, social scientists who concern themselves with learning treat technology as a given and are not analytic about its interrelations with other aspects of a community of practice. Becoming a full participant certainly includes engaging with the technologies of everyday practice, as well as participating in the social relations, production processes, and other activities of communities of practice. But the understanding to be gained from engagement with technology can be extremely varied depending on the form of participation enabled by its use. Participation involving technology is especially significant because the artifacts used within a cultural practice carry a substantial portion of that practice's heritage. For example, the alidade used by the quartermasters for taking bearings has developed as a navigational instrument over hundreds of years, and embodies calculations invented long ago (Hutchins in press). Thus, understanding the technology of practice is more than learning to use tools; it is a way to connect with the history of the practice and to participate more directly in its cultural life.

The significance of artifacts in the full complexity of their relations with the practice can be more or less *transparent* to learners. Transparency in its simplest form may just imply that the inner workings of an artifact are available for the learner's inspection: The black box can be opened, it can become a "glass box." But there is more to understanding the use and significance of an artifact: Knowledge within a community of practice and ways of perceiving and manipulating objects characteristic of community practices are encoded in artifacts in ways that can be more or less revealing. Moreover, the activity system and the social world of which an artifact is part are reflected in multiple ways in its design and use and can become further "fields of transparency," just as they can remain opaque. Obviously, the transparency of any technology always exists with respect to some purpose and is intricately tied to the cultural practice and social organization within which the technology is meant to function: It cannot be viewed as a feature of an artifact in itself but as a process that involves specific forms of participation, in which the technology fulfills a mediating function. Apprentice quartermasters not only have access to the physical activities going on around them and to the tools of the trade; they participate in information flows and conversations, in a context in which they can make sense of what they observe and hear. In focusing on the epistemological role of artifacts in the context of the social organization of knowledge, this notion of transparency constitutes, as it were, the cultural organization of access. As such, it does not apply to technology only, but to all forms of access to practice.

Productive activity and understanding are not separate, or even separable, but dialectically related. Thus, the term *transparency* when used here in connection with technology refers to the way in which using artifacts and under-standing their significance interact to become one learning process. Mirroring the intricate relation between using and understanding artifacts, there is an interest-ing duality inherent in the concept of transparency. It combines the two charac-teristics of *invisibility* and *visibility*: invisibility in the form of unproblematic interpretation and integration into activity, and visibility in the form of extended access to information. This is not a simple dichotomous distinction, since these two crucial characteristics are in a complex interplay, their relation being one of both conflict and synergy.

It might be useful to give a sense of this interplay by analogy to a window. A window's invisibility is what makes it a window, that is, an object through which the world outside becomes visible. The very fact, however, that so many things can be seen through it makes the window itself highly visible, that is, very salient in a room, when compared to, say, a solid wall. Invisibility of mediating technologies is necessary for allowing focus on, and thus supporting visibility of, the subject matter. Conversely, visibility of the significance of the technology is necessary for allowing its unproblematic—invisible—use. This interplay of con-flict and synergy is central to all aspects of learning in practice: It makes the design of supportive artifacts a matter of providing a good balance between these two interacting requirements. (An extended analysis of the concept of transpar-ency can be found in Wenger 1990.)

Control and selection, as well as the need for access, are inherent in com-munities of practice. Thus access is liable to manipulation, giving legitimate peripherality an ambivalent status: Depending on the organization of access, legitimate peripherality can either promote or prevent legitimate participation. In the study of the butchers' apprentices, Marshall provides examples of how access can be denied. The trade school and its shop exercises did not simulate the cen-tral practices of meat cutting in supermarkets, much less make them accessible to apprentices; on-the-job training was not much of an improvement. Worse, the master butchers confined their apprentices to jobs that were removed from activ-ities rather than peripheral to them. To the extent that the community of practice routinely sequesters newcomers, either very directly as in the example of appren-ticeship for the butchers, or in more subtle and pervasive ways as in schools, these newcomers are prevented from peripheral participation. In either case legit-imacy is not in question. Schoolchildren are legitimately peripheral, but kept from participation in the social world more generally. The butchers' apprentices participate legitimately, but not peripherally, in that they are not given produc-tive access to activity in the community of practitioners.

An important point about such sequestering when it is institutionalized is that it encourages a folk epistemology of dichotomies, for instance, between "abstract" and "concrete" knowledge. These categories do not reside in the world as distinct forms of *knowledge*, nor do they reflect some putative hierar-chy of forms of knowledge among practitioners. Rather, they derive from the nature of the new practice generated by sequestration. *Abstraction* in this sense stems from the disconnectedness of a particular cultural practice. Participation in that practice is neither more nor less abstract or concrete, experiential or cerebral, than in any other. Thus, legitimate peripheral participation as the core concept of relations of learning places the explanatory burden for issues such as "understanding" and "levels" of abstraction or conceptualization not on one type of learning as opposed to another, but on the cultural practice in which the learning is taking place, on issues of access, and on the transparency of the cultural environment with respect to the meaning of what is being learned. Insofar as the notion of transparency, taken very broadly, is a way of organizing activities that makes their meaning visible, it opens an alternative approach to the traditional dichotomy between learning experientially and learning at a distance, between learning by doing and learning by abstraction.

DISCOURSE AND PRACTICE

The characterization of language in learning has, in discussions of conventional contrasts between formal and informal learning, been treated as highly significant in classifying ways of transmitting knowledge. Verbal instruction has been assumed to have special, and especially effective properties with respect to the generality and scope of the understanding that learners come away with, while instruction by demonstration—learning by "observation and imitation"—is supposed to produce the opposite, a literal and narrow effect.

Close analysis of both instructional discourse and cases of apprenticeship raise a different point: Issues about language, like those about the role of masters, may well have more to do with legitimacy of participation and with access to peripherality than they do with knowledge transmission. Indeed, as Jordan (1989) argues, learning to become a legitimate participant in a community involves learning how to talk (and be silent) in the manner of full participants. In A. A. telling the story of the life of the nondrinking alcoholic is clearly a major vehicle for the display of membership. Models for constructing A. A. life stories are widely available in published accounts of alcoholics' lives and in the storytelling performances of old-timers. Early on, newcomers learn to preface their contributions to A. A. meetings with the simple identifying statement "I'm a recovering alcoholic," and, shortly, to introduce themselves and sketch the problems that brought them to A. A. They begin by describing these events in non-A. A. terms. Their accounts meet with counterexemplary stories by more-experienced members who do not criticize or correct newcomers' accounts directly. They gradually generate a view that matches more closely the A. A. model, eventually producing skilled testimony in public meetings and gaining validation from others as they demonstrate the appropriate understanding.

The process of learning to speak as a full member of a community of practice is vividly illustrated in an analysis of the changing performances of newcomer spirit mediums in a spiritist congregation in Mexico (Kearney 1977). This example is interesting partly because the notion of "proper speech" is so clearly crystallized in the collective expectations of the community, while at the same time, if the community were forced to acknowledge the idea that mediums must *learn* their craft, this would negate the legitimacy of spirit possession. That learning through legitimate peripheral participation nonetheless occurs makes this example especially striking.

Spiritist cult communities center around women who are adept at going into trance. They act as mediums, transmitting the messages of a variety of spirits. The spirits are arranged in a complex hierarchy of more- and less-important forms of deity. It takes a great deal of practice to speak coherently while in trance, especially while taking on a variety of personae.

> It is quite apparent from biographical data I have on mediums that they typically begin "working" with various [unimportant] exotic spirits who have idiosyncratic speech patterns, and then eventually switch to working with the [highly revered] Divinities who typically speak in a much more stereotypic manner. . . . Recently several novice mediums have been "entered" by "beings from outer space." These beings appeared quite intent on speaking to those present via the mediums, but of course their language was incomprehensible to the audience. During the course of repeated visits, however, and with help from nonpossessed spiritualists, they slowly "began to learn to speak the Spanish language," and to articulate their messages. . . . A . . . characteristic of advanced mediums as compared with novices is the large repertoire and wider range of identities displayed by the former [Kearney 1977].

In the *Psychology of Literacy*, Scribner and Cole (1981) speculate that asking questions—learning how to "do" school appropriately—may be a major part of what school teaches. This is also Jordan's conclusion about Yucatec midwives' participation in biomedical, state-sponsored training courses. She argues that the verbal instruction provided by health officials has the effect of teaching midwives how to talk in biomedical terms when required. Such talk only serves to give them "face validity" in the eyes of others who believe in the authoritative character of biomedicine. But Jordan argues that it has no effect on their existing practice.

This point about language use is consonant with the earlier argument that didactic instruction creates unintended practices. The conflict stems from the fact that there is a difference between talking *about* a practice from outside and talking *within* it. Thus the didactic use of language, not itself the discourse of practice, creates a new linguistic practice, which has an existence of its own. Legitimate peripheral participation in such linguistic practice is a form of learning, but does not imply that newcomers learn the actual practice the language is supposed to be about.

In a community or practice, there are no special forms of discourse aimed at apprentices or crucial to their centripetal movement toward full participation that correspond to the marked genres of the question—answer—evaluation format of classroom teaching, or the lecturing of college professors or midwife-training course instructors. But Jordan makes a further, acute, observation about language, this time about the role of *stories* in apprenticeship: She points out that stories play a major role in decision making (1989). This has implications for what and how newcomers learn. For apprenticeship learning is supported by conversations and stories about problematic and especially difficult cases.

> What happens is that as difficulties of one kind or another develop, stories of similar cases are offered up by the attendants [at a birth], all of whom, it should be remembered, are experts, having themselves given birth. In the ways in which these stories are treated, elaborated, ignored, taken up, characterized as typical and so on, the collaborative work of deciding on the present case is done. . . . These stories, then, are packages of situated knowledge. . . . To acquire a store of appropriate stories and, even more importantly, to know what are appropriate occasions for telling them, is then part of what it means to become a midwife [1989: 935].

Orr (in press) describes comparable patterns of story telling in his research on the learning of machine-repair work: Technicians who repair copier machines tell each other "war stories" about their past experiences in making repairs. Such stories constitute a vital part of diagnosing and carrying out new repairs. In the process, newcomers learn how to make (sometimes difficult) repairs, they learn the skills of war-story telling, and they become legitimate participants in the community of practice. In A. A. also, discussions have a dual purpose. Participants engage in the work of staying sober and they do so through gradual construction of an identity. Telling the personal story is a tool of diagnosis and reinterpretation. Its communal use is essential to the fashioning of an identity as a recovered alcoholic, and thus to remaining sober. It becomes a display of membership by virtue of fulfilling a crucial function in the shared practice.

It is thus necessary to refine our distinction between *talking about* and *talking within* a practice. Talking within itself includes both talking within (e.g., exchanging information necessary to the progress of ongoing activities) and talking about (e.g., stories, community lore). Inside the shared practice, both forms of talk fulfill specific functions: engaging, focusing, and shifting attention, bringing about coordination, etc., on the one hand; and supporting communal forms of memory and reflection, as well as signaling membership, on the other. (And, similarly, talking about includes both forms of talk once it becomes part of a practice of its own, usually sequestered in some respects.) For newcomers then the purpose is not to learn *from* talk as a substitute for legitimate peripheral participation; it is to learn *to* talk as a key to legitimate peripheral participation.

MOTIVATION AND IDENTITY: EFFECTS OF PARTICIPATION

It is important to emphasize that, during the extended period of legitimate participation typical of the cases of apprenticeship described here, newcomers participate in a community of practitioners as well as in productive activity.

Legitimate peripheral participation is an initial form of membership characteristic of such a community. Acceptance by and interaction with acknowledged adept practitioners make learning legitimate and of value from the point of view of the apprentice. More generally, learning in practice, apprentice learners know that there is a field for the mature practice of what they are learning to do—midwifing, tailoring, quartermastering, butchering, or being sober. The community of midwives, tailors, quartermasters, butchers, or nondrinking alcoholics and their productive relations with the world provide apprentices with these continuity-based "futures."

To be able to participate in a legitimately peripheral way entails that newcomers have broad access to arenas of mature practice. At the same time, productive peripherality requires less demands on time, effort, and responsibility for work than for full participants. A newcomer's tasks are short and simple, the costs of errors are small, the apprentice has little responsibility for the activity as a whole. A newcomer's tasks tend to be positioned at the ends of branches of work processes, rather than in the middle of linked work segments. A midwife's apprentice runs errands. Tailors' apprentices do maintenance on the sewing machine before the master begins work, and finishing details when the master has completed a pair of trousers; a lot of time in between is spent sitting beside the master on his two-person bench. For the quartermasters, the earliest jobs are physically at the periphery of the work space. In many cases, distinctions between play and work, or between peripheral activity and other work, are little marked. In all five cases of apprenticeship, however, it is also true that the initial, partial contributions of apprentices are useful. Even the A. A. newcomer, while reinterpreting his or her life, produces new material that contributes to the communal construction of an understanding of alcoholism. An apprentice's contributions to ongoing activity gain value in practice—a value which increases as the apprentice becomes more adept. As opportunities for understanding how well or poorly one's efforts contribute are evident in practice, legitimate participation of a peripheral kind provides an immediate ground for self-evaluation. The sparsity of tests, praise, or blame typical of apprenticeship follows from the apprentice's legitimacy as a participant.

Notions like those of "intrinsic rewards" in empirical studies of apprenticeship focus quite narrowly on task knowledge and skill as the activities to be learned. Such knowledge is of course important; but a deeper sense of the value of participation to the community and the learner lies in *becoming* part of the community. Thus, making a hat reasonably well is seen as evidence that an apprentice tailor is becoming "a masterful practitioner," though it may also be perceived in a more utilitarian vein in terms of reward or even value. Similarly, telling one's life story or making a Twelfth Step call confers a sense of belonging. Moving toward full participation in practice involves not just a greater commitment of time, intensified effort, more and broader responsibilities within the community, and more difficult and risky tasks, but, more significantly, an increasing sense of identity as a master practitioner.

When the process of increasing participation is not the primary motivation for learning, it is often because "didactic caretakers" assume responsibility for motivating newcomers. In such circumstances, the focus of attention shifts from co-participating in practice to acting upon the person-to-be-changed. Such a shift is typical of situations, such as schooling, in which pedagogically structured content organizes learning activities. Overlooking the importance of legitimate participation by newcomers in the target practice has two related consequences. First, the identity of learners becomes an explicit object of change. When central participation is the subjective intention motivating learning, changes in cultural identity and social relations are inevitably part of the process, but learning does not have to be mediated—and distorted—through a learner's view of "self" as *object*. Second, where there is no cultural identity encompassing the activity in which newcomers participate and no field of mature practice for what is being learned, exchange value replaces the use value of increasing participation. The commoditization of learning engenders a fundamental contradiction between the use and exchange values of the outcome of learning, which manifests itself in conflicts between learning to know and learning to display knowledge for evaluation. Testing in schools and trade schools (unnecessary in situations of apprenticeship learning) is perhaps the most pervasive and salient example of a way of establishing the exchange value of knowledge. Test taking then becomes a new parasitic practice, the goal of which is to increase the exchange value of learning independently of it use value.

CONTRADICTIONS AND CHANGE: CONTINUITY AND DISPLACEMENT

To account for the complexity of participation in social practice, it is essential to give learning and teaching independent status as analytic concepts. Primary reliance on the concept of pedagogical structuring in learning research may well prevent speculation about what teaching consists of, how it is perceived, and how—as perceived—it affects learning. Most analyses of schooling assume, whether intentionally or not, the uniform motivation of teacher and pupils, because they assume, sometimes quite explicitly, that teacher and pupils share the goal of the main activity (e.g., Davydov and Markova 1983). In our view, this assumption has several consequences. First, it ignores the conflicting viewpoints associated with teaching and learning, respectively, and obscures the distortions that ensue (Fajans and Turner in preparation). Furthermore, it reflects too narrowly rationalistic a perspective on the person and motivation. The multiple viewpoints that are characteristic of participation in a community of practice, and thus of legitimate peripheral participation, are to be found in more complex theories of the person-in-society, such as those proposed by critical psychologists. Finally, assumptions of uniformity make it difficult to explore the mechanisms by which processes of change and transformation in communities practice and processes of learning are intricately implicated in each other.

In considering learning as part of social practice, we have focused our attention on the structure of social practice rather than privileging the structure of pedagogy as the source of learning. Learning understood as legitimate peripheral participation is not necessarily or directly dependent on pedagogical goals or official agenda, even in situations in which these goals appear to be a central factor (e.g., classroom instruction, tutoring). We have insisted that exposure to resources for learning is not restricted to a teaching curriculum and that instructional assistance is not construed as a purely interpersonal phenomenon; rather we have argued that learning must be understood with respect to a practice as a whole, with its multiplicity of relations—both within the community and with the world at large. Dissociating learning from pedagogical intentions opens the possibility of mismatch or conflict among practitioners' viewpoints in situations where learning is going on. These differences often must become constitutive of the content of learning.

We mentioned earlier that a major contradiction lies between legitimate peripheral participation as the means of achieving continuity over generations for the community of practice, and the displacement inherent in that same process as full participants are replaced (directly or indirectly) by newcomers-become-old-timers. Both Fortes (1938) and Goody (1989) have commented on this conflict between continuity and displacement, which is surely part of all learning. This tension is in fact fundamental—a basic contradiction of social reproduction, transformation, and change. In recent accounts of learning by activity theorists (e.g., Engeström 1987), the major contradiction underlying the historical development of learning is that of the commodity. Certainly this is fundamental to the historical shaping of social reproduction as well as production. But we believe that a second contradiction—that between continuity and displacement—is also fundamental to the social relations of production and to the social reproduction of labor. Studies of learning might benefit from examining the field of relations generated by these interrelated contradictions. For if production and the social reproduction of persons are mutually entailed in the reproduction of the social order, the contradictions inherent in reproducing persons within the domestic group and other communities of practice do not go away when the form of production changes, but go through transformations of their own. How to characterize these contradictions in changing forms of production is surely the central question underlying a historical understanding of forms of learning, family, and of course, schooling.

The continuity-displacement contradiction is present during apprenticeship, whether apprentice and master jointly have a stake in the increasingly knowledgeable skill of the apprentice, as among the tailors and midwives, or whether there is a conflict between the master's desire for labor and the apprentice's desire to learn (see Goody 1982), as among the meat cutters. The different ways in which old-timers and newcomers establish and maintain identities conflict and generate competing viewpoints on the practice and its development. Newcomers are caught in a dilemma. On the one hand, they need to engage in the existing practice, which has developed over time: to understand it, to participate in it, and to become full members of the community in which it exists. On the other hand, they have a stake in its development as they begin to establish their own identity in its future.

We have claimed that the development of identity is central to the careers of newcomers in communities of practice, and thus fundamental to the concept of legitimate peripheral participation. This is illustrated most vividly by the experience of newcomers to A. A., but we think that it is true of all learning. In fact, we have argued that, from the perspective we have developed here, learning and a sense of identity are inseparable: They are aspects of the same phenomenon.

Insofar as the conflicts in which the continuity-displacement contradiction is manifested involve power—as they do to a large extent—the way the contradiction is played out changes as power relations change. Conflicts between masters and apprentices (or, less individualistically, between generations) take place in the course of everyday participation. Shared participation is the stage on which the old and the new, the known and the unknown, the established and the hopeful, act out their differences and discover their commonalities, manifest their fear of one another, and come to terms with their need for one another. Each threatens the fulfillment of the other's destiny, just as it is essential to it. Conflict is experienced and worked out through a shared everyday practice in which differing viewpoints and common stakes are in interplay. Learners can be overwhelmed, overawed, and overworked. Yet even when submissive imitation is the result, learning is never simply a matter of the "transmission" of knowledge or the "acquisition" of skill; identity in relation with practice, and hence knowledge and skill and their significance to the subject and the community, are never unproblematic. This helps to account for the common observation that knowers come in a range of types, from clones to heretics.

Granting legitimate participation to newcomers with their own viewpoints introduces into any community of practice all the tensions of the continuity-displacement contradiction. These may be muted, though not extinguished, by the differences of power between old-timers and newcomers. As a way in which the related conflicts are played out in practice, legitimate peripheral participation is far more than just a process of learning on the part of newcomers. It is a reciprocal relation between persons and practice. This means that the move of learners toward full participation in a community of practice does not take place in a static context. The practice itself is in motion. Since activity and the participation of individuals involved in it, their knowledge, and their perspectives are mutually constitutive, change is a fundamental property of communities of practice and their activities. Goody (1989) argues that the introduction of strangers into what was previously strictly domestic production (a change that occurred within an expanding market in West Africa in the recent past) led masters to think more comprehensively about the organization of their production activities. She points out that the resulting division of work processes into segments to be learned has been mirrored in subsequent generations in new, increasingly specialized occupations. Legitimate peripherality is important for developing "constructively naive" perspectives or questions. From this point of view, inexperience is an asset to be exploited. It is of use, however, only in the context of participation, when supported by experienced practitioners who both understand its limitations and value its role. Legitimacy of participation is crucial both for this naive involvement to invite reflection on ongoing activity and for the newcomer's occasional contributions to be taken into account. Insofar as this continual interaction of new perspectives is sanctioned, everyone's participation is legitimately peripheral in some respect. In other words, everyone can to some degree be considered a "newcomer" to the future of a changing community.

Part IV

Team Level

Chapter 9

From Action Learning to Learning from Action: Implementing the After Action Review

Lloyd Baird, Sandra Deacon and Phil Holland
Boston University School of Management

Change is a forgone conclusion. Technology innovation, the speed of information flow, shifts in demographics, globalization. etc. are all combining to make a crazy world. In fact, to start a discussion or article referring to the extensiveness and pace of change is becoming a cliché. The question is not whether change is happening, but how we respond. Can we learn fast enough to keep up? Can we adapt and respond in new ways rather than rely on old habits? Will our skills shift quickly enough to allow us to perform? Much of what we do in human resource management, leadership development and change management is designed to help people adapt to the new reality and it is good work, but often not fast enough. By the time skills are developed, culture modified, programs implemented or structure redesigned, the world has changed again. We have skills, culture and organizations perfectly designed to meet the needs of the past, but we never catch up with the future. Gordon Sullivan, recently retired Chief of Staff of the U.S. Army refers to this as making the past perfect. We are always behind and always responding to yesterday's problems. The critical issue is how we can learn and adapt fast enough to keep up with and stay ahead of the pace of change.

Consider, for example, the way we typically structure learning and development activities in organizations. Much of what we do assumes that by getting more real issues into the learning process, people are more likely to develop useable skills. We write real cases, focusing on current organization issues. We bring organization problems into the classroom. We adopt action learning programs; convene groups, help them get up to speed on their skills, and give them actual work related assignments. And most recently we go on-line with learning. Learning on demand, so people can ask for help and get input when and where they need it. With all of these efforts, we are trying to "get more performance into the learning process". We identify the skills needed to perform, establish a learning agenda, structure the development experience, and help develop the skills. All this makes a contribution, but often not fast enough or grounded enough in performance to keep up with the pace of change.

If we shift our perspective from "getting more performance into the learning process" to "getting more learning into the performance process", a whole new set of approaches can be added to our arsenal. This new perspective shifts us from action learning to learning from action. Now the issue becomes how to help individuals, groups and organizations learn from their performance. Performing and learning are not sequential or overlapping, but learning is a byproduct of performance. From this perspective, the objective is to get the plan and action steps "roughly right", use the skills you already have, get on with it, and learn as you go. Things change too quickly, so why waste time trying to predict and understand a future that is neither predictable nor understandable until you get there? Take the best guess you can, do the best you can and learn as you go.

One of the best examples of "getting more learning into the performance process" is toddlers learning to walk. They have a rough idea of what they want to do, spend very little time worrying about whether they can or cannot do it, move to action quickly, and learn as they go. They have no concept of failure. Falling simply means they are not walking yet. At no time does the toddler, having fallen to the ground yet again say, "Oh well I did not want to walk anyway, guess I will just stay down here on the ground." No, they just keep trying. But we can learn lessons from kids that go well beyond simply saying you need to stick it out.

First, for sure is their drive to perform. They are relentless. But second is how they learn. They learn as part of performing. They advance from sitting to crawling, and from crawling to taking steps while hanging onto the couch. All learned by trying and failing. They are now ready for the biggest event of their life, walking under their own power. And unlike adults, they have absolutely no problem with the concept that they will have to learn while trying to perform. They learn to walk by failing to walk. And it works the same for us. Learn while performing and apply quickly back into performance.

Third is the speed of their learning cycle. Kids try and fail, they learn, they try again. They can fail faster than any adult, and they get up and try again just as fast. As adults we spend far too much time worrying about whether we are going to fall. And we spend far too much time worrying about what we know. Rather than focusing on falling and knowing, we should focus on doing and learning. What you know does not count until it is applied. A lesson is not learned until behavior changes. Something has to happen. Kids are always involved in mischief because they are always trying out what they learned. Often in ways the adult does not quite understand or appreciate. Their learning cycle is very fast. As we strive to get more learning into our performance process we do have some advantages over children. We can think about what needs to be done and structure a process for learning.

THE CHALLENGE

Analog Devices "designs, manufactures, and markets a broad line of high-performance linear, mixed-signal and digital integrated circuits that address a wide range of real-world signal-processing applications" (1996, Annual Report). They compete in a marketplace that demands constant innovation and the rapid delivery of new products. If they do not learn quickly, they are out of business.

In the Transportation and Industrial Products Division (T & IPD) of the organization, which is responsible for new product development, engineers work with specific customers to design and deliver customized products. Three years ago, as part of a TQM initiative, the product development teams were redesigned and traditional functional groups were replaced by cross-functional product development (PD) teams assigned to a specific customer. Development times were reduced, costs went down and on-time delivery went up. But they had to do better. Too much time and too many resources were being wasted by each group working independently. Not only were they repeating the same mistakes, but they were not learning across teams. One team would do something to improve performance and other teams had no way of finding out what they did except through random conversations in the hall or on the company's intranet.

In the engineering culture, however, people were not interested in improving performance by learning new problem solving skills or developing more team processing capability. These were seen as "touch-feely" and the payoff too slow. The division needed an approach that focused on the task at hand rather than process. They needed to imbed learning into their performance process.

LEARNING FROM ACTION: THE AFTER ACTION REVIEW (AAR)

Curtis Davis, a Product Line Director in T & IPD, adapted the After Action Review from the U.S. Army to capture learning and improve communication within and across teams in his division. The After Action Review (AAR) is a way for a team to reflect on and learn while they are performing. Unlike other project reviews or post mortems, you do not wait until the patient is dead to figure out what went wrong. The objective is to learn as you perform, understand why the interim objectives were or were not accomplished, what happened, what lessons can be learned, and what can be quickly driven back into the performance process.

The few simple guidelines of the AAR imbed learning into performance (See Exhibit 1.) Focus on a few critical performance issues. The purpose is not to do a process debrief or discuss everything. The purpose is to focus on how to improve performance, find a few key factors and get back to performing. The AAR works best if done during the action, or very quickly afterwards. It should be a structured approach that involves a whole group or unit. Multiple

> **Exhibit 1**
> **An After Action Review works best if it is:**
>
> 1. *Focused* on the few critical issues
> 2. Done *immediately* after the action
> 3. *Inclusive* of the whole group
> 4. In accordance with a *structured* process
> 5. Leading *back to action* quickly

BOX 9.1

perspectives are included and a structured process is followed. And lastly, it works if learning can be captured and quickly moved back to action.

WHAT LEARNING FROM ACTION IS NOT

To understand an AAR, it also helps to understand what learning from action is not. First, it is not about fixing individual blame. Who did or did not do what they were supposed to. It does not grade the success or failure of an individual or a team. Instead, it is about learning how to improve the work process. As such, it cannot occur in an environment of fear and retribution. People must believe what they say will be used to drive improvement, not to punish.

Second, Learning from Action is not a replacement for other formal processes like quality management's Plan-Do-Check-Act. Both are about analysis, action and better results. The focus of a quality management process is to solve a given problem, to close a known gap between what is desired and what exists today. In contrast, the focus of Learning from Action is on recent action, whether successful or not. In fact, a group could engage in learning, for example, on how well it executed a quality management process. Finally, Learning from Action is not about discussion at the expense of action. Instead, it is *about* action: taking better future action by learning from current action. Members of large organizations, for example, often observe that one of their weaknesses is their inability to get to action after analysis and drive for results. Learning from Action should be a way to become more action-oriented, not a way to do more analysis.

THE AFTER ACTION REVIEW: A PROCESS OF LEARNING AS YOU GO

The After Action Review (see Exhibit 2 for guidelines on conducting an AAR), adapted from the United States Army where it has been in practice for a number of years, is a structured process for learning as you go.

**Exhibit 2
Conducting an AAR**

Who:
The AAR should involve all those who were the closest to the action, regardless of level. The goal is to gain all the needed perspectives, for both learning and action.

What:
You need not conduct an AAR after every event or action. Select those you can learn most from or where improvement would be most valuable.

When:
Conduct the AAR as soon after as possible, when memories are fresh.

Where:
Hold your AAR anywhere that promotes openness and learning: a conference room, meeting facility, or a place that is significant to a review of the events, such as where the action happened. Don't, however, let the choice of a location unduly delay you. The key is to do the AAR as close to the action in time and space as possible.

Why:
Again, the purpose of the AAR is to promote learning while the experience is fresh, and most importantly, to lead quickly to improved action.

How long:
A good AAR can be brief; less than an hour. Fifteen minutes is better, but enough time should be available to promote a full discussion and get the team to the next action step.

BOX 9.2

Step 1: What was the intent?
The first step of an AAR is to review what the intent was when the action began. What was the purpose of the action? What were you trying to accomplish? How was it to be accomplished? For example: Was the purpose of the meeting to communicate a certain message? Was the action an attempt to implement a faster business process?

Step 2: What happened?
What exactly happened? Why? How? What were the results? Recalling accurately what happened is usually difficult, but nevertheless essential if the team is to draw the right lessons and take better action in the future. This is why it is important to conduct AARs soon after the action and why multiple perspectives are valuable. For example: What was said to Jones prior to the product's being shipped? Who was involved in the design process? This is a

step for "getting out the facts," not in order to blame anyone, but to understand the steps taken by the team as it tried to achieve its intent.

There are two approaches that can be taken during the "what happened" discussion. The first is to ask members to reconstruct events chronologically. "First we did this, then that," and so on. The second is to ask the members to recall what they saw as key events. Events that they think are important to analyze further. "The reorganization was announced," or "the equipment arrived," might be examples. Either can achieve the same end: constructing a picture of what happened that the team agrees is valid.

Step 3: What have we learned?
Based on what we tried to do and what actually happened, what did we learn? What do we now know that we did not know before we started? What focused lessons have we learned? If someone else were to start down the same path, what advice would we give this person?

Step 4: What do we do now?
Based on what we know now, what should we do? Because the focus of an AAR is on action, and especially action that can be applied quickly to accelerate progress, it is important to think of action implications as occurring along three different "horizons:" short-term, mid-term and long-term. Thinking of what can be done in all three time horizons helps a team avoid the trap of just implementing actions that take a long time to produce benefits.

Short-term actions are those that can be taken quickly and will have immediate benefits. For example, making a phone call, stopping an activity, making an expenditure.

Mid-term actions are those that affect systems, policies, practices, and the organization. For example, implementing a bonus system, hiring people with new skills, starting up a learning network.

Long-term actions are those related to basic strategies, goals and values. For example, developing a better shared understanding of what "innovation" means, promoting better listening skills, redefining a strategic intent.

Step 5: Take action.
Lessons are of no use unless applied. A lesson is not learned until something changes.

Step 6: Tell someone else.
Who else needs to know what you have learned? What do they need to know? How are you going to tell them? Leverage what you know to other units and throughout the organization.

Leading an AAR

The leader's job is to promote focused, open, provocative, safe, reality-oriented exchange among the team so that in an AAR genuine learning can take place. The job is not to *have* the answers, but to facilitate a good discussion.

Follow the rule of objectivity. Because much of the AAR is about recreating the reality of events and getting out the facts, it is important that the team be objective. Jumping too quickly to what a given person thinks was "really going on," what so-and-so was "really up to" will only lead to misdiagnosis, misunderstanding and ineffective action. Likewise, you should try to stay away from referring to one's intent or purpose. The rule of objectivity, like Sergeant Joe Friday of the old Dragnet television series, asks AAR participants to give "Just the facts, ma'am."

What does it mean to give just the facts? It means sticking to descriptions of what could be observed, where what could be observed becomes primarily what individuals either *said* or *did*. For example, "John called me and told me that the new contract was signed."

Balance inquiry and advocacy. Because an AAR is about discovering the "why" behind what happened, the cause and effect relationships involved, and about planning effective actions, it is important that participants take care to understand each other and to feel comfortable that each has grasped what was said rather than talking past each other.

Balancing inquiry and advocacy asks us to focus less on advocating our own views and more on understanding others' views through inquiry. To engage in inquiry is to actively seek further understanding of another person's position. It requires one to probe, restate positions, and seek clarification. "So you're saying that . . .?" or "I understand your conclusion that there is a lot of red tape around; could you say more about how you think this caused our problem?" or "Can you give an example of what you mean?" are all examples of engaging in inquiry.

Climb the ladder of inference.

The *bottom* rung represents our experience at the level of direct observation. It is the raw material from which our conclusions come. People said things; people did things; these actions were followed by further words and deeds. This rung of the ladder represents our experience as a videotape recorder might capture it or as we might discuss it when we're practicing the rule of objectivity.

We don't focus on every detail of our experience. Instead we select what we think is relevant. Selecting, consolidating, and validating are on the second rung of the ladder.

Next, we compare our current and past experience. The next two rungs of the ladder represent this process: we apply our understanding from past experience to

BOX 9.3

our new experience, and in the process make assumptions about how to explain what we saw or heard.

At this point we reach the rung on the ladder that represents our final conclusions, which is followed by action. We arrive at a conclusion that represents a complex process of making inferences from directly observable data. Thus: the "ladder of inference."

What does this all have to do with learning from action? The purpose of the AAR is to arrive at a shared understanding not only of what happened in a given situation, but why it happened and what could be done differently next time. Shared understanding requires that we not only know what others have concluded, but why. What we their assumptions, past experiences, and biases for action? If we do not help others see how we got from what we observed to what we concluded, then however much we may not want, we will most likely, once again, simply contribute to a process of "talking past" one another.

Ready, fire, aim, aim, aim. The bias for action mentioned above is captured in the operating principle of "ready, fire, aim, aim, aim." Like the "smart-bomb" that fires and adjusts as it moves toward its target, the action too can begin, after a reasonable but not over-long analysis, and readjust as you move ahead. You plan, certainly; but we don't have to dot every "I" and cross every "t" before taking a step. The team can take action, learn from the results, correct, share with others, and stay in action until it achieves its goals.

BOX 9.3 *Continued*

IMPLEMENTING THE AAR

The product development teams at Analog integrated the AARs into their work activity at four different levels.

1. AAR and Product Development Teams: Adding Value within Teams

At any given point in time, each PD team is working on one project with many interrelated tasks, and weekly meetings are held to track progress on these various projects. Prior to the introduction of the AAR, the teams functioned more like a group of individuals than an interdependent team. Each week the team leader would struggle to get his/her members to quantify their progress and current status on the project. During the discussion, members would pay attention only when it was immediately relevant to them. Otherwise, they would drift off, attend to their individual business, etc.

The AAR was seen as a potential means of reducing redundancy, quantifying performance, and improving communication at the weekly team meetings. The AAR was introduced to one PD team using a facilitator who would capture the discussions on a flip chart. This format, while effective in illustrating the usefulness of the AAR process, proved to be extremely slow. This prompted the *team* to decide to implement a different format. On a weekly basis, each member would prepare a one-page overhead using the steps of the AAR to summarize their performance and progress. Then when they came together they were prepared to go through the steps much quicker and to quickly start talking about common issues.

The AAR has proven to be an extremely useful tool for tracking performance, and it has subsequently been adopted by the other PD teams. Of note here is that the successful implementation of the tool was the result of the team's decision to change the format. According to the team's facilitator, the team would have categorically rejected the idea if it had come from either the team leader or facilitator. It was still viewed as too "touchy feely."

Team leaders report that the AAR process adds value to the team; team meetings are more focused, time management is better, member participation has increased, more information is being shared, and the interdependencies among the team members are being illuminated and understood (e.g. "If you did X with your part, I need to do Y now.") Furthermore, the process of listing "just the facts" frequently gives people a different perspective on a problem; this helps to clarify differences and resolve conflicts more easily.

Chrysler is another corporation attempting to use the AAR process in their product development area. At critical points in the product development process the team stops and does an analysis of what they have accomplished and the lessons learned. They have found that there is substantial value to learning as you go and the real payoff comes when they apply their lessons learned back into their own work and aggressively share with others doing comparable work.

2. AAR and Semi-Quarterly Business Review (SQBR): Adding Value Across Teams

The same one-page AAR format is also used at the six-week Semi-Quarterly Business Review (SQBR). These meetings are attended by the team leaders of the various PD teams and the Product Line Director. Using the AAR, team leaders review the objectives and summarize the status of their projects. They also discuss any problems that their team encountered, the lessons learned, and the ways in which these problems were resolved. In this case, the AAR goes beyond tracking the performance of each team to learning across teams. The AAR provides the teams with a common language, format, and means of sharing and documenting lessons learned. What one teams learns can quickly be assessed and adapted by other teams.

Exhibit 3 illustrates the format used by the PD teams at Analog. Included on the chart is a compilation of various general examples taken from one SQBR meeting illustrating how AAR can be used to keep the process focused and communicate across business unit.

Exhibit 3
The Semi-Quarterly Business Review (AAR)

Step 1	Step 2			Step 3	Step 4/5	Step 6
Intent	What happened? Why?			Lessons Learned	Action	Disseminating
Objective	What happened?	Why did this happen?	What are the implications?	What are the lessons learned?	Who, what, and when?	Who needs to know?
Start correlation and Final Test board	Not started	Unrealistic estimate by team leader of time required for debugging	Unmet expectations	Get buy-in from team members for schedule estimates	Jack and Sue to update schedule for Test Dev . by . . . Jack and Sue to "start" correlation of Final Test board by next SQBR	Team leader
Complete debug of xyz board	Completed on schedule	John worked lots of overtime	Stress. Any unplanned problems would have pushed out schedule since we were already working max. hours. No buffer	Should have allowed more time in schedule to complete this task.	Review all trims to accommo-date package paristics	Schedule builders
Release trim	Trim not released	Sam T. is multiplexed between too many tasks and projects	Sam will continue to run produc-tion trim for #1 if trim is not released. Sam will not focus on #1 if he contin-ues to be distracted by other projects.	Release of program is jeopardized without focused resources	Release #1 trim by 2/1/98	Sponsors; Team leaders; Sam's manager
Deliver fully functional units in June 1998 to cus-tomer	Package cracks identified during engineering look-ahead	Assembly engineer performed tests prior to package qual.	Package being redesigned	Perform engineering look-ahead tests on new packages	Results of package redesign due late May by Assembly Engineer	Other team leaders

3. AAR and the Customer: Adding Value to the Customer Relationship

The AAR was also introduced by a PD team as a means of building more successful customer relationships. A Japanese customer came on site at Analog for a week to review the product design. At the conclusion of the weeklong visit, the team conducted a formal AAR with the customer with the explicit objective of reviewing the design issues and building a better relationship with the customer. In addition to surfacing some key design issues, this two-hour discussion served to illuminate some critical trust and communication deficiencies. As a result, the action steps focused on clarifying issues such as how to communicate with each other, where documents would be stored so that people could access relevant data, as well as on specific design issues. The final result of this AAR was to significantly increase the level of trust between the customer and the PD team. The customer was so impressed with the AAR that he wrote down the format so that he could take it with him back to Japan.

4. AAR and Improving the Product Development Process: Adding Value Across Divisions

A common product development process is used across divisions. The AAR became the way of capturing, showing, and driving improvement into the product development process itself. Analog has a formal review of each product four quarters after it has been released into production. The team does as AAR to identify the key issues and problems. They make recommendations, which are fed across divisions to other product development teams. The results from the multiple teams are then consolidated to make changes in the product development process itself.

British Petroleum has had similar experiences with the AAR in all four of these areas. BP was attracted to the AAR by the quickness with which it can be done and its direct relationships to the performance activity. They began by embedding the AAR in their meeting process to drive the effectiveness of drilling teams. British Petroleum then uses their video conferencing capability to disseminate the results of AARs throughout the organization and across the many functions needed to support drilling operations. This way the whole organization can learn rather than limiting payoff to one team. Next they began using the AAR process in Japan to build retail sites. Learning captured when one site is completed is quickly passed to the next one to be built, shortening production time and reducing costs. In Vietnam and other countries they are using it as a way to evaluate and improve customer and government relations. Some customers have been so impressed with the results that they have begun using the AAR process also.

THE PAYOFFS

The U.S. Army has the most experience with the After Action Review, having done them for ten years. Everyone is used to taking time quickly out of action to do a "hot wash" which happens in the action or a "cold wash" after the action is completed. For the Army, the payoff comes when insights are discovered and immediately moved back to action. For example, when the troops went into Haiti, AARs help them learn as they deployed and adjust to an ambiguous and new situation. This was the first time Army troops were deployed off of a Navy aircraft carrier and it was unclear if it was to be a peace keeping or a combat mission. As the 82nd Airborne and the 10th Mountain Division arrived in Haiti, units generated lessons learned using After Action Reviews. As would be expected, each unit began to learn and improve from its own perspective, based on its own experiences. But when efforts were consolidated, higher level solutions also began to emerge. One unit, for example, located on the aircraft carrier Eisenhower discovered an immediate problem. The hallways and stairs of an aircraft carrier are designed for efficient and quick movement of Navy personnel. Army personnel with 80 lb. packs can not easily go up and down the stairs, and it is impossible to pass in the hallways. The challenge, how to quickly move 3,000 troops from lower to higher decks. The solution developed in an AAR; use the large elevators designed to raise the aircraft to the upper decks to transport the troops and their gear.

Another unit discovered a shortage of water. The soldiers' water consumption was much higher than expected because of heat and humidity. The need for drinkable water increased dramatically. The AAR developed solutions that called for supply lines to be opened and units responsible for supplying drinkable water moved up quickly. Another unit looked at its supply of intravenous medical equipment and projected a shortage. The heat and humidity were causing dehydration problems. More soldiers than expected were passing out and needed IVs. The standard medical supply issue brought in by the troops needed to be modified. Solutions to these problems provided valuable lessons at the local level and improved operational efficiency.

As the lessons learned and their solutions were being fed to the Center for Army Lessons Learned, analysts examined all the units together and came to the conclusion that all three had related issues. The soldiers, carrying 80 lbs of equipment in high temperature and humidity, were losing more body fluid than normal. The suggested solution, have soldiers reduce what they carried to the bare essentials for a peacekeeping operation. This might reduce the physical exertion enough to prevent soldiers from perspiring so heavily, cutting down the loss of body fluid and therefore minimizing the need for so much water and IV. To test the principle, one unit was directed to reduce its carrying load. The test was successful. The command went out to all units to minimize pack loads.

Not only did the knowledge acquired by this solution have immediate effects, but it was also passed on to follow-on units that deployed to Haiti. Similar lessons collected during disaster assistance in the aftermath of Hurricane

Andrew in Florida, Somalia, Rwanda, and Bosnia have also been disseminated by CALL and archived for future peacekeeping operations. The AAR has proved to be an invaluable tool in assessing issues that have an impact on the ability of U.S. Army forces to complete their missions.

GTE is applying the same concepts in their management and executive development programs. In the programs managers learn how to and actually do AARs that capture learning from experience. These are consolidated and integrated into a knowledge base that is available throughout the corporation. Knowledge developed in one area has an impact on many.

Based on these experiences we can identify four reasons for pay off.

Structured, Purposeful Dialogue

When a structured process for learning is used, you are guided through a review of intent, what happened, lessons learned, and then into action. Following the proper steps ensures that the discussion progresses and is focused. The structure guides participants through a discussion toward a clear and valuable end.

Breaking Hierarchical Barriers

By emphasizing multiple perspectives, learning from action promotes an environment in which what is said becomes more important than who said it. Everyone's input is valued. While no formal process can guarantee this mind set, a structured process can promote it. The formal leader becomes facilitator, thus further breaking down hierarchical barriers. His or her role is not to give answers or decide content, but to promote an effective, productive discussion that leads to valuable learning lessons.

Reflection Close to Action

The skill of reflecting on one's actions may be the most important skill for any manager or leader. Through reflection we come to understand ourselves better, as well as others and our business. From this understanding comes continuous improvement. Experience and action are continuous teachers, but only for those who are able and willing to use them. AARs promote reflection by offering a formal process to practice it. Widespread use of AARs will encourage us to learn and reflect as a matter course.

Recorded Lessons

One of the last steps is to record what has been learned from analysis. Recording lessons has a number of important benefits. First, the act of writing down both lessons and action plans prompts us to clarify our thinking, condense our words, and weed out ambiguity in our conclusions. Second, recording lessons helps to retain them. They endure as a reference and are not easily forgotten. Lessons lost are typically those not written down. Finally, recorded lessons are easier to share with others. People across the business can benefit from what one team has done. Sharing learning in this way will accelerate the rate of organizational improvement.

WHEN THINGS DON'T GO WELL

Drawing from the experiences across these and other organizations, we can identify three potential explanations if you do not get payoff.

1. Improper Use of the AAR: A One-Person Show

The AAR was used by one particular team leader as a vehicle for lecturing his team about what he saw as the problems they were facing. Instead of engaging everyone who had been involved in the action in an AAR, he came to the meeting with his own perspective and agenda and made a presentation to the team. Since then his team was very reluctant to engage in future AARs. Such an example highlights the importance of having the entire team *participate* in the discussion, working together to discover what happened and why. Team leaders who have used the tool successfully have found that the insight gained from the multiple perspectives is one of the biggest advantages of the AAR.

2. The Wrong Motive: AAR Used to Punish

In a second example, the AAR was used inappropriately to control and punish a team member whose performance was not meeting the team's expectations. Since the team was experiencing some difficulties, the Team Facilitator suggested that all team members prepare in advance for an AAR by writing out their own, one-page mini-AAR on their performance. When the team gathered for the AAR, the Team Leader opted to have the questionable performer present. Rather than using this opportunity to conduct an AAR discussion with all team members, the Team Leader used the tool to criticize and punish one member. Following this, the other team members balked. Viewing it as a form of punishment and control, they refused to present their own mini-reviews, calling it "micromanagement." Not surprisingly, this team has a very negative view of the AAR.

3. Not Moving to Action

Another team kept doing the AAR correctly but nothing ever happened. It would come to conclusions that were not implemented. Next time the team came together, not surprisingly members were not willing to spend much real energy in reviewing what they had learned during the last phase of the product development process.

SOME CONCLUDING THOUGHTS

Few managers today would argue with the value of learning from action. The After Action Review is a one tool useful for getting "more learning into the performance process". Its payoff comes from two main sources: much of today's work is done in teams, and one of the greatest sources of learning is learning from experience—both consistent with the purpose and method of AAR. The payoffs are immediate and cost nothing to implement. Combined with action learning tools already available, learning and performance become even more tightly integrated. Consider the following:

- The process of listing facts, rather than opinions, helps clarify problems
- The non-blaming approach allows for new perspectives to emerge
- Many and varied perspectives on a problem lead to new learning
- It provides a common language for addressing performance and learning needs
- It helps to build customer relationships
- The lessons learned from other teams saves both time and effort by reducing repetitive errors

Providing a clear structure, After Action Reviews guide an effective learning process, all the way to action. However, they also promote better dialogue and constructive conflict. This way, AARs have a dual purpose: to achieve immediate results while building the capability to achieve even better results in the future.

BIOGRAPHICAL STATEMENTS

Lloyd Baird

Dr. Baird served for eight years as Executive Director of the Leadership Institute which he helped found at Boston University. He is currently a principal at the Systems Research Center focusing on learning and knowledge management. In addition, Dr. Baird is a Professor of Management at Boston University.

Working with many corporations he has been able to do a full analysis of the Corporation and help them understand the risks and the potential of corporate wide learning initiatives. For other leading corporations he has analyzed corporate strategy and culture, developed learning initiatives to bring corporate culture into alignment and worked directly with top executives to help them understand organizational transformation. He is currently helping firms assess and manage their knowledge capabilities. With all of these projects the objective is to improve organizational performance.

In addition to his work with firms, Dr. Baird is active directing and managing several consortia of corporations. He is a partner of the Center for Enterprise Leadership, a collection of twenty-five corporations which jointly sponsor consulting and research. He also serves as Director of Research for the Executive Development Roundtable and is a Faculty Partner of the Human Resources Policy Institute. Each brings together top executives from leading national and international corporations collaborating to lead their own firms. His is author of numerous books and articles on the topics of human resource management and executive development.

He received his B.S. degree from Utah State University and his M.B.A. and Ph.D. from Michigan State University.

Philip Holland

Philip Holland is a principal at The Center for Executive Development, Cambridge, Massachusetts. He holds a bachelor's degree in Industrial Engineering from Stanford University and a master's degree in Public Administration from Harvard University, and has authored many case studies and notes for the Graduate School of Business at Harvard. Two of his case studies have been reprinted in Todd Jick, *Managing Change: Cases and Concepts* (1993). Prior to his graduate studies he was an engineering manager at IBM. His research focus has been in the areas of corporate culture, leadership and organizational learning. For ten years he was worked with leading corporations around the world, including Lucent Technologies, Chrysler, Johnson and Johnson, ARCO and Merrill Lynch, on how companies can use education processes as a force for change.

Sandra Deacon

Sandra Deacon has a Ph.D. from Northeastern University in Counseling Psychology, an M.Ed. from Boston University in Counseling, and a B.A. from Amherst College. She is a faculty member at Boston University's School of Management where she teaches in the undergraduate program. She is also the Team Consultant for the undergraduate program at Boston University's Center for Team Learning, and has been involved with several Executive Education programs. As Team Consultant she works with faculty who use team learning across the curriculum, provides course support, and consults with student teams on a variety of team-related issues. Her research interests include team and organizational learning, knowledge management, and team dynamics. In addition to her work at Boston University, Sandi is a licensed psychologist and has several years of experience in the healthcare industry. As a management consultant, she provides leadership and team development training, executive coaching, and team process consultation.

SELECTED BIBLIOGRAPHY

For an extensive overview of the field of knowledge management and learning see *Knowledge and Knowledge Management in Organizations* by Rob Cross (Systems Research Center, Boston University, 1998). Ikujiro Nonaka and Hirotaka Takeuchi have written the best description of knowledge management in corporations (see Nonaka, I. & Takeuchi, H., *The Knowledge-Creating Company*, Oxford University Press, 1995). For a review of knowledge creation and knowledge transfer see Tom Davenport and Larry Prusak's book on *Working Knowledge* (Harvard University Press, Boston, Mass, 1997).

The best source for a thorough description of the After Action Review is the Army's manual "A Leader's Guide to After-Action Reviews" (TC-25-20). The manual is most easily available through the Center for Army Lessons Learned (CALL) web site at *HTTP://CALL.ARMY.MIL.CALL.HTML* under the category of training products. For a full description of how CALL uses the After Action Review and other techniques to get learning into the performance process see Lloyd Baird, John Henderson, and Stephanie Watts article "Learning From Action: An Analysis of the Center for Army Lessons Learned (CALL)" (*Human Resource Management*, Winter 1997, pp. 385–395). CALL's use of AARs are also described in Thomas Ricks article "Army Devises System to decide What Does and Does Not Work" (*Wall Street Journal*, 5/23/97).

The skills needed to learn from action are best described in Peter Senge's seminal work *The Fifth Discipline* (Doubleday, New York, 1990) and Chris Argyris's article of learning "Education for Leading-Learning" (*Organizational Dynamics*, Summer, 1992). The leadership skills required are described by Richard Pascale, Mark Milleman, and Linda Gioja's article "Changing the Way We Change" (*Harvard Business Review*, November/December 1997).

EXECUTIVE SUMMARY

Change is a forgone conclusion. The question is can we keep up. Can we change our skills and ways of working fast enough to stay ahead of the pace of change? Most of our techniques and processes are devoted to "getting more performance into the learning process". We write real cases, we bring organizational issues into the classroom and adopt action learning processes. All good but often not fast enough. Our challenge is how to "get more learning into the performance process". How can we get people to learn as they go, rather than needing to structure separate learning activities? If learning becomes an integral part of employees' ongoing responsibilities on the job and directly linked to improving performance we will have removed many barriers to getting employees to learn and change quickly. The After Action Review developed and used for the past ten years by the U.S. Army is a proven process for moving from action learning to learning from action. More and more corporations are using it to drive not only learning but performance. It is simple, easily done and directly related to performance. After an event a team need only ask themselves, What was our intent? What actually happen? What have we learned? What do we do now? And who else should we tell? The learning captured is then driven directly back into action. The more people do After Action Reviews the more learning becomes a natural part of the performance process and the quicker lessons learned are driven back into higher levels of performance.

Chapter 10

Learning from Mistakes is Easier Said Than Done: Group and Organizational Influences on the Detection and Correction of Human Error[*]

Amy C. Edmondson[**]
Harvard University

This research explores how group-and organizational-level factors affect errors in administering drugs to hospitalized patients. Findings from patient care groups in two hospitals show systematic differences not just in the frequency of errors, but also in the likelihood that errors will be detected and learned from by group members. Implications for learning in and by work teams in general are discussed.

[*] Reprinted by permission.
[**] *This project was funded by the Agency for Health Care Policy and Research as part of the Prevention of Drug Related Complications Study at the Harvard School of Public Health. The author benefited from the support and advice of Lucien Leape, David Bates, and David Cullen (the three principal investigators of the study), and two other members of the project team, Kathy Porter and Martha Vander Vliet. Andy Molinsky contributed enormously to this article by conducting much of the qualitative research. Clayton Alderfer and two anonymous reviewers provided many helpful suggestions that greatly improved the final version of this article. Finally, I am indebted to Richard Hackman who provided invaluable advice and feedback at each stage of this research.*

Amy C. Edmondson is a doctoral candidate in the joint program in organizational behavior at the Harvard Business School and Department of Psychology. Her current research explores issues related to organizational learning and work team effectiveness.

The evening nurse reported for work at 3 p.m. in the surgical intensive care unit of University Hospital[1] and began her first round. Checking on a patient admitted to the unit more than 24 hours earlier after a successful cardiac operation, she noticed that the bag of medication hanging upside-down in the intravenous drip was not heparin—a clot-preventing blood thinner routinely administered after heart surgery—but was instead lidocaine. Lidocaine, an anesthetic and heart rhythm stabilizer, is not likely to harm a patient for whom it is not prescribed; however, the absence of heparin might have been fatal. Fortunately the patient suffered no ill effects from the error in this case, which subsequently was investigated by the author as part of a larger interdisciplinary study seeking to understand causes of these kinds of errors in hospitals.[2]

The average hospitalized patient receives 10 to 20 doses of medication each day and stays for 5 or 6 days (Leape et al., 1991), thus risking exposure to errors such as this about 85 times. Bates, Boyle, Vander Vliet, Schneider, and Leape (1995) recently found an average of 1.4 *medication errors* per patient per hospital stay, with 0.9% of these errors ultimately leading to serious drug complications. In an earlier population study, 0.35% of 80,000 patients in New York State Hospitals suffered "a disabling injury" caused by medications during hospitalization (Leape et al., 1991). These different frequencies—0.35% to 140%—reflect a range of drug error phenomena, from infrequent but disabling injuries to less consequential but far more frequent errors in medication dosage or timing. One fact is clear: Mistakes in administering drugs in hospitals occur and some patients are harmed by these errors.

Patient injuries related to drugs are called adverse drug events, or ADEs. ADEs are classified here as either *preventable* (the result of human error) or *nonpreventable* (not involving human error, as in an unpredictable allergic reaction) (Leape et al., 1991). The present study explores underlying causes of preventable errors in drug administration. As these errors occur in organizational contexts, this study examined organizational and group influences on the process of administering drugs to patients, toward a goal of supplementing existing research that has focused on classifying types of errors and identifying which individuals or professions are more likely to make them.

The Heparin Event

To illustrate how organizational systems affect error rates, consider further the heparin case. First, we might ask who was responsible for this

---

[1] This study involved two urban tertiary care hospitals; University Hospital and Memorial Hospital are pseudonyms.

[2] The Prevention of Drug Complications Study at the Harvard School of Public Health was funded by the Agency for Health Care Policy and Research. Physicians, nurses, and social psychologists collaborated to explore the phenomenon of drug errors from diverse perspectives.

life-threatening mistake. The answer is not completely straightforward. Between the point at which the operating surgeon prescribed the routine administration of heparin and the evening nurse discovered the error, no fewer than six health care professionals were responsible for the patient's care. The perfusionist, a medical technician in the operating room, hung the wrong bag in the intravenous drip. In an interview with the author, he claimed to have pulled the bag off the shelf where heparin belongs, and he noted that the bags look alike. (Did pharmacy mistakenly stock lidocaine where heparin should be? Perhaps, but should not the perfusionist have checked the bag carefully without assuming it to be heparin?)

An anesthesiologist wheeled the patient to the surgical intensive care unit and failed to notice the error. Then, another nurse, on duty the afternoon the patient arrived in the intensive care unit, was responsible for checking medications. How could she have missed the perfusionist's mistake? Easily, according to cognitive psychologists. The human tendency to perceive what one expects to see rather than what is actually there is a well-documented psychological phenomenon (Norman, 1980, 1981; Reason, 1984; Rumelhart, 1980). A heparin bag hanging by the bedside of postcardiac surgery patients is utterly routine—making it all too easy for caregivers to assume the presence of heparin and miss the error. This nurse was replaced by another at 11 p.m., and another at 7 a.m. the next morning. All of them could have detected the mistake before the next evening nurse with whom this episode opened came on duty.

Had the patient experienced an adverse drug event, it would have been technically difficult to assign blame to one person, for it was in the job descriptions of several individuals to avoid and to check for such errors. Drug administration is a collective undertaking—inviting the question of whether drug error rates can be explained as a function of group or hospital unit properties, rather than focusing exclusively on individual characteristics such as ignorance, fatigue, or carelessness. Moreover, in terms of preventing ADEs, individual errors cannot ever be completely eliminated. Indeed, even when everything "goes right" in the hospital setting, errors undoubtedly have occurred without notice or consequence. When an ADE caused by human error is documented, that error is likely to have involved multiple errors—such as the repeated errors of failing to detect and correct the discrepancy, as described above. Secondary errors of not noticing are as critical as primary errors that start a potentially harmful chain of events.

In summary, the system of drug administration in a modern hospital is complex, involving multiple handoffs in the journey from physician decision making all the way through to the receipt of a medication by a patient. Bates, Leape, and Petrycki (1993) have identified 10 points at which an error can occur (or be caught): (a) physician prescription, (b) initial delivery to a unit secretary who (c) transcribes the order, which then (d) must be picked up by a nurse who (e) verifies and transcribes again and (f) hands off to the pharmacist who (g) dispenses the medication and (h) sends it back to a nurse who (i) administers to a patient who (j) receives the drug. The present study explores organizational influences on the execution of these loosely coupled tasks, all of which take place within the context of hospital patient care "units." In the next section, I review approaches to understanding errors and accidents in organizations at three levels of analysis, to set a context for the design of the present study.

THE SOCIAL PSYCHOLOGY OF ERRORS AND ACCIDENTS

Medical researchers, psychologists, and organizational theorists have conceptualized errors and accidents in at least two different ways, and their research has investigated both the causes of errors and the efficacy of preventive strategies. One approach focuses on the individual and the other on the role of the system in which individuals operate in inducing or preventing accidents. A third perspective, proposed here, integrates system and individual levels of analysis by focusing on the work group as the point where organizational and cognitive effects meet and play out in enabling or preventing errors.

Individual-Level Analysis

In general, medical researchers have tended to emphasize the role of individual caregivers in studies of errors, and to blame physiological or educational deficits for adverse events (e.g., Lesar et al., 1990; Melmon, 1971). Many studies have been conducted to detect the frequency of errors among hospitalized patients and to identify responsible individuals. For example, physicians have been identified as more often responsible for such mistakes than nurses, pharmacists, or other personnel (Bates et al., 1993). Suggested strategies for prevention include individual-focused devices such as computerized order entry to prevent errors caused by poor handwriting and physician remedial education (Classen, Pestotnik, Evans, & Burke, 1991; Cohen, 1977; Massaro, 1992).

Psychologists have offered both cognitive and affective explanations for human error. According to schema theory, perceivers' expectations, or frames, have the power to steer attention away from actual visual data, enabling perceptual processes to construct images consistent with expectations (Rumelhart, 1980). If we see what we expect to see, we can make mistakes such as administering lidocaine instead of heparin. Similarly, well-learned activities can be carried out without conscious attention, allowing us to make odd slips such as putting a cereal box in the refrigerator (Norman, 1981; Reason, 1984). This automatic quality is indeed present in some drug errors; "I wasn't thinking" or "I can do [a particular task] in my sleep" are frequent phrases used by nurses interviewed, describing how an obviously wrong medication was given or not noticed. Such cognitive explanations for error have no need for Freud's "hidden impulses" to generate "slips" (Goleman, 1985); however, the unconscious effects of emotions such as anger or anxiety also can induce error, by distracting people's attention from the task at hand. Although the current social psychological literature emphasizes cognitive explanations for human behavior (Fiske &

Taylor, 1991), in examining group-level influences below, we reconsider the role of emotions.

System-Level Analysis

Certain sociologists and organizational theorists have focused on the properties of *systems* in understanding error (e.g., Perrow, 1984). Rather than trying to explain why slips are made by individuals, this approach examines the design of systems and how systems give rise to human error. The nature of the system both influences the actions of individual operators and determines the consequences of errors. Perrow (1984) describes a "normal accident" as a predictable consequence of a system that has both interactive complexity and tight coupling. *Interactive complexity* is characterized by irreversible processes and multiple, nonlinear feedback loops. Interactively complex systems thus involve hidden interactions; the consequences of one's actions cannot be seen (Perrow, 1984). Giving a patient the wrong medication has this quality; immediate feedback is typically not present. *Tightly coupled* systems have little slack; actions in one part of the system directly and immediately affect other parts. The system of drug administration to hospitalized patients offers considerable interactive complexity; however, because the procedures linking medications to patients are loosely coupled, failures in a part of the system can be caught and corrected without causing harm. Although the modern hospital thus does not fit Perrow's worst case scenario, the interactive complexity of medications does create considerable potential risk for patients.

In Perrow's model, individual human error is taken as a given; the critical question is, under what conditions is the ever-present potential for human error dangerous? When do simple slips trigger an irreversible chain of events—by virtue of properties of the system—that ends in disaster? He challenges "the ready explanation of operator error" (Perrow, 1984, p. 26) and proposes that certain systems are accidents waiting to happen.

Just as the design of a system can invite accidents, straightforward solutions—implemented to prevent specific kinds of errors that have occurred in the past—can lead to unintended negative consequences. Organizational systems tend to resist straightforward solutions to problems (Forrester, 1971). When only the superficial symptoms of complex problems are addressed, the underlying problem typically remains unsolved, and even can be exacerbated if the solution feeds into a vicious cycle (such as providing food as direct aid, which relieves starvation but perpetuates the problem of population growth in inhospitable climates; Senge, 1990). This perspective suggests that strategies such as remedial education of physicians who have written incorrect prescriptions in the past, or use of warning stickers to remind caregivers of allergies, may have limited effectiveness in preventing drug errors, as they fail to consider the nature of the system that consists of many individuals and technical systems interacting in administering drugs to patients.

Organizational systems also transmit broader social forces that affect attitudes and behaviors related to error—including social forces that preclude "embracing error" (Michael, 1976) and thus inhibit learning. A widely held view in society of error as indicative of incompetence leads people in organizational hierarchies to systematically suppress mistakes and deny responsibility (Michael, 1976). Hierarchical structures thus discourage the kind of systematic analysis of mistakes that would allow people to better design systems to prevent them.

In summary, systemic approaches expand the scope of analysis of errors and accidents beyond the idiosyncrasies of individual behavior. Moreover, they introduce the variable of how errors that have been made are treated in the system, and how systems for error prevention can be designed. Some of these theories focus on technical and structural features of macro systems that primarily influence the outcomes of error and thwart simple preventative strategies; others focus on societal forces that shape attitudes toward error. However, these theories are less useful for understanding variance in behavior within a given organization or system. Thus we turn to the social psychology of groups for insight into how small social systems such as work teams may operate to prevent or catch errors.

Group-Level Analysis

Individual skills, motivation, and cognition are imperfect. Organizational systems are inevitably flawed. Hackman (1993) proposes that, facing this ever-present potential for error, teams in organizations can act as "self-correcting performance units." Members of a superb team have a way of coordinating task, anticipating and responding to each other's actions, and often appearing to perform as a seamless whole. Consider, for example, the study by Foushee, Lauber, Baetge, and Acomb (1986) on the effects of fatigue on flight crew errors. These researchers found, to their surprise, that crews who had just logged several days flying together (fatigue condition) made significantly fewer errors *as teams* than well-rested crews who had not yet worked together. As expected, the fatigued individuals made more errors than others; however, functioning as teams they were able to compensate for these, presumably because they were better able to coordinate and to catch each other's mistakes.

Such differences in group behavior and performance have been examined by two research traditions in the social psychology literature. One research tradition has focused on social, affective, and unconscious influences on groups and their members, whereas another tradition is rooted in cognition, goals, and structures.[3] The former tradition finds its origins in the late 19th-century work of

---

[3] I thank Clayton Alderfer for this insight, which has helped me to view this study in a new way. Although the research design relied on the latter (structural/intellectual) tradition, the results required me to take a new look at the former (emotional/unconscious) tradition.

Gustave Le Bon, who proposed that unconscious processes of a crowd or group could manifest themselves in the actions of individual members (Alderfer, 1987). Similarly, the Hawthorne studies reported that emotions and tacit group norms could exert a greater influence on performance than working conditions or economic incentives (Roethlisberger & Dickson, 1939), and sociotechnical theorists later described the importance of a strong social unit in motivating workers (Rice, 1958; Trist & Bamforth, 1951). Finally, the intergroup perspective has explored how membership in identity groups (such as gender or race) or organizational groups (such as rank or function) can affect communication and motivation in task groups (Alderfer, 1987), which could lead to errors due to lack of coordination. When members of a work team communicate across tacit boundaries imposed by rank or identity group, this can inhibit the transfer of valid data (Argyris, 1985). Along these lines, nurses and physicians working as part of the same team (hospital unit) face identity group boundaries confounded with status differences that can affect within-team communication and thereby influence the process of administering drugs to patients.

The other research tradition emphasizes intellectual formulations such as structure and design, minimizing attention to emotional processes. The emphasis is on identifying conditions that help teams work together and solve problems (e.g., Hackman & Morris, 1975; Maier, 1967), such as early research that examined what leadership style would enable positive group outcomes (Lewin, Lippitt, & White, 1939). Recent work in this tradition has focused on the importance of practice (Senge, 1990) and members' interpersonal skills (Helmreich & Foushee, 1993) as influences on team performance. The structure of the team, the design of its task, and the supportiveness of the organizational context (reward, information, and educational systems) have also been central concerns in this tradition (Hackman, 1987). Both research traditions share the understanding that a group is more than the sum of its members and that group-level phenomena exist and influence task performance (Alderfer, 1987; Hackman, 1990). Although the design of the present study drew almost exclusively from the latter tradition, the results, as discussed more fully below, suggest that the story of drug errors cannot be told fully without attention to the constructs of the former.

Hospital units are one kind of work group, and group research may help explain differences in error rates. Hospital units are primarily managed and staffed by nurses, whereas physicians and pharmacists affiliated with each unit interact with the nursing teams. Preliminary observation revealed considerable flexibility in carrying out work processes; units vary in the way work is done and in how people work together. When and by whom the various tasks will be accomplished is left largely up to the discretion of the unit members, suggesting that critical performance outcomes such as the prevalence of drug errors can vary. Based on this perspective, the present study focused on hospital units as the unit of analysis in attempting to gain insight into causes and prevention of medication errors. The guiding question—rather than what causes people to make mistakes—was thus, are some work groups better than others at catching and correcting human error before it becomes consequential? Further, are such groups better able to learn from the inevitable errors that do occur and to avoid making the same ones in the future?

THE STUDY

Previous research suggested that error rates vary widely across units within the same hospital (Bates et al., 1993). Similarly, unit error rates obtained in the current study of drug complications range from 2.3 to 23.7 errors per thousand patient days. (Table 10.6, discussed in the Results section, displays the data for each unit.) What accounts for these differences? One possibility is that unit characteristics (such as team stability, norms, and work structure) influence error rates. Starting with the proposition that team behaviors are influenced by organizational context, team leader behaviors, task design, resource adequacy, and team composition (Hackman, 1987), the present study tests the hypothesis that error rates vary with these unit characteristics. Figure 10.1 depicts a model of proposed influences on, and outcomes of, hospital unit work processes. In this model, unit outcomes such as error rates and members' assessments of unit performance are group-level characteristics.

The research question guiding the present study was, are differences in work group (unit) properties associated with differences in error rates? And do members' perceptions of how their unit performs and of the quality of unit relationships vary with the "hard" data of drug error rates?[4] Thus the study explores the extent to which certain group-level properties contribute to understanding differences in drug error rates in hospital units.

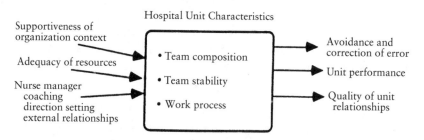

FIGURE 10.1 Model of Unit-Level Influences on Drug Error Rates and Other Performance Outcomes

---

[4] It is important to note that this "hard" measure consists of those drug errors identified by the research team, and thus is not one and the same as "actual error rates." More will be said about this distinction in the Results and Discussion section.

Method

The study used a comparative nonexperimental research design. Eight hospital unit teams were randomly selected for study from two urban teaching hospitals affiliated with the same medical school. No known differences in unit composition, skill, professionalism, or workload existed between the two hospitals.

Three parallel data collection activities were conducted in the units studied. Independent of the present study, potentially harmful drug-related errors were identified over a 6-month period by trained medical investigators through daily chart review, daily informal visits to each unit to inquire about unusual drug events, and a confidential system to allow unit members to report incidents in writing. Previous research (Bates et al., 1993) found this combination of activities to uncover more errors than other methods.

Dependent Variables

Data were collected for four variables related to patient adverse drug events (ADEs), each expressed as a number of incidents per thousand patient days: (a) nonpreventable ADEs (adverse drug events unrelated to error), (b) preventable ADEs, (c) potential ADEs (or PADEs) (consequential errors that did not harm patients despite having the potential to cause injury, such as the heparin incident described above), and (d) interceptions (errors caught and corrected before reaching patients). The first two variables (nonpreventable ADEs and preventable ADEs) were measured by a combination of patient chart review and voluntary reporting. The second two variables (PADEs and interceptions) could only be measured through voluntary reporting of events by unit members. To capture the construct of human error, the primary dependent variable for the present study ("detected error rates") is the sum of preventable ADEs and potential ADEs.

Work Group Measures

To address the main research question of how unit properties influenced these outcome variables, two independent methods were employed (survey and observation) to develop a full picture of how the hospital units studied functioned and how they differed. First, the author developed a survey to assess the social and organizational properties of hospital units, based on a prior instrument designed to study the performance of cockpit crews (Hackman, 1990). The new survey measures include leadership behaviors of nurse managers, organization context (adequacy of training, information, and equipment), team characteristics (stability, composition, quality of unit relationships, and performance outcomes), and individual satisfaction and motivation. Figure 10.1 depicts relationships among these variables.

Next, another researcher, blind to both error rates and survey results, observed nursing teams in the eight units for several days each over a 2-month period; his goal was to observe behavioral dynamics in support of the larger project goal of understanding conditions surrounding drug errors.[5] He interviewed all nurse managers, several nurses, and members of the support staff in each unit, using a semistructured interview format that included open-ended questions to elicit interviewees' own descriptions of how mistakes are handled and perceived in their unit.

Sample

Eight units in two urban hospitals were included in the study. Five units from one, referred to as Memorial Hospital, include three intensive care units and two general care units. The three units from the other, referred to as University Hospital, are all general care units. Two hundred and eighty-nine surveys were distributed to nurses physicians, and pharmacists identified by hospital personnel as full- or part-time members of the eight units. Fifty-five percent (159) of the surveys were completed and returned.[6] Surveys were filled out at the end of the second month of the 6 month during which drug errors were tracked.[7]

Survey Variables

Survey items include unit descriptions such as "This unit operates as a real team" as well as individual satisfaction items such as "I am satisfied with the amount of pay I receive." (Table 10.2 shows items for selected scales as illustration.) Each descriptive statement is followed by a 7-point Likert-type scale (7 = *strong agreement*, 1 = *strong disagreement*), except for the items describing nurse manager behaviors, which are followed by a 5-point scale ranging from *never* to *frequently*. As shown in Table 10.1, the individual items combine to create 12 variables in five categories: leadership behavior, organization context, unit characteristics, unit outcomes, and individual satisfaction. (These categories map to the research model in Figure 10.1.) Single-item variables include members' perceptions of the frequency of drug errors, of the degree of reporting of such errors, and of the consequences of making a mistake in their unit.

---

[5] I am indebted to Andy Molinsky who conducted most of the on-site interviews and observations; his qualitative data are summarized in Tables 10.5 and 10.6 and form the basis of the four individual cases described in the Results section.

[6] The respondents include 123 nurses, 19 physicians, and 4 pharmacists. Nurses are full-time members of the eight units; pharmacists and physicians who work with or rotate through the units were asked to judge—as relative outsiders—how units that they know well function. Thus, although 77% of the surveys returned and analyzed were from the full-time unit staff, responses from nurses and physicians were similar; we tested for differences across these groups and found none.

[7] Adam Galinsky's assistance in administering the survey and his endless supply of ideas and enthusiasm during this project are acknowledged with great appreciation.

TABLE 10.1 Summary Statistics for Survey-Based Measures

Scale	Mean	SD	Internal Consistency Reliability
Leadership behaviors			
Nurse manager direction setting	3.78	0.86	0.90
Nurse manager coaching	3.60	0.88	0.90
Nurse manager external relations	3.79	0.88	0.90
Organization context			
Supportiveness of organization context	4.96	0.94	0.74
Unit characteristics			
Team composition	4.43	1.15	0.67
Team stability	4.76	0.95	0.68
Unit outcomes			
Unit performance outcomes	5.06	0.93	0.77
Quality of interpersonal relationships	4.12	0.84	0.80
Individual satisfaction			
Internal motivation	6.14	0.71	0.70
General satisfaction	4.63	0.57	0.73
Satisfaction with work relationships	5.74	0.66	0.68
Satisfaction with growth opportunities	5.51	0.85	0.72
Single items			
"Drug-related errors occur frequently in this unit"	2.88	1.25	
"In this unit, drug-related errors are always reported"	4.43	1.54	
"If you make a mistake in this unit it is held against you"	3.24	1.20	

Analytic Strategy

Preparatory analyses assessed (a) the adequacy of the psychometric properties of the new survey instrument, and (b) whether the survey scales were meaningful group-level variables. As the research questions examine relationships between unit attributes and unit error rates, it is important to establish that the survey variables in question are meaningful as unit-level properties (Kenny & LaVoie, 1985). Spearman rank order correlations were then used to examine substantive relationships between unit properties and detected error rates, interceptions, and nonpreventable ADEs. Finally, qualitative data were analyzed independently to understand ways in which unit climates and nurse behaviors differ, and units were ranked according to openness in discussing mistakes, a variable that surfaced during observation and analysis as differing across units. These qualitative results subsequently were compared to the quantitative survey and drug error data.

TABLE 10.2 Survey Items for Selected Scales

Selected Scale	Items
Nurse manager direction setting	The nurse manager takes initiatives to establish strong standards of medical excellence and professionalism in this team.
	The nurse manager sets clear goals and objectives for this team.
	The nurse manager is clear and explicit about what he or she expects from unit members.
	The nurse manager actively encourages nurses in this unit to stretch their level of performances.
Nurse manager coaching	The nurse manager takes initiatives to build the unit as a team.
	The nurse manager actively coaches individual unit members.
	The nurse manager shares leadership with other experienced members of the unit.
	The nurse manager is an ongoing "presence" in the unit—someone who is readily available.
Quality of interpersonal relationships	Members of this unit care a lot about it and work together to make it one of the best in the hospital.
	Working with the members of this unit is an energizing and uplifting experience.
	Some people in this team do not carry their fair share of the overall workload. (R)
	Every time someone attempts to straighten out a team member whose behavior is not acceptable, things seem to get worse rather than better. (R)
	There is a lot of unpleasantness among members of this team. (R)
Unit performance outcomes	Recently, this unit seems to be "slipping" a bit in its level of performance and accomplishments.
	Patients often complain about how this unit functions. (R)
	The quality of care this unit provides to patients is improving over time.
	Drug-related errors occur frequently in this unit. (R)
	This unit shows signs of falling apart as an organization.
	Attending physicians often complain about how this unit functions.
	In this unit, drug-related errors are always reported.

NOTE: (R) = reverse scored.

Survey psychometrics: Analysis of the psychometric properties of the survey results yielded satisfactory results, demonstrating the validity and internal consistency reliability of the scales as shown in Table 10.1. Internal consistency reliabilities range from 0.67 for team composition to 0.90 for each of the three nurse manager behaviors.

Unit-level properties: To assess the degree to which the organizational attributes measured by the survey are meaningful as group-level variables, two complementary measures of within-unit agreement about unit properties were computed. Measures of within-unit agreement also provide an indication of interrater reliability in measuring unit characteristics with this survey. The first, the intraclass correlation coefficient (ICC), uses one-way analysis of variance (ANOVA) to compare between- and within-unit variance. The second, the interrater reliability coefficient (IRR) derived by James, Demaree, and Wolf (1984), compares actual variance to a measure of "expected variance" to assess within-group agreement, without between/within comparisons.

ICCs for survey variables assessing unit characteristics were examined first; Kenny and LaVoie (1985) maintain that an ICC greater than zero indicates that a variable is meaningful at the group level. In many organizations, however, institutional forces restrict variance, leaving strong similarities across work groups, which suggests that allowing the magnitude of between-group differences to determine whether a variable is meaningful at the group level may not always be sensible in real organizational settings. For example, in these data, several variables designed to measure unit-level attributes have very low positive ICCs, such as team composition (0.08) and unit performance outcomes (0.06). Does this indicate lack of within-team agreement? Perhaps not. IRRs for the same variables (0.80 and 0.88, respectively) provide a measure of within-group agreement that

TABLE 10.3 Intraclass Coefficients (ICC) and Interrater Reliability Coefficients (IRR) Compared Across Units

	ICC	*Median IRR*
Supportiveness of organization context	0.12^*	0.85
Nurse manager direction setting	0.22^*	0.88
Nurse manager external relationships	0.21^*	0.89
Nurse manager coaching	0.18^*	0.82
Team composition	0.08^*	0.80
Team stability	0.10^*	0.83
Unit performance outcomes	0.06	0.88
Satisfaction with growth opportunities	0.04	0.91
"Drug-related errors occur frequently"	0.08^*	0.67

[*] One-way ANOVA for each of these variables by unit is significant ($p < 0.05$).

is unaffected by between-group similarities, and these values suggest high levels of within-team agreement (see Table 10.3). As many organizational features are similar across units, the critical sources of variance among units may be largely due to those features that are noticeably different, such as leadership behaviors of nurse managers.

The IRR is appealing as an absolute measure of within-unit agreement; however, its expected variance term is derived based on an assumption that survey responses are rectangularly distributed, thus posing a different limitation. Positive leniency in responding to items about unit performance is likely, which limits variance and can inflate estimates of agreement (see James, Demaree, & Wolf, 1984).[8] Thus response bias makes it difficult to assess absolute levels of unit agreement. However, examining both coefficients shows which variables have greater between-group differences while having similar within-group agreement levels. To facilitate comparison of the two kinds of unit-agreement coefficients, ICCs and median IRRs are shown for eight variables in Table 10.3.[9]

The ICC's between/within comparison is useful in showing which variables stand out as attributes that vary across, and hence best distinguish among, units. For example, nurse managers' direction setting (0.22) has the highest ICC in the sample, reflecting the greater variance between units in perceived behavior of nurse managers, compared to variables describing less tangible unit characteristics such as performance outcomes (ICC = 0.06). ICCs for each of the three leadership scales are significant ($p < 0.001$). This result is consistent with the author's on-site observations of the nurse managers' behaviors; each unit has a different nurse manager, in some cases with strikingly contrasting management styles. In contrast, the variable "unit performance outcomes" has low between-unit variance (ICC = 0.08) despite having the same level of within-unit agreement (IRR = 0.88) as nurse manager direction setting.

In sum, IRRs and ICCs provide different, complementary measures of within-group agreement. In these data, the IRRs reveal the high within-unit agreement levels for variables, such as unit performance outcomes, which lack high between-unit differences and thus have low ICCs. Together these coefficients allow us to have confidence that these measures are meaningful as group- or unit-level variables.

---

[8] In the case of positive leniency, the denominator (expected variance) will be too large to represent accurately the response patterns reasonably expected for this survey, such that James's formula (unity minus actual variance divided by expected variance) will produce an inflated IRR.

[9] The IRR also differs from the ICC in that it provides individual coefficients for each unit, enabling cross-unit comparisons.

RESULTS AND DISCUSSION

As discussed above, this study employed two distinct methods to investigate organizational factors that may account for variance in drug error rates across hospital units. In this section, I first review the quantitative results, and then present results from the qualitative research. These two lenses provide distinct and complementary pictures of the phenomenon.

Relationships between Error Rates and Unit Characteristics

Correlational analyses of the relationships between unit characteristics and error rates yielded unexpected results. We expected to find higher error rates to

TABLE 10.4 Organizational Influences on the Detection of Error: Spearman Rank Order Correlations between Survey Variables and Drug Error Variables

	Correlation
Detected error rates and . . .	
Nurse manager coaching	0.74[*]
Nurse manager direction setting	0.74[*]
Unit performance outcomes	0.76[*]
Quality of unit relationships	0.74[*]
Willingness to report errors	0.55
Mistakes (are not held against you)[a]	0.44
Intercepted errors and . . .	
Nurse manager coaching	0.71[*]
Nurse manager direction setting	0.83[*]
Unit performance outcomes	0.71[*]
Quality of unit relationships	0.76[*]
Willingness to report errors	0.62
Mistakes (are not held against you)	0.45
Nonpreventable drug complications and . . .	
Nurse manager coaching	−0.10
Nurse manager direction setting	−0.09
Unit performance outcomes	0.11
Quality of unit relationships	−0.07
Willingness to report errors	0.09
Mistakes (are not held against you)	0.07

NOTE: All correlations are between unit means for each survey variable and the dependent drug error variable.
[a] The survey item that reads "If you make a mistake in this unit it is held against you" is reverse scored in analyzing the data.
[*] $p < 0.03$, two-tailed.

be associated with lower mean scores on perceived unit performance, quality of unit relationships, and nurse manager leadership behaviors. Exactly the opposite result was found. As shown in Table 10.4, detected error rates are strongly associated with high scores on nurse manager direction setting ($r = 0.74$), coaching ($r = 0.74$), perceived unit performance outcomes ($r = 0.76$), and quality of unit relationships ($r = 0.74$), with $p < 0.03$ in each case. These relationships between nurse manager behaviors and the independently collected error rates are noteworthy, and at first glance an odd result indeed. Do better coached teams make more mistakes?

An alternative interpretation of these findings also merits careful consideration: In certain units, the leaders may have established a climate of openness that facilitates discussion of error, which is likely to be an important influence on detected error rates. Awareness of the labor intensiveness and difficulty of tracking drug-related errors—and of how easy and natural it is for human beings to underreport error—suggests that measuring errors in each unit is not a trivial undertaking. The difficulty of assessing actual error rates is shown in a recent study in which a hospital in Salt Lake City was able to increase the number of ADEs identified forty-fold after instituting a new computing system to predict and track errors (Evans et al., 1992). The magnitude of this increase indicates how few of the errors made in hospital units are reported, and suggests also that variance in error rates caused by differences in patient severity and complexity across general and intensive care units can be overwhelmed by the influence of lack of reporting of errors (see Note 10). In short, detected error rates are a function of at least two influences—actual errors made and unit members' willingness to report errors. Moreover, in organizational settings in which errors are consequential, willingness to report may be a greater influence on the error rates obtained than is variance in actual errors made. These observations suggest that positive correlations between error rates and nurse manager coaching, perceived unit performance, and quality of unit relationships may be explained by examining the role of members' willingness and ability to catch and report drug errors.

The Role of Willingness to Report Errors

Higher detected error rates in units with higher mean scores on nurse manager coaching, quality of unit relationships, and perceived unit performance may be due in part to members' perceptions of how safe it is to discuss mistakes in their unit. Several other survey variables provide support for this hypothesis. First, a variable labeled "willingness to report errors" was computed for each unit; this is the difference between two item means—"in this unit, drug errors are always reported" and "drug errors occur frequently in this unit." This difference score, which ranges from −4 to 5 in these data, measures perceived willingness to report errors controlling for perceived frequency of error. Detected error rates then were found to be correlated with willingness to report errors ($r = 0.55$). Second, a single-item variable measuring unit members' perceptions that making a mistake in their unit will not be held against them is also correlated with detected error rates ($r = 0.44$; see Table 10.4). Moreover, one-way ANOVA reveals significant between-unit differences for both of these single-item variables ($p < 0.05$), suggesting that unit climates vary significantly in perceptions of the risk of discussing mistakes.

Examining relationships between these two survey variables and another dependent variable, the number of interceptions in each unit, provides additional support for the hypothesis that willingness to report error influences ability to detect errors in a unit (see Table 10.6 for means and standard deviations of interceptions and other drug error data). Recall that the concept of self-correcting performance units highlights the role of catching errors before they become consequential; the number of interceptions in a unit provides an indication of unit members' attentiveness to their interdependence in caring for patients, as well as a measure of their ability to function as a self-correcting performance unit. Analysis of the data shows that units with a greater number of interceptions (team self-correcting behaviors) also tend to have relatively higher scores on nurse manager direction setting ($r = 0.83$), coaching ($r = 0.71$), performance outcomes ($r = 0.71$) and quality of unit relations ($r = 0.76$), with $p < 0.03$ in each case. Further, correlations between interceptions and willingness to report ($r = 0.62$) and between interceptions and unit tolerance of mistakes ($r = 0.45$) suggest that interceptions are more prevalent in units in which members are less concerned about being caught making a mistake. Figure 10.2 depicts a model that summarizes these relationships. The model proposes that nurse manager leadership behaviors—especially related to how mistakes are handled—create an ongoing, continually reinforced climate of openness or of fear about discussing drug errors. The more readily errors are reported and discussed, the more willing unit members may be to report error in the future, and the more they may believe that making a mistake will not be held against them. A feedback loop indicates how these

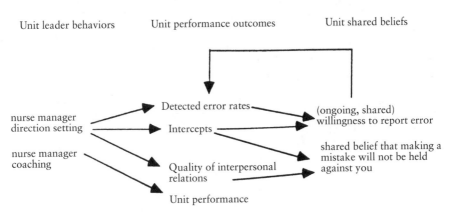

FIGURE 10.2 Model of Influence of Willingness to Report Error on Detected Error Rates

perceptions contribute to a self-perpetuating cycle of learning, or else of defensiveness.

Finally, if willingness to discuss mistakes is indeed an important influence on detected error rates, then nonpreventable ADEs should not be correlated with the unit characteristics discussed above. The results in fact do reveal a consistent lack of association between nonpreventable ADEs and unit variables such as nurse manager direction setting ($r = -0.09$), coaching ($r = -0.10$), unit tolerance of mistakes ($r = 0.07$), and willingness to report errors ($r = 0.09$). Although error rates show significant correlations with these unit characteristics, there is simply no relationship between nonerror drug complications and these survey variables.

Error Suppression in Authoritarian Units

In the above discussion, I offer an explanation for the unexpected reversal of the direction of the correlations between drug error rates and unit characteristics, and I support this with additional quantitative results that are consistent with this interpretation.[10] Fortunately, however, there are other independent data available that corroborate the proposed phenomenon.

Qualitative data gathered by a researcher blind to the quantitative results (for both drug and survey data) support the hypothesis that these units vary in terms of openness in discussing mistakes (see Note 5). The social climate was

---

[10] Because patients in oncological and intensive care units receive more medications each day than patients in general medical or surgical units, several of the physicians involved in the larger drug study suggested that I adjust the dependent variables for exposure to medications, to make these values more comparable across units. Moreover, the positive correlations may indicate simply that ICUs have more actual drug errors while also having better coordinated teams and more active nurse manager coaches. Thus, following this suggestion, I reexamined the correlations between unit survey variables and drug rates, using drug error data adjusted for exposure. (Each dependent variable was divided by mean number of drugs per patient per day in that unit and multiplied by the mean across units, thus deflating ICU values and inflating values for general care units.) The result, rather than weakening the reported correlations, was an overall strengthening of the relationships, as follows:

Detected Error rates and . . .	Correlation	Correlation Using Adjusted Data
Nurse manager coaching	0.74[*]	0.76[*]
Nurse manager direction setting	0.74[*]	0.88[*]
Unit performance outcomes	0.76[*]	0.74[*]
Quality of unit relationships	0.74[*]	0.88[*]
Willingness to report errors	0.55	0.69
Mistakes (are not held against you)	0.44	0.67

[*] $p < 0.03$.

noticeably different across the eight units, including differences in nurse-physician relationships, and appeared to be influenced by nurse managers whose behavioral styles varied widely. Several behavioral patterns related to mistakes were observed and described in interviews. In analyzing these data, the qualitative researcher identified several variables that distinguished among units, such as unit climate (blame oriented vs. learning oriented), openness, nurse manager attire, nurses' trust in their nurse manager, and perceived supportiveness of both nurse manager and peers. He then ranked each unit as high, medium, or

Intercepted Errors and . . .	Correlation	Correlation Using Adjusted Data
Nurse manager coaching	0.71[*]	0.69
Nurse manager direction setting	0.83[*]	0.81[*]
Unit performance outcomes	0.71[*]	0.64
Quality of unit relationships	0.76[*]	0.67
Willingness to report errors	0.62	0.62
Mistakes (are not held against you)	0.45	0.33

[*] $p < 0.03$.

The results reported in the article use the original detected error data, as the phenomenon discussed is that of reporting differences across units. With this perspective, each instance of a nurse willingly reporting a drug error is an illustration of proactive, learning-oriented behavior, which contributes to the prevention of future errors. The actual count of the number of times such a behavior occurs in each unit is thus a better dependent variable for this study than the more conservative adjusted error data.

The principal investigators of the drug study also suggested that I do the above analyses using only PADEs, which can be only obtained through voluntary reporting, instead of using the current dependent variable of total error rates (PADEs plus preventable ADEs, the latter measure being obtained by chart review and voluntary reporting). Separating PADEs and ADEs illustrates the relatively stronger relationships between unit characteristics and those errors only voluntarily reported, supporting the interpretation that unit differences in willingness to report errors accounts for much of the variance in detected error rates. Moreover, the existence of (weaker) correlations between unit characteristics and ADEs (obtained in chart review and voluntary reporting) support the hypothesis of a relationship between error reporting and error rates.

PADEs and . . .	Correlation	Correlation Using Adjusted PADEs
Nurse manager coaching	0.79[*]	0.81[*]
Nurse manager direction setting	0.76[*]	0.93[*]
Unit performance outcomes	0.64	0.69
Quality of unit relationships	0.62	0.74[*]
Willingness to report errors	0.33	0.50
Mistakes (are not held against you)	0.33	0.52

[*] $p < 0.03$.

low on openness, and arranged the eight units in a table from most authoritarian to most open. Table 10.5 displays these results, which are strikingly consistent with quantitative results, as juxtaposed in Table 10.6. Only one unit is noticeably out of place, Memorial 4, which has fewer errors than six of the other units along with a nurse manager who is perceived as relatively open and accessible.

A more in-depth look at four of the units will illustrate the phenomenon of authoritarian suppression of error that I propose may explain much of the variance in the dependent variable of detected error rates. These units illustrate four distinct leadership styles and climates; they range from a highly supportive to a highly authoritarian environment, and each illustrates a different way of dealing with mistakes. Differences in willingness to collaborate across professions are also evident, which is highly relevant to catching and correcting drug errors, as will be illustrated below. I start with a description of the most open unit, then proceed to the most authoritarian, and then fill in the middle with two other units.

Memorial 1

This unit is run by a nurse manager described uniformly by nurses, physicians, and others interviewed as highly accessible and as inspiring top performance. Observed on the job wearing blood-stained scrubs, she is a hands-on manager who actively invites questions and concerns. Her own descriptions of the unit reveal a high degree of respect for her subordinates: "The nurses problem solve together . . . they have good relationships." Further, she reports that "attending physicians" on the unit are "respectful of nurses' expertise," and that relations between nurses and physicians working in the unit are smooth. Other nurses concur, with one describing relations between physicians and nurses as "more collaborative here than in other units." By volunteering these observations, several nurses reveal that physician-nurse relationships are salient to them and suggest that harmonious relations are not the norm in the hospital. As will be illustrated below, these relations are relevant to correcting drug errors.

In an interview, the nurse manager explains that a "certain level of error will occur," so a "nonpunitive environment" is essential to deal with this error

ADEs and . . .	Correlation	Correlation Using Adjusted PADEs
Nurse manager coaching	0.31	0.24
Nurse manager direction setting	0.41	0.38
Unit performance outcomes	0.52	0.64
Quality of unit relationships	0.48	0.41
Willingness to report errors	0.45	0.50
Mistakes (are not held against you)	0.45	0.50

TABLE 10.5 Units Ranked According to Analysis of Qualitative Data

	Memorial 1	University 1	University 3	Memorial 2	Memorial 4	Memorial 5	University 2	Memorial 3
Interviewer's overall rating on openness	High	High	Medium/High	Medium/High	Medium	Medium/Low	Low	Very Low
Espoused attitudes toward drug errors: blame vs. learn	Learn	Tends toward learning	Learn	Neutral	Blame, fear	Blame, fear	Neutral	Blame
"Nurse vs. manager": staff views of nurse manager	70% Nurse/ 30% Manager	25%/75%	50%/50%	50%/50%	10%/90%	0%/100%	50%/50%	10%/90%
Nurse manager: hands on vs. hands off	Hands on	Hands off, but "approachable"	Hands on	Hands on	Hands on, but "controlling"	Hands off	Hands off	Hands off, and "controlling"
Nurse manager attire	Scrubs	Scrubs	Usually scrubs	Scrubs	Business suit/ dress	Business suit/ dress	Scrubs or dress	Business suit
Nurse manager's views of staff	"They are too hard on themselves," "They are capable and seasoned"	"Doctors are independent and don't take nurses' advice," "Nurses should talk to each other first before coming to me with a concern"	"Nurses feel a lot of guilt," "Nurses see mistakes as larger than life"	"Nurses are hard on themselves," Advocates 'compassionate confrontation'	"Nurses are nervous and defensive about mistakes"	"Nurses are nervous about being called into [my] 'the principal's office'"	"Nurses are always assessing and judging each other"	Views residents as kids needing discipline, treats nurses in same way, pays careful attention to reporting structures
Staff's views of nurse manager	A superb nurse and leader	"A counselor, not a boss"	"A rule person," "She talks to us individually, avoids public discussion of mistakes"	"Distracted," helpful, nonpunitive, nonjudgmental	"Controlling and overbearing" "Makes you feel guilty," "Makes you want to cover your butt"	"Tends to blame individuals for mistakes"	Punitive, "Gives you the silent treatment," "Makes you feel guilty"	"Treats you as guilty if you make a mistake," "Treats you like a two-year-old"

TABLE 10.5 *Continued*

Staff's views of errors	Natural, normal, important to document	"Mistakes are serious because of the toxicity of drugs, so you're never afraid to tell the nurse manager"	Mistakes happen because we get interrupted doing our work	"Med errors are not a big deal here"	"Reluctance to report, because people get in trouble"	"Individuals get blamed for mistakes; you don't want to make them"	"The environment is unforgiving," "Heads will roll!"	"You get put on trial"

TABLE 10.6 Units Ranked According to Quantitative Data (Detected Error Rates) and Juxtaposed with Independent Qualitative Ranking from Table 10.5

	Memorial 1	University 1	University 3	Memorial 2	Memorial 4	Memorial 5	University 2	Memorial 3
Detected error rates[a]	23.68	17.23	13.19	11.02	10.31	9.37	8.6	2.34
Interviewer's overall rating on openness	High	High	Medium/High	Medium/High	Medium/Low	Low	Medium	Very Low

[a] All preventable ADEs and potential ADEs per 1,000 patient days. Mean detected error rate = 11.97 interceptions per 1,000 patient days ($SD = 6.33$); mean interceptions = 3.30 interceptions per 1,000 patient days ($SD = 2.03$), per 1,000 patient days ($SD = 4.75$).

productively. All three staff nurses interviewed offered descriptions of how mistakes are handled that suggest a nonpunitive environment has indeed been established. One nurse describes a recent drug error, saying "there is no punishment; you just let the doctor know and fill out an incident report." Another nurse says that there is an "unspoken rule here to help each other and check each other," and a third volunteers, "people feel more willing to admit to errors here, because [the nurse manager] goes to bat for you." Interestingly, the nurse manager explained that "nurses tend to beat themselves up about errors; they are much tougher on themselves than I would ever be," revealing a managerial philosophy that renders a punitive stance unnecessary—as well as unproductive in serving the larger goal of learning and improving.

A recent prevented drug error in this unit illustrates how errors can be intercepted by the collaborative tendencies described above. A nurse on duty noticed that a particular medication order appeared to be too high a dose. She telephoned the physician on call at home, who confirmed the nurse's concern and agreed with her recommendation to cut the dose in half, and a potential ADE was avoided. This interdependence and communication across professional group boundaries facilitates catching errors and is not in evidence in all of the units, as will be seen below.

Memorial 3

Interviews and observation in another unit in Memorial Hospital reveal a very different climate. One nurse told us that the unit "prides itself on being clean, neat and having an appearance of professionalism." The nurse manager is dressed impeccably in a business suit and has discussions with unit nurses behind the closed door of her office. Several nurses volunteered that making a mistake here means "you get in trouble," and one nurse describing an incident in which she had hurt a patient while drawing blood said that the nurse manager made her feel like she was "on trial; it was degrading, like I was a two-year-old." She continued, "I'll probably get in trouble for telling you this." Many referred to the need to place the blame for mistakes. Another nurse in this unit explained that Memorial Hospital "doesn't support nurses; doctor condescend, and they bite your head off if you" make a mistake. Moreover, "nurse are blamed for mistakes"—revealing a degree of tension between professional group in this unit that leads to resentment and blame across group boundaries.

In an interview, the nurse manager was tense and agitated, and expressed anger about having to "discipline the interns for repeatedly leaving their room messy." Late walking by an interview between the researcher and a pharmacist, she commented without warmth or visible humor, "it looks like you're plotting a revolution." We also noted that she required us to wear badges at all times, whereas in all other units except one, badges were never mentioned, and wearing them was not required. This too will be illustrative of intergroup tensions; as researchers we felt less welcome here than other units.

Memorial 2

Another unit, rated as high to medium on openness based on the qualitative data illustrates a different way of being open. Without featuring the active coaching by the nurse manager that was evident in Memorial 1, this unit is characterized by the apparently very high willingness to speak openly about mistakes and other threatening issues. The nurse manager also wears scrubs, which she explicitly mentioned in interview as a way of "building commonality" with nurses. She also describes efforts to engage unit members in team building and quality improvement processes, which themselves "require open discussion of mistakes." In discussing drug errors, she echoes an earlier comment from the nurse manager in Memorial 1 by saying that nurses are "much harder on themselves" than she would ever be on them.

Nurses in this unit describe their manager as "distracted," and "not quite focusing on you when you're talking to her," but she "helps at the drop of a hat with unpleasant tasks." One nurse reports that the nurse manager "is cool about incident reports," and that "you feel bad already and are not made to feel worse." Another says, "medication errors are not a big deal around here," and "problems exist here, but we have very candid conversation about them." She also notes that another unit (not one of those studied here) is "very blame oriented, [unlike this one]." Indeed, observations of behavior in this unit reinforce these descriptions, as nurses were seen talking openly and audibly in candid conversations about errors, with no apparent concern whether they could be overheard by the nurse manager. Members of Memorial 2 do not seem to convey the same spirit of collaboration and trust that characterizes Memorial 1. Instead, they describe a distracted but decidedly nonpunitive manager who—even though she does not actively "go to bat" for them—is completely approachable and not a source of threat. Their candid, nonfearful behavior supports this view.

University 2

Finally, a unit at University Hospital, rated as medium to low on openness based on the qualitative data, is run by another apparently authoritarian nurse manager who is described by nurses interviewed as "an authority not a coworker." Her office is somewhat removed from the unit, and according to nurses interviewed, the "door is always closed." As in Memorial 3, she consistently wears a business suit rather than nursing scrubs, and is viewed by unit nurses as "uncomfortable to deal with" and "inconsistent" in being supportive. In an interview, she explains that mistakes should be learning experiences, but observes that "people are nervous about being called into the principal's office" to talk to her about them. One nurse reports that the nurse manager has a tendency to blame individuals for mistakes, and that "people don't advertise error here; if there's no adverse event, then don't report it."

The behavior of nurses in this unit is noticeably less collaborative and supportive than in Memorial 1 or 2. Those interviewed describe "backstabbing" and "cliques," and during observations on the unit, one nurse was overheard making a mean-spirited comment behind the back of another nurse while explaining why she refused to help the other nurse.

Summary

Interviews and observations in the eight units reinforce quantitative findings that shared perceptions about the consequences of making mistakes influence the climate and reporting behaviors within a unit team. A picture emerges from the qualitative results described above that is consistent with the earlier interpretation of the unexpected quantitative results. It appears that nurse manager behaviors are an important influence on unit members' beliefs about the consequences and discussability of mistakes. In addition to the influence of what is said by the nurse manager, the ways past errors have been handled are noticed, and conclusions are drawn, which then are strengthened by ongoing conversations among unit members. In this way, perceptions may become reality, as the perception that something is not discussable leads to avoidance of such discussions. These kinds of perceptions, when shared, contribute to a climate of fear or of openness, which can be self-reinforcing, and which further influences the ability and willingness to identify and discuss mistakes and problems. These climates are characterized in part by the nature of relationships within and between professional identity groups.

IMPLICATIONS AND CONCLUSIONS

This article reports a positive answer to the question guiding this study; differences in unit properties do appear to be associated with differences in error rates. However, the relationship discovered here was an unexpected one, suggesting that a primary influence on detected error rates is unit members' willingness to discuss mistakes openly. Thus a model is proposed in which leadership behavior influences the way errors are handled, which in turn leads to shared perceptions of how consequential it is to make a mistake. These perceptions influence willingness to report mistakes, and may contribute to a climate of fear or of openness that is likely to endure and further influence the ability to identify and discuss problems.

In this research, as in organizational life, actual errors are confounded inextricably with detected errors. Despite its thoroughness, the process of documenting errors is still partly dependent upon organizational members' willingness and ability to detect and report errors within their units. Thus there are at least two sources of influence on the dependent variable of detected errors—actual differences in errors made and willingness to expose them—and disentangling the relative contribution of each source is not feasible in most naturalistic organizational settings. Organizational characteristics influence both of these behavioral outcomes; however, conditions that foster making errors are likely to be different from those that foster catching, correcting, discussing, and learning from errors.

We can speculate that actual medication error may be lower in units that perform as more tightly coordinated teams and have more accessible, open nurse managers; however, from these data we cannot support this hypothesis directly. What we do learn is that willingness to report errors varies systematically with perceived openness of unit leaders, and we can speculate that these attributes may overwhelm differences in actual error rates. This speculation is supported by other research discussed above that reveals that the rare of detection of actual drug errors is orders of magnitude below 100%.

These findings provide evidence that the detection of error is influenced by organizational characteristics, suggesting that the popular notion of learning from mistakes faces a management dilemma. Detection of error may vary in such a way to make those teams that most need improvement least likely to surface errors—to data that fuel improvement efforts. This has important implications for quality improvement efforts that rely upon work teams' participation in detecting and correcting error, by suggesting that there may be barriers that prevent some (more than other) teams from doing so. Communication failures caused by intergroup tensions may also affect the ability of teams to discuss and correct mistakes. Michael (1976) has suggested that embracing error is feasible when organizations reward such behaviors, and this study is supportive of that proposition. Organizational and group interventions may be needed to encourage detection and discussion of error, although strategies for accomplishing this are beyond the scope of this article.

Finally, this research suggests that the group level of analysis offers a useful perspective for investigating the phenomenon of errors in organizations. Research at the individual level of analysis tends to suggest educational and technical interventions to reduce the incidence of errors, whereas researchers at the systems level of analysis warn of the perverse effects of targeted technical solutions. Given that human error will never disappear from organizational life, an important management issue thus becomes the design and nurturance of work environments in which it is possible to learn from mistakes and collectively to avoid making the same ones in the future. This research contributes to this goal by pointing to conditions at the group level that may influence the degree to which errors are caught and corrected by work teams.

REFERENCES

Alderfer, C. (1987). An intergroup perspective on group dynamics. In J. W. Lorsch (Ed.). *Handbook of organizational behavior.* Englewood Cliffs, NJ: Prentice Hall.

Argyris, C. (1985). *Strategy, change, and defensive routines,* Boston: Ballinger.

Barker, K. N., & McConnell, W. E. (1962). Detecting errors in hospitals. *American Journal of Hospital Pharmacy,* 19, 361–369.

Bates, D. W., Boyle, D. L., Vander Vliet, M. B., Schneider, J., & Leape, L. L. (1995). Relationship between medication errors and adverse drug events. *Journal of General Internal Medicine,* 10, 199–205.

Bates, D. W., Leape, L. L., & Petrycki, S. (1993). Incidence and preventability of adverse drug events in hospitalized patients. *Journal of General Internal Medicine*, 8, 289–294.

Classen, D. C., Pestotnik, S. L., Evans, R. S., & Burke, J. P. (1991). Computerized surveillance of adverse drug events in hospital patients. *Journal of the American Medical Association*, 266(20), 2847–2851.

Cohen, M. R. (1977). Medication error reports. *American Journal of Hospital Pharmacy*, 12(1), 42–44.

Evans, R. S., Pestotnik, S. L., Classen, D. C., Bass, S. B., Menlove, R. L., Gardner, R. M., & Burke, J. P. (1992). Development of a computerized adverse drug event monitor. In *Proceedings of the Annual Symposium on Computerized Applications for Medical Care*, pp. 23–27.

Fiske, S. T., & Taylor, S. E. (1991). *Social cognition*. New York: McGraw-Hill.

Forrester, J. W. (1971). Counterintuitive behavior of social systems. *Technology Review*, 73(3), 52–68.

Foushee, H. C., Lauber, J. K., Baetge, M. M., & Acomb, D. B. (1986). *Crew factors in flight operations III: The operational significance of exposure to short-haul air transport operations* (Technical Memorandum No. 88342). Moffett Field, CA: NASA-Ames Research Center.

Goleman, D. (1985). *Vital lies simple truths: The psychology of self-deception*. New York: Simon & Schuster.

Hackman, J. R. (1987). The design of work teams. In J. W. Lorsch (Ed.), *Handbook of organizational behavior*. Englewood Cliffs, NJ: Prentice Hall.

Hackman, J. R. (1990). New directions in crew-oriented flight training. Unpublished proceedings of the ICAO Human Factors Seminar, Leningrad.

Hackman, J. R. (1993). Teams, leaders, and organizations: New directions for crew-oriented flight training. In E. L. Wiener, B. G. Kanki, & R. L. Helmreich (Eds.), *Cockpit resource management*. Orlando, FL: Academic Press.

Hackman, J. R., & Morris, C. G. (1975). Group tasks, group interaction process, and group performance effectiveness. In H. H. Blumberg, A. P. Hard, V. Kent, & M. Davies (Eds.), *Small groups and social interaction* (Vol. 1). Chichester, UK: Wiley.

Helmreich, R. L., & Foushee, H. C. (1993). Why crew resource management? Empirical and theoretical bases of human factors training in aviation. In E. L. Wiener, B. G. Kanki, & R. L. Helmreich (Eds.), *Cockpit resource management*. Orlando, FL: Academic Press.

James, L. R., Demaree, R. G., & Wolf, G. (1984). Estimating within-group interrater reliability with and without response bias. *Journal of Applied Psychology*, 69(1), 85–98.

Kenny, D. A., & LaVoie, L. (1985). Separating individual and group effects. *Journal of Personality and Social Psychology*, 48(2), 339–448.

Leape, L. L., Brennan, T. A., Laird, N., Lawthers, A. G., Localio, A. R., Barnes, B. A., Hebert, L., Newhouse, J. P., Wyler, P. C., & Hiatt, H. (1991). The nature of adverse events in hospitalized patients: Results of the Harvard Medical Practice Study II. *New England Journal of Medicine*, 324(6), 377–384.

Lesar, T. S., Briceland, L. L., Delcoure, K., Parmalee, J. C., Masta-Gomic, V., & Pohl, H. (1990). Medication prescribing errors in a teaching hospital. *Journal of American Medicine*, 263, 2329–2334.

Lewin, K., Lippitt, R., & White, R. (1939). Patterns of aggressive behavior in experimentally created social climates. *Journal of Social Psychology*, 10, 271–299.

Maier, N. R. F. (1967). Assets and liabilities in group problem solving: The need for an integrative function. *Psychological Review*, 74, 239–249.

Massaro, T. A. (1992). Introducing physician order entry at a major academic medical center: II. Impact on medical education. *Academic Medicine*, 68, 25–30.

Melmon, K. L. (1971). Preventable drug reactions: Causes and cures. *New England Journal of Medicine*, 284(24), 1361–1368.

Michael, D. N. (1976). *On learning to plan and planning to learn.* San Francisco: Jossey-Bass.

Norman, D. A. (1980). Post-Freudian slips. *Psychology Today*, 13, 42–50.

Norman, D. A. (1981). Categorization of action slips. *Psychological Review*, 88, 1–15.

Perrow, C. (1984). *Normal accidents.* New York: Basic Books.

Reason, J. (1984). Lapses of attention in everyday life. In R. Parasuraman & D. R. Davies (Eds.), *Varieties of attention* (pp. 515–549). Orlando, FL: Academic Press.

Rice, A. K. (1958). *Productivity and social organization: The Ahmedabad experiment.* London: Tavistock.

Roethlisberger, F. J., & Dickson, W. (1939). *Management and the worker.* Boston: Harvard University Press.

Rumelhart, D. E. (1980). Schemata: The building blocks of cognition. In R. J. Spiro, B. C. Bruce, & W. F. Brewer (Eds.), *Theoretical issues in reading comprehension: Perspectives from cognitive psychology, linguistics, artificial intelligence and education* (pp. 33–58). Hillsdale, NJ: Lawrence Erlbaum.

Senge, P. (1990). *The fifth discipline: The art and practice of the learning organization.* New York: Doubleday.

Trist, E. A., & Bamforth, K. W. (1951). Some social and psychological consequences of the Longwall method of coal-getting. In D. S. Pugh (Ed.), *Organization theory* (pp. 393–419). London: Penguin.

Chapter 11

Taking Flight: Dialogue, Collective Thinking, and Organizational Learning

William N. Isaacs

A report from the Center for Organizational Learning's Dialogue Project lays out a promising new way of promoting collective learning and dealing with lingering conflicts—in union-management relations, among urban leaders, and in South African politics.

I think there is a beginning to dialogue, but I do not think there is an end—President of Local Union, United Steelworkers of America

Commenting on the G7 Summit in July of 1993, former Israeli Foreign Minister Abba Eban noted that the attending leaders "bring an extraordinary concentration of power, but their meetings don't seem to produce anything." His core observation: "Perhaps it's because each of the leaders is thinking individually, not collectively."

Given the nature of global and institutional problems, thinking alone at whatever level of leadership is no longer adequate. The problems are too complex, the interdependencies too intricate, and the consequences of isolation and fragmentation too devastating. Human beings everywhere are being forced to develop their capacity to think together—to develop collaborative thought and coordinated action.

This capacity is also rapidly becoming acknowledged as central to management effectiveness. According to Alan Webber, former editor of the *Harvard Business Review*, conversation is the means by which people share and often develop what they know. He says, "the most important work in the new economy is creating conversations." In fact, some writers have gone so far as to conceive of organizations themselves as networks of conversation.

During a single conversation, a management team may navigate through a variety of forms of group talk, each with its own effects on the quality of the team's results. Unfortunately, most forms of organizational conversation, particularly around tough, complex, or challenging issues lapse into debate (the root of which means "to beat down"). In debate, one side wins and another loses; both parties maintain their certainties, and both suppress deeper inquiry. Such exchanges do not activate the human capacity for collective intelligence. Dialogue is a discipline of collective thinking and inquiry, a process for transforming the quality of conversation and, in particular, the thinking that lies beneath it.

What makes dialogue (as we are now defining it) unique is its underlying premise: that human beings operate most often within shared, living fields of assumptions and constructed embodied meaning, and that these fields tend to be unstable, fragmented, and incoherent. As people learn to perceive, inquire into, and allow transformation of the nature and shape of these fields, and the patterns of individual thinking and acting that inform them, they may discover entirely new levels of insight and forge substantive and, at times, dramatic changes in behavior. As this happens, whole new possibilities for coordinated action develop.

Our standard way of thinking suggests that coordinated action occurs when different people reach a shared agreement, then create an "action plan." Dialogue proposes that some levels of coordinated action do not require this rational planning at all. In fact, some of the most powerful forms of coordination may come through participation in unfolding meaning, which might even be perceived differently by different people. A flock of birds suddenly taking flight from a tree reveals the potential coordination of dialogue: this is movement all at once, a wholeness and listening together that permits individual differentiation but is still highly interconnected.

At The Dialogue Project at MIT, we have begun to learn how to nurture this coordination in the context of diverse organizations and social systems— including a steel mill with a troubled labor-management history, an entire health-care community in the Midwest riddled with competitive antagonisms, South African professionals and leaders, managers in corporations, and a group of urban leaders in a major U.S. city. This discipline, which involves reflection on ways of knowing, on language, and on the embodied experience of meaning, turns out to have exceedingly practical applications, and suggests equally powerful applications for cultivating learning within organizations.

This article reviews our emerging theory of dialogue and reports on early evidence of its impact in practical settings.

DIALOGUE: A WORKING DEFINITION

The word dialogue comes from two Greek roots, *dia* and *logos*, suggesting "meaning flowing through." This sense of the word stands in stark contrast to what we normally think of as "dialogue"—a mechanistic and unproductive debate between people seeking to defend their views against one another. In dialogue, as we use the term, people gradually learn to suspend their defensive exchanges and further, to probe into the underlying reasons for *why* those exchanges exist. However, this probing into defenses is not the central purpose of a dialogue session: the central purpose is simply to establish a field of genuine meeting and inquiry (which we call a container)—a setting in which people can allow a free flow of meaning and vigorous exploration of the collective background of their thought, their personal predispositions, the nature of their shared attention, and the rigid features of their individual and collective assumptions.

Dialogue can be initially defined as *a sustained collective inquiry into the processes, assumptions, and certainties that compose everyday experience.* Yet this is experience of a special kind—the experience of the meaning embodied in a

William N. Isaacs is the director of the Dialogue Project at MIT's Organizational Learning Center, which is part of the Sloan School of Management. Funded initially by a grant from the W. K. Kellogg Foundation, The Dialogue Project has conducted action research experiments on dialogue and organizational learning in a variety of settings around the world.

Dr. Isaacs received his doctorate from Oxford University. His research has focused on the perils of shared ideals, dialogue, and organizational learning. For the past seven years, Bill has consulted with senior management of *Fortune* 500 companies and leaders in communities and in health care systems.

FIGURE 11.1

community of people. All organizations, even dysfunctional organizations, are full of a rich store of meaning—it is what produces the commonality of behaviors across any complex organization, and what gives communities the power to torment and stifle their members. Yet often that meaning is incoherent, full of fragmented interpretations that guide behavior, yet go untested and unexplored.

If people can be brought into a setting where they, at their choice, can become conscious of the very process by which they form tacit assumptions and solidify beliefs, and be rewarded by each other for doing so, then they can develop a common strength and capability for working and creating things together. This free flow of inquiry and meaning allows new possibilities to emerge. This capability exists in every community, but in most organizations it is dormant. Dialogue allows it to be awakened.

Unlike most forms of inquiry, the inquiry in dialogue is one that places primacy on the whole. Dialogue's aim is to take into account the impact one speaker has on the overall system, giving consideration to the timing of comments, their relative strength, their sequence, and their meaning to others. Dialogue seeks to unveil the ways in which collective patterns of thinking and feeling unfold—both as conditioned, mechanistic reflexes, and potentially as fluid, dynamically creative exchanges.

Dialogue is an old term. Some evidence suggests that human beings have gathered in small groups to talk together for millennia; to claim this is a new art is a mistake. Indeed, it is because dialogue is, at its core, very natural to human beings that there seems real possibility for its use in modern settings, despite a range of institutionalized barriers.

Dialogue vs. Consensus

In consensus building, people seek some rational means to limit options and focus on the ones that are logically acceptable to most people. Often, the purpose of a consensus approach (the root of the word means "to feel together") is to find a view that reflects what most people in a group can "live with for now." This assumes that shared action will arise out of a shared position. This assumption is questionable. While consensus approaches may create some measure of agreement, they do not alter the fundamental patterns that led people to disagree at the outset. Consensus approaches generally do not have the ambition of exploring or altering underlying patterns of meaning.

By contrast, dialogue seeks to have people learn how to think together—not just in the sense of analyzing a shared problem, but in the sense of surfacing fundamental assumptions and gaining insight into why they arise. Dialogue can thus produce an environment where people are consciously participating in the creation of shared meaning. Through this they begin to discern their relationship to a larger pattern of collective experience. Only then can the shared meaning lead to new and aligned action.

For example, in 1992, the labor and management representatives from a troubled steel company in the Midwest realized that, if their company was to survive intensified competitive pressure, they would have to find a way to resolve intractable differences between them—differences they had maintained for more than 30 years. They turned to dialogue to explore those differences, to see what sort of mutual learning they could create, and to discover whether that might lead to performance differences in the mill. At that time, representatives from both sides could barely speak without shouting at each other or walking out at the first signs of anger. Less than one year later, the two sides have grown so accustomed to talking together that they regularly make joint presentations—not as "first management speaks, and then the union speaks," but as presentations made by a third entity that contains both management and union. This particular group has transformed an intense adversarial relationship into one where there is genuine and serious inquiry into taken-for-granted ways of thinking. It's significant that the allegiances to management and union have not disappeared. Dialogue, instead, has given birth to a metaphorical container—with their steel mill background, these people call it a "cauldron"—that is large enough to contain the allegiance to union and management within it.

In a recent presentation by this dialogue group to 80 managers from a variety of companies, one union participant said, "We have learned to question fundamental categories and labels that we have applied to each other." A manager in the audience shot up his hand and said, "Can you give us an example?" "Yes. Labels like *management* and *union*." The manager's face registered evident surprise. Perhaps, in his company, no one would have even voiced the fact that these labels existed, for fear of raising questions about "class" and "worth" and "status" that people would be afraid they couldn't confront. The union president is articulate about what has changed:

> . . . they hired me from the neck down. They never hired any of us from the neck up . . . I was given the opportunity to say and do and make things happen myself and voice my opinion. And you know, I didn't do too bad. I was shocked with some of the things that I actually said, that came out of my mouth. Things that we couldn't have done several years ago.

In another setting, we brought together major health care providers for a city—the CEOs of the major hospitals, doctors, nurses, insurance agents, a legislator, and technicians. The group was, in effect, a microcosm of the healthcare system. Within that setting, people were able to mutually inquire into some of the underlying assumptions and forces that seem to make this field so chaotic. Said one senior physician during a session, "I am struck by my schizophrenia: the difference between how I treat my patients and how I treat all of you." In another session, participants confronted the collective pain levied by the inhuman demand that they should assume responsibility for all the illness of a community.

In these sessions, this group has begun to inquire openly about underlying—and deeply taboo—subjects, such as feelings of self-protection and anomie among health care professionals, and how these feelings, themselves, are a key source of the counterproductivity inherent in the healthcare system; they lead to costly isolation, misplaced competitiveness, and lack of coordination. Dialogue produces insights into collective challenges that can alter people's ways of thinking and acting in their systems.

By focusing on underlying thinking, dialogue appears to be directed away from producing results. This perception, however, may stem from our expectations about *how* common direction and results are produced. One story, recently told to the author, illustrates the power of a dialogue-like kind of exchange.

In the late 1960s, the dean of a major U.S. business school was appointed to chair a committee to examine whether the university, which had major government contracts, should continue to design and build nuclear bombs on its campus. People were in an uproar over the issue. The committee was somewhat like Noah's ark: two of every species of political position on the campus. The chairman had no idea how to bring all these people together to agree on anything, so he changed some of the rules. The committee would meet, he said, every day until it had produced a report. Every day meant exactly that—weekends, holidays, everything. People objected: "You can't do that." He insisted, "Yes we can. We will continue to meet. If you can't be there, that's okay."

The group eventually met for 36 days straight. Consistent with our emerging theory of dialogue, for the first two weeks, they had no agenda. People just talked about anything they wanted to talk about—the purpose of the university, how upset they were, their deepest fears, and their noblest aims. They eventually turned to the report they were supposed to write. By this time, people had been drawn quite close to one another.

To the surprise of many, the group eventually produced a unanimous statement. They agreed that the university should gradually phase out the building of weapons. This was not a consensus process in the traditional sense, in that the dean did not seek to find common ground among the competing views, or insist on agreement by compromise. What was striking was that they agreed on a direction, but for different reasons. Some felt the laboratories were extremely expensive and administratively complex; others felt the presence of the weapons was morally wrong. An important lesson showed itself here: people did not have to have the same reasons to agree with the direction that emerged.

DIALOGUE AND ORGANIZATIONAL LEARNING

The discipline of dialogue is central to organizational learning because it holds promise as a means for promoting collective thinking and communication. Three factors point to the need for new levels of practical improvement on this score:

First, organizations today face a degree of complexity that requires intelligence beyond that of any individual. To solve problems in complex systems, we must learn to tap the collective intelligence of groups of knowledgeable people. Yet in the face of complex, highly conflictual issues, teams typically break down, revert to rigid and familiar positions, and cover up deeper views. One result of this is "abstraction wars"—people lobbing abstract opinions across meeting rooms, without exploring what the opinions of others mean. Another result is "dilemma paralysis"—people find themselves stuck: raising the issues leads to polarization; failing to raise these issues means ineffectiveness is likely to continue.

Second, most of the current efforts at fostering collective thinking and learning in organizations backfire. While all organizations are continuously learning, some seem to be supporting learning that maintains a dysfunctional status quo. Paradoxically, our very efforts to produce learning can be counterproductive. The Challenger disaster is one of many sad examples of how organizations (in this case, a network of organizations working with NASA) can learn systematically to distort information and block communication channels, despite rigorous attempts to avoid this. Carefully defined procedures and checkpoints did not stop people from withholding their doubts and preventing or delaying productive debate about possible dangers; they were following "official" protocols and unofficial face-saving rules.

One antidote to problems of this sort has revolved around efforts to promote learning by introducing "vision" and "values" into the daily lexicon and practice of managers. Yet organizations that use ideals in this way are particularly susceptible to creating behavioral rigidity; people make "ideal-images" of these same values, of themselves, and of their performance. These images devolve into superficial ideology and blind people to the numbing self-deception and enormous dilemmas they create for people seeking to live up to them. And when organizations learn a pattern that produces breakthrough results, they often become locked into that same trajectory, staying with it even after it begins to head toward downfall.

The work of The Dialogue Project indicates that breakdowns like these are reflective of a broader crisis in the very nature of how human beings perceive the world and take action in it. To address this crisis, humankind will require radically new approaches. The essence of the crisis is based in the fact that people have learned to divide the world into categories in thought and make distinctions within those categories. Though these categories are a natural mechanism to develop meaning, we have a tendency to become almost hypnotized by them, forgetting that we created them. We act mindlessly, as if our assumptions and categories of thought were perfectly representative of reality. Our own creations, our thoughts, take on a seemingly independent power over us. Perhaps most striking is the realization that we do this collectively. Organizational learning will not advance substantially, it seems, without a collective discipline for inquiring into this subtle and yet profoundly influential domain.

A central and serious manifestation of the crisis of perception is the problem of "fragmentation" in thought, as described by Fred Kofman and Peter Senge in "Communities of Commitment." (See lead article in this issue.) We have divided our experience into numerous isolated bits that seem to have no connection to one another. As a result, specialists in most fields cannot talk across specialties. Nowhere does this fragmentation become more apparent than when human beings seek to communicate and think together about difficult issues. Rather than reason together, people defend their "part."

Yet recent developments in both quantum theory and cognitive science make strong cases to support the notion that perceiving the world in terms of separate fragments is based in a fictitious way of thinking. In quantum theory, the discovery of what Niels Bohr called the "quantum wholeness" suggests that there is an irreducibility of observer and observed when it comes to looking at small particles of matter. According to quantum theory, light can behave like a particle or a wave depending on how you set up the experiment. What you perceive, in other words, is not determined by independent external properties of "parts" of reality, but is a function of the ways in which you try to perceive that reality. At the most fundamental level, the work of dialogue rests upon an understanding that noted physicist and author David Bohm and others found articulated in quantum physics theory. As Bohm puts it:

> . . . fragmentation is now very widespread, not only throughout society, but also in each individual; and this is leading to a kind of general confusion of the mind, which creates an endless series of problems and interferes with our clarity of perception so seriously as to prevent us from being able to solve most of them. . .

> The notion that all these fragments are separately existent is evidently an illusion, and this illusion cannot do other than lead to endless conflict and confusion.

The practice of dialogue focuses on uncovering and inquiring into the feedback loop between our internal interpretive structures (our tendency to name events in certain ways) which then influence the world and (eventually) our internal structures. It seems increasingly clear that our perceptions and thought can literally create our worlds. Bohm and Edwards give the example of walking down a dark street late at night, where one might see a shadow, suddenly finding one's heart pounding and breath quickening. Naming the perception of the shadow as an attacker leads us to behave in particular ways; when we discover it is only a shadow we relax. Our internal interpretation of an external stimulus produces a physical response. We constantly do this in our worlds, naming external stimuli in certain automatic ways and responding to them, all the while directly producing our own internal experience of them.

Finally, to understand the pervasive nature of fragmentation, it is important not to think of fragmentation as a problem and dialogue as its solution.

Fragmentation is a condition of thought, and dialogue is one tentatively demonstrated strategy for stepping back from the way of thinking produced by fragmentation and incorporating another way of thinking. Dialogue is an attempt to perceive the world with new eyes, not merely to solve problems using the thought that created them in the first instance.

Dialogue and Triple-Loop Learning

One approach to ameliorating these problems within the field of organizational learning attempts to help individuals and organizations examine and change the underlying assumptions, or the theories behind their actions. Instead of merely trying to improve along a particular set of standards or dimensions, "double-loop" learning (a concept developed by Chris Argyris and Donald Schon) focuses on the assumptions underlying these standards.

An organization that *does* successfully modify some of its underlying values or standards has thus achieved a remarkable result. The consequences of this can be impressive. The mini-mill phenomenon in the American steel industry is one example: an industry based on large scale integrated mills has been transformed by powerful competition and now accepts a premise that would have not have been considered 15 years ago: that success and quality can come from small, flexible mills. But the question remains as to whether such organizations have actually learned about the underlying reasons that rigidity and limited assumptions ruled at the outset. Without learning about learning at this next level, the cycle is likely to repeat itself.

Gregory Bateson used the term "learning III" to describe this form of learning about the context of learning. It could also be called "triple-loop learning." If Argyris and Schon's "double-loop learning" answers the question, "What are alternative ways of seeing this situation that could free me to act more effectively?" triple-loop learning would answer the question, "What is leading me and others to have a predisposition to learn in this way at all? Why these goals?" Double-loop learning encourages learning for increasing effectiveness. Triple-loop learning is the learning that opens inquiry into underlying "why's." It is the learning that permits insight into the nature of paradigm itself, not merely an assessment of which paradigm is superior.

While this type of learning may seem abstract or risky, especially when people understand how vulnerable it might make them feel, experience has begun to show that it can be quite practical and actionable by managers and employees in organizations, and that it can have a transformative and creative effect on their lives.

THE THEORY OF DIALOGUE

To create an operational theory of how a reflective learning process—dialogue—can produce "triple-loop" learning, we began by drawing on the work of three key Twentieth-Century thinkers. The philosopher Martin Buber used the term *dialogue* in 1914 to describe a mode of exchange among human beings in which there is a true turning to one another and a full appreciation of another person, not as an object in a social function but as a genuine being. Psychologist Patrick DeMaré suggested in the 1980s that large group "socio-therapy" meetings could enable people to engage in understanding and altering the cultural meanings present within society—to heal the sources of mass conflict and violence or ethnic bigotry, for example.

David Bohm, with his understanding of the changing view of the nature of physical matter, suggested that this new form of conversation should focus on bringing to the surface, and altering, the "tacit infrastructure" of thought. Bohm suggested that as groups of people learned to watch and articulate the assumptions and pressures inherent in individual and collective thought, they might catch and alter their self-defeating and self-deceptive processes.

While each of these thinkers has stressed important dimensions of dialogue—Buber's emphasis was on "being," DeMaré's on cultural meaning, Bohm's on thought—the development of a theory of dialogue remains in an embryonic stage. In our research project, we have been exploring ways of combining elements of these theories and producing dialogue in the world, examining its impact in action, and in so doing, extending the theory behind it.

To understand dialogue and its contribution to collective learning, one must explore the domain of collective thought, and in particular, the underlying processes that seem to govern it. This opens an inquiry into the nature of "tacit thought" as it is held by individuals and collectives.

Most people know how to ride a bicycle. Once you learn, you never forget. But trying to explain how you ride could cause you to fall off! Philosopher Michael Polanyi called this "tacit knowledge." You know more than you can say. Other examples include our knowledge of how to digest, and how (without consciously thinking about it) to follow the roads that lead to our workplace. Finally, and most importantly, our use of language is tacit—and collective. People who communicate share an understanding not simply of words, but of how to form words to make meaning.

As Bohm conceived it, dialogue would kindle a new mode of paying attention, to perceive—as they arise—the assumptions taken for granted, the flow of the polarization of opinions, the rules for acceptable and unacceptable conversation, and the methods for managing differences. Since these are collective, individual reflection would not be enough to bring these matters to the surface. And since reflection, by its nature, looks back at what has already taken place, it is innately limited for anticipating assumptions, opinions, rules, and differences that are only now emerging. The mindfulness embodied in dialogue involves awareness of the living experience of thinking, not reflection after the fact about it. For us to gain insight into the nature of our tacit thought, we must somehow learn to watch or experience it, in action. This work would require a form of collective attention and learning. Dialogue's purpose is to create a setting where conscious collective mindfulness can be maintained.

CREATING FIELDS OF INQUIRY

Dialogue is a discipline that conducts "field experiments"—i.e., experiments that attempt to make conscious the underlying field in which different frames and different choices for action emerge. The notion of a "field" of influence can be traced to one of the pioneers in the study of groups and social interaction—Kurt Lewin. Lewin noted that human association could be understood as shared fields, with forces that could be measured and influenced. Though seemingly ephemeral, fields are obviously tangible forces: a current of electricity running through a wire creates, as a byproduct, a weak magnetic field that is invisible and yet has impact.

Our emergent dialogue theory and practice builds on this notion, claiming that shared tacit thought among a group comprises a field of "meaning" and that such fields are the underlying constituent of human experience. As these fields are altered in a variety of subtle ways, their influence on peoples' behavior changes too. In many cases, the social fields in which people live are unstable and incoherent. That is, there are many different "tacit programs" in motion, in conflict, leading people to hold images of the world that they experience as literally true and obvious. The images that one person holds might be very different from the images held by his or her neighbors. People also tend to defend these images, particularly under conditions of threat and embarrassment. This creates organizational defensive routines of the sort articulated by Argyris. An unstable social field supports defensive routines.

Based on his work in quantum physics, David Bohm has compared dialogue to superconductivity. In superconductivity, electrons cooled to very low temperatures act more like a coherent whole than as separate parts. They flow around obstacles without colliding with one another, creating no resistance and very high energy. At higher temperatures, however, they began to act like separate parts, scattering into a random movement and losing momentum. Depending on the environment in which they operate, electrons behave in dramatically different ways. The field in which the electrons operate changes.

When confronting tough issues, people act more like separate, high-temperature electrons. Their associations are unstable and incoherent, in the sense that they collide with one another at times. Dialogue seeks to alter this by producing a "cooler" shared environment, by refocusing the group's shared attention. When this takes place, people can spend time in high-energy interactions with reduced friction, without ruling out differences between them. Negotiation tactics, in contrast, often try to cool down interactions among people, but do so by bypassing the most difficult issues and narrowing the field of exchange to something manageable. They produce somewhat cooler interactions, but lose energy and intelligence in the process. In dialogue the aim is to produce a special, "super cooled" environment in which a different kind of relationship among the parts can come into play.

Traditional forms of inquiry focus on the nature of the parts of the system and their causal interrelationships. Following the analogy here, this might be called "hot inquiry." Dialogue can permit the emergence of a form of inquiry that requires a new repertoire of collective attention called "cool inquiry." Cool inquiry focuses people's attention on collective thought and shared assumptions, and the living social processes that sustain them.

The Practice of Dialogue

Dialogue poses several paradoxes in practice. While it seeks to allow greater coherence to emerge among a group of people (not necessarily agreement), it does not impose coherence. Beginning a dialogue exposes another paradox: while the process encourages people to have a shared intention for inquiry, it does not have an agenda, a leader, or a task. Dialogue does require a facilitator initially, who can help set up this field of inquiry and who can embody its principles and intention. But by deliberately not trying to solve familiar problems in a familiar way, dialogue opens a new possibility for shared thinking.

Dialogue in Action: Case Study in a Steel Mill

The case of the steel mill provides examples of all these facets of dialogue. The management-union structure that prompted the dialogue effort still exists, but participants can stand beside it with far more perspective. This plant has experienced the pain of intense downsizing typical of much of the American steel industry. From 5,000 employees in 1980, the largest plant now has shrunk to fewer than 1,000.

When we entered the scene in 1992, we heard stories about confrontations in which people had thrown chairs at one another or stormed out of meetings, slowed down work, and called each other names. Both union and management were skeptical about the possibility of genuine reconciliation—and vociferous about the lack of trust that they felt for the other. Competition from mini-mills, however, had forced them to recognize the need to cooperate. Consequently, they had recently agreed to a participative total quality improvement process, formed joint committees to solve problems, and set up an individual reward system for cost-saving improvements.

In our earliest conversations, held separately with labor leaders in one group and senior managers of the plant and division in the other, we explored ways each group was projecting blame for problems onto the other. There people developed an initial grasp of inquiry skills, such as how to detect an abstract

---

EXHIBIT 1
INITIAL GUIDELINES FOR DIALOGUE

- Suspend assumptions and certainites
- Observe the observer
- Listen to your listening
- Slow down the inquiry
- Be aware of thought
- Befriend polarization

BOX 11.1

statement and invite people to explain their thinking. We introduced the set of initial guidelines for our time together shown in Box 11.1.

The metaphor of a "crucible" emerged in these conversations as a powerful influence on the initial thinking and connection of all parties. Steelmaking involves intense heat and pressure under control; this was an image for dialogue that made immediate sense to the steelworkers. Human intensity under control allows forces to be brought to bear and change to be wrought. Typically, however, there is no "container," or field, in which such changes can be made. The steel mill participants still sometimes speak of how a meeting got "hot," that someone was "burned." The heat analogy refers to intensity of human exchange. One central concern was how to create a setting where the intensity of years of adversarial relationship could be transformed.

Eventually both groups met together. In the initial two-day gathering, people found that talking together was not as horrendous as they had expected. They began to relax and say what was really on their minds, expressing their worries, their concerns, their beliefs about the business. But they did this in ways that sparked old conflicts. Someone went "ballistic" and people began to feel that all was lost.

To manage this intensity, we asked people to step deliberately into their anger, and to step back from their collective (and hopelessly stuck) reasoning. To achieve this, we created a map of their interactions, then sought to "suspend" the map—to look at it without trying to fix it, but simply to see it together, and see its impact on the organization.

Together, we succeeded in seeing the conflict as a patterned behavioral response in the group's shared field, and allowed it to change. This proved to be a turning point: members of the group gained insight into (and to some degree arrested) familiar conflicts that previously they had felt helpless to change. This encouraged people to, as one manager subsequently put it, "play along."

Following this two-day session, the group agreed to meet once every two weeks in an open setting. At each meeting, the group sits in a circle, and each person is typically given a chance to say something about what is on his mind. There is no agenda and no effort to solve problems directly. Topics emerge.

People learn to see how others are thinking and feeling about critical plant matters and about each other. They learn to inquire into the nature of the assumptions behind their thinking. This free flowing exchange has not only allowed new insight, it has altered fundamental assumptions about the union's relationship to the business. The union president, speaking about the progress they have made, put it this way:

> When we first started . . . the only thing that we ever talked about was the past: How you've screwed me in the past. How you've lied to me in the past. How you went from 5,000 workers down to 1,000. How you've promised us job security and right on down the line. You know, we don't hear that any more. That went away. That's gone. Now we're looking at the future. . . .

People report change of this sort across the group. A manager in one session said:

> I was very antsy about this at first—to dedicate that much time, a half a day every other week—I thought Lordy, that's a lot of time. But what we've done is to dedicate the time, to slow down and then create a space to listen to each other so that people can collectively learn the values of a lot of various people as opposed to the same people.

Perhaps the most dramatic effects of this are evident not in the dialogue sessions themselves, but in all other activities. For the first time managers and union personnel have been talking together and thinking about their business. This has evoked a sense of mutually seeing one another's opinions as valid and as part of a single system.

Over the months, there has been a remarkable change in the pattern of relationship and quality of inquiry among this group. After one recent session, a union man said, "you know, I can't tell who is on what side anymore." Initially the union men would never disagree with each other publicly, in front of the managers. Their story was singular: all the problems in the plant were the manager's faults, and any new program or plan was essentially intended to take advantage of them. Now, some months later, they openly disagree and inquire with one another, and they challenge one another to think together, instead of separately.

One critical factor in this group has been the openness of the CEO, who participates fully in the dialogue meetings. He has demonstrated a profound willingness to learn, and to admit publicly when he makes a mistake. As he put it, "The process became a method of exchanging thoughts and realizing that none of us have *the* answer, but together we might have a better answer."

LEVELS AND STAGES OF DIALOGUE: THE DEVELOPMENT OF COOL INQUIRY

Mapping the evolution of dialogue through time has been one of our initial research aims. We have attempted to articulate a practical theory of dialogue by naming elements of this process and identifying the individual behaviors and collective skills that seem to compose it. A central factor in this has been to uncover the concrete ways dialogue requires the creation of a series of increasingly conscious environments or fields of inquiry. These environments, which we have called "containers," can be developed as a group of people become aware of the requirements and discipline of creating them. A container can be understood as the sum of the collective assumptions, shared intentions, and beliefs of a group. These manifest in part as a collective "atmosphere" or climate.

Figure 11.2 displays the evolution of dialogue. One could think of the evolving stages as enfolded within one another. In one sense, they are all present simultaneously, though one may seem dominant. Moreover, a group may pass through one level, then return to a lower level. Passing through from one level to the next seems to entail meeting different types of individual and collective crises.

1. Instability of the Container. When any group of individuals comes together, they bring with them a wide range of tacit, unexpressed differences in paradigms and perspectives. The first challenge for participants is to recognize this, and to accept that the purpose of the dialogue is not to hide these differences but to find a way of letting them be explored.

EXHIBIT 2
EVOLUTION OF DIALOGUE

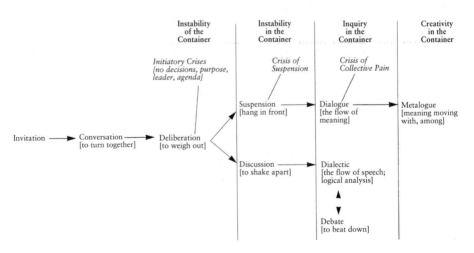

FIGURE 11.2 Evolution of Dialogue

Dialogue requires a container. To some degree in all settings, conflict and "defensive routines" will tend to make the container unstable. To begin a dialogue requires somehow altering these patterns of interaction in a system so that the group of people can directly observe them. In contrast to conventional intervention methods, this does not then lead to deliberate attempts to fix these structures, but only to explore them collectively in a skillful manner. The core of the theory of dialogue builds on the premise that the effect of people's shared attention can alter the quality and level of inquiry possible at any particular time. People can gradually learn to refine their modes of collective awareness to promote increasingly more subtle and intelligent modes of interaction. The process is very demanding, and at times frustrating; it is also deeply rewarding.

Dialogue begins with conversation. The root of the word conversation means "to turn together." People begin by speaking together, and from that flows deliberation. To deliberate is to "weigh out." Consciously and unconsciously, people weigh out different views, finding some with which they agree, and others that they dislike. They selectively pay attention, noticing some things, missing others. At this point, people face the first crisis, a decision point that can lead either to the further refinement and evolution of the dialogue environment, or to greater instability. This "initiatory crisis" comes because people recognize that despite their best intentions, they cannot force dialogue to take place. In their terms, they cannot comprehend, much less *impose* coherence on the diversity of differences of view.

For the steelworkers, the initial experience was of instability and overt hostility, as well as a gradual willingness to step back from the conflict. Said one manager during the first two-day session:

> I can see the pattern of the old pattern. I can feel it. "We want this and this.
> . . . Well, no way can you have this and if we give you this, you have got to
> give us this." And that's two containers. That's us against them.

But gradually people recognize that they can either begin to defend their points of view, finding others as somewhat or totally wrong, or suspend their view, and begin to listen without coming to a hard and fast conclusion about the validity of any of the views yet expressed. They become willing to loosen the "grip of certainty" about all views, including their own.

2. Instability *in* the Container. A recognition of this "initiatory" crisis begins to create an environment in which people know that they are seeking to do something different from the usual. Groups often begin to oscillate between suspending views and "discussing" them. (The root of the word discussion means "to break apart.") People will feel the tendency to fall into the familiar habit of analyzing the parts, instead of listening for the incoherence of the whole. At this stage, people may find themselves feeling frustrated, principally because the underlying fragmentation and incoherence in everyone's thought begins to appear. They may, for example, tend to defend their views, despite evidence that they may be wrong. They may see their behavior as principally a function of how others think and behave, and discount the ways their own thought deeply influences their experience. Normally, all this is either taken for granted or kept below the surface. In dialogue, we deliberately seek to make observable and accessible these general patterns of thought and feeling, and more critcally, the tacit influences that sustain them.

People begin to see and explore the range of assumptions that are present. They ask: Which are true? Which are false? How far is the group willing to go to expose itself? At this point, people begin to feel as if they were in a giant washing machine. No point of view seems to hold all the truth any longer; no conclusion seems definitive.

This leads to a second crisis, namely the "crisis of suspension." Points of view that used to make sense no longer do. People feel that they can't tell where the group is heading; they feel disoriented, and perhaps marginalized or constrained by others. Polarization comes up. Extreme views become stated and defended. All of this "heat" and instability is exactly what *should* be occurring. The fragmentation that has been hidden is surfacing in the container.

In our healthcare dialogue sessions, at this stage, people began to talk about the long-suppressed "myths" different groups held about each other (physicians and administrators, for example), and the anger that they felt about each other. Though expressing conflict of this sort was traditionally anathema to "caring" people, the group explored it directly—not strictly as a set of interpersonal issues, but as a function of the collective images of one another.

Similarly, in the steel mill sessions, conflict "of the same old kind" emerged. Some participants felt helpless and defeated, others went "ballistic." Yet they did not walk out. They stayed to explore the ways in which they had each contributed to the unproductive dynamics. The facilitators presented them with a "map" of their conflict (similar to that shown in Figure 11.3), then gave them a chance to reflect on it and consider whether to sustain the pattern shown.

Maps of this sort can be used as guides to correct behavior; in this instance, it was used to raise awareness and encourage responsibility for the shared field in which the participants were operating. People acknowledged that this was an accurate reflection of their actions; we placed a copy of the map on the wall. In the very next interchange, the same dynamic appeared again. Several in the group pointed (literally) to the map, and then to the people; it dawned on them and others that they were caught in the same back-eddy of the stream of thought. The dynamic changed in that moment for the group; it has not appeared in that way since. Polarizations still come up, but tend to be handled in a very different fashion.

To manage the crisis of collective suspension that arises at this stage, everyone must be adequately awake to what is happening. People may then avoid taking an internal "vote" about any position—not panic and withdraw, not choose to fight, not categorize things as "this" or "that," but listen and inquire: "What is this? What is the meaning of this?" They do not merely listen to others, but to themselves. They ask: "Where am I listening from? What is the disturbance going

EXHIBIT 3
A CONFLICT MAP

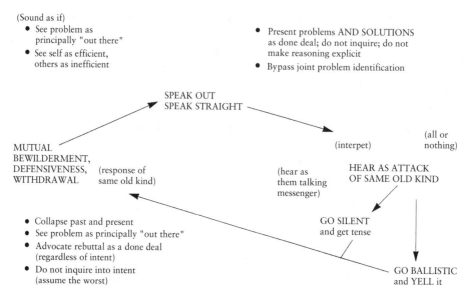

FIGURE 11.3 A Conflict Map

on in me (not others)? What can I learn if I slow things down and inquire (to seek within)?" Another union man said in one dialogue session:

> At the last meeting, I was very motivated to go and find out what I thought were negatives coming up in the container, what I could do to fix them. And I think some other people did too. I used to have a very significant impulse to attack an issue. I would feel like I would have to at least get my position in, or there was going to be trouble. And I'm not having that impulse—hardly at all anymore . . . if somebody says something I don't particularly agree with . . . it's almost like, so what?

This crisis is where skilled facilitation is most critical. The facilitator, however, is not seeking to "correct" or impose order on what is happening, but to model how to suspend what is happening to allow greater insight into the order that is present.

3. Inquiry in the Container. If a critical mass of people stay with the process beyond this point, the conversation begins to flow in a new way. In this "cool" environment people begin to inquire together as a whole. New insights often emerge. The energy that had been trapped in rigid and habitual patterns of thought and interaction begins to be freed up. People notice, for example, that they differ in their pace and timing of speaking and thinking, and begin to inquire into and respect these facts.

Our experience with a dialogue in South Africa among leading black and white businessmen and women, community organizers, and educators provides an example. We found that people came to the point of reflecting on apartheid in ways that surprised them. They were able to stand beside the tension of the topic without being identified with it. Similarly, the steelworkers recognized that they had far more in common with management than they had previously realized or expected. And they realized that they could inquire together in ways that previously would have surprised them. In the healthcare dialogue, it was at this point that people began to discuss their "god-like" status and stopped blaming others in the "system" for the difficulties they saw.

Sometimes in this phase the flow takes on a powerful and undeniable intensity. Inquiry within this phase of the container is subtle; people here can become sensitive to the cultural "programs" for thinking and acting that they have unwittingly accepted as true. In these later stages of dialogue, the term "container" becomes limiting. It is more accurate to describe it as a kind of shared "field" in which meaning and information are being exchanged.

While people participate, they also begin to watch the session in a new way. One participant from an urban leaders' dialogue in Boston likened this experience to seeing the inside of their minds performing together in a theater. People become sensitive to the ways in which the conversation is affecting all the participants in the group. In particular, they can begin to look for the embodied manifestations of their thoughts.

This phase can be playful and penetrating. Yet it also leads to another crisis. People gradually realize that deeper themes exist, behind the flow of ideas. They come to understand and feel the impact that holding fragmented ways of thinking has had on them, their organizations, and their culture. They sense their separateness. While people may understand intellectually that they have had limits to their vision, they may not yet have experienced the fact of their isolation. Such awareness brings pain—both from loss of comforting beliefs and from the exercise of new cognitive and emotional muscles. People recognize that their thoughts—in the form of collective assumptions and choices—create and sustain fragmentation and separation.

The "crisis of collective pain" is the challenge of embracing these self-created limits of human experience. This crisis is one that can lead to transformation of fundamental patterns of interaction. Areas in which wholeness is lacking become evident. As they are collectively observed, they change, freeing up rigidity and old habits of attention and communication. Moving through this crisis is by no means a given nor necessary for "success" in dialogue. Groups may develop the capacity for moving to the final level of dialogue over a considerable period of time. It is a deep and challenging crisis, one that requires considerable discipline and collective trust.

4. Creativity in the Container. If this crisis can be navigated, a new level of awareness opens. People begin to know consciously that they are participating in a pool of common meaning because they have sufficiently explored each other's views. They still may not agree, but their thinking takes on an entirely different rhythm and pace. At this point, the distinction between memory and thinking becomes apparent. People may find it hard to talk together using the rigid categories of previous understanding. The net of their existing thought is not fine enough to begin to capture the subtle and delicate understandings that begin to emerge. This too may be unfamiliar or disorienting. People may find that they do not have adequate words and fall silent. Yet the silence is not an empty void, but one replete with richness. Rumi, a 13th century Persian poet, captures this experience:

> Out beyond ideas of rightdoing
> and wrongdoing
> There is a field
> I will meet you there
> When the soul lies down in that grass
> The world is too full to talk about

In this experience, the world is too full to talk about; too full to use language to analyze it. Yet words can also be evocative, creating narratives that convey richness of meaning. Though we may have few words for such experiences, dialogue raises the possibility of speech that clothes subtle meaning, instead of words merely pointing towards it. I call this kind of experience "metalogue," or "meaning flowing with." Metalogue reveals a conscious, intimate, and subtle relationship between the structure and content of an exchange and its meaning. The medium and the message are linked: Information from the process conveys as much meaning as the content of the words exchanged. The group does not "have" meaning, in other words, it *is* its meaning. This kind of exchange entails learning to think and speak together for the creation of breakthrough levels of thought, and to know the aesthetic beauty of shared speech. Such loosening of rigid thought patterns frees energy that now permits new levels of intelligence and creativity in the container.

CONCLUSION

Our experience with the discipline of dialogue suggests that there is a new horizon opening up for the field of management and organizational learning. Several key elements stand out in this respect. First, dialogue is an advance on double-loop learning processes, and represents triple-loop learning. That is, dialogue involves learning about context and the nature of the processes by which people form their paradigms, and thus take action. Second, this field suggests a new range of skills for managers that involve learning how to set up environments or "fields" in which learning can take place. These environments are "safely dangerous," in that they allow people to risk while feeling safe in doing so. Third, this discipline stresses the power of collective observation of patterns of collective thought that typically speed by us or influence our behavior without our noticing. There seems to be leverage on this score to begin to explore deeply held underlying patterns of association and meaning.

Finally, dialogue is an emerging and potentially powerful mode of inquiry and collective learning for teams. It balances more structured problem-solving approaches with the exploration of fundamental habits of attention and assumption behind traditional problems of thinking. Traditional modes of solving problems are clearly necessary. However, the same thinking that created our most pressing problems cannot be used to solve them. Unless we find ways of transforming the ground out of which all of our thinking and acting emerges, we are likely to repeat the kinds of entrained errors and produce the unintended effects we now witness. By providing a setting in which these subtle and tacit influences on our thinking can be altered, dialogue holds the potential for allowing entirely new kinds of collective intelligence to appear.

SELECTED BIBLIOGRAPHY

For more information on double-loop learning and defensive routines, see Chris Argyris, *Overcoming Organizational Defenses* (Allyn and Bacon, 1990) and C. Argyris and D. Schon, *Organizational Learning: A Theory of Action Perspective* (Reading, MA: Addison-Wesley, 1978). For an extension of these concepts into "learning III," see Gregory Bateson, *Steps to an Ecology of Mind* (New York: Chandler Publishing Company, 1972); Mario Cayer, "Bohm's Dialogue and Action Science: Two Different Approaches," unpublished paper for the Saybrook Institute, 1993; and Peter Hawkins, "The Spiritual Dimension of the Learning Organization," *Management Education and Development*, Vol. 22, Part 3, pp. 172–187.

Both conversation with and a number of works by David Bohm have significantly influenced our thinking. See, especially, his *Wholeness and the Implicate Order* (Routledge and Kegan Paul, 1980); *Unfolding Meaning* (Mickleton: Foundation House, 1985, epilogue); and *On Dialogue* (Ojai, CA, 1989). See also *Changing Consciousness* (Harper San Francisco, 1991), co-authored with M. Edwards.

For Martin Buber's foundational thoughts on the nature of dialogue, see his *The Knowledge of Man* (Atlantic Highlands, N.J: Humanities Press International, Inc., 1988). For Kurt Lewin's influence, see his *Field Theory and Social Science* (New York: Harper and Row, 1951).

Other works cited in this article include: P. DeMaré, R. Piper, and S. Thompson, *Koinonia: From Hate Through Dialogue to Culture in the Large Group*, 1st ed. (London: Karnac Books, 1991); E. Eisenberg and H. L. Goodall, Jr. *Organizational Communication* (New York: St. Martin's Press, 1993); E. J. Langer, *Mindfulness* (Reading, Mass.: Addison-Wesley Pub. Co., 1989); D. Miller, *The Icarus Paradox: How Exceptional Companies Bring About Their Own Downfall* (Harper Business, 1990); Michael Polanyi, *The Tacit Dimension* (New York: Doubleday and Co., 1967).

The metaphor of birds in flight used in the opening section was first suggested by Risa Kaparo.

Chapter 12

Teams as Learners: A Research-Based Model of Team Learning*

Elizabeth Kasl**
California Institute of Integral Studies

Victoria J. Marsick
Columbia University

Kathleen Dechant
University of Connecticut

Organizational literature heralds the value of team learning but does not provide a research-based description of it. This article describes a model of team learning that was derived empirically from case studies in two companies, one with a cross section of employees in a petrochemical company and the second in a data-processing unit that had been reorganized into self-managed teams in a manufacturing company. The authors draw conclusions about changes in learning processes,

* The thinking on which this article is based arises from joint writing and joint development of ideas among all three authors over an extensive period of collaboration. Reprinted with permission.
** Elizabeth Kasl, Ph.D., is a professor of integral studies in the School for Transformative Learning, Califonia Institute of Integral Studio, San Francisco.
Victoria J. Marsick, Ph.D., is a professor of adult and continuing education in the Department of Organization and Leadership, Teachers College, Columbia University, New York.
Kathleen Dechant, Ed. D., is an assistant professor of management in the Department of Management, School of Business Administration, University of Connecticut, Stamford.

253

conditions, and perceptions of time and explore research implications regarding human dynamics.

As organizations move away from the steep hierarchies common to the industrial era toward flatter, more integrative networks appropriate for the knowledge era (Savage, 1990), teams are being used to solve highly complex problems (Katzenbach & Smith, 1993). Corporations are searching for ways to enhance the effectiveness of teams. Recently, some theorists have pointed to the potential value of team learning to help organizations achieve breakthrough innovation (Marsick, Dechant, & Kasl, 1993; Savage, 1990; Senge, 1990). Senge, for example, emphasizes that "teams, not individuals, are the fundamental learning unit in modern organizations. This [is] where 'the rubber meets the road'; unless teams can learn, the organization cannot learn" (p. 10).

Although the organizational literature advocates team learning, it offers neither a definition nor a clear description of what it is. This article presents a research-based model of team learning. Our purpose is to describe what we found when we raised the question: What does team learning look like? We begin by describing our research methods, the team learning model, and how team-learning concepts differ from group dynamics. Next, we tell the stories of three teams and use our model to interpret their experience. We conclude with some implications for future research around team learning.

RESEARCH METHODS AND MODEL BUILDING

We began the project with traditional case study research (Yin, 1989) in a petrochemical company that had introduced high-involvement management (Lawler, 1986) to promote autonomy in work teams and decentralization of decision making. We interviewed 28 employees representing a diagonal, cross-functional slice of the organization. Using content analysis and elements of grounded theory (Strauss & Corbin, 1990), we coded transcripts for learning processes and conditions that facilitated or impeded learning in the company teams. At two different stages of our coding process, additional analysts were recruited to code a number of transcripts independently and cross-check our interpretation. We returned to the case study site and presented our tentative findings to a group of our interviewees, as well as to a cross section of managers, all of whom confirmed that our emerging description of team learning was a valid description of their experience. The model for team learning we derived from the petrochemical case study focused on team-learning processes and conditions (Dechant & Marsick, 1991), although we began to speculate, based more on theoretical inference than data, about developmental stages in teams as learning systems (Dechant, Marsick, & Kasl, 1993).

We continued our research with a second case study, this time of a single department within a manufacturing company that we named the Brewster

Company. During a five-month period in 1990, we interviewed 23 of 25 members of a data-processing unit who had been reorganized into three self-managed teams. We began our analysis by coding the same transcripts and refreshing our capacity for intercoder agreement of? team-learning processes and conditions. We then divided the interviews, recorded approximately 800 pages of transcripts. Each of us independently coded the interviews from a single team and wrote a case analysis of that team's learning. Differences among the three teams were striking. We at first suspected that our inter-coder agreement, in this case disagreement, accounted for differences in the case analyses. A process of cross-checking led us to realize that the differences among teams were real, and that these differences could be characterized by the stages of team learning about which we had been speculating.

Thus the team-learning model was derived partially from the petrochemical data and enhanced by the Brewster data. However, the two cases are not the only source of our interpretation and analysis. Working in a constructivist paradigm, we are aware that as our perspective changes, so does our understanding of team learning. The three of us have worked together on team-learning research for about five years. Our experience helped us to understand the phenomenon we are studying (Kasl, Dechant, & Marsick, 1993), along with insights we have gained as individuals through other research collaborations.

TEAM-LEARNING MODEL

We define team learning as a process through which a group creates knowledge for its members, for itself as a system, and for others. Our model describes team-learning processes, conditions that support learning, and modes of functioning as a learning system.

Team-Learning Processes and Conditions

In an earlier report on our study's findings (Dechant et al., 1993), we portrayed team learning as an interrelated set of processes in which collective thinking and action play a central role.[1] These processes are described in Table 12.1. Although we differentiate several processes in this thinking-acting interaction, it is important to emphasize that the processes are interdependent, interacting with

---

[1] In an empirical study of four teams in the research-and-development unit of a large high-technology manufacturing company, Brooks (1994) derived similar concepts to describe collective team learning from her data.

TABLE 12.1 Definition of Team-Learning Processes

Learning Process	Definition
Framing	Framing is the group's initial perception of an issue, situation, person, or object based on past understanding and present input.
Reframing	Reframing is the process of transforming that perception into a new understanding or frame.
Experimenting	Group action is taken to test hypotheses or moves, or to discover and assess impact.
Crossing boundaries	Individuals seek or give information, views, and ideas through interaction with other individuals or units. Boundaries can be physical, mental, or organizational.
Integrating perspectives	Group members synthesize their divergent views such that apparent conflicts are resolved through dialectical thinking, not compromise or majority rule.

NOTE: All the learning processes are clearly represented in our data and validated through several rounds of asking outsiders to code our transcripts. However, the work of Schön (1983) and Mezirow (1991) strongly influenced our early conceptualization of "framing/reframing" and "experimenting."

each other to produce new knowledge. Enabling conditions within the team, which we describe in Table 12.2,[2] affect its ability to learn.

Modes of Team Learning

Earlier, we posited four evolutionary stages that we believed to be developmental. Our Brewster data demonstrate how teams can and do move back and forth between these stages. Although we still believe that a team's capacity for learning is characterized by a broad developmental arc, we recognize that use of the term *stage* connotes a one-way, stepwise progression that does not capture the complexity of a team's development as a learning system. To suggest nonlinear change, we now choose the term *mode* to refer to the configuration

---

[2] Conditions are derived empirically. Gail Robinson worked with us to create Likert-type items that represented conditions identified from open coding of the petrochemical interview data. The resulting survey was administered to a large sample of petrochemical company employees and to University of Connecticut MBA students. Factor analysis created clusters that equate to the learning conditions. Robinson tested construct validity with a team-effectiveness instrument used in a Fortune 500 company involved in extensive team building. A diagnostic instrument, the Team Learning Survey, was created to measure the conditions. The manual for this instrument provides statistics about the factor analysis and the validity test (Dechant & Marsick, 1993).

TABLE 12.2 Definition of Team-Learning Conditions

Condition	Definition
Appreciation of teamwork	This condition includes the openness of team members to hearing and considering others' ideas. It also reflects the degree to which members value playing a team role and the extent to which they act in ways that help the team build on the synergy of its members.
Individual expression	Reflected in this condition is the extent to which team members have the opportunity to give their input in forming the team's mission and goals, influence the team's operation on an ongoing basis, as well as feel comfortable expressing their objections in team meetings.
Operating principles	This condition reflects the extent to which the team has organized itself for effective and efficient operation; how well the team has established a set of commonly held beliefs, values, purpose, and structure; and how effectively the team has balanced working on tasks with building relationships within the group.

of learning processes and conditions that typify a team's operation as a learning system. We name these modes Fragmented, Pooled, Synergistic, and Continuous.[3]

In the Fragmented mode, individuals learn separately, but the group does not learn as a holistic system. Members retain their separate views and are often not committed to working as a group. In the Pooled mode, individuals begin to share information and perspectives in the interest of group efficiency and effectiveness. Sometimes, small clusters of individuals learn together, but the group as an entire unit does not learn; there is not yet an experience of having knowledge that is uniquely the group's own. In the Synergistic mode, members create knowledge mutually. Divergent perspectives are integrated through dialectical processes that create shared meaning schemes. Simple phrases or metaphors from the team's experience often become code words for more elaborate meanings. Because each individual contributes to the team's knowledge, individuals integrate team knowledge into personal meaning schemes. As a result, knowledge created in a synergistic mode is frequently shared outside the group. Our concept of the Continuous mode describes a team in which synergistic learning becomes habitual. This mode continues to be posited, not data-based, and is not discussed in this article.

---

[3] In our earlier descriptions of the developmental stages of team learning, we used different labels. The words—*contained, collected, constructed*—are now replaced by *fragmented, pooled,* and *synergistic.* The conceptualization of the stages has also evolved, but the major constructs are largely unchanged.

We use a metaphor of color to illuminate qualitative differences among the learning modes in how knowledge is used. Imagine a large sheet of paper on which the team's knowledge is painted. In the Fragmented mode, the colors that characterize each individual's knowledge are separate. Bold shapes of red, blue, and yellow are discretely formed and stand out as isolated splotches on the paper. In Pooled learning, the colors are carefully arranged with an eye for pattern and relationships. Perhaps the painting evokes a patchwork quilt or a mosaic. Although individual units of color remain separate and distinct, they are interrelated and complementary. These harmonious patterns contrast with the random splotches of color that represent the Fragmented mode. In Synergistic learning, colors are blended to form completely new ones. Instead of joining individual knowledge and insights into a mosaic of team capacity, individual contributions pour forth to mingle with others, forming new colors that had not been seen before.

Team Learning and Group Dynamics

The literature on group dynamics and team building helps to explain how teams manage tasks and interpersonal relationships (Forsyth, 1990; Otter, 1996; Worchel, Wood, & Simpson, 1992). Capacity for task management is related to the learning condition that we call "operating principles," and interpersonal relationships to the conditions that we call "appreciation of teamwork" and "individual expression." Thus the group dynamics and team-building literature provides a rich description of many conditions that are essential for team learning to occur. Healthy group dynamics is prerequisite for team learning because it provides a fertile ground in which learning can germinate and grow. For example, conflict can occur when team members cross boundaries to gain new perspectives. Before members can learn through the conflict, they need a process for confronting it (operating principles), they need to be open to hearing and considering each other's ideas (appreciation of teamwork), and everyone has to have the opportunity to offer input (individual expression).

However, having healthy group dynamics in place does not guarantee collective learning. More is needed. The team-learning processes that are fostered by supportive conditions include cognitive processes (framing, reframing, integrating perspectives) and two specific, linked behaviors (crossing boundaries, experimenting) that are not fully addressed in the organizational literature. Teams can work their way through the developmental stages of forming, norming, storming, and performing (Tuckman, 1965), yet never challenge dysfunctional assumptions or create new knowledge through strategies such as reframing or perspective integration.

THE BREWSTER COMPANY: AN ILLUSTRATION OF TEAM LEARNING

We now illustrate our team-learning model by telling the stories of three self-managed teams from Brewster Company, the site for our second case study. Pseudonyms are used for both the company and the individuals in these stories.

Brewster Company takes a commodity raw material and converts it into a number of consumer products that are sold in retail markets; it also processes and sells the raw material in several forms to other industries. During the 25 years since its founding, the Brewster Company has grown to encompass nearly 175 plants and offices in North America and Europe with a total of 50,000 employees and annual sales of $6 billion. After years of rapid expansion, growth stalled. The company was faced with rising costs and heated competition. Old ways of working did not seem to work as well anymore.

The story of the data-processing and information systems group that is the focus of this case study begins at the point where the Brewster Company—recognizing its declining profit margins and unrealistic growth expectations—had decided to undergo reforms. Around this time, Norman arrived as a new director of the systems group's parent department, bringing new initiatives that catalyzed discussions between Marie, the systems group manager, and her staff. As a result, Marie suggested that her group split into self-managed teams and turned them loose to organize themselves. This reorganization, which involved matrix management, took three months of extensive discussions. Marie recounted, "It was beginning to be interminable. You can imagine trying to get 25 people to agree on anything."

The Logistics group was the first to declare itself a team. Its members had been working together on the logistics project prior to Marie's tenure as their manager. Ultimately, two additional teams emerged—Production Systems and Distributed Systems. In the next section, we describe important events that characterize each team's development and interpret each team's experience by using the concepts from our team-learning model.

The Production Systems Team Story

Members of the Production Systems team were diverse in technical knowledge and background. Walt, with an operations background, was the most senior in both age and experience. Stephen was an engineer. The remaining members we interviewed—John, Roland, and Nick—were experts in different types of software and hardware. We were unable to interview Lee, the sixth member of the team.

Prior to reorganization, members of this group had been working on a variety of mill-related projects. Following reorganization, they were assembled into a group dedicated to the task of linking process applications in the mills to data processing. At the outset, the team met to organize and establish a mission, holding a series of meetings—daily at first, then biweekly. Members viewed these early sessions as "figuring out what each of us was doing. . . . Everybody brought in their projects talked about those projects so we understood what was happening and who the customers were."

However, members attained neither a common vision nor a commitment to working collaboratively, a state reflected in members' replies when the interviewer asked, "How does your team work?" For example, Nick answered, "There's a group of us—subgroups if you will—that are working on certain projects, but the team itself is not working on one massive project. . . . I think we're still trying to find a definition of ourselves." John noted, "Everybody was working on their own." The inclination of people to think and act as individuals rather than as members of a team became the bane of the Production Systems team's existence. Here are a few examples of how the team operated on the basis of this mind-set.

My Project or Yours?

The First Story is About a Disagreement between Lee and Roland. Lee was already working on a project when Marie assigned Roland. to work on it also because he had different expertise. It was evident from the start that Lee and Roland saw things differently. Roland's view was that "there was an ownership issue with Lee . . . a perception [that] someone else was taking over her project . . . the two of us being more or less lead analysts." Although we never spoke to Lee, we do know about some of the actions she took to resolve the dispute. She proposed, for example, that scheduling be split up into two areas, one to be managed by her and one to be managed by Roland. The conflict was presented to the Production Systems team for discussion but was not resolved. Shortly thereafter, Roland went out of town, finding upon his return that the team had met and handed over sole ownership for the project to Lee. Roland reported that he preferred to move on to other projects rather than continue the conflict.

The Betrayal

The second story is told by John, who was the leader of a project to which Stephen had also been assigned. John felt betrayed when he discovered that Stephen was making individual arrangements to work with clients:

> And a lot of times I would voice everything to Stephen and say, "I had this conversation, this is what's going on." We've had conference calls with Stephen being included, and then after the conference call, a few days later, I find out that Stephen had independent meetings with the vendor over the phone. He's planning trips to go out to their site or planning trips to go to one of our mills. . . . I'm supposedly the leader of the project, and he's handling these things individually without letting me know.

None of My Business

The third story illustrates the team's emergent operating norm. The group fell into the habit of meeting only to talk about projects as they arose, prioritizing them according to significance for the business, then assigning them on the basis of members' personal interests. Once this was done, members went off to work as individuals, reporting on progress in subsequent meetings. Roland elaborated, "People felt [at meetings] that if something was being discussed that didn't relate to them directly, they would be better off doing some work than sitting there listening to a status update." Consequently, it was common for members to skip those team meetings when they had nothing to report, or to get up and leave if they felt what was being reported was not relevant to their immediate work.

Interpretive Discussion: Fragmented Team Learning in Production Systems

The Production Systems group represents the initial or Fragmented mode of team learning. The group as a whole never shared a joint purpose; members seldom worked interactively on projects. They remained individually responsible for project outcomes.

The way this team functioned is typical of systems professionals. Based on expert analysis at the launch of a project, a master plan is created. People are assigned work on the basis of their expertise. By contrast, the Brewster Company's vision for self-managed teams required each individual to take on a wide variety of projects, some of which might fall outside of his or her primary expertise. Tasks were to be rotated and responsibility shared. The Production Systems members never enacted the company's vision for self-managed teams. Walt reported, "Some people are still comfortable with the old mode of 'leave me alone; I don't really need to know what you're doing or to know some of these skills that you have.'"

Team-learning processes, as defined in Table 12.1, are in their most rudimentary form when teams function in the Fragmented mode. Having failed to reframe their way of thinking about how teams work, members of Production Systems did not cross boundaries or integrate perspectives. The conditions, listed in Table 12.2, that foster team learning are, for the most part, absent or negative. Because members did not appreciate teamwork, they found themselves without compelling reasons to foster individual expression or to create effective operating principles. Conflict was repressed or suppressed, as illustrated in Roland's reassignment from Lee's project while he was on a field trip. Norms reflected the valuing of the individual over the group, as illustrated in the tacit agreement that it was OK to walk out of a team meeting if a member did not find it relevant to his or her immediate work.

Production Systems never moved beyond the Fragmented mode of team learning. Members learned individually rather than collectively. In contrast, there are a number of incidents from the Distributed Systems team experience that illustrate the Synergistic learning mode. We turn next to this team's story.

The Distributed Systems Team Story

Distributed Systems was the smallest of the three teams. It supported "new related administrative types of projects or systems" in the mills. Its members included software specialists Amy, Peter, and Leroy; hardware specialists Dale and Robert; and John who moved from Production Systems to Distributed Systems after a department reorganization in July 1990. Many on the team attributed its success, in part, to the background of its members. They were young and did not have long histories at Brewster. Three had been there less than a year and no one more than six years. No-one had prior managerial experience, although several did talk about prior experience in successful teams. Unlike other teams, members were "all working on the same platform, using the same types of systems and the same hardware."

Like Production Systems, when this team began working together, it did not have a clear idea of a common vision. The group somewhat mechanically followed recommended steps for getting started, which included regular meetings, specialized training, and shared leadership roles. All team members reported in their interviews that an unanticipated crisis in March was the force that helped them coalesce as a real team.

Weathering the Crisis

The crisis was a production deadline for a software project that had been "on the back burner" for about a year and a half. As Leroy, the original project manager tells it, he was behind schedule, but this only became a problem when the software, which he demonstrated to the new users in March, had to be up and running by April. When Amy joined Leroy to help prepare the prototype, she realized how much work was needed to meet the April deadline. She called on Peter to help. Hardware specialists Robert and Dale were not as active at this early stage but were part of team meetings where progress and problems were aired. Everyone "chipped in . . . did what it took." Disagreements were solved reasonably by thinking together about different perspectives and options. The team was proud that it was able to complete the project by deadline.

Nonetheless, Amy and Peter found Leroy's behavior erratic during the crisis. He worked creatively but not systematically. Amy observed that he would make "a quick change on just the one piece, and that one piece works, but he never retests" for impact on other parts of the program. To make matters more complicated, Leroy missed deadlines and was tardy or absent from work without adequate notice. Leroy, however, did not realize others were dissatisfied. For his part, Leroy thought that the organization was not sufficiently respectful of family values. The culture of the organization demanded that people work late if needed. His wife worked, which left him with "half an hour or 45 minutes to get home at the end of the day, relieve the babysitter so that the children weren't left alone."

Giving Leroy Feedback

After the crisis, Distributed Systems members heard that Human Resources (HR) was consulting with Marie about Leroy's performance problem. The team had grown close as it worked together to weather the crisis. Peter reported that the team decided to challenge Marie and HR: "I thought if we're really a team, we should be addressing this issue ourselves. . . . [Marie and HR] were a bit hesitant, but then they said, 'If we're going to do this [self-managed teams], we're going to have to do it all the way.'"

With help from an HR-sponsored training program that taught team members how to give each other feedback, the Distributed Systems team focused on Leroy's issues for the better part of a day. Marie, who was present as a silent observer, noted that "they discussed a very delicate performance issue openly, honestly, and it was very obvious that it was hard for them to do, that they were not doing it to pick on this person."

Maturing as a Learning Team

Distributed Systems thought that the experience of handling these events propelled them to more effective team performance. Robert pointed to another key to the team's successful learning:

> None of us really have [sic] a major ego problem about discussing something and either having their [sic] mind changed or at least seeing the different opinion and supporting that particular opinion . . . instead of thinking *I* have to do this, it's *we* have to do this. . . . If there's a problem, it's not *you* have to solve it . . . *we have to solve it.* We have to work with other teams as a team. [italics added]

In contrast to the Production Systems team, Distributed Systems valued regular meetings, often daily, for joint planning, problem solving, and for cross-training. Peter comments, "We're trying to get it so that the whole group will be aware of what you're currently doing so that if there would be any need to help out with something that becomes a hot spot, the group" could pitch in. John, who transferred from Production Systems as part of the July reorganization, was not used to working in the open, direct way practiced by his new team. Team members described how they socialized John into being more open and challenging in their team meetings, teasing him when he kept quiet.

Distributed Systems began to flex its team muscles and increasingly challenge others' practices. For example, when Marie requested that all members of the department rate each other so that performance review would be collaborative, members of this team challenged her plan, explaining that they did not know people outside of their team well enough to do the ratings. Marie modified her strategy for performance review. In a second example, in a culture in which the user was considered king, the team began to challenge users' requests if it thought the requested project would not be "value-added."

Interpretive Discussion: Synergistic Team Learning in Distributed Systems

The Distributed Systems group functioned in the Synergistic mode. The team turned crisis into learning—first, by helping Leroy meet his deadline rather than leaving him to sink or swim alone; and then, by giving Leroy difficult feedback even though the immediate crisis had passed. This cycle of action during crisis, followed by reflection during the feedback, enabled the group to reflect together at a deeper level and thus convert short-term solutions into longer term learning about how the team should work together.

This team regularly employed the learning processes outlined in Table 12.1. Experimentation was frequent and bold, leading to new frames not only for the team but for others. The team challenged taken-for-granted personnel practices in the larger system as well as the company-wide value that user needs supersede technical judgment. It evolved a norm of active participation that is a hallmark of integrating perspectives in synergistic learning. The team found it easy to cross boundaries by gathering needed information from outside sources as well as from each other. The team also took pride in transporting the team's learning into the larger organization. When others complained that their teams did not function well, Distributed Systems encouraged them to go back to their teams and work things out together, as they in Distributed Systems had learned to do.

The conditions that facilitate team learning, outlined in Table 12.2, were present and highly favorable in the Distributed Systems group. Norms emphasized the value of teamwork, the importance of each person's participation and opinions. As Amy observed, "Usually, we all listen to each other. I don't think there's a member on the team that we don't hear out, and if we agree, we agree; and if we don't, then we just talk about it."

The Production and Distributed Systems stories illustrate teams that function primarily in a single mode. We now turn to the Logistics team, whose experience illustrates how a team moves back and forth between the modes.

The Logistics Team Story

The Logistics project had a four-year history at the time of the research interviews. Dean, one team member, called the project "a sort of a grand idea" that would have altered fundamentally the working relationships among the mills as well as between the mills and headquarters. Gradually, in response to limits in resources of time and money, the grand idea of the original logistics project vision was scaled back, and the system was reconceptualized from a mainframe to a personal computer (PC).

Not surprisingly, with four years elapsed time and major reconceptualiza-tion in the system design, the logistics project experienced significant personnel turnover. When we began our research in June 1990, the Logistics team had eight persons, seven of whom we interviewed. Some had been with the project as long as two years, and the newest member for only a few weeks. The story of the Logistics group is punctuated by four events that provide context for interpreting how the team learned.

Prototype Fails

In October 1989, several logistics programmers demonstrated a prototype to representatives from the user community who were pleased with what they saw. As the team later discovered, the demonstration was problematic because it did not include connections to the rest of the system, nor did it include real data. When the logistics team started trying to make those real-world connections, it ran into trouble.

War Room Games

After a few months, Marie asked two persons who were not on the team to take a look at the prototype and figure out why it was performing poorly. Stephen, a technical specialist, and Barbara, a trusted assistant, set up "a war room." Barbara explains, "We took a conference room for two weeks and set up the PCs and brought in the software and then brought in two of the people that had worked specifically on this piece." After systematically "trying everything;" Stephen and Barbara reported to Marie that the software in the prototype "was totally inappropriate. Just bag it!"

In his interview, Rodney reported that he had tried, shortly after his arrival at Brewster, to tell the team exactly what Stephen and Barbara would discover a full year later—that the software was inadequate for the intended task. Rodney remembers telling the team, "'That software's not going to work. . . . What you're designing on paper is fine, how it looks on paper is great. When you get to actually programming that software, it ain't going to work.' . . . That's exactly what happened." The team disregarded his warning. Rodney observed that the person who had selected the software interpreted his assessment as a criticism of her personally rather than of the software.

Black Wednesday

Shortly after the War Room revelation, Marie arranged an all-day meeting with the Logistics team and its users—a meeting that came to be called Black Wednesday. Dean explained, "Basically, we got yelled at by Marie and the users about how frustrated they were, . . . that if we all knuckled down harder and applied ourselves even more, that we could do this." Wynona described it as a critical turning point. "Marie blamed everybody. . . . It was just like a big ranting session. Shot morale right below the floor."

At issue was a series of missed deadlines and the users' increasing frustration. Although Marie believed that the team wasn't working hard enough, the team saw it differently. Kay observed that management, under pressure from users, set deadlines without regard for team members' technical expertise. Dean agreed:

> If we say something was going to take a year and a half, our best estimate, . . . there were several times when the user community and Marie . . . [would] say, "That's unacceptable. So we'll make it shorter.". . . The question I asked at a couple of meetings was, "Just by saying that it's going to take a year now, instead of a year and a half, will that make it actually happen faster?". . . But I was kind of chastised [by Marie and Barbara] for being antiteam.

After Black Wednesday, some members left the company; others worked on disheartened. Wynona explained, "The focus after that really was more like 'Just do your work.' . . . We just stopped having our weekly meetings with the little team and sharing stuff and trying to move forward." Dean reported that the team

> became the laughingstock of the whole company and the people who weren't involved in it at all, the people who worked on a different floor would walk right in and say, "How's logistics, ha ha ha?" They heard about it, it was like this big disaster.

The World Brightens

After Black Wednesday and at Marie's directive, the Logistics team met daily with the users to keep them updated on progress. About the beginning of June, another event catalyzed a brighter view for the team. Rodney explained that he "was getting aggravated" and approached a fellow worker to suggest that the Logistics team "should get together as a team without managers and decide what our problem is and then present it to them as a unified team, because whenever we did it one at a time, it didn't seem to get the message across." A few minutes before a scheduled team meeting, Rodney was talking to Barbara about his idea and "everybody started walking into the room and she started writing it down on a flip chart, . . . just different things that I was naming at random, and the more I brought it out, it got the others . . . to open up." The result was a list of about 25 difficulties with work on the Logistics team.

As they gazed at the list, group members saw that the users had played a major role in the difficulties. Users' lack of clarity and their continuing requests for change combined with the team's pattern of accommodating those requests, had stymied the project. The group then created a plan for fixing these problems. When the team reported its analysis to Marie, she backed it up and suggested a meeting with the users.

Kay reported, "This is really the first time that we've challenged the users and said that we need to do this analysis, and we need to take the time to do it right." The result, Kay believed, was an important change for the Logistics team:

> This group is pretty stable and I would say that out of all the groups within the [department], we are the most cohesive at this point. . . . The personality problems have been ironed out and people have gotten either used to each other or learned how to deal with one another.

Kay observed that in the past, when people had problems, they would "just sit there and try to do it by themselves. . . . And now . . . it's much more of a group effort. . . . So usually, the problem gets solved faster, even though there's not any more knowledge."

Interpretive Discussion: Team Learning in Logistics

In telling their stories, Logistics team members reported on experiences that the team had over the last 18 months. During this time, the team seems to have moved from Pooled to Fragmented and Synergistic modes. The team's movement among learning modes facilitates comparison of learning processes and conditions.

The Pooled Learning Mode

Prior to Black Wednesday, when the Logistics team was functioning in a Pooled learning mode, our data suggest that the reframing process was qualitatively different from the reframing that happened subsequently during synergy. New frames in the Pooled mode were imposed on the team by outside forces. The first example, scaling back the project scope, took place because of budget and resource considerations. The second example is Marie's intervention. When Marie brought in Stephen and Barbara to troubleshoot, she substituted a new problem frame by asking them to find out, "Why doesn't the prototype work?" Marie moved the Logistics team out of the frame in which members had been stuck, "How can we make the prototype software perform more efficiently?"

The Logistics data also help us see that there is a quantitative, not qualitative, difference in the way that perspectives are integrated in the Pooled learning mode versus the Fragmented mode. Learning in both modes is primarily individual, not collective. However, in the Pooled mode, individuals learn more because members are more open in expressing their ideas, sharing information, listening to each other, and seeking help.

During the Pooled mode, team-learning conditions in the Logistics group were favorable. Wynona spoke glowingly about the group's positive experience before Black Wednesday when the team enjoyed its "weekly meetings . . . [when we were] sharing stuff and trying to move forward." Although team members seemed to appreciate teamwork and developed some effective operating principles, concern for building relationships was probably unattended. The data include several examples of interpersonal discord that went unresolved, like the example mentioned by Rodney when he described how his attempt to redirect the project away from the ill-fated software was interpreted as personal criticism.

The Fragmented Learning Mode

After Black Wednesday, the team disintegrated into a Fragmented mode where learning processes and conditions closely resemble those in the Production Systems story. The team could neither think nor act together. Individuals adopted the attitude summed up by Wynona, "Just do your work." Disheartened by a sense of being abandoned by their manager and ridiculed in the larger organization, the team members saw no reason to appreciate teamwork, to express personal views, or to function according to the operating principles that the team had crafted in its earlier work.

Although there is a resemblance here to the Production Systems story, similarities are surface. The lack of cohesion in Production Systems grew from individualistic values that were never reframed. In contrast, lack of cohesion in the Logistics team was a reaction to an outside assault that left members feeling devastated and demoralized.

The Synergistic Learning Mode

In the June meeting, the group reframed its understanding of the problem and came to realize that the users had been a primary force in stymieing the project. The result, Kay reports, was a new level of group cohesion and creative interdependence. Our analysis of the June meeting helps us understand why breakthrough thinking is associated with synergistic learning. In the Fragmented and Pooled modes, individual team members integrate perspectives to craft problem solutions. Although teams in the Synergistic learning mode continue this process—and probably do so more efficiently and more often—there is a qualitative leap in the team's ability to create knowledge mutually. This new capacity is for synchronous insight, the moment of a group "aha!" For example, as the Logistics team members absorbed the meaning of the lists that Barbara had written on flipchart paper, the group experienced an insight that was holistic and mutual. As a team, the group realized that the users, not they, were the problem.

CONCLUSIONS AND OBSERVATIONS

In this section, we draw some conclusions about how the conditions and learning processes change as the team adopts different modes of team learning. We then offer our observations about the roles of time and human dynamics.

Development of Team-Learning Conditions that Support Team-Learning Processes

Team learning is a dynamic process in which both learning processes and the conditions that support them change qualitatively as the team adopts Fragmented, Pooled, or Synergistic modes of learning. Table 12.3 summarizes these differences.[4]

TABLE 12.3 Team-Learning Conditions and Processes at Each Team-Learning Stage

Team-Learning Conditions	*Team-Learning Processes*
	Fragmented learning stage
Teamwork is perceived as unnecessary to task accomplishment; little interest is taken in developing as a team.	Team members retain initial frames.
	Little or no boundary crossing occurs except to seek information that meets individual needs.
Members show impatience in listening to others' views and do not value interdependence.	Experimentation occurs at the individual rather than group level.
Group-operating principles support individual, separately conceived, pieces of the work; little attention is paid to relationships.	Perspective integration is limited because members do not willingly attend meetings, are not interested in others' views, and are not open to reframing.
	Pooled learning stage
Teams are valued both as a context for individual learning and also as an efficient, effective mechanism for coordinating complex tasks.	Reframing occurs, but our data suggest it is externally imposed or catalyzed.
Members are open to hearing others' views to reach task objectives.	Members cross boundaries to share information when they see a clear relationship to task accomplishment.
Operating principles allow negotiation of differences and interpersonal conflict to	Experimentation is, for the most part, focused on individual learning.

[4]   A preliminary conceptualization of changes in team-learning processes can be found in Marsick, Dechant, and Kasl (1991).

TABLE 12.3 *Continued*

achieve the goal. Members may repress comments irrelevant to the goal.	Perspective integration occurs sometimes but is impeded by suppression of interpersonal conflict.

Synergistic learning stage

Teamwork is valued as an enriching modus operandi that can lead to breakthrough thinking.	Members reframe views individually and collectively based on internal and external insights.
Ideas are freely and openly expressed; members see the potential payoff of all contributions, even when they might at first seem irrelevant.	The team becomes boundary-less as information is sought and given freely.
	Experimentation is frequent and bold; it is both individual and collective.
Operating principles go beyond task accomplishment to include attention to relationships and to each other's growth, learning, and development.	Members seek out views that may be disconfirming or challenging. The team acquires collective memories that enable sudden leaps of insight.

Team-Learning Conditions

The first condition, appreciation of teamwork, strongly influences the remaining two. The meaning that individuals attach to teams is the context for both individual expression and operating principles. In the Fragmented mode, the focus is on meeting the needs and enhancing the value of the individual contributor. In the Pooled mode, members continually balance individual needs against the group's need. In the Synergistic mode, members have acquired a deep understanding of the creative potential in teams.

Team-Learning Processes

A team evolving toward a Synergistic learning mode reframes more frequently and develops capacity to be self-directing in its reframing. Reframing frequently sets off a chain reaction where one new frame induces another, leading a team to challenge deeply held assumptions. For example, when the Distributed Systems team reframed itself as self-managing in relation to Leroy's performance, its action challenged both Marie and HR to rethink personnel management practices.

To reframe, team members must explore new ideas and perspectives, which can originate from within or outside the group. Whether and how boundaries are crossed depends on what team members perceive to be relevant. In Fragmented learning, only information or ideas that meet individual needs are sought, as in the example of members of the Production Systems team who developed a norm of walking out of meetings when the topic did not relate directly to an individual's current project. Stephen went even further, by actively withholding information from John, the project leader. In Pooled learning, boundaries are crossed to give and get ideas that contribute to what the team has defined as its task. In Synergistic learning, team members do not construct artificial boundaries between the issues they tackle within the team and their modus operandi elsewhere in the organization, a phenomenon that has been described as the "boundary-less quality" of team learning (Bray, 1995; Gerdau, 1995; Smith, 1995; Yorks, 1995; Zelman, 1995).

> Each time the group convenes, each individual brings new experiences and insights accrued since the group's last meeting. Each time the group adjourns, individuals go into the world with new insights and experiences. . . . [The] group represents a dynamic, ever-changing intersection of individuals' perspectives in which boundaries between personal and group knowledge become blurred. (Group for Collaborative Inquiry & thINQ, 1994, pp. 58–59)

Integrating perspectives involves much more than being willing to listen to the viewpoints of others; it ultimately involves enabling others to express their views and actively seeking out views that are disconfirming or challenging. In Synergistic learning, members acquire a deep capacity to enter into the mind-set of others on the team.

The Role of Time in Team Learning

In addition to the changes in learning conditions and processes that are outlined in Table 12.3, our analysis provides insight into the role of time in team learning. Gersick (1989) recently drew attention to the importance of time when she found that for teams to achieve their goals, members had to reach a point of relatively smooth, cohesion operation about halfway through the time frame they had allotted to their task. This was so whether groups were to achieve their tasks within days, months, or longer. In this study, we found that time is perceived differently in the three learning modes and that changes in perception influence the kind of team learning that is possible. In the Fragmented and Pooled modes, time is seen as a resource, and in the Synergistic mode time is understood to be a dimension of learning.

In Fragmented learning, time is an individual resource to be conserved and used to advance individual needs and agendas, as was the case in Production Systems. In Pooled learning, team members begin to think of time as belonging to the group and are concerned about conserving and investing time wisely. Team members are sometimes willing to add to the team's resource by donating time that might otherwise be spent on individual tasks. For example, the Distributed

Systems team, in its crash effort to bring Leroy's project in under deadline, made "extra" time by working long hours and pushing aside other responsibilities.

When time is perceived as a resource that can be expanded in order to meet a team's needs, there is also a potential danger. As Dean pointed out in the context of his comments about decision making, "[management] can't just arbitrarily set a date and expect that the project will come in on time . . . as if we're not working hard enough and by putting a little extra effort in, that's all that's required." In addition to being a resource, time can also be seen as a dimension of learning. As such, time functions in three ways—an ingredient of learning, as a context for incubation, and as a context for shared history.

Time is an ingredient of learning when members take time to explore ideas for which relevance is not immediately apparent. These "time-outs" often lead to the generative thinking that typifies synergistic learning. For example, in its June meeting the Logistics team allowed itself to follow the activity begun spontaneously by Rodney and Barbara. By abandoning the planned agenda and indulging in associative thinking, the team accomplished an insight and a plan for dealing with the users that launched it into a new stage of cohesion. Although we do not have examples in the Brewster data to support this claim, we have learned in other contexts that as synergistic learning becomes habitual, teams learn to choose strategic moments to suspend their concern with time (ARL™ Inquiry, 1995; Group for Collaborative Inquiry, 1991; Kasl et al., 1993).

The second way in which time serves as a dimension of learning is as an incubator. Learning proceeds in cycles of reflection and action that often cannot be accelerated. Incubation is a context in which intuitive knowing finds its way into the learning mix.

Third, time is a dimension of learning when it is the context for shared history. When teams share the joys and pride of achievement, as typified by the Distributed Systems team experience, and moments of pain, as typified by Black Wednesday for the Logistics team, they develop shared-meaning schemes. Shared-meaning schemes enhance the team's capacity for sudden insight, as in the case of the Logistics team's June meeting. "The 'aha' of synchronous group response" is composed of an intuitive recognition that a solution to a problem has been found as well as a capacity to articulate the intuitive knowing (thINQ, 1994, pp. 354–355). Shared history also creates the store of interpersonal interactions that contribute to team members' capacity for deep understanding of the other's perspective.

Further Research on the Human Dynamics of Team Learning

The team-learning model derived from our research focuses on rational, cognitive learning processes, but not on the affective interactions that influence a group's capacity to execute these processes. Many of the factors that govern these affective interactions are described in the group dynamics literature. We argued earlier that healthy group dynamics is a prerequisite for collective learning,

although not sufficient as a guarantee. Here, we identify elements in this literature—interpersonal conflict, power, ego, and emotion—that may have special
relevance to team learning and call for further research about their role.[5] We sus-
pect that, as with the role of time, team members' perceptions about the nature
of these elements have an important effect on the team's capacity to learn.
Because our case study did not focus on these factors, our data are limited, but
suggestive.

First, we perceive that teams in the synergistic learning mode may reframe
their understanding of interpersonal conflict. The group dynamics literature
(Forsyth, 1990) teaches us that effective groups evolve from strategies for avoid-
ing conflict to strategies for confronting it constructively. Teams that learn must
evolve similarly, but they do more. They recognize that conflict and the differences that produce it can be valuable resources for generative learning, as happened in the handling of Leroy's performance problems. A second issue, related
to conflict and reflected in our data, is the management of power dynamics.
Brooks (1994) examined power in some detail in her research on team learning.

Third, research could better illuminate the interaction between individual
ego and the team's need for healthy interdependence. In Western culture, success
has been framed as an individual accomplishment. Recently, educational and
business institutions have begun to foster collaborative learning and management
but must counteract deeply held cultural values of individualism. As Brooks
(1994) observed,

> We frequently view . . . our success as having been won in competition with
> others. . . . Thus, the shift to working in teams in many U.S. work organiza-
> tions represents not just a structural change in how work is done, but a signif-
> icant historical and cultural shift. (p. 231)

Logistics team member Rodney echoes Brooks: "You're trained from
school, from grade school to high school to college, for that matter, to work as
an individual and to excel as an individual, and when you go into a team effort,
all of a sudden there's no more competition." In Synergistic learning, members
acquire a team identity. They reframe ego as an individual characteristic to ego as
a group attribute, as Robert describes regarding the Distributed Systems team's
success: "None of us really have [sic] a major ego problem." Members of the
group learned a new way of team thinking.

Finally, socioemotional roles have been recognized in the group dynamics
literature as important for effective group functioning (Forsyth, 1990). More
recently, the adult learning literature has blossomed with additional insights
(Belenky, Clinchy, Goldberger, Tarule, 1986; Boud, Cohen, & Walker, 1993;

---

[5] Team learning as a developmental process should also be studied in real time and over
time, through longitudinal design. Our team-learning model is based on two case studies.
Data from a variety of companies and teams are needed to understand the way in which
our case study contexts affected the model we created.

Loughlin, 1993). Yet emotions are anathema in the workplace. Research can explore how work teams can reframe emotion as a resource for team learning.

Over the course of time, we have changed our awareness about the dynamic character of this model. Although we always postulated that the team evolved through stages of maturity in its learning capacity, in this analysis we clarify how the team learning processes and conditions change qualitatively to create distinct modes of learning. Our analysis of the role of time is also an extension of our work.

REFERENCES

ARL™ Inquiry. (1995, May). Life on the seesaw: Tensions in an action reflection learning program. In P. Collette, B. Einsiedel, & S. Hobden (Eds.), *Proceedings of the 36th Annual Adult Education Research Conference* (pp. 1–6). Edmonton, Alberta, Canada: University of Alberta.

Belenky, M. F., Clinchy, B. M., Goldberger, N. R., & Tarule, J. M. (1986). *Women's ways of knowing: The development of self, voice, and mind.* New York: Basic Books.

Boud, D., Cohen, R., & Walker, D. (Eds.). (1993). *Using experience for learning.* Buckingham, UK, and Bristol, PA: Society for Research Into Higher Education & Open University Press.

Bray, J. (1995). The noetic experience of learning in collaborative inquiry groups—From descriptive, hermeneutic, and eidetic perspectives. *Dissertation Abstracts International, 56*(07), 2524. (University Microfilms No. AAC95–39779)

Brooks, A. (1994). Power and the production of knowledge: Collective team learning in work organizations. *Human Resource Development Quarterly, 5*(1), 213–236.

Dechant, K., & Marsick, V. J. (1991). In search of the learning organization: Toward a conceptual model of collective learning. In A. Herd (Ed.), *Proceedings of the Eastern Academy of Management* (pp. 225–228). Hartford, CT: Eastern Academy of Management.

Dechant, K., & Marsick, V. (1993). *Team learning survey and facilitator guide.* King of Prussia, PA: Organization Design & Development.

Dechant, K., Marsick, V., & Kasl, E. (1993). Toward a model of team learning. *Studies in Continuing Education, 15*(1), 1–14.

Forsyth, D. R. (1990). *Group dynamics* (2nd ed.). Pacific Grove, CA: Brooks/Cole.

Gerdau, J. (1995). Learning in adulthood through collaborative inquiry. *Dissertation Abstracts International, 56*(07), 25247. (University Microfilms No. AAC95–39807)

Gersick, C. J. G. (1989). Marking time: Predictable transitions in task groups. *Academy of Management Journal, 32*(2), 274–309.

Group for Collaborative Inquiry. (1991, October). There must be some meaning to this: Storytelling as a research method. In *Professionals' Ways of knowing and the Implications for CPE, Pre-Conference Proceedings of the Commission for Continuing Professional Education of the American Association of Adult and Continuing Education Annual Conference* (pp. 6–10). New York and Calgary, Canada: Teachers College and University of Calgary.

Group for Collaborative Inquiry & thINQ. (1994). Collaborative inquiry for the public arena. In A. Brooks & K. E. Watkins (Eds.), *The emerging power of action inquiry technologies, new directions for adult and continuing education* (pp. 57–67). San Francisco: Jossey-Bass.

Kasl, E., Dechant, K., & Marsick, V. J. (1993). Living the learning: Internalizing our model of group learning. In D. Boud, R. Cohen, & D. Walker (Eds.), *Using experience for learning* (pp. 143–156). Buckingham, UK, and Bristol, PA: Society for Research into Higher Education and Open University Press.

Katzenbach, J. R., & Smith, D. K. (1993). *The wisdom of teams—Creating the high-performance organization.* Boston: Harvard Business School Press.

Lawler, E. (1986). *High involvement management.* San Francisco: Jossey-Bass.

Loughlin, K. (1993). *Women's perceptions of transformative learning experiences within consciousness-raising.* San Francisco: Mellen Research University Press.

Marsick, V. J., Dechant, K., & Kasl, E. (1991). Group learning among professionals: The Brewster Company case study. In *Professionals' Ways of Knowing and the Implications for CPE, Pre-Conference Proceedings of the Commission for Continuing Professional Education of the American Association of Adult and Continuing Education Annual Conference* (pp. 138–142). New York and Calgary, Canada: Teachers College and University of Calgary.

Marsick, V. J., Dechant, K., & Kasl, E. (1993). Team learning. In K. E. Watkins & V. J. Marsick, *Sculpting the learning organization: Lessons in the art and science of systemic change* (pp. 96–117). San Francisco: Jossey-Bass.

Mezirow, J. (1991). *Transformative dimensions of adult learning.* San Francisco: Jossey-Bass.

Otter, K. (1996). *The relevance of group dynamics research in the facilitation of learning communities: A critical review of the literature.* Manuscript in preparation, California Institute of Integral Studies, School for Transformative Learning, San Francisco.

Savage, C. M. (1990). *5th generation management.* Bedford, MA: Digital Press.

Schön, D. (1983). *The reflective practitioner.* New York: Basic Books.

Senge, P. (1990). *The fifth discipline.* New York: Doubleday.

Smith, L. L. (1995). Collaborative inquiry as an adult learning strategy. *Dissertation Abstracts International* 56(07), 2533. (University Microfilms No. AAC95–39867)

Strauss, A. L., & Corbin, J. (1990). *Basics of qualitative research: Grounded theory procedures and techniques.* Newbury Park, CA: Sage.

thINQ. (1994, May). Phenomenology as an interpretive frame: The evolution of a research method for understanding how learning is experienced in collaborative inquiry groups. In M. Hyams, J. Armstrong, & E. Anderson (Eds.), *Proceedings of the 35th Annual Adult Education Research Conference* (pp. 354–359). Knoxville: University of Tennessee at Knoxville.

Tuckman, B. W. (1965). Developmental sequence in small groups. *Psychological Bulletin, 63,* 384–399.

Worchel, S., Wood, W., & Simpson, J. A. (Eds.). (1992). *Group process and productivity.* Newbury Park, CA: Sage.

Yin, R. K. (1989). *Case study research: Design and methods* (2nd ed.). Newbury Park, CA: Sage.

Yorks, L. (1995). Understanding how learning is experienced through collaborative inquiry: A phenomenological study. *Dissertation Abstracts International*, 56(07), 2534. (University Microfilms No. AAC9-39884)

Zelman, A. (1995). Answering the question: "How is learning experienced through collaborative inquiry?" *Dissertation Abstracts International*, 56(07), 2534. (University Microfilms No. AAC95-39885)

PART V

Individual Level

Chapter 13

Teaching Smart People How to Learn*

Chris Argyris**

Every company faces a learning dilemma: the smartest people find it the hardest to learn.

Any company that aspires to succeed in the tougher business environment of the 1990s must first resolve a basic dilemma: success in the marketplace increasingly depends on learning, yet most people don't know how to learn. What's more, those members of the organization that many assume to be the best at learning are, in fact, not very good at it. I am talking about the well-educated, high-powered, high-commitment professionals who occupy key leadership positions in the modern corporation.

Most companies not only have tremendous difficulty addressing this learning dilemma; they aren't even aware that it exists. The reason: they misunderstand what learning is and how to bring it about. As a result, they tend to make two mistakes in their efforts to become a learning organization.

First, most people define learning too narrowly as mere "problem solving," so they focus on identifying and correcting errors in the external environment. Solving problems is important. But if learning is to persist, managers and employees must also look inward. They need to reflect critically on their own behavior, identify the ways they often inadvertently contribute to the organization's problems, and then change how they act. In particular, they must learn how the very way they go about defining and solving problems can be a source of problems in its own right.

* Reprinted with permission.
** Chris Argyris is the James B. Conant Professor at the Harvard graduate schools of business and education. His most recent book, *Overcoming Organizational Defenses*, was published by Allyn and Bacon in 1990. Among his previous HBR articles are "Double Loop Learning in Organizations" (September-October 1977) and "Skilled Incompetence" (September-October 1986).

I have coined the terms "single loop" and "double loop" learning to capture this crucial distinction. To give a simple analogy: a thermostat that automatically turns on the heat whenever the temperature in a room drops below 68 degrees is a good example of single-loop learning. A thermostat that could ask, "Why am I set at 68 degrees?" and then explore whether or not some other temperature might more economically achieve the goal of heating the room would be engaging in double-loop learning.

Highly skilled professionals are frequently very good at single-loop learning. After all, they have spent much of their lives acquiring academic credentials, mastering one or a number of intellectual disciplines, and applying those disciplines to solve real-world problems. But ironically, this very fact helps explain why professionals are often so bad at double-loop learning.

Put simply, because many professionals are almost always successful at what they do, they rarely experience failure. And because they have rarely failed, they have never learned how to learn from failure. So whenever their single-loop learning strategies go wrong, they become defensive, screen out criticism, and put the "blame" on anyone and everyone but themselves. In short, their ability to learn shuts down precisely at the moment they need it the most.

The propensity among professionals to behave defensively helps shed light on the second mistake that companies make about learning. The common assumption is that getting people to learn is largely a matter of motivation. When people have the right attitudes and commitment, learning automatically follows. So companies focus on creating new organizational structures—compensation programs, performance reviews, corporate cultures, and the like—that are designed to create motivated and committed employees.

But effective double-loop learning is not simply a function of how people feel. It is a reflection of how they think—that is, the cognitive rules or reasoning they use to design and implement their actions. Think of these rules as a kind of "master program" stored in the brain, governing all behavior. Defensive reasoning can block learning even when the individual commitment to it is high, just as a computer program with hidden bugs can produce results exactly the opposite of what its designers had planned.

Companies can learn how to resolve the learning dilemma. What it takes is to make the ways managers and employees reason about their behavior a focus of organizational learning and continuous improvement programs. Teaching people how to reason about their behavior in new and more effective ways breaks down the defenses that block learning.

All of the examples that follow involve a particular kind of professional: fast-track consultants at major management consulting companies. But the implications of my argument go far beyond this specific occupational group. The fact is, more and more jobs—no matter what the title—are taking on the contours of "knowledge work." People at all levels of the organization must combine the mastery of some highly specialized technical expertise with the ability to work effectively in teams, form productive relationships with clients and customers, and critically reflect on and then change their own organizational practices. And the nuts and bolts of management—whether of high-powered consultants or service representatives, senior managers or factory technicians—increasingly consists of guiding and integrating the autonomous but interconnected work of highly skilled people.

HOW PROFESSIONALS AVOID LEARNING

For 15 years, I have been conducting in-depth studies of management consultants. I decided to study consultants for a few simple reasons. First, they are the epitome of the highly educated professionals who play an increasingly central role in all organizations. Almost all of the consultants I've studied have MBAs from the top three or four U.S. business schools. They are also highly committed to their work. For instance, at one company, more than 90% of the consultants responded in a survey that they were "highly satisfied" with their jobs and with the company.

I also assumed that such professional consultants would be good at learning. After all, the essence of their job is to teach others how to do things differently. I found, however, that these consultants embodied the learning dilemma. The most enthusiastic about continuous improvement in their own organizations, they were also often the biggest obstacle to its complete success.

As long as efforts at learning and change focused on external organizational factors—job redesign, compensation programs, performance reviews, and leadership training—the professionals were enthusiastic participants. Indeed, creating new systems and structures was precisely the kind of challenge that well-educated, highly motivated professionals thrived on.

And yet the moment the quest for continuous improvement turned to the professionals' *own* performance, something went wrong. It wasn't a matter of bad attitude. The professionals' commitment to excellence was genuine, and the vision of the company was clear. Nevertheless, continuous improvement did not persist. And the longer the continuous improvement efforts continued, the greater the likelihood that they would produce ever-diminishing returns.

What happened? The professionals began to feel embarrassed. They were threatened by the prospect of critically examining their own role in the organization. Indeed, because they were so well paid (and generally believed that their employers were supportive and fair), the idea that their performance might not be at its best made them feel guilty.

Far from being a catalyst for real change, such feelings caused most to react defensively. They projected the blame for any problems away from themselves and onto what they said were unclear goals, insensitive and unfair leaders, and stupid clients.

Consider this example. At a premier management consulting company, the manager of a case team called a meeting to examine the team's performance on a recent consulting project. The client was largely satisfied and had given the team relatively high marks, but the manager believed the team had not created the value added that it was capable of and that the consulting company had promised. In the spirit of continuous improvement, he felt that the team could do better. Indeed, so did some of the team members.

The manager knew how difficult it was for people to reflect critically on their own work performance, especially in the presence of their manager, so he took a number of steps to make possible a frank and open discussion. He invited to the meeting an outside consultant whom team members knew and trusted—"just to keep me honest," he said. He also agreed to have the entire meeting tape-recorded. That way, any subsequent confusions or disagreements about what went on at the meeting could be checked against the transcript. Finally, the manager opened the meeting by emphasizing that no subject was off limits—including his own behavior.

"I realize that you may believe you cannot confront me," the manager said. "But I encourage you to challenge me. You have a responsibility to tell me where you think the leadership made mistakes, just as I have the responsibility to identify any I believe you made. And all of us must acknowledge our own mistakes. If we do not have an open dialogue, we will not learn."

The professionals took the manager up on the first half of his invitation but quietly ignored the second. When asked to pinpoint the key problems in the experience with the client, they looked entirely outside themselves. The clients were uncooperative and arrogant. "They didn't think we could help them." The team's own managers were unavailable and poorly prepared. "At times, our managers were not up to speed before they walked into the client meetings." In effect, the professionals asserted that they were helpless to act differently—not because of any limitations of their own but because of the limitations of others.

The manager listened carefully to the team members and tried to respond to their criticisms. He talked about the mistakes that he had made during the consulting process. For example, one professional objected to the way the manager had run the project meetings. "I see that the way I asked questions closed down discussions," responded the manager. "I didn't mean to do that, but I can see how you might have believed that I had already made up my mind." Another team member complained that the manager had caved in to pressure from his superior to produce the project report far too quickly, considering the team's heavy work load. "I think that it was my responsibility to have said no," admitted the manager. "It was clear that we all had an immense amount of work."

Finally, after some three hours of discussion about his own behavior, the manager began to ask the team members if there were any errors *they* might have made. "After all," he said, "this client was not different from many others. How can we be more effective in the future?"

The professionals repeated that it was really the clients' and their own managers' fault. As one put it, "They have to be open to change and want to learn." The more the manager tried to get the team to examine its own responsibility for the outcome, the more the professionals bypassed his concerns. The best one team member could suggest was for the case team to "promise less"—implying that there was really no way for the group to improve its performance.

The case team members were reacting defensively to protect themselves, even though their manager was not acting in ways that an outsider would consider threatening. Even if there were some truth to their charges—the clients may well have been arrogant and closed, their own managers distant—the *way* they presented these claims was guaranteed to stop learning. With few exceptions, the professionals made attributions about the behavior of the clients and the managers but never publicly tested their claims. For instance, they said that the clients weren't motivated to learn but never really presented any evidence supporting that assertion. When their lack of concrete evidence was pointed out to them, they simply repeated their criticisms more vehemently.

If the professionals had felt so strongly about these issues, why had they never mentioned them during the project? According to the professionals, even this was the fault of others. "We didn't want to alienate the client," argued one. "We didn't want to be seen as whining," said another.

The professionals were using their criticisms of others to protect themselves from the potential embarrassment of having to admit that perhaps they too had contributed to the team's less-than-perfect performance. What's more, the fact that they kept repeating their defensive actions in the face of the manager's efforts to turn the group's attention to its own role shows that this defensiveness had become a reflexive routine. From the professionals' perspective, they weren't resisting; they were focusing on the "real" causes. Indeed, they were to be respected, if not congratulated, for working as well as they did under such difficult conditions.

The end result was an unproductive parallel conversation. Both the manager and the professionals were candid; they expressed their views forcefully. But they talked past each other, never finding a common language to describe what had happened with the client. The professionals kept insisting that the fault lay with others. The manager kept trying, unsuccessfully, to get the professionals to see how they contributed to the state of affairs they were criticizing. The dialogue of this parallel conversation looks like this:

> Professionals: "The clients have to be open. They must want to change."
> Manager: "It's our task to help them see that change is in their interest."
> Professionals: "But the clients didn't agree with our analyses."
> Manager: "If they didn't think our ideas were right, how might we have convinced them?"
> Professionals: "Maybe we need to have more meetings with the client."
> Manager: "If we aren't adequately prepared and if the clients don't think we're credible, how will more meetings help?"
> Professionals: "There should be better communication between case team members and management."
> Manager: "I agree. But professionals should take the initiative to educate the manager about the problems they are experiencing."
> Professionals: "Our leaders are unavailable and distant."
> Manager: "How do you expect us to know that if you don't tell us?"

FIGURE 13.1 It's Not Enough to Talk Candidly. Professionals Can Still Find Themselves Talking Past Each Other

Conversations such as this one dramatically illustrate the learning dilemma. The problem with the professionals' claims is not that they are wrong but that they aren't useful. By constantly turning the focus away from their own behavior to that of others, the professionals bring learning to a grinding halt. The manager understands the trap but does not know how to get out of it. To learn how to do that requires going deeper into the dynamics of defensive reasoning—and into the special causes that make professionals so prone to it.

DEFENSIVE REASONING AND THE DOOM LOOP

What explains the professionals' defensiveness? Not their attitudes about change or commitment to continuous improvement; they really wanted to work more effectively. Rather, the key factor is the way they reasoned about their behavior and that of others.

It is impossible to reason anew in every situation. If we had to think through all the possible responses every time someone asked, "How are you?" the world would pass us by. Therefore, everyone develops a theory of action—a set of rules that individuals use to design and implement their own behavior as well as to understand the behavior of others. Usually, these theories of actions become so taken for granted that people don't even realize they are using them.

One of the paradoxes of human behavior, however, is that the master program people actually use is rarely the one they think they use. Ask people in an interview or questionnaire to articulate the rules they use to govern their actions, and they will give you what I call their "espoused" theory of action. But observe these same people's behavior, and you will quickly see that this espoused theory has very little to do with how they actually behave. For example, the professionals on the case team said they believed in continuous improvement, and yet they consistently acted in ways that made improvement impossible.

When you observe people's behavior and try to come up with rules that would make sense of it, you discover a very different theory of action—what I call the individual's "theory-in-use." Put simply, people consistently act inconsistently, unaware of the contradiction between their espoused theory and their theory-in-use, between the way they think they are acting and the way they really act.

What's more, most theories-in-use rest on the same set of governing values. There seems to be a universal human tendency to design one's actions consistently according to four basic values:

1. To remain in unilateral control;
2. To maximize "winning" and minimize "losing";
3. To suppress negative feelings; and
4. To be as "rational" as possible—by which people mean defining clear objectives and evaluating their behavior in terms of whether or not they have achieved them.

The purpose of all these values is to avoid embarrassment or threat, feeling vulnerable or incompetent. In this respect, the master program that most people use is profoundly defensive. Defensive reasoning encourages individuals to keep private the premises, inferences, and conclusions that shape their behavior and to avoid testing them in a truly independent, objective fashion.

Because the attributions that go into defensive reasoning are never really tested, it is a closed loop, remarkably impervious to conflicting points of view. The inevitable response to the observation that somebody is reasoning defensively is yet more defensive reasoning. With the case team, for example, whenever anyone pointed out the professionals' defensive behavior to them, their initial reaction was to look for the cause in somebody else—clients who were so sensitive that they would have been alienated if the consultants had criticized them or a manager so weak that he couldn't have taken it had the consultants raised their concerns with him. In other words, the case team members once again denied their own responsibility by externalizing the problem and putting it on someone else.

In such situations, the simple act of encouraging more open inquiry is often attacked by others as "intimidating." Those who do the attacking deal with their feelings about possibly being wrong by blaming the more open individual for arousing these feelings and upsetting them.

Needless to say, such a master program inevitably short-circuits learning. And for a number of reasons unique to their psychology, well-educated professionals are especially susceptible to this.

Nearly all the consultants I have studied have stellar academic records. Ironically, their very success at education helps explain the problems they have with learning. Before they enter the world of work their lives are primarily full of successes, so they have rarely experienced the embarrassment and sense of threat that comes with failure. As a result, their defensive reasoning has rarely been activated. People who rarely experience failure, however, end up not knowing how to deal with it effectively. And this serves to reinforce the normal human tendency to reason defensively.

In a survey of several hundred young consultants at the organizations I have been studying, these professionals describe themselves as driven internally by an unrealistically high ideal of performance: "Pressure on the job is self-imposed." "I must not only do a good job; I must also be the best." "People around here are very bright and hardworking; they are highly motivated to do an outstanding job." "Most of us want not only to succeed but also to do so at maximum speed."

These consultants are always comparing themselves with the best around them and constantly trying to better their own performance. And yet they do not appreciate being required to compete openly with each other. They feel it is somehow inhumane. They prefer to be the individual contributor—what might be termed a "productive loner."

Behind this high aspiration for success is an equally high fear of failure and a propensity to feel shame and guilt when they do fail to meet their high standards. "You must avoid mistakes," said one. "I hate making them. Many of us fear failure, whether we admit it or not."

To the extent that these consultants have experienced success in their lives, they have not had to be concerned about failure and the attendant feelings of shame and guilt. But to exactly the same extent, they also have never developed the tolerance for feelings of failure or the skills to deal with these feelings. This in turn has led them not only to fear failure but also to fear the fear of failure itself. For they know that they will not cope with it superlatively—their usual level of aspiration.

The consultants use two intriguing metaphors to describe this phenomenon. They talk about the "doom loop" and "doom zoom." Often, consultants will perform well on the case team, but because they don't do the jobs perfectly or receive accolades from their managers, they go into a doom loop of despair. And they don't ease into the doom loop, they zoom into it.

As a result, many professionals have extremely "brittle" personalities. When suddenly faced with a situation they cannot immediately handle, they tend to fall apart. They cover up their distress in front of the client. They talk about it

FIGURE 13.2 When Professionals Don't Do Their Jobs Perfectly, They Zoom into a "Doom Loop"

constantly with their fellow case team members. Interestingly, these conversations commonly take the form of bad-mouthing clients.

Such brittleness leads to an inappropriately high sense of despondency or even despair when people don't achieve the high levels of performance they aspire to. Such despondency is rarely psychologically devastating, but when combined with defensive reasoning, it can result in a formidable predisposition against learning.

There is no better example of how this brittleness can disrupt an organization than performance evaluations. Because it represents the one moment when a professional must measure his or her own behavior against some formal standard, a performance evaluation is almost tailor-made to push a professional into the doom loop. Indeed, a poor evaluation can reverberate far beyond the particular individual involved to spark defensive reasoning throughout an entire organization.

At one consulting company, management established a new performance-evaluation process that was designed to make evaluations both more objective and more useful to those being evaluated. The consultants participated in the design of the new system and in general were enthusiastic because it corresponded to their espoused values of objectivity and fairness. A brief two years into the new process, however, it had become the object of dissatisfaction. The catalyst for this about-face was the first unsatisfactory rating.

Senior managers had identified six consultants whose performance they considered below standard. In keeping with the new evaluation process, they did all they could to communicate their concerns to the six and to help them improve. Managers met with each individual separately for as long and as often as the professional requested to explain the reasons behind the rating and to discuss what needed to be done to improve—but to no avail. Performance continued at the same low level and, eventually, the six were let go.

When word of the dismissal spread through the company, people responded with confusion and anxiety. After about a dozen consultants angrily complained to management, the CEO held two lengthy meetings where employees could air their concerns.

At the meetings, the professionals made a variety of claims. Some said the performance-evaluation process was unfair because judgments were subjective and biased and the criteria for minimum performance unclear. Others suspected that the real cause for the dismissals was economic and that the performance-evaluation procedure was just a fig leaf to hide the fact that the company was in trouble. Still others argued that the evaluation process was antilearning. If the company were truly a learning organization, as it claimed, then people performing below the minimum standard should be taught how to reach it. As one professional put it: "We were told that the company did not have an up-or-out policy. Up-or-out is inconsistent with learning. You misled us."

The CEO tried to explain the logic behind management's decision by grounding it in the facts of the case and by asking the professionals for any evidence that might contradict these facts.

Is there subjectivity and bias in the evaluation process? Yes, responded the CEO, but "we strive hard to reduce them. We are constantly trying to improve the process. If you have any ideas, please tell us. If you know of someone treated unfairly, please bring it up. If any of you feel that you have been treated unfairly, let's discuss it now or, if you wish, privately."

Is the level of minimum competence too vague? "We are working to define minimum competence more clearly," he answered. "In the case of the six, however, their performance was so poor that it wasn't difficult to reach a decision." Most of the six had received timely feedback about their problems. And in the two cases where people had not, the reason was that they had never taken the responsibility to seek out evaluations—and, indeed, had actively avoided them. "If you have any data to the contrary," the CEO added, "let's talk about it."

Were the six asked to leave for economic reasons? No, said the CEO. "We have more work than we can do, and letting professionals go is extremely costly for us. Do any of you have any information to the contrary?"

As to the company being antilearning, in fact, the entire evaluation process was designed to encourage learning. When a professional is performing below the minimum level, the CEO explained, "we jointly design remedial experiences with the individual. Then we look for signs of improvement. In these cases, either the professionals were reluctant to take on such assignments or they repeatedly failed when they did. Again, if you have information or evidence to the contrary, I'd like to hear about it."

The CEO concluded: "It's regrettable, but sometimes we make mistakes and hire the wrong people. If individuals don't produce and repeatedly prove themselves unable to improve, we don't know what else to do except dismiss them. It's just not fair to keep poorly performing individuals in the company. They earn an unfair share of the financial rewards."

Instead of responding with data of their own, the professionals simply repeated their accusations but in ways that consistently contradicted their claims. They said that a genuinely fair evaluation process would contain clear and documentable data about performance—but they were unable to provide firsthand examples of the unfairness that they implied colored the evaluation of the six dismissed employees. They argued that people shouldn't be judged by inferences unconnected to their actual performance—but they judged management in precisely this way. They insisted that management define clear, objective, and unambiguous performance standards—but they argued that any humane system would take into account that the performance of a professional cannot be precisely measured. Finally, they presented themselves as champions of learning—but they never proposed any criteria for assessing whether an individual might be unable to learn.

In short, the professionals seemed to hold management to a different level of performance than they held themselves. In their conversation at the meetings, they used many of the features of ineffective evaluation that they condemned— the absence of concrete data, for example, and the dependence on a circular logic of "heads we win, tails you lose." It is as if they were saying, "Here are the features of a fair performance-evaluation system. You should abide by them. But we don't have to when we are evaluating you."

Indeed, if we were to explain the professionals' behavior by articulating rules that would have to be in their heads in order for them to act the way they did, the rules would look something like this:

1. When criticizing the company, state your criticism in ways that you believe are valid—but also in ways that prevent others from deciding for themselves whether your claim to validity is correct.
2. When asked to illustrate your criticisms, don't include any data that others could use to decide for themselves whether the illustrations are valid.
3. State your conclusions in ways that disguise their logical implications. If others point out those implications to you, deny them.

Of course, when such rules were described to the professionals, they found them abhorrent. It was inconceivable that these rules might explain their actions. And yet in defending themselves against this observation, they almost always inadvertently confirmed the rules.

LEARNING HOW TO REASON PRODUCTIVELY

If defensive reasoning is as widespread as I believe, then focusing on an individual's attitudes or commitment is never enough to produce real change. And as the previous example illustrates, neither is creating new organizational structures or systems. The problem is that even when people are genuinely committed to improving their performance and management has changed its structures in order to encourage the "right" kind of behavior, people still remain locked in defensive reasoning. Either they remain unaware of this fact, or if they do become aware of it, they blame others.

There is, however, reason to believe that organizations can break out of this vicious circle. Despite the strength of defensive reasoning, people genuinely strive to produce what they intend. They value acting competently. Their self-esteem is intimately tied up with behaving consistently and performing effectively. Companies can use these universal human tendencies to teach people how to reason in a new way—in effect, to change the master programs in their heads and thus reshape their behavior.

People can be taught how to recognize the reasoning they use when they design and implement their actions. They can begin to identify the inconsistencies between their espoused and actual theories of action. They can face up to the fact that they unconsciously design and implement actions that they do not intend. Finally, people can learn how to identify what individuals and groups do to create organizational defenses and how these defenses contribute to an organization's problems.

Once companies embark on this learning process, they will discover that the kind of reasoning necessary to reduce and overcome organizational defenses is the same kind of "tough reasoning" that underlies the effective use of ideas in strategy, finance, marketing, manufacturing, and other management disciplines. Any sophisticated strategic analysis, for example, depends on collecting valid data, analyzing it carefully, and constantly testing the inferences drawn from the data. The toughest tests are reserved for the conclusions. Good strategists make sure that their conclusions can withstand all kinds of critical questioning.

So too with productive reasoning about human behavior. The standard of analysis is just as high. Human resource programs no longer need to be based on "soft" reasoning but should be as analytical and as data-driven as any other management discipline.

Of course, that is not the kind of reasoning the consultants used when they encountered problems that were embarrassing or threatening. The data they collected was hardly objective. The inferences they made rarely became explicit. The conclusions they reached were largely self-serving, impossible for others to test, and as a result, "self-sealing," impervious to change.

How can an organization begin to turn this situation around, to teach its members how to reason productively? The first step is for managers at the top to examine critically and change their own theories-in-use. Until senior managers become aware of how they reason defensively and the counterproductive consequences that result, there will be little real progress any change activity is likely to be just a fad.

Change has to start at the top because otherwise defensive senior managers are likely to disown any transformation in reasoning patterns coming from below. If professionals or middle managers begin to change the way they reason and act, such changes are likely to appear strange—if not actually dangerous—to those at the top. The result is an unstable situation where senior managers still believe that it is a sign of caring and sensitivity to bypass and cover up difficult issues, while their subordinates see the very same actions as defensive.

The key to any educational experience designed to teach senior managers how to reason productively is to connect the program to real business problems. The best demonstration of the usefulness of productive reasoning is for busy managers to see how it can make a direct difference in their own performance and in that of the organization. This will not happen overnight. Managers need plenty of opportunity to practice the new skills. But once they grasp the powerful impact that productive reasoning can have on actual performance, they will have a strong incentive to reason productively not just in a training session but in all their work relationships.

One simple approach I have used to get this process started is to have participants produce a kind of rudimentary case study. The subject is a real business problem that the manager either wants to deal with or has tried unsuccessfully to address in the past. Writing the actual case usually takes less than an hour. But then the case becomes the focal point of an extended analysis.

For example, a CEO at a large organizational-development consulting company was preoccupied with the problems caused by the intense competition among the various business functions represented by his four direct reports. Not only was he tired of having the problems dumped in his lap, but he was also worried about the impact the interfunctional conflicts were having on the organization's flexibility. He had even calculated that the money being spent to iron out disagreements amounted to hundreds of thousands of dollars every year. And the more fights there were, the more defensive people became, which only increased the costs to the organization.

In a paragraph or so, the CEO described a meeting he intended to have with his direct reports to address the problem. Next, he divided the paper in half, and on the right-hand side of the page, he wrote a scenario for the meeting—much like the script for a movie or play—describing what he would say and how his subordinates would likely respond. On the left-hand side of the page, he wrote down any thoughts and feelings that he would be likely to have during the meeting but that he wouldn't express for fear they would derail the discussion.

But instead of holding the meeting, the CEO analyzed this scenario *with* his direct reports. The case became the catalyst for a discussion in which the CEO learned several things about the way he acted with his management team.

He discovered that his four direct reports often perceived his conversations as counterproductive. In the guise of being "diplomatic," he would pretend that a consensus about the problem existed, when in fact none existed. The unintended result: instead of feeling reassured, his subordinates felt wary and tried to figure out "what is he *really* getting at."

The CEO also realized that the way he dealt with the competitiveness among department heads was completely contradictory. On the one hand, he kept urging them to "think of the organization as a whole." On the other, he kept calling for actions—department budget cuts, for example—that placed them directly in competition with each other.

Finally, the CEO discovered that many of the tacit evaluations and attributions he had listed turned out to be wrong. Since he had never expressed these assumptions, he had never found out just how wrong they were. What's more, he learned that much of what he thought he was hiding came through to his subordinates anyway—but with the added message that the boss was covering up.

The CEO's colleagues also learned about their own ineffective behavior. They learned by examining their own behavior as they tried to help the CEO analyze his case. They also learned by writing and analyzing cases of their own. They began to see that they too tended to bypass and cover up the real issues and that the CEO was often aware of it but did not say so. They too made inaccurate attributions and evaluations that they did not express. Moreover, the belief that they had to hide important ideas and feelings from the CEO and from each other in order not to upset anyone turned out to be mistaken. In the context of the case discussions, the entire senior management team was quite willing to discuss what had always been undiscussable.

In effect, the case study exercise legitimizes talking about issues that people have never been able to address before. Such a discussion can be emotional— even painful. But for managers with the courage to persist, the payoff is great: management teams and entire organizations work more openly and more effectively and have greater options for behaving flexibly and adapting to particular situations.

When senior managers are trained in new reasoning skills, they can have a big impact on the performance of the entire organization—even when other employees are still reasoning defensively. The CEO who led the meetings on the performance-evaluation procedure was able to defuse dissatisfaction because he didn't respond to professionals' criticisms in kind but instead gave a clear presentation of relevant data. Indeed, most participants took the CEO's behavior to be a sign that the company really acted on the values of participation and employee involvement that it espoused.

Of course, the ideal is for all the members of an organization to learn how to reason productively. This has happened at the company where the case team meeting took place. Consultants and their managers are now able to confront some of the most difficult issues of the consultant-client relationship. To get a sense of the difference productive reasoning can make, imagine how the original conversation between the manager and case team might have gone had everyone engaged in effective reasoning. (The following dialogue is based on actual sessions I have attended with other case teams at the same company since the training has been completed.)

FIGURE 13.3 The Professional Who Reasons Productively Casts a Critical Eye on Her Own Role in a Company's Problem

First, the consultants would have demonstrated their commitment to continuous improvement by being willing to examine their own role in the difficulties that arose during the consulting project. No doubt they would have identified their managers and the clients as part of the problem, but they would have gone on to admit that they had contributed to it as well. More important, they would have agreed with the manager that as they explored the various roles of clients, managers, and professionals, they would make sure to test any evaluations or attributions they might make against the data. Each individual would have encouraged the others to question his or her reasoning. Indeed, they would have insisted on it. And in turn, everyone would have understood that act of questioning not as a sign of mistrust or an invasion of privacy but as a valuable opportunity for learning.

The conversation about the manager's unwillingness to say no might look something like this:

Professional #1: "One of the biggest problems I had with the way you managed this case was that you seemed to be unable to say no when either the client or your superior made unfair demands." [Gives an example.]

Professional #2: "I have another example to add. [Describes a second example.] But I'd also like to say that we never really told you how we felt about this. Behind your back we were bad-mouthing you—you know, 'he's being such a wimp'—but we never came right out and said it."

Manager: "It certainly would have been helpful if you had said something. Was there anything I said or did that gave you the idea that you had better not raise this with me?"

Professional #3: "Not really. I think we didn't want to sound like we were whining."

Manager: "Well, I certainly don't think you sound like you're whining. But two thoughts come to mind. If I understand you correctly, you were complaining, but the complaining about me and my inability to say no was covered up. Second, if we had discussed this, I might have gotten the data I needed to be able to say no."

Notice that when the second professional describes how the consultants had covered up their complaints, the manager doesn't criticize her. Rather, he rewards her for being open by responding in kind. He focuses on the ways that he too may have contributed to the cover-up. Reflecting undefensively about his own role in the problem then makes it possible for the professionals to talk about their fears of appearing to be whining. The manager then agrees with the professionals that they shouldn't become complainers. At the same time, he points out the counterproductive consequences of covering up their complaints.

Another unresolved issue in the case team meeting concerned the supposed arrogance of the clients. A more productive conversation about that problem might go like this:

Manager: "You said that the clients were arrogant and uncooperative. What did they say and do?"

Professional #1: "One asked me if I had ever met a payroll. Another asked how long I've been out of school."

Professional #2: "One even asked me how old I was!"

Professional #3: "That's nothing. The worst is when they say that all we do is interview people, write a report based on what they tell us, and then collect our fees."

Manager: "The fact that we tend to be so young is a real problem for many of our clients. They get very defensive about it. But I'd like to explore whether there is a way for them to freely express their views without our getting defensive.

"What troubled me about your original responses was that you assumed you were right in calling the clients stupid. One thing I've noticed about consultants—in this company and others—is that we tend to defend ourselves by bad-mouthing the client."

Professional #1: "Right. After all, if they are genuinely stupid, then it's obviously not our fault that they aren't getting it!"

Professional #2: "Of course, that stance is anti-learning and overprotective. By assuming that they can't learn, we absolve ourselves from having to."

Professional #3: "And the more we all go along with the bad-mouthing, the more we reinforce each other's defensiveness."

Manager: "So what's the alternative? How can we encourage our clients to express their defensiveness and at the same time constructively build on it?"

Professional #1: "We all know that the real issue isn't our age; it's whether or not we are able to add value to the client's organization. They should judge us by what we produce. And if we aren't adding value, they should get rid of us— no matter how young or old we happen to be."

Manager: "Perhaps that is exactly what we should tell them."

In both these examples, the consultants and their manager are doing real work. They are learning about their own group dynamics and addressing some generic problems in client-consultant relationships. The insights they gain will allow them to act more effectively in the future—both as individuals and as a team. They are not just solving problems but developing a far deeper and more textured understanding of their role as members of the organization. They are laying the groundwork for continuous improvement that is truly continuous. They are learning how to learn.

Chapter 14

Learning from Experience Through Reflection

Marilyn Wood Daudelin[*]

Everyone, of course, reflects on life events in an effort to learn from experience. New research suggests that guiding the process can the learning.

The forces affecting business environments change rapidly, frequently, and unpredictably. Gone are the days when managers could predict the future and prepare themselves to meet its demands with relatively stable, five-year plans. Instead, they find themselves imagining three or four possible future scenarios, then developing action plans that can be modified in response to impossible-to-predict technological or social changes.

How do managers prepare themselves to survive, let alone be successful, in such an environment?

The more traditional avenues of development—MBA degrees, executive education programs, and management workshops and seminars—face the same turbulence. The designers of these educational experiences do their best to predict the kinds of knowledge, skills, and attitudes that will be most helpful. Yet there is an inherent game of "catch up" within this system. By the time these designers understand existing issues and trends, develop cases, write texts, and create workshop designs, a new wave of business challenges appears.

Without question, we need a more adaptable, responsive system of helping managers learn. Recent studies have shown that the day-to-day experiences of managers as they confront challenges and problems on the job are rich sources of learning—perhaps more appropriate "classrooms" than the traditional venues described above. Consider, for example, recent research conducted by the Center

[*] Reprinted with permission.

for Creative Leadership in Greensboro, North Carolina. By studying 616 descriptions of experiences that 191 successful executives claimed made a lasting developmental difference, researchers were able to identify 16 types of experiences or "key events" that are critical to the development of specific managerial competencies.

UNCOVERING HIDDEN LEARNING POTENTIAL

The Center for Creative Leadership study recognizes the immense learning potential hidden in everyday experience. But such recognition is not enough. Managers need support in these efforts to make sense out of their developmental experiences. The word "experience" derives from the Latin word *experientia*, meaning trial, proof, or experiment. Thus challenging work experiences may be described as trial-and-error experiments that produce learning. Viewed this way, what is needed is a process of analysis that explores causes, develops and tests hypotheses, and eventually produces new knowledge.

Rather than creating a new system—with the danger of adding one more fad to those that surface repeatedly in management practice—we turn to a process that has roots as deep as the ancient Greek philosophers: the process of reflection.

Using Reflection to Learn from Experience

Reflection is a natural and familiar process. In school, we wrote papers, answered questions, engaged in classroom discussions, and analyzed cases, all as ways to develop new insights. In the business world, we analyze experiences and summarize our learning in reports, performance review sessions, and problem-solving processes. In our personal lives, we discuss troubling situations with friends, spouses, counselors, or support groups. Reflection occurs in less formal ways as well. We may have experienced breakthroughs while jogging, showering, or mowing the lawn.

Reflection as a way of learning has ancient roots. Socrates may have been one of the first to use this process as he tried to discover the nature of goodness by asking questions of others. He constantly challenged the statements and beliefs of his students, including Plato, whose work developed as a consequence of Socrates' training in how to reflect. Other early proponents of reflection as a way of learning include Sophocles, who declared that one learns by observing what one does time and time again, and John Locke, who believed that knowing is purely a function of thoughtful reaction to experience.

If the process of reflection is so natural and familiar, what keeps organizations from embracing formal reflective practices as a way to encourage learning? One explanation is that managers have always placed a higher value on action than reflection. Twenty years ago, Henry Minztberg wrote in the *Harvard*

Business Review, "Study after study has shown that managers work at an unrelenting pace, that their activities are characterized by brevity, variety and discontinuity, and that they are strongly oriented to action and dislike reflective activities." More recently, Rosabeth Moss Karter identified short-term managerial incentives and demands as forces working against managers' ability to pause and reflect.

Recognizing Existing Reflection Practices

In spite of these tendencies to resist reflection, evidence exists that it is becoming a part of the lifeblood of organizations today. Many of the tools taught and practiced in total quality management programs, for example, are actually

Dr. Marilyn W. Daudelin has had over twenty years of experience as an in-house trainer, consultant, and program manager for Polaroid Corporation in Cambridge, Massachusetts. She has spent much of that time designing and implementing unique internal development programs. Her consulting, writing, and speaking engagements have focused on programs she developed for human resources professionals, executives and secretaries.

Marilyn now provides consultation to a variety of organizations in the greater Boston area. Her current interests include helping managers in corporations learn from their challenging work experiences by using reflection tools and practices.

Marilyn received her Ed.D. in human resources education from Boston University, her Me.D. in human resources development from Northeastern University, and her undergraduate degree in English from Boston University. She has served on several university executive education advisory boards and has been the recipient of a variety of academic and professional awards.

BOX 14.1

processes of reflection. They allow individuals to call a halt, at least briefly, to the frantic pace of action and engage in processes that permit individuals to reflect upon important areas such as customer needs, root causes of problems, and dysfunctional work-flow patterns. In many companies, the improvements and innovations resulting from these processes have had a direct and powerful effect on both company profits and employee satisfaction.

Also, the trend toward greater employee involvement in corporate decision making has changed the relationship between leaders and followers in corporations. As the values of empowerment and participation increasingly appear in corporate vision and mission statements, the manager's role has shifted from that of charismatic leader (a person who has all the answers) to that of coach—a person who works with employees to help them discover the answers. This shift occurs when managers use reflective approaches to running the business: When they ask challenging questions from a position of mutual discovery; when they provide the time and the structure to reflect upon challenging work situations, both individually and collectively; and when they are open to and supportive of ideas that emerge from these processes.

Finally, the trend toward greater accountability to external shareholders, to boards of directors, and, most recently, to employee-owners for corporate performance has led to a new examination of the age-old method of planning and evaluating *individual* performance: the performance appraisal process.

This examination has, in turn, led to new techniques such as 360 degree feedback (soliciting data on strengths and weaknesses from immediate managers, peers, and direct reports) and customer input processes (collecting performance feedback from internal and external customers). These new practices place more emphasis on the need to reflect on prior performance over the course of a year, or longer. The skills applied in that reflection may then be used to plan for improvements in the following year's performance.

These two key elements of performance management—evaluation and planning—represent two important conditions for learning from experience: developing insights from past events and applying them to future actions.

Thus, as managers use quality improvement tools, as they empower others to participate in decision making, and as they develop procedures to measure performance, they have the opportunity to engage more actively in reflection. Taking the time to formally reflect during these processes is the key to whether the processes become mechanisms to unearth new and important meaning or simply the latest in a series of new management gimmicks.

The Need for More Formal Reflective Practices

Even though reflection has been an important part of traditional educational experiences since ancient times, its power is just beginning to be harnessed as a deliberate tool of managerial learning. A recent *Fortune* article titled "Leaders Learn to Heed the Voice Within" reports that companies such as AT&T,

PepsiCo, and Aetna are developing ways to introduce more introspection into their management development programs. In addition, Exxon, Motorola, General Motors, and Hewlett-Packard are just a few of the companies that are using a system called Action-Reflection Learning (ARL) to explore and find answers to important business problems.

These efforts signal an increased interest in using this powerful tool in corporate decision making. What is now needed is (a) an understanding of the core processes that make up reflection, (b) an understanding of which of these processes are most likely to promote learning from work experiences, and (c) a set of tools to help managers use reflection as a way of learning. The rest of this article addresses itself to these three needs.

THE NATURE OF REFLECTION

Reflection is a highly personal cognitive process. When a person engages in reflection, he or she takes an experience from the outside world, brings it inside the mind, turns it over, makes connections to other experiences, and filters it through personal biases. If this process results in learning, the individual then develops inferences to approach the external world in a way that is different from the approach that would have been used, had reflection not occurred. While the catalyst for the reflection is external, and while others may help in the process by listening, asking questions, or offering advice, the reflection occurs within the mental self.

Reflection and learning may therefore be defined in this context as follows: Reflection is the process of stepping back from an experience to ponder, carefully and persistently, its meaning to the self through the development of inferences; learning is the creation of meaning from past or current events that serves as a guide for future behavior.

Like many other cognitive activities, reflection is often spontaneous, and, at times, outside an individual's awareness. In fact, the "sorting through" nature of the reflection process is most efficient while we sleep. In his book *Sleep*, J. Allan Hobson, professor of psychiatry at Harvard Medical School and the director of the Laboratory of Neurophysiology at the Massachusetts Mental Health Center, explains that sleep reduces the level of incoming sensory data and allows for the reorganization and efficient storage of information already in the brain, thus better preparing us to handle the demands of our waking hours.

The same sort of spontaneous sorting through of existing information occurs during certain mindless, rhythmic physical activities like jogging, swimming laps, or mowing the lawn; or during habitual routines that no longer need the conscious brain's full attention, such as showering or commuting on the same route each day. Just as it does during sleep, this spontaneous process of reflection allows one to momentarily suspend the intense flow of new information to the brain. This enhances the processing of existing information, thereby better preparing the person to handle the demands of the rapidly changing environment.

The Stages in the Reflection Process

Spontaneous reflection is often stimulated by the nagging, unresolved problems or challenges that are a normal part of any manager's job. Reflection then progresses through four distinct stages: (a) articulation of a problem, (b) analysis of that problem, (c) formulation and testing of a tentative theory to explain the problem, and (c) action for deciding whether to act.

Let's explore these four stages by considering the hypothetical example in the box.

The first stage of reflection, articulation of a problem, defines the issue that the mind will work on during the process of reflection. It is often preceded by what John Dewey calls "a state of doubt, hesitancy, perplexity, or mental difficulty." The clear articulation of a problem is often an insight in itself, and rewarding to the manager who has struggled to identify a vague sense of discomfort or dissatisfaction.

In our hypothetical example, Joe enters this first stage as he realizes what the problem is *not*. It is not the product of the review, which both he and Hector judged to be fair. It is not the completion of the task, which was timely. It is, in this case, some still-to-be-discovered element of the performance review process that caused a less-than-satisfactory feeling. Joe's process of problem articulation is a result of discarding possibilities and is based on what he defines as a negative situation. Others may find themselves in situations where they must discover what went *right* during a very positive experience, perhaps for the purpose of summarizing their learning in a report, coaching others, or relating past successes to similar but more challenging experiences. In either cases, clarifying the problem or challenge sets the stage for the next step in the process.

The second step, analysis of the problem, consists of a search for possibilities: in Joe's case, possible reasons for the problem as he has defined it. To quote Dewey once again, analysis is "an act of searching, hunting, or inquiring to find material that will resolve the doubt, and settle or dispose of the perplexity." It may involve asking and answering a series of questions about the situation, put forth by oneself or others. It may consist of searching the memory for similar situations or imagining how someone else might handle the same issue. It involves reviewing past behavior with intensity, as though under a microscope.

When Joe decided to review the hour-long performance discussion from the moment Hector entered the room, he was searching for important clues—ideas that were perhaps stored in the mind but still out of his conscious reach. During this stage, it is important to be ready to grasp elusive but potentially relevant thoughts that may enter the consciousness. In Joe's case, Sally's words from his own performance review came to mind. When he applied them to the current situation, he came up with a tentative hypothesis.

This generation of a hypothesis that addresses the problem is the first part of stage three of the reflection process: formulation and testing of a tentative theory to solve the problem. The tentative theory that Joe developed in stage three is the following: his desire to do a good job led him to such a thorough and well-presented analysis of Hector's strengths and weaknesses that there was little time or opportunity left for Hector's contribution. After testing this possibility against the comments he had received from Sally in the past, it seemed to be a sound theory.

Stage four, action (or deciding whether to act) brings closure to the cycle and is the final "test" of the hypothesis. It is only through this last stage that true learning occurs. Learning, as defined earlier, is the creation of meaning from past or current events that serves as a guide for future behavior. Thus, this final stage involves the articulation of a new way of acting in the future. Even though Joe has been engaged in the process of reflection (stepping back from an experience

---

Jogging for Answers

■ Joe lifts his foot onto the concrete wall bordering the stairs leading from his office building. As he reties the lace on one of his new Nikes, he thinks again how glad he is that the renovation of this building included a shower and locker room in the basement. It was just the incentive he needed to introduce some much-needed exercise into the frantic pace of his work week.

He crosses the busy two-lane highway, turns left onto the jogging path he discovered along the river, and settles in to a comfortable pace and rhythm. The first person he passes raises a hand in hello, and Joe thinks how much this fellow jogger looks like one of his employees, Hector. His mind turns to the performance review discussion he had with Hector earlier this week.

■ Although the review resulted in a fairly positive description of how Hector performed against the defined goals and objectives, it was an uncomfortable session. Joe has been perplexed about the source of the discomfort ever since. He resolves to get at the heart of this before his next three reviews—all with employees who have not been performing as well as Hector.

"What exactly is the problem here?" Joe wonders. It isn't the result: Joe completed the task in a timely manner, and the evaluation was fair, as evidenced by Hector's willingness to sign the acknowledgment at the bottom of the form.

■ Suddenly he remembers comments made at his own performance review last year. Joe's boss, Sally, was trying to express a concern she had regarding the way he managed his people. She felt he did not include them in the decisions that affected them. Maybe this is an example of what Sally meant.

As Joe thinks about what transpired from the time Hector entered his office to the time he signed the bottom of the form, he doesn't remember Hector saying very much. Joe suddenly realizes that his desire to do a good job led him to such a thorough and carefully presented analysis of Hector's strengths and weaknesses that there was little time or opportunity left for Hector's contribution.

■ Joe catches sight of the big steeple clock across the river, and realizes he must head back or he will be late for his project review meeting with Sally. While showering and changing, he resolves to take a few minutes of his upcoming meeting to tell Sally about this insight and enlist her help in working on the issue.

BOX 14.2 Jogging for Answers

to carefully and persistently ponder its meaning to the self through the development of inferences) since the beginning of his run, he has not yet truly learned.

We leave him at the end of stage three. Hopefully, as a result of his discussion with Sally, he will be able to develop an action plan that will guide his future behavior in performance reviews. This four-stage reflection process can be applied repeatedly to the many problems or challenges that arise in challenging work situations.

The Power of Questions

One of the techniques for increasing the learning power of reflection is the posing and answering of questions. School systems have long recognized the power of questioning as a tool for reflection and learning. Questions form the basis of class discussions; they become topics for papers; they stimulate debates; they guide case analyses; and, when used in quizzes and tests, reinforce learning. Counselors and therapists use provocative questions to guide clients through the discovery process. And the best managers in corporations realize that posing thoughtful questions is often a better way to gain commitment than providing concise answers.

The types of questions that are most effective in enhancing reflection vary depending on the stage of reflection.

During problem articulation, "what" questions allow one to fully describe the situation: "What occurred?" "What did you see, think, feel?" "What was the most important thing?" These questions are useful in arriving at a thorough understanding of the problem to be solved or the challenge to be addressed.

In the problem analysis stage, "why" questions are most helpful: "Why was that important?" "Why do you think it happened?" "Why were you feeling that way?"

During hypothesis generation, "how" questions allow an individual to begin to formulate a tentative theory to explain or address the problem: "How is this situation similar and different from other problems?" "How might you do things differently?"

Finally, during the action stage, "what" questions become important once again: "What are the implications of all this for future action?" "What should you do now?"

The most useful questions are rarely profound yet often produce powerful results. A simple "what else?" can open the mind to a myriad of possibilities previously untapped. The age-old one-word question "why?" has guided scientists and philosophers to discoveries and insights that have changed our world. Introducing an intervention with the question "may I?" performs the powerful functions of indicating respect, ascertaining readiness, and lowering defensive barriers.

Examples of solitary reflection	Examples of reflection with helper or small group
■ Spontaneous thinking during rhythmic, repetitive, mindless physical exercise (jogging, swimming laps, mowing the lawn) or routine habits (driving an established route, showering, shaving) ■ Meditation ■ Prayer ■ Journal writing ■ Business writing (project reports, professional papers, evaluations) ■ Assessment instruments	■ Performance appraisal discussions ■ Counseling sessions ■ Individual or group therapy ■ Problem-solving meetings ■ Project review sessions ■ Informal discussions with friends/colleagues ■ Interviews ■ Mentoring ■ Feedback discussions

BOX 14.3

Questions are thus one of the most basic and powerful elements of the reflection experience. They are used in the process of learning from challenging work situations in three ways: to open up possibilities, to clarify meaning, and to structure the progression through the four stages.

Alone or with Others?

Individuals differ in the way they think about and make sense out of their challenges in life. One of these individual differences is whether one tends to reflect alone or with others. In the hypothetical case presented earlier, Joe is an introverted thinker who tends to work out problems by thinking about them on his own. He eventually recognized the need to get help from his boss, but it was not the first and most natural way for him to tackle a challenging situation. Others may do their best thinking out loud, bouncing ideas off trusted colleagues or friends. The box, above, lists a variety of examples of reflection in both categories.

In the case of reflecting alone, a major distinction is whether or not writing is involved. The ability to write out reflections (and the propensity to do so) varies greatly with individuals. In those cases where one is comfortable with the tool, writing can be a powerful vehicle to produce insights during the reflection process.

Reflection with others may be with one other person or in small groups. When only one other person is involved, that person often takes on a helper role. In the world of work, individuals often discuss challenging situations or problems with those who have greater experience (immediate managers, mentors) or with those who are helpful facilitators (career counselors, employee advocates, human resource professionals, organizational development consultants). Outside of work, people turn to clergy, therapists, astrologers, friends, parents, or spouses when they need to think through challenging situations.

When reflection takes place in a small group, ideas are generated by the sharing of different perspectives. For example, self-help support groups that unite people who face similar challenges assist participants in discovering important information about themselves. Although the total discussion time each individual has in these settings is less than in coaching discussions, the total reflection time is no less. While one person is sharing his or her experience, the others are relating the information to their own challenges. Thus, whether conducted alone or with others, reflection occurs and learning results if the four-stage process of problem articulation, problem analysis, theory formulation, and action planning takes place.

THE RESEARCH STUDY

Which of these three ways of reflecting—alone, with a helper, or in a small group—is most effective in helping managers enhance learning from challenging work experiences? The experiment described here was designed to answer that question, and thus bridge the gap between our understanding of the nature of reflection and our ability to recommend tools to enhance managerial learning.

The participants in the study were 48 managers from a wide variety of functional disciplines in a *Fortune* 500 corporation. The corporation is an international research, design, manufacturing, and sales organization with approximately 10,000 employees. Headquartered in the Northeast, it has been in business since 1937 and has recently experienced a large-scale restructuring of its major product lines.

The experiment took place in corporate classrooms at two locations used for company retreats and special meetings. Both locations have a combination of large, appropriately equipped classrooms as well as many small, comfortable break-out rooms. They are located in areas bordering fields and woods, providing a relaxed atmosphere that encourages reflective activity.

The Intervention

The participants were randomly divided into four groups and each group participated in a one-hour reflection session. Those managers assigned to the first group, labeled the "individual" group, engaged in the reflection activity by themselves. The managers in the second group, labeled the "helper group," were asked to bring a coach with them to their reflection session. (We provided guidelines to ensure that the helper was someone the individuals were comfortable with and someone who had good facilitation skills.) The managers assigned to the third group, known as the "peer group," joined three or four others from the study with whom they had no hierarchical relationship. The fourth group was the control group, consisting of managers who did not participate in a reflection session.

At the beginning of the reflection session, participants in each group were asked to select a current, challenging work experience that fit into one of the five types of experiences identified as highly developmental by the Center for Creative Leadership: (a) building something from nothing; (b) fixing/stabilizing a failing operation; (c) leading a project assignment; (d) managing a significant increase in people, dollars, or functions; or (e) moving from a line to a corporate role.

In each group, participants spent the next hour reflecting on that situation. All groups were asked to follow the same four-stage reflection process described here and to use reflection questions similar to those explored in this article. We provided each group with a set of guidelines for effective reflection.

After receiving general instructions with others in their respective groups, the participants moved to comfortable, quiet, isolated parts of the training center—either alone, in pairs, or in their assigned small groups. The individual group members spent the hour thinking about and writing down answers to the reflection questions. The "helper" groups engaged in a discussion of the situation chosen with the helper guiding the conversation using the reflection questions and the participant jotting down insights as they occurred. The small groups began their reflection with a statement from each member about their challenging situation. They then engaged in an unstructured group conversation beginning with one individual's specific challenge. The sessions were videotaped.

The Questionnaires

At the conclusion of the one hour of reflection, each participant completed a questionnaire. Part Three of the questionnaire asked participants to record the insights or lessons that occurred as a result of the process, and to indicate the meaning that the lesson had for future action. They were directed to use any notes they had taken during the reflection process to help with this task. The questionnaire also asked for responses about the challenging experience they selected, the learning statements they recorded, and the reflection process itself.

Members of the control group completed the questionnaire over the telephone. They identified a challenging work experience and listed their learning from it without having participated in the reflection session.

A follow up questionnaire was distributed by mail ten days after the reflection intervention to collect information on subsequent learning.

The primary emphasis of the study was to discover the effect of the independent variable: type of reflection (individual, helper, or peer-group) on the dependent variable: amount of learning. "Amount of learning" was measured by counting the number of insights or lessons listed by participants.

In addition, the questionnaire was designed to collect information about the effect of moderator variables (type of experience, length of the experience, importance of the experience, positive or negative nature of the experience) on the dependent variable: amount of learning.

The following additional data were also collected and analyzed:

- Subjects' satisfaction with the learning recorded (amount, quality, impact)
- Subjects' satisfaction with the reflection process (amount of time, performance of researcher, performance of others in group)
- Follow-up data (additional reflection time, discussions with others, additional learning)
- Written comments under each scale
- Descriptions of learning
- Videotapes from the three peer-group sessions

The Results

Both the individual and the helper groups had a statistically significant greater number of learnings than the control group; however, the peer group did not. An analysis of the videotapes and the descriptive comments from the questionnaires provide three explanations for the lower number of learnings recorded by the peer-group members.

First, the members of the small groups tended to search for similarities among experiences, placing less emphasis than the other groups on learning that was unique to themselves. Many interactions were introduced by statements such these: "Listening to you, Paul, a similar thing happened to me . . ." and "I ran into a similar situation . . ." and "There's a common thread here. . ."

Second, the need to discuss several different subjects' experiences discouraged the group from detailed probing that may have elicited more learning. Efforts to ensure that all members had a chance to talk caused members to shift focus before developing depth.

Third, none of the participants in the three separate small groups followed the instruction to take notes or to use the reflection questions in their discussion. This is in direct contrast to the individual group, where each person considered all reflection questions and summarized their thoughts in writing; and to the helper group, where the questions guided the entire discussion, and where participants made note of insights throughout the hour.

This finding reinforces the need to use reflection questions and to capture learning throughout a reflection experience. It also suggests the need for future research into the nature of reflection in small groups. For instance, it would be interesting to know whether the small group could be equally effective with a facilitator and more time. Because the research is inconclusive on this, it is important to withhold judgment about the value of reflection in small groups.

When the learning statements of all three treatment groups were analyzed, statistically significant differences emerged in the type of learning recorded. The individual and helper groups recorded mostly intrapersonal learning, or learning about themselves. Examples of insights recorded for these groups include "I've become even more aware that I need details to function—I need to know how things work and why in order to be satisfied"; "I should spend more time coaching my staff members"; and "I spend too much time 'caretaking' other people's problems, not enough on my own."

The peer-group participants recorded mostly interpersonal learning (learning about others) and contextual learning (learning about the culture of the corporation). Examples of interpersonal learning statements include "The strength of our team came from a good balance of different talents" and "Treat others as you wish to be treated." Examples of contextual learning include, "In our culture, action is rewarded more than planning" and "There is a tendency to resist change and enhance fadishness—the challenge is to identify what is fad and when change is needed."

None of the moderator independent variables (type of experience, length of experience, importance of experience, negative or positive nature of the experience) affected the amount of learning recorded. Four implications arise from this: first, all five categories of challenging work experiences are equally effective as a focus for the reflection experience; second, just as much can be learned in the beginning of an experience as in the middle or end; third, the relative importance of the experience to one's career in the corporation does not affect the amount of learning derived from it; and fourth, one may learn just as much from negative experiences as from positive ones.

No statistically significant differences between treatment groups were found in satisfaction with the learnings recorded or in satisfaction with the reflection experience. Most participants indicated general satisfaction with both the learnings that emerged and with the reflection process itself.

No statistically significant differences between treatment groups were found in amount of time spent reflecting after the session, nor in subjects' tendency to discuss their results with others. Participants spent, on average, one and one-half hours reflecting after the session, and tended to talk most frequently about the experience with co-workers or spouses.

Finally, there was no statistically significant increase in learning after the session; rather, participants reported a reaffirmation of previous learning. Many participants spent the follow-up reflection time thinking about the process of reflection rather than the original work experience or the learning from it.

IMPLICATIONS

What do these results tell us about the role of reflection in learning from managers' challenging work experiences? They tell us that just one hour spent reflecting on one aspect of a challenging situation, using some general questions and guidelines, either alone or with a helper, can significantly increase the learning from that situation. If corporations spent a portion of their training and development budgets on introducing formal reflection practices, they could provide support to managers like our fictional character Joe as they try to make sense out of these learning opportunities.

Management development organizations are in a unique position to provide this support. Reflection processes could be built into classroom training by adding one hour of reflection at the conclusion of each experience. However, as the research described here shows, it is important that the goal of the process chosen matches the outcome desired. If the goal is to reinforce as much individual learning as possible (perhaps for future personal goal setting), reflection should take place individually or with a helper. If the goal is to develop an understanding of the learning of the entire group (perhaps for future curriculum design or group impact studies), peer-group reflection strategies may be more appropriate.

In addition, non-classroom reflection activities could be added to the products and services currently provided by management development organizations. These might include personal learning guides developed and widely distributed for use by managers in two ways: (a) to help them uncover learning from their own challenging work experiences, and (b) to help them assist others in surfacing learning from their experiences. Structured reflection sessions could be established for all managers following challenging experiences such as job rotations, on-the-job training exercises, or external executive development activities. Finally, formal individual and helper-based reflection processes could become a standard element of corporate succession planning activities. Succession planning candidates could use formal reflection sessions to become aware of the learning attained from each job rotation, thus contributing their own assessment of readiness to that of upper management.

A tool called The Reflection Workbook, developed by the author and used in her work with managers at Polaroid Corporation, combines many of these suggestions. It has two major sections. The first section describes the three tools used in the Workbook—the learning journal, the learning log, and the learning conversation—and provides guidelines for their use. The second section contains the journal pages and learning logs used to explore and record the random thoughts and summary learning statements that occur throughout a work experience.

While the Workbook was designed to be used independently or with one other person who acts as a learning coach, an interactive, small-group process was also developed to help users get used to writing in the Workbook and to share their learning with others. The exercise, called "Community Reflection," takes approximately 90 minutes. Participants are introduced to the process, agree to a set of ground rules, then spend 20 minutes reflecting by themselves (using the learning journal, the learning log, or both). During this individual reflection time, they are asked to think and write about their learning in four specific categories using a set of reflection questions as prompts. For the next 50 minutes, a facilitator leads the group through a process that allows participants to share their individual learning. The exercise ends with a brief discussion of additional learning that surfaced as a result of the process.

As one might predict from the research described earlier, Polaroid managers who are using these tools report surfacing a large amount of personal learning that would otherwise have gone unrecognized. However, one group of managers involved in a particularly challenging new role reported three additional unforeseen benefits of the Community Reflection exercise. First, they found that both the individual and the group reflection time created a sense of fellowship, of "we're in this together." The act of revealing learning from both positive and negative experiences created a sense of trust and friendship that had not previously existed. Second, they indicated that the session provided a much needed opportunity to slow down and reflect quietly and spontaneously on what had already been learned. This proved to be a relief from the rapid and continuous assault of new learning that is a regular part of their particular developmental experience.

Finally, in addition to the personal insights and lessons that were shared, dilemmas and questions emerged that were captured for exploration during future developmental activities.

SUMMARY

Given the fast pace of change confronting managers today, it is critical that they develop capacities to learn from current work situations and adapt this learning to new situations. This need is driven by elaborate techniques and new processes that emerge regularly—initiatives that often require corporate-wide behavioral changes beginning at the top of the organization. In the midst of these time-consuming and expensive initiatives lies the simple and time-tested tool of reflection. To use it effectively, managers need only recognize that it has value, then create an amazingly small amount of time and structure for it to take place. With this process, managers take responsibility for their own learning—a responsibility that is, in some cases, too quickly turned over to workshop leaders, university professors, or consultants. No matter how qualified these educational providers may be, it is unlikely that any of them could create case studies with greater relevance or challenge than a manager's own work experiences.

SELECTED BIBLIOGRAPHY

For more information on learning from experience in organization, see: M. McCall, Jr., "Developing Executives Through Work Experiences," *Human Resources Planning*, 1988, Vol. 11, No. 1, pp. 1–11; M. McCall, Jr., M. Lombardo, and A. Morrison, *The Lessons of Experience* (Lexington Books, 1988); G. Robinson and C. Wick, "Executive Development That Makes a Business Difference," *Human Resource Planning*, 1992, Vol. 15, No. 1, pp. 63–76; K. Dechant, "Making the Most of Job Assignments: An Exercise in Planning for Learning," *Journal of Management Education*, 1994, Vol. 18, No. 2, pp. 198–211; S. Hoberman and S. Mailick,

Experiential Management Development: From Learning to Practice (Quorum Books, 1992); D. Schon, *The Reflective Practitioner* (Basic Books, 1983). D. Boud, R. Cohen, and D. Walker, *Using Experience for Learning* (The Society for Research into Higher Education & Open University Press, 1993); K. Watkins and V. Marsick, *Sculpting the Learning Organization* (Jossey-Bass, 1993); V. Marsick, "Action Learning and Reflection in the Workplace," in J. Mezirow, *Fostering Critical Reflection in Adulthood* (Jossey-Bass, 1990); and V. Marsick, L. Cederholm, E. Turner, and T. Pearson, "Action-Reflection Learning," *Training and Development*, August 1992, pp. 63–66.

Readers interested in the ways that reflection has been used to enhance learning in traditional education settings should read J. Calderhead, "Reflective Teaching and Teacher Education." *Teaching and Teacher Education*, 1989, Vol. 5, No. 1, pp. 43–51; C. Knapp, *Lasting Lessons: A Teacher's Guide to Reflecting on Experience* (Appalachia Educational Laboratory, 1992); E. Boyd and A. Fales, "Reflective Learning: Key to Learning from Experience" *Journal of Humanistic Psychology*, Vol. 23, No. 2, pp. 99–117; C. Canning, "What Teachers Say about Reflection," *Educational Leadership*, Vol. 48, No. 6, pp. 18–21; T. Fulwiler, *The Journal Book* (Heinemann Educational Books, 1987); B. Horwood, "Reflections on Reflection," *The Journal of Experiential Education*, Vol. 12, No. 2, pp. 5–6; and K. Osterman, "Reflective Practice: A New Agenda for Education," *Education and Urban Society*, Vol. 22, No. 2, pp. 133–152.

To learn more about underlying mental processes that guide reflection and learning, see C. Argyris, "The Executive Mind and Double-Loop Learning," *Organizational Dynamics*, 1982, Autumn, pp. 5–22; C. Argyris and D. Schoen, *Organizational Learning: A Theory of Action Perspective* (Addison-Wesley, 1978); A. Bandura, *Social Foundations of Thought and Action: A Social Cognitive Theory* (Prentice-Hall, 1986); J. Bartunek and M. Louis, "The Design of Work Environments to Stretch Managers' Capacities for Complex Thinking," *Human Resource Planning*, Vol. 11, No. 1, pp. 13–22; J. Hobson, *Sleep* (Scientific American Library, 1989); S. Brookfield, *Developing Critical Thinkers: Challenging Adults to Explore Alternative Ways of Thinking and Acting*, (Jossey-Bass, 1987); J. Dewey, *How We Think*, (D.C. Heath and Company, 1910); H. Hullfish and P. Smith, *Reflective Thinking: The Method of Education*, (Dodd, Mead & Company, 1961); P. Hutchings and A. Wultzdorff, *Knowing and Doing: Learning through Experience* (Jossey-Bass, 1988); D. Kolb, *Experiential Learning*, (Prentice Hall, 1984); J. Mezirow, *Transformative Dimensions of Adult Learning*, (Jossey-Bass, 1991); R. Paul & A. Binker, "Socratic Questioning," in R. Paul, *Critical Thinking* (Center for Critical Thinking and Moral Critique, 1990); and R. Revans, *The Origins and Growth of Action Learning* (Studedntilleratur, 1982).

Chapter 15

The Process of Experiential Learning*

D. Kolb

We shall not cease from exploration
And the end of all our exploring
Will be to arrive where we started
*And know the place for the first time.***

Experiential learning theory offers a fundamentally different view of the learning process from that of the behavioral theories of learning based on an empirical epistemology or the more implicit theories of learning that underlie traditional educational methods, methods that for the most part are based on a rational, idealist epistemology. From this different perspective emerge some very different prescriptions for the conduct of education, the proper relationships among learning, work, and other life activities, and the creation of knowledge itself.

This perspective on learning is called "experiential" for two reasons. The first is to tie it clearly to its intellectual origins in the work of Dewey, Lewin, and Piaget. The second reason is to emphasize the central role that experience plays in the learning process. This differentiates experiential learning theory from rationalist and other cognitive theories of learning that tend to give primary emphasis to acquisition, manipulation, and recall of abstract symbols, and from behavioral learning theories that deny any role for consciousness and subjective experience in the learning process. It should be emphasized, however, that the aim of this work is not to pose experiential learning theory as a third alternative to behavioral and cognitive learning theories, but rather to suggest through

* Reprinted by permission.
** From Little Gidding in FOUR QUARTETS,© 1943 by T. S. Eliot; renewed 1971 by Esme Valerie Eliot. Reprinted by permission of Harcourt Brace Jovanovich, Inc.

experiential learning theory a holistic integrative perspective on learning that combines experience, perception, cognition, and behavior. This chapter will describe the learning models of Lewin, Dewey, and Piaget and identify the common characteristics they share—characteristics that serve to define the nature of experiential learning.

THREE MODELS OF THE EXPERIENTIAL LEARNING PROCESS

The Lewinian Model of Action Research and Laboratory Training

In the techniques of action research and the laboratory method, learning, change, and growth are seen to be facilitated best by an integrated process that begins with here-and-now experience followed by collection of data and observations about that experience. The data are then analyzed and the conclusions of this analysis are fed back to the actors in the experience for their use in the modification of their behavior and choice of new experiences. Learning is thus conceived as a four-stage cycle, as shown in Figure 15.1. Immediate concrete experience is the basis for observation and reflection. These observations are assimilated into a "theory" from which new implications for action can be deduced. These implications or hypotheses then serve as guides in acting to create new experiences.

Two aspects of this learning model are particularly noteworthy. First is its emphasis on *here-and-now concrete experience* to validate and test abstract concepts. Immediate personal experience is the focal point for learning, giving life, texture, and subjective personal meaning to abstract concepts and at the same time providing a concrete, publicly shared reference point for testing the implications and validity of ideas created during the learning process. When human beings share an experience, they can share it fully, concretely, and abstractly.

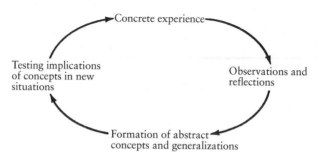

FIGURE 15.1 The Lewinian Experiential Learning Model

Second, action research and laboratory training are based on *feedback processes*. Lewin borrowed the concept of feedback from electrical engineering to describe a social learning and problem-solving process that generates valid information to assess deviations from desired goals. This information feedback provides the basis for a continuous process of goal-directed action and evaluation of the consequences of that action. Lewin and his followers believed that much individual and organizational ineffectiveness could be traced ultimately to a lack of adequate feedback processes. This ineffectiveness results from an imbalance between observation and action—either from a tendency for individuals and organizations to emphasize decision and action at the expense of information gathering, or from a tendency to become bogged down by data collection and analysis. The aim of the laboratory method and action research is to integrate these two perspectives into an effective, goal-directed learning process.

Dewey's Model of Learning

John Dewey's model of the learning process is remarkably similar to the Lewinian model, although he makes more explicit the developmental nature of learning implied in Lewin's conception of it as a feedback process by describing how learning transforms the impulses, feelings, and desires of concrete experience into higher-order purposeful action.

> *The formation of purposes is, then, a rather complex intellectual operation. It involves: (1) observation of surrounding conditions; (2) knowledge of what has happened in similar situations in the past, a knowledge obtained partly by recollection and partly from the information, advice, and warning of those who have had a wider experience; and (3) judgment, which puts together what is observed and what is recalled to see what they signify. A purpose differs from an original impulse and desire through its translation into a plan and method of action based upon foresight of the consequences of action under given observed conditions in a certain way. . . . The crucial educational problem is that of procuring the postponement of immediate action upon desire until observation and judgment have intervened. . . . Mere foresight, even if it takes the form of accurate prediction, is not, of course, enough. The intellectual anticipation, the idea of consequences, must blend with desire and impulse to acquire moving force. It then gives direction to what otherwise is blind, while desire gives ideas impetus and momentum. [Dewey, 1938, p. 69]*

Dewey's model of experiential learning is graphically portrayed in Figure 15.2. We note in his description of learning a similarity with Lewin, in the emphasis on learning as a dialectic process integrating experience and concepts, observations, and action. The impulse of experience gives ideas their moving force, and ideas give direction to impulse. Postponement of immediate action is essential for observation and judgment to intervene, and action is essential for

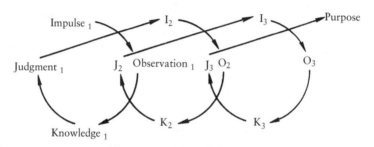

FIGURE 15.2 Dewey's Model of Experiential Learning

achievement of purpose. It is through the integration of these opposing but symbiotically related processes that sophisticated, mature purpose develops from blind impulse.

Piaget's Model of Learning and Cognitive Development

For Piaget, the dimensions of experience and concept, reflection, and action form the basic continua for the development of adult thought. Development from infancy to adulthood moves from a concrete phenomenal view of the world to an abstract constructionist view, from an active egocentric view to a reflective internalized mode of knowing. Piaget also maintained that these have been the major directions of development in scientific knowledge (Piaget, 1970). The learning process whereby this development takes place is a cycle of interaction between the individual and the environment that is similar to the learning models of Dewey and Lewin. In Piaget's terms, the key to learning lies in the mutual interaction of the process of *accommodation* of concepts or schemas to experience in the world and the process of *assimilation* of events and experiences from the world into existing concepts and schemas. Learning or, in Piaget's term, intelligent adaptation results from a balanced tension between these two processes. When accommodation processes dominate assimilation, we have imitation—the molding of oneself to environmental contours or constraints. When assimilation predominates over accommodation, we have play—the imposition of one's concept and images without regard to environmental realities. The process of cognitive growth from concrete to abstract and from active to reflective is based on this continual transaction between assimilation and accommodation, occurring in successive stages, each of which incorporates what has gone before into a new, higher level of cognitive functioning.

Piaget's work has identified four major stages of cognitive growth that emerge from birth to about the age of 14–16. In the first stage (0–2 years), the child is predominantly concrete and active in his learning style. This stage is called the sensory-motor stage. Learning is predominantly enactive through feeling, touching, and handling. Representation is based on action—for example, "a hole is to dig." Perhaps the greatest accomplishment of this period is the development of goal-oriented behavior: "The sensory-motor period shows a remarkable evolution from non-intentional habits to experimental and exploratory activity which is obviously intentional or goal oriented" (Flavell, 1963, p. 107). Yet the child has few schemes or theories into which he can assimilate events, and as a result, his primary stance toward the world is accommodative. Environment plays a major role in shaping his ideas and intentions. Learning occurs primarily through the association between stimulus and response.

In the second stage (2–6 years), the child retains his concrete orientation but begins to develop a reflective orientation as he begins to internalize actions, converting them to images. This is called the representational stage. Learning is now predominantly ikonic in nature, through the manipulation of observations and images. The child is now freed somewhat from his immersion in immediate experience and, as a result, is free to play with and manipulate his images of the world. At this stage, the child's primary stance toward the world is divergent. He is captivated with his ability to collect images and to view the world from different perspectives. Consider Bruner's description of the child at this stage:

> What appears next in development is a great achievement. Images develop an autonomous status, they become great summarizers of action. By age three the child has become a paragon of sensory distractibility. He is victim of the laws of vividness, and his action pattern is a series of encounters with this bright thing which is then replaced by that chromatically splendid one, which in turn gives way to the next noisy one. And so it goes. Visual memory at this stage seems to be highly concrete and specific. What is intriguing about this period is that the child is a creature of the moment; the image of the moment is sufficient and it is controlled by a single feature of the situation. [Bruner, 1966b, p. 13]

In the third stage (7–11 years), the intensive development of abstract symbolic powers begins. The first symbolic developmental stage Piaget calls the stage of concrete operations. Learning in this stage is governed by the logic of classes and relations. The child in this stage further increases his independence from his immediate experiential world through the development of inductive powers:

> The structures of concrete operations are, to use a homely analogy, rather like parking lots whose individual parking spaces are now occupied and now empty; the spaces themselves endure, however, and leave their owner to look beyond the cars actually present toward potential, future occupants of the vacant and to-be-vacant spaces. [Flavell, 1963, p. 203]

Thus, in contrast to the child in the sensory-motor stage whose learning style was dominated by accommodative processes, the child at the stage of concrete operations is more assimilative in his learning style. He relies on concepts and theories to select and give shape to his experiences.

Piaget's final stage of cognitive development comes with the onset of adolescence (12–15 years). In this stage, the adolescent moves from symbolic processes based on concrete operations to the symbolic processes of representational logic, the stage of formal operations. He now returns to a more active orientation, but it is an active orientation that is now modified by the development of the reflective and abstract power that preceded it. The symbolic powers he now possesses enable him to engage in hypothetico-deductive reasoning. He develops the possible implications of his theories and proceeds to experimentally test which of these are true. Thus his basic learning style is convergent, in contrast to the divergent orientation of the child in the representational stage:

> We see, then, that formal thought is for Piaget not so much this or that specific behavior as it is a generalized orientation, sometimes explicit and sometimes implicit, towards problem solving; an orientation towards organizing data (combinatorial analysis), towards isolation and control of variables, towards the hypothetical, and towards logical justification and proof. [Flavell, 1963, p. 211]

This brief outline of Piaget's cognitive development theory identifies those basic developmental processes that shape the basic learning process of adults (see Figure 15.3).

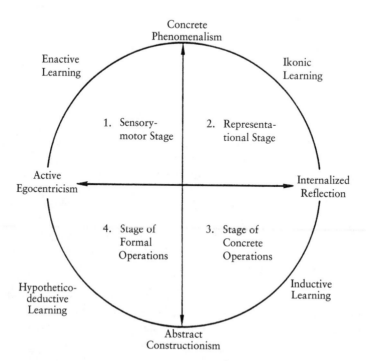

FIGURE 15.3 Piaget's Model of Learning and Cognitive Development

CHARACTERISTICS OF EXPERIENTIAL LEARNING

There is a great deal of similarity among the models of the learning process discussed above.[1] Taken together, they form a unique perspective on learning and development, a perspective that can be characterized by the following propositions, which are shared by the three major traditions of experiential learning.

Learning Is Best Conceived as a Process, Not in Terms of Outcomes

The emphasis on the process of learning as opposed to the behavioral outcomes distinguishes experiential learning from the idealist approaches of traditional education and from the behavioral theories of learning created by Watson, Hull, Skinner, and others. The theory of experiential learning rests on a different philosophical and epistemological base from behaviorist theories of learning and idealist educational approaches. Modern versions of these latter approaches are based on the empiricist philosophies of Locke and others. This epistemology is based on the idea that there are elements of consciousness—mental atoms, or, in Locke's term "simple ideas"—that always remain the same. The various combinations and associations of these consistent elements form our varying patterns of thought. It is the notion of constant, fixed elements of thought that has had such a profound effect on prevailing approaches to learning and education, resulting in a tendency to define learning in terms of its outcomes, whether these be knowledge in an accumulated storehouse of facts or habits representing behavioral responses to specific stimulus conditions. If ideas are seen to be fixed and immutable, then it seems possible to measure how much someone has learned by the amount of these fixed ideas the person has accumulated.

Experiential learning theory, however, proceeds from a different set of assumptions. Ideas are not fixed and immutable elements of thought but are formed and re-formed through experience. In all three of the learning models just reviewed, learning is described as a process whereby concepts are derived from and continuously modified by experience. No two thoughts are ever the same, since experience always intervenes. Piaget (1970), for example, considers the creation of new knowledge to be the central problem of genetic epistemology, since each act of understanding is the result of a process of continuous construction and invention through the interaction processes of assimilation and accommodation (compare Chapter 5, p. 99). Learning is an emergent process whose outcomes represent only historical record, not knowledge of the future.

When viewed from the perspective of experiential learning, the tendency to define learning in terms of outcomes can become a definition of nonlearning, in the process sense that the failure to modify ideas and habits as a result of

---

[1] There are also points of disagreement, which will be explored more fully in the next chapter.

experience is maladaptive. The clearest example of this irony lies in the behaviorist axiom that the strength of a habit can be measured by its resistance to extinction. That is, the more I have "learned" a given habit, the longer I will persist in behaving that way when it is no longer rewarded. Similarly, there are those who feel that the orientations that conceive of learning in terms of outcomes as opposed to a process of adaptation have had a negative effect on the educational system. Jerome Bruner, in his influential book, *Toward a Theory of Instruction*, makes the point that the purpose of education is to stimulate inquiry and skill in the process of knowledge getting, not to memorize a body of knowledge: "Knowing is a process, not a product" (1966, p. 72). Paulo Freire calls the orientation that conceives of education as the transmission of fixed content the "banking" concept of education:

> *Education thus becomes an act of depositing, in which the students are the depositories and the teacher is the depositor. Instead of communicating, the teacher issues communiques and makes deposits which the students patiently receive, memorize, and repeat. This is the "banking" concept of education, in which the scope of action allowed to the students extends only as far as receiving, filing, and storing the deposits. They do, it is true, have the opportunity to become collectors or cataloguers of the things they store. But in the last analysis, it is men themselves who are filed away through the lack of creativity, transformation, and knowledge in this (at best) misguided system. For apart from inquiry, apart from the praxis, men cannot be truly human. Knowledge emerges only through invention and reinvention, through the restless, impatient, continuing, hopeful inquiry men pursue in the world, with the world, and with each other. [Friere, 1974, p. 58]*

Learning is a Continuous Process Grounded in Experience

Knowledge is continuously derived from and tested out in the experiences of the learner. William James (1890), in his studies on the nature of human consciousness, marveled at the fact that consciousness is continuous. How is it, he asked, that I awake in the morning with the same consciousness, the same thoughts, feelings, memories, and sense of who I am that I went to sleep with the night before? Similarly for Dewey, continuity of experience was a powerful truth of human existence, central to the theory of learning:

> *. . . the principle of continuity of experience means that every experience both takes up something from those which have gone before and modifies in some way the quality of those which come after. . . . As an individual passes from one situation to another, his world, his environment, expands or contracts. He does not find himself living in another world but in a different part or aspect of one and the same world. What he has learned in the way of knowledge and skill in one situation becomes an instrument of understanding and dealing effectively with the situations which follow. The process goes on as long as life and learning continue. [Dewey, 1938, pp. 35, 44]*

Although we are all aware of the sense of continuity in consciousness and experience to which James and Dewey refer, and take comfort from the predictability and security it provides, there is on occasion in the penumbra of that awareness an element of doubt and uncertainty. How do I reconcile my own sense of continuity and predictability with what at times appears to be a chaotic and unpredictable world around me? I move through my daily round of tasks and meetings with a fair sense of what the issues are, of what others are saying and thinking, and with ideas about what actions to take. Yet I am occasionally upended by unforeseen circumstances, miscommunications, and dreadful miscalculations. It is in this interplay between expectation and experience that learning occurs. In Hegel's phrase, "Any experience that does not violate expectation is not worthy of the name experience." And yet somehow, the rents that these violations cause in the fabric of my experience are magically repaired, and I face the next day a bit changed but still the same person.

That this is a *learning* process is perhaps better illustrated by the nonlearning postures that can result from the interplay between expectation and experience. To focus so sharply on continuity and certainty that one is blinded to the shadowy penumbra of doubt and uncertainty is to risk dogmatism and rigidity, the inability to learn from new experiences. Or conversely, to have continuity continuously shaken by the vicissitudes of new experience is to be left paralyzed by insecurity, incapable of effective action. From the perspective of epistemological philosophy, Pepper (1942) shows that both these postures—dogmatism and absolute skepticism—are inadequate foundations for the creation of valid knowledge systems. He proposes instead that an attitude of provisionalism, or what he calls partial skepticism, be the guide for inquiry and learning (compare Chapter 5, p. 107).

The fact that learning is a continuous process grounded in experience has important educational implications. Put simply, it implies that all learning is relearning. How easy and tempting it is in designing a course to think of the learner's mind as being as blank as the paper on which we scratch our outline. Yet this is not the case. Everyone enters every learning situation with more or less articulate ideas about the topic at hand. We are all psychologists, historians, and atomic physicists. It is just that some of our theories are more crude and incorrect than others. But to focus solely on the refinement and validity of these theories misses the point. The important point is that the people we teach have held these beliefs whatever their quality and that until now they have used them whenever the situation called for them to be atomic physicists, historians, or whatever.

Thus, one's job as an educator is not only to implant new ideas but also to dispose of or modify old ones. In many cases, resistance to new ideas stems from their conflict with old beliefs that are inconsistent with them. If the education process begins by bringing out the learner's beliefs and theories, examining and testing them, and then integrating the new, more refined ideas into the person's belief systems, the learning process will be facilitated. Piaget (see Elkind, 1970, Chapter 3) has identified two mechanisms by which new ideas are adopted by an individual—integration and substitution. Ideas that evolve through integration tend to become highly stable parts of the person's conception of the world. On the other hand, when the content of a concept changes by means of substitution, there is always the possibility of a reversion to the earlier level of conceptualization and understanding, or to a dual theory of the world where espoused theories learned through substitution are incongruent with theories-in-use that are more integrated with the person's total conceptual and attitudinal view of the world. It is this latter outcome that stimulated Argyris and Schon's inquiry into the effectiveness of professional education:

> *We thought the trouble people have in learning new theories may stem not so much from the inherent difficulty of the new theories as from the existing theories people have that already determine practices. We call their operational theories of action* theories-in-use *to distinguish them from the* espoused *theories that are used to describe and justify behavior. We wondered whether the difficulty in learning new theories of action is related to a disposition to protect the old theory-in-use.* [Argyris and Schon, 1974, p. viii]

The Process of Learning Requires the Resolution of Conflicts Between Dialectically Opposed Modes of Adaptation to the World

Each of the three models of experiential learning describes conflicts between opposing ways of dealing with the world, suggesting that learning results from resolution of these conflicts. The Lewinian model emphasizes two such dialectics—the conflict between concrete experience and abstract concepts and the conflict between observation and action.[2] For Dewey, the major dialectic is between the impulse that gives ideas their "moving force" and reason that gives desire its direction. In Piaget's framework, the twin processes of accommodation of ideas to the external world and assimilation of experience into existing conceptual structures are the moving forces of cognitive development. In Paulo Freire's work, the dialectic nature of learning and adaptation is encompassed in his concept of *praxis*, which he defines as "reflection and action upon the world in order to transform it" (1974, p. 36). Central to the concept of praxis is the process of "naming the world," which is both active—in the sense that naming

---

[2] The concept of dialectic relationship is used advisedly in this work. The long history and changing usages of this term, and particularly the emotional and ideological connotations attending its usage in some contexts, may cause some confusion for the reader. However, no other term expresses as well the relationship between learning orientations described here—that of mutually opposed and conflicting processes the results of each of which cannot be explained by the other, but whose merger through confrontation of the conflict between them results in a higher order process that transcends and encompasses them both. This definition comes closest to Hegel's use of the term but does not imply total acceptance of the Hegelian epistemology (compare Chapter 5, p. 117).

something transforms it—and reflective—in that our choice of words gives meaning to the world around us. This process of naming the world is accomplished through dialogue among equals, a joint process of inquiry and learning that Freire sets against the banking concept of education described earlier:

> As we attempt to analyze dialogue as a human phenomenon, we discover something which is the essence of dialogue itself: the word. But the word is more than just an instrument which makes dialogue possible; accordingly, we must seek its constitutive elements. Within the word we find two dimensions, reflection and action, in such radical interaction that if one is sacrificed—even in part—the other immediately suffers. There is no true word that is not at the same time a praxis. Thus, to speak a true word is to transform the world.
>
> An unauthentic word, one which is unable to transform reality, results when dichotomy is imposed upon its constitutive elements. When a word is deprived of its dimension of action, reflection automatically suffers as well; and the word is changed into idle chatter, into verbalism, into an alienated and alienating "blah." It becomes an empty word, one which cannot denounce the world, for denunciation is impossible without a commitment to transform, and there is no transformation without action.
>
> On the other hand, if action is emphasized exclusively, to the detriment of reflection, the word is converted into activism. The latter—action for action's sake—negates the true praxis and makes dialogue impossible. Either dichotomy, by creating unauthentic forms of existence, creates also unauthentic forms of thought, which reinforce the original dichotomy.
>
> Human existence cannot be silent, nor can it be nourished by false words, but only by true words, with which men transform the world. To exist, humanly, is to name the world, to change it. Once named, the world in its turn reappears to the namers as a problem and requires of them a new naming. Men are not built in silence, but in word, in work, in action-reflection.
>
> But while to say the true word—which is work, which is praxis—is to transform the world, saying that word is not the privilege of some few men, but the right of every man. Consequently, no one can say a true word alone—nor can he say it for another, in a prescriptive act which robs others of their words. [Freire, 1974, pp. 75, 76]

All the models above suggest the idea that learning is by its very nature a tension- and conflict-filled process. New knowledge, skills, or attitudes are achieved through confrontation among four modes of experiential learning. Learners, if they are to be effective, need four different kinds of abilities—*concrete experience* abilities (CE), *reflective observation* abilities (RO), *abstract conceptualization* abilities (AC), and *active experimentation* (AE) abilities. That is, they must be able to involve themselves fully, openly, and without bias in new experiences (CE). They must be able to reflect on and observe their experiences from many perspectives (RO). They must be able to create concepts that integrate their observations into logically sound theories (AC), and they must be able to use these theories to make decisions and solve problems (AE). Yet this ideal is difficult to achieve. How can one act and reflect at the same time? How can one be concrete and immediate and still be theoretical? Learning requires abilities that are polar opposites, and the learner, as a result, must continually choose which set of learning abilities he or she will bring to bear in any specific learning situation. More specifically, there are two primary dimensions to the learning process. The first dimension represents the concrete experiencing of events at one end and abstract conceptualization at the other. The other dimension has active experimentation at one extreme and reflective observation at the other. Thus, in the process of learning, one moves in varying degrees from actor to observer, and from specific involvement to general analytic detachment.

In addition, the *way* in which the conflicts among the dialectically opposed modes of adaptation get resolved determines the level of learning that results. If conflicts are resolved by suppression of one mode and/or dominance by another, learning tends to be specialized around the dominant mode and limited in areas controlled by the dominated mode. For example, in Piaget's model, imitation is the result when accommodation processes dominate, and play results when assimilation dominates. Or for Freire, dominance of the active mode results in "activism," and dominance of the reflective mode results in "verbalism."

However, when we consider the higher forms of adaptation—the process of creativity and personal development—conflict among adaptive modes needs to be confronted and integrated into a creative synthesis. Nearly every account of the creative process, from Wallas's (1926) four-stage model of incorporation, incubation, insight, and verification, has recognized the dialectic conflicts involved in creativity. Bruner (1966a), in his essay on the conditions of creativity, emphasizes the dialectic tension between abstract detachment and concrete involvement. For him, the creative act is a product of detachment and commitment, of passion and decorum, and of a freedom to be dominated by the object of one's inquiry. At the highest stages of development, the adaptive commitment to learning and creativity produces a strong need for integration of the four adaptive modes. Development in one mode precipitates development in the others. Increases in symbolic complexity, for example, refine and sharpen both perceptual and behavioral possibilities. Thus, complexity and the integration of dialectic conflicts among the adaptive modes are the hallmarks of true creativity and growth.

Learning Is an Holistic Process of Adaptation to the World

Experiential learning is not a molecular educational concept but rather is a molar concept describing the central process of human adaptation to the social and physical environment. It is a holistic concept much akin to the Jungian theory of psychological types (Jung, 1923), in that it seeks to describe the emergence of basic life orientations as a function of dialectic tensions between basic modes of relating to the world. To learn is not the special province of a single specialized realm of human functioning such as cognition or perception. It involves the integrated functioning of the total organism—thinking, feeling, perceiving, and behaving.

This concept of holistic adaptation is somewhat out of step with current research trends in the behavioral sciences. Since the early years of this century and the decline of what Gordon Allport called the "simple and sovereign" theories of human behavior, the trend in the behavioral sciences has been away from theories such as those of Freud and his followers that proposed to explain the totality of human functioning by focusing on the interrelatedness among human processes such as thought, emotion, perception, and so on. Research has instead tended to specialize in more detailed exploration and description of particular processes and subprocesses of human adaptation—perception, person perception, attribution, achievement motivation, cognition, memory—the list could go on and on. The fruit of this labor has been bountiful. Because of this intensive specialized research, we now know a vast amount about human behavior, so much that any attempt to integrate and do justice to all this diverse knowledge seems impossible. Any holistic theory proposed today could not be simple and would certainly not be sovereign. Yet if we are to understand human behavior, particularly in any practical way, we must in some way put together all the pieces that have been so carefully analyzed. In addition to knowing how we think and how we feel, we must also know when behavior is governed by thought and when by feeling. In addition to addressing the nature of specialized human functions, experiential learning theory is also concerned with how these functions are integrated by the person into a holistic adaptive posture toward the world.

Learning is the major process of human adaptation. This concept of learning is considerably broader than that commonly associated with the school classroom. It occurs in all human settings, from schools to the workplace, from the research laboratory to the management board room, in personal relationships and the aisles of the local grocery. It encompasses all life stages, from childhood to adolescence, to middle and old age. Therefore it encompasses other, more limited adaptive concepts such as creativity, problem solving, decision making, and attitude change that focus heavily on one or another of the basic aspects of adaptation. Thus, creativity research has tended to focus on the divergent (concrete and reflective) factors in adaptation such as tolerance for ambiguity, metaphorical thinking, and flexibility, whereas research on decision making has emphasized more convergent (abstract and active) adaptive factors such as the rational evaluation of solution alternatives.

The cyclic description of the experiential learning process is mirrored in many of the specialized models of the adaptive process. The common theme in all these models is that all forms of human adaptation approximate scientific inquiry, a point of view articulated most thoroughly by the late George Kelly (1955). Dewey, Lewin, and Piaget in one way or another seem to take the scientific method as their model for the learning process; or to put it another way, they see in the scientific method the highest philosophical and technological refinement of the basic processes of human adaptation. The scientific method, thus, provides a means for describing the holistic integration of all human functions.

Figure 15.4 shows the experiential learning cycle in the center circle and a model of the scientific inquiry process in the outer circle (Kolb, 1978), with models of the problem-solving process (Pounds, 1965), the decision-making process (Simon, 1947), and the creative process (Wallas, 1926) in between. Although the models all use different terms, there is a remarkable similarity in concept among them. This similarity suggests that there may be great payoff in the integration of findings from these specialized areas into a single general adaptive model such as that proposed by experiential learning theory. Bruner's work on a theory of instruction (1966b) shows one example of this potential payoff. His integration

FIGURE 15.4 Similarities Among Conceptions of Basic Adaptive Processes: Inquiry/Research, Creativity, Decision Making, Problem Solving, Learning

of research on cognitive processes, problem solving, and learning theory provided a rich new perspective for the conduct of education.

When learning is conceived as a holistic adaptive process, it provides conceptual bridges across life situations such as school and work, portraying learning as a continuous, lifelong process. Similarly, this perspective highlights the similarities among adaptive/learning activities that are commonly called by specialized names—learning, creativity, problem solving, decision making, and scientific research. Finally, learning conceived holistically includes adaptive activities that vary in their extension through time and space. Typically, an immediate reaction to a limited situation or problem is not thought of as learning but as *performance*. Similarly at the other extreme, we do not commonly think of long-term adaptations to one's total life situation as learning but as *development*. Yet performance, learning, and development, when viewed from the perspectives of experiential learning theory, form a continuum of adaptive postures to the environment, varying only in their degree of extension in time and space. Performance is limited to short-term adaptations to immediate circumstance, learning encompasses somewhat longer-term mastery of generic classes of situations, and development encompasses lifelong adaptations to one's total life situation.

Learning Involves Transactions Between the Person and the Environment

So stated, this proposition must seem obvious. Yet strangely enough, its implications seem to have been widely ignored in research on learning and practice in education, replaced instead by a person-centered psychological view of learning. The casual observer of the traditional educational process would undoubtedly conclude that learning was primarily a personal, internal process requiring only the limited environment of books, teacher, and classroom. Indeed, the wider "real-world" environment at times seems to be actively rejected by educational systems at all levels.

There is an analogous situation in psychological research on learning and development. In theory, stimulus-response theories of learning describe relationships between environmental stimuli and responses of the organism. But in practice, most of this research involves treating the environmental stimuli as independent variables manipulated artificially by the experimenter to determine their effect on dependent response characteristics. This approach has had two outcomes. The first is a tendency to perceive the person-environment relationship as one-way, placing great emphasis on how environment shapes behavior with little regard for how behavior shapes the environment. Second, the models of learning are essentially decontextualized and lacking in what Egon Brunswick (1943) called ecological validity. In the emphasis on scientific control of environmental conditions, laboratory situations were created that bore little resemblance to the environment of real life, resulting in empirically validated models of learning that accurately described behavior in these artificial settings but could not easily be generalized to subjects in their natural environment. It is to me not surprising that the foremost proponent of this theory of learning would be fascinated by the creation of Utopian societies such as Walden II (Skinner, 1948); for the only way to apply the results of these studies is to make the world a laboratory, subject to "experimenter" control (compare Elms, 1981).

Similar criticisms have been made of developmental psychology. Piaget's work, for example, has been criticized for its failure to take account of environmental and cultural circumstances (Cole, 1971). Speaking of developmental psychology in general, Bronfenbrenner states, "Much of developmental psychology as it now exists is *the science of the strange behavior of children in strange situations with strange adults for the briefest possible periods of time*" (1977, p. 19).

In experiential learning theory, the transactional relationship between the person and the environment is symbolized in the dual meanings of the term *experience*—one subjective and personal, referring to the person's internal state, as in "the experience of joy and happiness," and the other objective and environmental, as in, "He has 20 years of experience on this job." These two forms of experience interpenetrate and interrelate in very complex ways, as, for example, in the old saw, "He doesn't have 20 years of experience, but one year repeated 20 times." Dewey describes the matter this way:

> *Experience does not go on simply inside a person. It does go on there, for it influences the formation of attitudes of desire and purpose. But this is not the whole of the story. Every genuine experience has an active side which changes in some degree the objective conditions under which experiences are had. The difference between civilization and savagery, to take an example on a large scale, is found in the degree in which previous experiences have changed the objective conditions under which subsequent experiences take place. The existence of roads, of means of rapid movement and transportation, tools, implements, furniture, electric light and power, are illustrations. Destroy the external conditions of present civilized experience, and for a time our experience would relapse into that of barbaric peoples. . . .*
>
> *The word "interaction" assigns equal rights to both factors in experience—objective and internal conditions. Any normal experience is an interplay of these two sets of conditions. Taken together . . . they form what we call a situation.*
>
> *The statement that individuals live in a world means, in the concrete, that they live in a series of situations. And when it is said that they live in these situations, the meaning of the word "in" is different from its meaning when it is said that pennies are "in" a pocket or paint is "in" a can. It means, once more, that interaction is going on between an individual and objects and other persons. The conceptions of situation and of interaction are inseparable from each other. An experience is always what it is because of a transaction taking place between an individual and what, at the time, constitutes his environment, whether the latter consists of persons with whom he is talking about some topic or event, the subject talked about being also a part of the situation; the book he is reading (in which his environing conditions at the*

time may be England or ancient Greece or an imaginary region); or the mate-
rials of an experiment he is performing. The environment, in other words, is
whatever conditions interact with personal needs, desires, purposes, and
capacities to create the experience which is had. Even when a person builds a
castle in the air he is interacting with the objects which he constructs in fancy.
[Dewey, 1938, p. 39, 42–43]

Although Dewey refers to the relationship between the objective and subjective conditions of experience as an "interaction," he is struggling in the last
portion of the quote above to convey the special, complex nature of the relationship. The word *transaction* is more appropriate than *interaction* to describe the
relationship between the person and the environment in experiential learning
theory, because the connotation of interaction is somehow too mechanical,
involving unchanging separate entities that become intertwined but retain their
separate identities. This is why Dewey attempts to give special meaning to the
word *in*. The concept of transaction implies a more fluid, interpenetrating relationship between objective conditions and subjective experience, such that once
they become related, both are essentially changed.

Lewin recognized this complexity, even though he chose to sidestep it in his
famous theoretical formulation, $B = f(P,E)$, indicating that behavior is a function
of the person and the environment without any specification as to the specific
mathematical nature of that function. The position taken in this work is similar
to that of Bandura (1978)—namely, that personal characteristics, environmental
influences, and behavior all operate in reciprocal determination, each factor
influencing the others in an interlocking fashion. The concept of reciprocally
determined transactions between person and learning environment is central to
the laboratory-training method of experiential learning. Learning in T-groups is
seen to result not simply from responding to a fixed environment but from the
active creation by the learners of situations that meet their learning objectives:

The essence of this learning experience is a transactional process in which the
members negotiate as each attempts to influence or control the stream of
events and to satisfy his personal needs. Individuals learn to the extent that
they expose their needs, values, and behavior patterns so that perceptions and
reactions can be exchanged. Behavior thus becomes the currency for transac-
tion. The amount each invests helps to determine the return. [Bradford, 1964,
p. 192]

Learning in this sense is an active, self-directed process that can be applied
not only in the group setting but in everyday life.

Learning is the Process of Creating Knowledge

To understand learning, we must understand the nature and forms of
human knowledge and the processes whereby this knowledge is created. It has

already been emphasized that this process of creation occurs at all levels of sophistication, from the most advanced forms of scientific research to the child's discovery that a rubber ball bounces. Knowledge is the result of the transaction between social knowledge and personal knowledge. The former, as Dewey noted, is the civilized objective accumulation of previous human cultural experience, whereas the latter is the accumulation of the individual person's subjective life experiences. Knowledge results from the transaction between these objective and subjective experiences in a process called learning. Hence, to understand knowledge, we must understand the psychology of the learning process, and to understand learning, we must understand epistemology—the origins, nature, methods, and limits of knowledge. Piaget makes the following comments on these last points:

> Psychology thus occupies a key position, and its implications become increasingly clear. The very simple reason for this is that if the sciences of nature explain the human species, humans in turn explain the sciences of nature, and it is up to psychology to show us how. Psychology, in fact, represents the junction of two opposite directions of scientific thought that are dialectically complementary. It follows that the system of sciences cannot be arranged in a linear order, as many people beginning with Auguste Comte have attempted to arrange them. The form that characterizes the system of sciences is that of a circle, or more precisely that of a spiral as it becomes ever larger. In fact, objects are known only through the subject, while the subject can know himself or herself only by acting on objects materially and mentally. Indeed, if objects are innumerable and science indefinitely diverse, all knowledge of the subject brings us back to psychology, the science of the subject and the subject's actions.
>
> . . . it is impossible to dissociate psychology from epistemology . . . how is knowledge acquired, how does it increase, and how does it become organized or reorganized? . . . The answers we find, and from which we can only choose by more or less refining them, are necessarily of the following three types: Either knowledge comes exclusively from the object, or it is constructed by the subject alone, or it results from multiple interactions between the subject and the object—but what interactions and in what form? Indeed, we see at once that these are epistemological solutions stemming from empiricism, apriorism, or diverse interactionism. . . . [Piaget, 1978, p. 651]

It is surprising that few learning and cognitive researchers other than Piaget have recognized the intimate relationship between learning and knowledge and hence recognized the need for epistemological as well as psychological inquiry into these related processes. In my own research and practice with experiential learning, I have been impressed with the very practical ramifications of the epistemological perspective. In teaching, for example, I have found it essential to take into account the nature of the subject matter in deciding how to help students learn the material at hand. Trying to develop skills in empathic listening is a different educational task, requiring a different teaching approach from that of teaching fundamentals of statistics. Similarly, in consulting work with organizations, I have often seen barriers to communication and problem solving that at root are epistemologically based—that is, based on conflicting assumptions about the nature of knowledge and truth.

The theory of experiential learning provides a perspective from which to approach these practical problems, suggesting a typology of different knowledge systems that results from the way the dialectic conflicts between adaptive modes of concrete experience and abstract conceptualization and the modes of active experimentation and reflective observation are characteristically resolved in different fields of inquiry. This approach draws on the work of Stephen Pepper (1942, 1966), who proposes a system for describing the different viable forms of social knowledge. This system is based on what Pepper calls world hypotheses. World hypotheses correspond to metaphysical systems that define assumptions and rules for the development of refined knowledge from common sense. Pepper maintains that all knowledge systems are refinements of common sense based on different assumptions about the nature of knowledge and truth. In this process of refinement he sees a basic dilemma. Although common sense is always applicable as a means of explaining an experience, it tends to be imprecise. Refined knowledge, on the other hand, is precise but limited in its application or generalizability because it is based on assumptions or world hypotheses. Thus, common sense requires the criticism of refined knowledge, and refined knowledge requires the security of common sense, suggesting that all social knowledge requires an attitude of partial skepticism in its interpretation.

SUMMARY: A DEFINITION OF LEARNING

Even though definitions have a way of making things seem more certain than they are, it may be useful to summarize this chapter on the characteristics of the experiential learning process by offering a working definition of learning.[3] *Learning is the process whereby knowledge is created through the transformation of experience.* This definition emphasizes several critical aspects of the learning process as viewed from the experiential perspective. First is the emphasis on the process of adaptation and learning as opposed to content or outcomes. Second is that knowledge is a transformation process, being continuously created and recreated, not an independent entity to be acquired or transmitted. Third, learning transforms experience in both its objective and subjective forms. Finally, to understand learning, we must understand the nature of knowledge, and vice versa.

---

[3] From this point on, I will drop the modifier "experiential" in referring to the learning process described in this chapter. When other theories of learning are discussed, they will be identified as such.

Index